AD SALES:

WINNING SECRETS
of the
MAGAZINE PROS

VOLUME II

Helen Berman

Edited by Diane Cyr

BERMAN PUBLISHING COMPANY.

AD SALES:
Winning Secrets of the Magazine Pros

By Helen Berman

Published by:
The Berman Publishing Company
12021 Wilshire Blvd., Suite 177
Los Angeles, CA 90025-1200
(310) 820-7312

Library of Congress Catalog Number: 96-96212

Volume II - ISBN: 0-9649716-2-3
Volume I - ISBN: 0-9649716-1-5
Volume Set - ISBN: 0-9649716-0-7

Printed in the United States of America
1 2 3 4 5 6 7 8 9 0

DISCLAIMER

This publication is designed to provide the reader with information that will benefit and aid in the sales process. Figures, sources and other specific data are as up-to-date as possible within the parameters of this publishing. They are real figures that have been faithfully researched to the time of this printing. They are meant for comparison of media and other factors. This data changes minimally from year to year.

Photograph of Helen Berman by Helen K. Garber Photography

In Memorial

This book is dedicated to Gene Silverman, who perished
with his family on TWA flight #800.
Gene modeled how we can combine brilliance and
assertiveness with caring and compassion.
He made a difference in our lives.

ACKNOWLEDGMENTS

I owe many thanks to my peers and colleagues for their help with Volume II of *Ad Sales: Winning Secrets of the Magazine Pros.*

First, my appreciation and gratitude to the team who stayed through countless hours and incarnations of Volume II. My editor, Diane Cyr once again helped me express my ideas with logic, intelligence and sparkle. I'm grateful to have been able to call on her many years of magazine publishing experience. I also want to thank Carolyn Porter and Alan Gadney of One on One Book Production and Marketing. Carolyn spent many months tranforming hundreds of pages of copy and art into an orderly and crisp book, while Alan shared with me his encouragement, excitment and marketing savvy. My thanks also to my assistant, Sheba Roy, who deserves a medal for her copy editing, late hours and good humor..

My deepest thanks to many of my publishing colleagues for their invaluable experience, contribution and peer review: Jim Fischer, *The New York Observer* who helped with "Selling the Value of Your Circulation;" Rita Stollman, president of Editorial Management Strategies, for her insight in "Selling the Value of Your Editorial;" David Orlow, president of Periodical Studies Service for his contribution to "Using the Rate Card as a Selling tool;" Lori Fein at Simmons Research and Gretchen Vandenburg and Lisa Budwick, both at Cowles Media, for their help with "The Dynamics of Research;" Anne Mille, president of Chiron Associates, who shared valuable negotiation strategies and Julie Laitin, president of Julie Laitin Associates for her review of "If You're Asked to Cut Rates." Also thanks to Jack Sweger for his contribution to "Sales Letters that Get Action."

Lastly, special thanks to all the magazine publishing executives who provided art work to run in this book. Their cooperation helps us all share and learn from great selling minds.

ABOUT HELEN BERMAN

A magazine publisher recently called Helen Berman "...the best teacher I ever met! No one else stimulates advertising sales people and opens minds to new ideas and possibilities the way she does."

Interestingly, Helen started out in life as a budding English professor. Midway through her doctorate she realized that the academic life wasn't for her. What did excite her was the world of business where she could base her income on her skills instead of tenure. Her love of words led her career path to magazine publishing. She started out as a rep and quickly found ad sales to be continually motivating, stimulating and challenging— *the ultimate career frontier.*

Over the years she's progressed through the magazine business as an ad director, marketing director and publisher. Then in 1984, her career came full circle; Helen was able to combine her predisposition to teaching with her magazine publishing experience by opening her own sales training company. Since then, she has worked with hundreds of consumer and trade magazines and thousands of sales people. Today, her "disciples" can be found throughout the magazine industry, many in top management positions. While she does offer open training to the industry, most of her work involves doing customized in-house training that focuses on the individual sales challenges each magazine faces.

Helen likes to think of herself as a "career catalyst," a motivator who gets people fired up about selling advertising space as a profession. In fact, she feels very strongly about space selling as a *profession* where a good rep becomes a marketing partner with the client. And just as in any other profession, proficiency requires training. She knows from practical experience that good sales people aren't born, they're trained.

Helen still remembers her first space selling job when the manager handed her a rate card, a list of names and a telephone and said, "Go sell!" This "sink or swim" plunge into the business—and the difficulties it presented—is one of the reasons she felt it so essential that newcomers to the profession have a book they could turn to when they began planning and making their calls. It gives newcomers and sales veterans as well a kind of "sales coach" that is a continual support to them in their sales career.

A very popular speaker at *Folio:* shows, as well as at most of the other major publishing associations around the country, Helen is also a regular contributor to *Folio:* magazine. She has also produced an intensive eight-hour audio sales training program called "The Advertising Sales Solution."

TABLE OF CONTENTS

Introduction

WHAT ELSE DO YOU NEED to KNOW for SALES SUCCESS?

❖ ❖ ❖

Remember the Tyrolean Traverse? In Volume I of *Ad Sales: Winning Secrets of the Magazine Pros*, you may recall, the Traverse was one of the more diabolic challenges on the "ropes" course I once braved in the name of conquering fear. It was, simply, a rope hanging slack across a crevasse. My goal was to cross the crevasse hand over hand, from one cliff edge to the other.

I completed the first half easily. Hand over hand down the rope—no problem! Then I reached the middle and froze. Ahead of me, the rope stretched upward through air. Below me...nothing. If not for the loud encouragement shouted by my "ropes" team on the other side, I think I'd be dangling there still, ostensibly with no clue as to how to keep moving my hands, one over the other, to reach other side.

In a sense, that's where you are now. You're halfway to where you need to be in sales. Having read Volume I, you've already done the hard part of getting on the rope and starting across. Perhaps at this point it's tempting to stop!

After all, you now know how to sell as a marketing consultant. You know how to read your magazine's sales materials and how to understand rates and circulation. You can ably diagnose client needs, ask appropriate questions and turn your magazine's features into client benefits. You even know how to put together power presentations!

But to complete the job of sales—to reach your full potential with clients—you must continue to learn. That's what Volume II of *Ad Sales* brings to you. Page by page, it will serve as a bridge over the sales chasm. Stay where you are, and you risk having a sales career of missed opportunities and stilted performance. Stay the course and your new-found knowledge will boost you towards exceptional growth and success. You'll learn how to join the ranks of prosperous sales executives.

What's left to learn? For one thing, the secrets of positioning. In this volume, you'll learn to sell the unique value of your circulation, market and editorial.

You'll also develop a skill for research. You'll know how to understand the arcana that comes out of your magazine's research department, and learn how to translate those surveys and studies into powerful marketing tools.

Volume II also targets the tough sale. Does one prospect keep telling you that your rates are too high, regardless of the advertising value you've demonstrated? Does another tell you he doesn't have the budget? How about someone who believes your magazine is great, but simply won't commit? You'll learn how to deal with every situation. Countering objections with knowledge is the key to turning potential minefields into goldmines.

Most important, you'll learn the strategies of closing. Without the skills to ask for the sale, you cannot sell, no matter how beautiful, organized and powerful your presentation. In this volume you'll learn to identify obstacles to closing, how to develop the right closing attitude, and how to correct misunderstandings your client may have about your marketing solutions.

Volume II also offers detailed strategies for writing sales letters that get action, and for adding value to the sale through appropriate merchandising. Moreover, you'll learn to streamline your work habits by learning how to organize, manage your time and territory, prioritize target accounts and sell at trade shows.

Additionally, Volume II demonstrates how to negotiate calmly, professionally and effectively—without underminding the integrity of your magazine. You'll also learn about the psychological skills of top sales reps, including intuition, observation and adapting the "sales chameleon" approach for dealing with difficult clients. Even better, you'll discover how to handle that stickiest of sales clients, the "Deal-Cutter."

Throughout this book and throughout your career, you'll also come to appreciate your most valuable sales tool: the Advertising Syllogism. As you might recall from "Sales Basics" (Vol. I, Ch. 4), this is how it goes:

1. *This is your prospect.*

2. *This is our reader.*

3. *Your prospect is our reader.*

4. *Your prospect—our reader—reads this magazine.*

5. *Your prospect's buying behavior is affected by reading this magazine.*

6. *Therefore, you can sell your prospect—our reader—by advertising in the pages of our magazine.*

7. *Here are our advertising recommendations.*

8. *Close the sale.*

Whenever you get stuck with a tough client, feel you're losing your sale, or can't seem to close, call on the Advertising Syllogism. As long as you remember that "your prospect is our reader," you've got the key to the sale.

So keep going. The more you know about sales, the less likely you'll be left dangling in a nowhere sales career. At this point, you've got nowhere to go but *up*.

Section I

SELLING THE VALUE OF YOUR MAGAZINE

1

WHAT YOU MUST KNOW to POSITION YOUR MAGAZINE

"In science the credit goes to the man who convinces the world, not to the man to whom the idea first occurs."
—Sir William Osler (1849-1919)
Canadian physician

We're all familiar with paint-by-number paintings. You fill in the numbered areas of a pattern using the corresponding colors and... voila! A painting. Not a very good one, but a painting nonetheless. Fortunately, we're also familiar with Claude Monet, who also painted by organizing colors in a pattern. In Monet's case, however, the colors are organized with artistic intent and are expressive and alive. They complement each other to form the glowing, ghostly facade of a cathedral, or a haystack as brilliant as a sunrise.

In a sense, it's the same in magazine ad sales. Any capable salesperson could sum up a magazine's strong points using compelling charts, reader studies and circulation statements. Put them together in an orderly fashion, and they would present a very nice picture of a publication and what it delivers.

The drawback is, they would only create a "paint-by-number" presentation. The result might look professional, but it would lack unity: in style, in movement, or both.

So how does one turn a lackluster presentation into a "Monet"? Through *positioning.* Instead of laying out audit statements and subscriber surveys in a dull logical pattern, you can position the materials to harmonize and sing.

Essentially, positioning is a magazine's statement of what it is, whom it reaches, and what makes it *special, unique* and *different.* (That's SUD.) Positioning *distinguishes* a magazine from its competitors, not only in terms of circulation and sales, but in terms of its editorial attitude, mission, and market perception.

> **Essentially, positioning is a magazine's statement of what it is, who it reaches, and what makes it *special, unique* and *different*.**

TARGETING WITHIN THE NICHE

Every magazine positions itself within a particular market *niche.* Consider the teen market. Most magazines in the category position themselves to reach teenage girls with editorials about dating, career choices and grooming. In other words, no matter which teen magazine you pick up, you undoubtedly find articles about teenage boys, fashion and adolescent angst.

Each magazine, however, also differentiates itself by focusing on a particular niche in the teen market, positioning itself to address only certain topics or readers.

Consider, for instance, *YM, Teen* and *Seventeen,* the leading magazines in the teen category. Here's my approximation of their respective positions:

> ◆ *YM:* Positioned for fast-paced, guy-crazy teenagers, 15-19, with lots of gossip and jazzy features on fashion, grooming, dating, and how to attract boys. It's *Cosmopolitan's* baby sister.

> ◆ *Teen:* Positioned for middle-American teens, 13-18, with reassuring articles about dating boys, and how to comfortably handle the full range of adolescent issues. There's also a healthy dose of fashion and grooming advice.

> ◆ *Seventeen:* Positioned as the lead title for young women, 15 to college age, with trustworthy editorial and authoritative advice on sex, young men, career choices and the challenges of growing up.

The magazine's *mission* determines its positioning.

In each case, the magazine's *mission* determines its positioning. *YM's* mission is to tell girls the stuff they most want to know. *Teen's* is to be the reassuring big sister. *Seventeen's* is to provide accurate, believable information. Each one of these editorial missions slightly skews the title's position offering distinct messages to readers and advertisers.

To an outsider, of course, the above editorial differences may be very subtle. What 45-year-old male media supervisor (unless he has teenage daughters) can immediately understand why *YM* is a hotter read than *Teen*?

That's why it's critical for any magazine to develop a strong, individual position within its market. Without positioning, magazines can't show how they are editorially compatible with their advertisers, nor how they address market-specific audiences.

Advertisers make informed media choices only when they understand what makes a magazine special, unique and different.

It's a sales rep's job to use positioning to tie together the elements of the presentation. Advertisers make informed media choices only when they understand what makes a magazine special, unique and different. Positioning is what would enable a car advertiser, for instance, to pick *Seventeen* for its

9

print budget, while an advertiser for pre-teen bras might pick *Teen*.

THE STICKY PROBLEM OF DUAL POSITIONING

Here's where positioning starts to get complicated. The fact is, every magazine works from not one, but two positions:

◆ Advertising position

◆ Editorial position

As a sales rep, it's your job to illustrate how the two positions can be coordinated to the advertiser's benefit.

A magazine's *advertising position*, of course, is the message that the title creates to appeal to advertisers. You'll find the advertising position stated in the title's media kit and trade advertising.

Cooking Light, for instance, has positioned itself in its trade ads as "The Recipe for Living," attracting "readers with an appetite for living well." *Family Circle* has positioned itself as the magazine responsive to family issues, regardless of how modern the family may be. *Good Housekeeping* has positioned itself as reaching "new traditionalists," women who have redefined the roles of mother and homemaker. In each case, the title's position addresses the magazine's readership qualities as well as its editorial thrust.

A magazine's *editorial position*, however, can be slightly different from its advertising stance. This position is simply the entire message conveyed by the magazine's text and graphics. What articles and features does it highlight? What overall image does it present? How sophisticated or unsophisticated is its language and design? Most importantly, does the magazine appear to deliver to the readers what the advertising positioning says it does?

10

For selling purposes, it's crucial that the advertising and editorial position jibe. Consider a hypothetical magazine: *Fit Forever*. Let's say that its advertising position is "for readers who love all aspects of the good life." This suggests that *Fit Forever*'s readers are interested not only in exercise, but in gourmet cooking, vacationing, travel, fine home decor, and all other aspects of good living.

In other words, through its advertising position, *Fit Forever* tells non-health advertisers that its readership is the right market for their products. Moreover, let's assume the magazine has the reader research to back up those claims.

Now take a look at editorial position. Let's assume that *Fit Forever* focuses editorially on health and exercise. It does not carry articles about cooking. It does not provide travel tips for healthy vacations. It includes no articles on choosing fine china or stereo equipment. Nor does it carry advertising from cruise lines, cookware manufacturers, vacation planners or other advertisers associated with "living well."

In short, *Fit Forever*'s editorial position doesn't jibe with its advertising position. Advertisers get the message that they're only reaching readers who never leave the gym.

Naturally, the further apart the advertising and editorial positions, the tougher the sales rep's task. The readers the editors believe they are reaching may not be the same readers advertisers believe the magazine reaches.

In the long term, when advertising and editorial positions clash, a magazine can end up in big trouble. Eventually, poor response to advertising tells clients that they're simply not reaching the readers they thought they were.

Consider *Venture* magazine, which died rather suddenly in the mid-'80s. The magazine had marketed itself as a publication targeting high-growth, high-tech, top-of-the-line ven-

> For selling purposes, it's crucial that the advertising and editorial position jibe.

ture companies looking to go public. Advertisers, which included venture capitalists and other investment companies, thought they were reaching the Apple Computer companies of tomorrow.

It turned out, though, that because of the title's *content* the readership base actually consisted of small, undercapitalized mom-and-pop businesses that didn't have a chance of going public. Once advertisers failed to get the reader response they expected, they started pulling back their support for the magazine. Without its advertisers, it was "sayanora *Venture.*"

Of course, if your magazine isn't delivering the readers it needs to stay afloat, it's not your job to fix the problem. Instead, your publisher and editor-in-chief may have to hash over the positioning dilemma, and perhaps even reposition the magazine to appeal to the readers your advertisers want.

So what's your job if your magazine suffers from split-personality positioning? Find out how well your magazine delivers on its advertising position. Use your common sense. Believe me, advertisers don't swallow whole all the wonderful things in your media kit and trade advertising. Expect them to look through your magazine, check out your advertisers and study your readership to find out how well you deliver on your positioning. (That means, of course, that you should read your own magazine every month. Don't let your advertisers become more familiar with your title than you are!)

Whether your magazine is positioned to top-level computer technicians or to Eagle Scouts, make sure you back it up. Have your publisher statements, readership surveys and other factual information at hand. After all, you can't paint a picture of your publication without using the right materials!

PERCEPTION VERSUS REALITY

Closely tied to positioning, of course, is perception. Positioning tells your advertisers what you want them to know about your magazine. Perception is what your advertisers tell you. You can't change the latter, of course, without changing the former.

To grasp your magazine's perception, first take a moment to think about how your clients and readers currently react to your magazine. What do they say about it? Be honest. Do they call it "the industry bible?" An "also ran," "tabloid," "stuffy," "gorgeous," "trendy?" "Really on top of the market?"

No matter how polished you are as a salesperson, no matter how your clients love your sales story, people have their own opinions about your magazine. How they feel about your title will affect how they respond to you.

Granted, perception often doesn't have a lot to do with reality. Personally, I'd like a dollar for every publisher complaint I've heard about being "misunderstood" in the marketplace.

The truth is, many magazines often become a "must buy" because of clever or unique positioning, not necessarily because of their quality. They've been able to convince advertisers that their publications stand out among the myriad marketing choices—that their publications are special, unique and different.

More importantly, many of these "must-buys" have also positioned themselves as influential. They have convinced advertisers that their editorial is accurate, believable and actionable. That's important, because readers who have faith in a magazine's editorial are likely to have faith in its advertisers as well.

Other titles have a tougher task in positioning themselves. Advertisers may not like one book because it had a

Whatever the perception, that's the material with which you have to work—or change—when constructing your presentation.

history of running rehashed press releases. They may not like another because it fired an editor three years ago. Obviously, many newcomer titles have a tough time positioning, as do "number three" books in a field.

Consider a title like *Soap Opera Digest*. At one time, the magazine's selling story emphasized that upscale, professional women bought *SOD* to catch up on the soaps they were too busy to watch. While that may have been nice positioning, it would have taken a lot more to change advertisers' perception of the magazine as a low-budget read for underworked housewives. Only total editorial repositioning—including upscaled graphics, design and sophisticated language—could probably have altered that ingrained perception.

Clearly, perceptions are not easy to change. But they are not unalterable genetic traits, like short fingers. Essentially, to change perceptions, you have to change positions. Each changes in tandem with the other.

FIXING YOUR POSITION

To understand your magazine's position, you don't start by asking what you want to say about the magazine. You start by asking how you are already perceived by your prospects, your advertisers, your competitors, your readers, even your publishing team. As Al Riese and Jack Trout put it in their book *Positioning: The Battle for Your Mind* (1986, McGraw-Hill), "positioning is thinking in reverse. Instead of asking what you are, you ask what position you already own in the minds of the prospect." In other words, "What's your image?"

To work on your own position, you must first look at what your competitors currently say about you and about themselves. Analyze your competitors' media kits, audits, subscriber studies and promotional literature. Then take a look at your own magazine in light of your competition. See

14

how your own media kit and magazine come across to your advertisors and your competitors. How would you feel about your magazine if you didn't work for it?

From there, look at how the market perceives your competitors. Check their ad pages. Are your competitors attracting a certain type of client that you're not? Maybe they're getting more local than national accounts. Maybe they're accepting "prestige" advertisers only, leaving out classified or direct-response ads. Maybe they appeal only to upscale prospects, or to mass market ones. The kinds of advertisers drawn to your publication—and to your competitors'—will tell you a lot about how the titles are perceived.

Changing your positioning has to do with changing the mind of the prospect.

Positioning, of course, starts with what your magazine is—its editorial, its design, its content. But as I've already noted, positioning and perceptions change in tandem. To change your positioning, you have to change the mind of your prospect.

HOW IT STARTED

Positioning actually started as an advertising concept. It was seen as a way to make one product stand out from another.

Back in the '50s, for instance, one could sell a product on quality alone. It was the "build a better mousetrap" era. Sales reps focused on product features and customer benefits. But as technology enabled competitors to create me-too products, the "image" era came to the fore. At this point, companies switched the focus to branding. They found that reputation, or image, sold better than any product or product feature.

By the '70s, though, the deluge of brands meant advertisers needed a new method for standing out. That brought us to today's emphasis on positioning. Positioning looks beyond both the product and its image to "create a comparative position in the mind of the prospective buyer."

15

Avis, for example, created one of the first and most successful positioning campaigns with "We're number two, so we try harder." The company recognized where it stood in the marketplace and actually positioned that as an advantage to its customers.

How does that now apply to magazines? Simple. Just as agencies can use positioning to sell product, so you, too, can use positioning to sell magazines.

Sales reps and their publishers alike would benefit by perusing a book by Ries and Trout, titled *The 22 Immutable Laws of Marketing* (1993, Harper Business). Although these "laws" apply to product marketing, they say a lot about what it takes to make your magazine stand out in a world of competitors.

1. The Law of Leadership: *It's best to be first than it is to be better.*

Some "first" products have become such an institution that they're practically generic. When you want a copy of a report, you ask for a "Xerox." When you need to blow your nose, you reach for "Kleenex." When you want a soda, you ask for a "Coke."

Likewise, the first magazine in a field gets a head start with influencing the minds of the readers and the advertisers. It is perceived as the leader by virtue of being first. The Cowles magazines *Catalog Age* was first in the market addressing the catalog industry. Although it's been followed by many competitors, it has yet to be knocked from first place.

2. The Law of the Category: *If you can't be first in a category, set up a new category.*

For example, if your title is one of the dozens to address the women's service market, good luck. Look at the millions of dollars Bauer Publishing spent to launch *First for Women* as the "eighth sister" among the Seven Sisters women's magazines.

However, look at the success of *Allure*. Even though it's ostensibly a women's beauty title, it became successful by creating its own niche in a crowded category. It addressed the needs of women who were more interested in the science and process of beauty than in merely looking more beautiful.

3. **The Law of the Mind:** *It's better to be first in the mind than to be first in the marketplace.*

Look at IBM. It wasn't first in the computer field with its mainframe. Remington Rand was, with UNIVAC. But who remembers Remington Rand? It was IBM's massive marketing campaign that gave it the category. Being first only works if you can take advantage of the position to get into the buyer's mind.

It's the same in the magazine world. Those magazines that establish themselves early as something new usually end up the "category killers." Consider *People Magazine*. Before *People*, the market had plenty of movie and gossip magazines. But *People*, with the vast resources of Time Inc., could afford the marketing necessary to establish itself. In turn, *People* spawned dozens of imitators, none of which have come close to matching its sales and positioning.

It's not so much the merits of the product that win the hearts of buyers; it's the image.

4. **The Law of Perception:** *Marketing is not a battle of products. It's a battle of perceptions.*

We've already talked about this as the key concept to positioning. It's not so much the merits of the product that win the hearts of buyers; it's the image.

Often in the magazine world, clients don't so much notice which magazine is "best" as much as they do which

17

magazines have a "buzz." That's why *Seventeen* continues to pack in the ad pages, even though the teen market is loaded with competitors. It's the power of perception. It's also why *Wired* magazine got so much notice, even as it launched into a market already packed with computer titles. Magazines seen as the "best" or the "freshest" or the "most authoritative" can win over advertisers.

5. The Law of Focus: *The most powerful cconcept in marketing is owning a word in the prospect's mind.*

Consider the following brands. If you did a word association, it would sound something like this:

Crest	cavities
Volvo	safety
Domino's	delivery
Pepsi-Cola	youth

It's the same thing with magazines. Try it in reverse:

television	TV Guide
cars	Motor Trend
fashion	Vogue
retirement	Modern Maturity

The most established and successful magazines are those that have a rock-hard identity within their category.

6. The Law of Exclusivity: *Two companies can't win the same word in the prospect's mind.*

It wouldn't help Burger King, for instance, to tell customers "You deserve a break today." And only one beer gets to be "The king of beers." So it is in the magazine world. Who else but *Good Housekeeping* could, for instance, have a "Seal of Approval?" If your magazine has a word or phrase associated

If your magazine has a word or phrase associated with it, that's golden for winning the battle for readers' minds and hearts.

with it, that's golden for winning the battle for readers' minds and hearts.

7. The Law of the Ladder: *The strategy to use depends on which rung of the ladder you occupy.*

Avis, as we know, has been the number two rental-car company for years. Instead of fighting that ranking, the company claimed it to create its classic positioning slogan: "We try harder."

However, with magazines, numbers two and three in a category can't get away with a simple image campaign. They need to explain *why* they're the better choice, whether it's because of superior readership, targeted circulation or quality editorial.

Which leads us to this point: If you're not among the market leaders—the number ones, the Bibles of the Industry—what can you do to make yourself stand out? That's what we'll take up in the next section.

CHANGING PERCEPTIONS

Let's go back to the example from "The Power Presentation" (Vol. I, Ch. 22). You may recall that when I created a presentation for *Apparel Industry*, I led clients to accept this conclusion: Even though our magazine wasn't the industry bible, it did possess "SUD." Clients could reach more of their market with *Apparel Industry* than with our competition, *The Bobbin*.

What I did was position our magazine right up against the competition. You too, can position your magazine against your competitors—or against other types of media, or even other types of magazines.

A lot depends on the kinds of perceptions you need to create. *The American Bar Association Journal*, for instance, wanted to crack upscale, national accounts. So, rather than

19

compare itself to other lawyer publications, it compared the financial worth of its readers with that of readers of *The Wall Street Journal*, *Forbes*, and *Fortune*.

ABA Journal Has a Higher Median HH Income			
Median Household Income			
ABA Journal	*Wall Street Journal*	*Forbes*	*Fortune*
$129,600	$105,400	$100,800	$97,200

Every magazine, no matter where it sits in its market, has some unique attribute or benefit that gives it a position of value. It can position itself by editorial, circulation, graphics, frequency, or ad sales and rates. It can position its market niche. It can position its readership.

However a magazine chooses to position itself, positioning becomes the glue that holds together its sales presentations. Put another way, presentations are positioning statements.

As you close your presentation, you want to see your client nod in agreement with your carefully built proposal. You want to weave a story for your client, to lead him through every pivotal point in a seamless, effortless transition. To do it, you may have to make a number of odd pieces fit: subscriber studies, audit reports and editorial awards. But if you let your positioning be your guide, you'll have a solid base for a sale.

Look at how *Good Housekeeping* used positioning in the in the early '90s. At that time, the magazine's sizable task was not only to position itself against competitors, but to make a wholesale change in how buyers perceived the magazine.

My belief, and probably that of many women of my generation, was that *Good Housekeeping* was a magazine my mother read. The advertising community believed this too, despite demographic and subscriber data to the contrary. The challenge for the publisher was to reposition *Good Housekeeping* in the minds of future advertisers.

The first step was to get advertisers to accept how change has occurred in society, and how the magazine has mirrored those changes. To do it, *Good Housekeeping* walked advertisers step by step through the life cycle of the baby boomer (the hot target market), explaining the shift in culture from the "Childhood '50s" to the "Protest '60s," "Feminist '70s" and "Yuppie '80s."

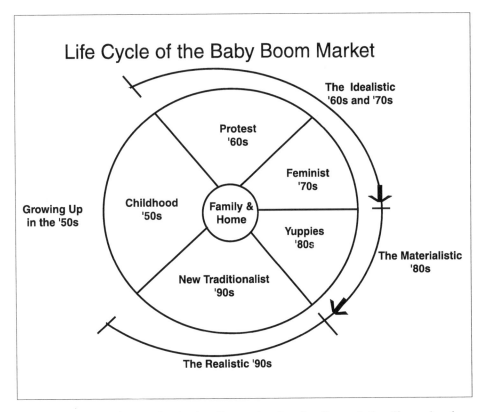

Good Housekeeping *walked advertisers step by step through the life cycle of the baby boomer.*

Then, using a term coined by research company Yankelovich & Associates, it showed advertisers that the "New Traditionalist '90s" actually completed the circle. The '90s value system of stability and equilibrium was actually just one step away from the traditionalist '50s of boomer childhoods. With this cyclical logic, *Good Housekeeping* sales reps made it easy for advertisers to accept the conclusion that society had entered its "New Traditionalist" phase—and that *Good Housekeeping* was the magazine to address it.

The title's media kit inserts showed—through strong visual images, not statistics—that its readers were not strictly housewives and members of sewing circles, but professional and family-oriented women of the 1990s.

The series of ads themselves first took a gentle approach to the new concept. The first showed a mother ("The contemporary woman whose values are rooted in tradition"); the second a trio of doctors ("They still find time to help their kids with homework"), and the third a hard-hatted laborer ("The new traditionalist. She's a woman who loves her job, even when icicles form on her hard hat"). All told, they added up to a new image for Good Housekeeping, one that proved potent in creating a new "buzz" for the magazine among advertisers.

THE NEW TRADITIONALIST.

A NEW KIND OF WOMAN WITH DEEP-ROOTED VALUES
IS CHANGING THE WAY WE LIVE.

There's a rebirth in America.

There's a renewal, a reaffirmation of values, a return to quality and quality of life.

We have seen it approaching, we have felt it happening, it has begun to affect our lives.

And now, suddenly, it is upon us in full force.

To us it's a woman who has found her identity in herself, her home, her family. She is the contemporary woman whose values are rooted in tradition.

The quality of life she has chosen is the embodiment of everything that Good Housekeeping has stood for.

The values she is committed to are the values we have always represented — the Magazine, the Seal, the Institute.

Who else can speak to the New Traditionalist with that kind of authority and trust?

That's why there's never been a better time than now for Good Housekeeping.

AMERICA IS COMING HOME TO GOOD HOUSEKEEPING

23

THE NEW TRADITIONALISTS.

HOW TO DELIVER 300 BABIES A YEAR AND STILL HAVE TIME TO BE A MOTHER.

Here are three of the busiest doctors you'll ever meet. They delivered over 300 babies last year. Yet they still find time to help their kids with homework and go out with their husbands on Saturday night.

To make time for family and career

they formed a joint practice. "We share responsibilities, cover for each other," says Dr. Laura Corio (center). She and her partners, Dr. Lynn Friedman (left) and Dr. Lee Morrone (right), have built a very successful practice, and are living "very fulfilling" lives.

No magazine is more dedicated to the values women are seeking today, or can speak to the New Traditionalist with the authority and trust of Good Housekeeping. She believes in Good Housekeeping – the Magazine , the Institute, the Seal.

AMERICA BELIEVES IN GOOD HOUSEKEEPING

THE NEW TRADITIONALIST.

SHE'S A WOMAN WHO LOVES HER JOB —
EVEN WHEN ICICLES FORM ON HER HARDHAT.

When winter storms hit the Blue Ridge Mountains, Emily McCoy straps on her tools, and works through the night on high voltage lines.

Nobody said it was easy. Emily trained for the job when she was divorced and a single mother.

But today she's "real happy" about her job, her paycheck and her life with her 8-year old daughter and her new husband.

Her energy, her attitudes, and her values embody the New Traditionalist movement that now affects almost every aspect of American life.

No magazine can speak to the New Traditionalist with the authority and trust of Good Housekeeping.

That's why there has never been a better time for Good Housekeeping – the Magazine, the Institute, and the Seal.

AMERICA BELIEVES IN GOOD HOUSEKEEPING

25

CREATE A THOROUGH PRESENTATION

Once you've determined your own magazine's SUD—its position in the marketplace—you, too, must present it thoroughly and comprehensively. You can't just make a bold statement. If *Good Housekeeping,* for instance, had simply announced "We reach more professional women than you think," it's very unlikely anyone would have paid attention.

Let's walk through a typical categorical presentation to show how you might use positioning to your own advantage. Say you sell for a title we'll call *Sports Car Illustrated* and you're presenting to hubcap manufacturers. You don't simply announce "Our magazine reaches hard-core enthusiasts in the sports-car market." In the hearts and minds of hubcap buyers, you need to show that your title is better positioned than any other title in the market.

How do you do it? First determine what's special, unique and different about your publication. After laying out your competitor's magazines and studying their editorial and advertisers, you may discover that *Sports Car Illustrated* is user-friendly, not just another showcase for fancy cars. It's the kind of magazine that gets torn and oil-smeared from sitting around the garage, always ready to inspire the reader to try new mechanical feats. It's the magazine for people who love to spend Saturdays browsing in auto-parts stores looking for new chrome customizing goodies.

So, you can position your magazine as the resource for tinkering addicts: "It's the next best thing to having a friendly mechanic coaching readers right in their own garage."

That makes *Sports Car Illustrated* the perfect place for a hubcap manufacturer to find people who love hubcaps. All you have to do now is tie that positioning into your presentation. You can use the Sales Presentation Worksheet (Vol I, Ch. 22).

Sales Presentation Worksheet

	Sales Point	Facts	Story	Visual	Anticipated Objections
1. Opening					
-attention getter					
-client objectives					
2. Market					
-description		✓			
-size/scope	✳	✓	✓	✓	
-sales volume					
-description					
-buying behavior					
-growth				✓	
-history					
-trends					
3. Publication					
-circ./demographics		✓		✓	
-readership		✓			
-editorial					
-cost		✓			
4. Proposal					
-pages					
-added-value					
5. Confirmation					
6. Implementation					

This worksheet helps you prioritize the points of your sales story.

1. *Restate your client's needs and commitment to the market.* "We know sports-car enthusiasts comprise 45 percent of your market. And we'll show you that our readers are not only enthusiasts but spend more than $30 million annually on sports car hubcaps." Then discuss the details of how your publication delivers the market, looking at circulation, demographics, editorial, readership and advertising. At this point, you can tie in your strong visuals: maybe photographs of readers in their garages or with their customized cars. You might even throw a blackened dog-eared copy of the magazine onto the presentation table.

27

2. *Address your client's advertising goals and objectives.* Don't just talk about the size and scope of the hubcap market, the sales volume available to your client, or how readers buy hubcaps. Think about how your client already reaches the sports car market, and whether he's having trouble finding distributors or reaching buyers. Is the client meeting his own sales goals? If he isn't, maybe it's because he's not reaching the real down-and-dirty enthusiasts who will spend their last dollar on a great set of wheels.

   You might also address trends in the hubcap market, like the decline of wire wheels, or opportunities in aluminum wheels. Talk about how your readers replace their own hubcaps yearly, or how 40 percent switch from standard to custom hubcaps when buying a new car.

3. *Talk about how you deliver the market.* "Our readers comprise one-quarter of all sports car buyers, and they spend 50 percent more on parts than the readers of our competition." Now is the time to talk about reach and numbers, the geographic regions your magazine covers, titles, job functions, growth, renewal, whether you have exclusive readers or pass-along readers, and what your audit shows about your magazine versus your competitors. Remember to emphasize that parts aren't sold to people who day-dream about family cars—they're sold to parts freaks like your readers.

4. *Show your readers' level of involvement.* "*Sports Car Illustrated* readers spend more time with our magazine than they do with any other magazine they receive at home. We generate 5,000 letters to the editor every month, and have received 16 editorial awards from the Sports Car Association of America." Talk here about the quality of your editorial, about how many pages are devoted each

month to the hubcap business. Bring letters from readers, or talk about how they call editors daily asking for help and advice in choosing parts.

5. *Show competitive advertising effectiveness.* "If you advertise with our magazine, you'll spend half as much to reach each hubcap prospect as you would with our competition." Show the effective reach of your CPM among your client's buyers. If you can demonstrate a low cost-per-contact, or high return on investment, you'll have added gravy to the meat of your marketing story.

6. *Propose an advertising program.* "With your 12-month-schedule, we'll showcase your hubcaps exclusively at our booth at the annual Sports Car Trade Show. We'll also highlight your product in our annual car-giveaway promotion." Talk about your full advertising program, merchandising and the total client investment.

And be sure to add how your readers—your client's buyers—will be swarming all over the booth to get first crack at the latest news in parts.

If you've carefully constructed your presentation around your *positioning statement*, you'll have your buyers' full attention at this crucial stage. By this time, your advertisers should be focused on the enthusiastic audience and hands-on editorial that make *Sports Car Illustrated* special, unique and different. They should leave with a clear perception that your magazine is the perfect vehicle for their advertising.

When you follow the logic of the Sales Presentation Worksheet, you can't help but create a compelling buy for your client—provided you've got the right positioning to tie it all together.

By working on its positioning, a magazine can become a better marketing partner for its clients. You can make your clients feel that your title meets their needs. There's no better way to do this than to tailor your position.

But remember, you alone can't position your magazine. Positioning is a company effort, something taken on by editorial, sales, circulation and promotion working under a strong vision. After all, changing market perception is a huge task: look how Chrysler had to regroup after its financial fiascoes of the early '80s.

However, you can, at least, understand positioning. To sell effectively, you must understand your own magazine's position and work with it. No matter what your marketplace image, whether you're seen as the the Number One leader or industry muckraker, you can do your part to improve or transcend your magazine's positioning.

2

SELLING the VALUE of YOUR MARKET

*"Last year our customers bought more than one million quarter-inch drill bits
and none of them wanted to buy the product.
They all wanted quarter-inch holes."*
—Anonymous

By now, you've probably got a good idea of how you can position your title in the marketplace. You know the strengths and weaknesses of your competitors, you've got a handle on your magazine's niche and you know what makes your title special, unique and different.

But how well can you position your *market*?

It's tricky. "Market" is not the same as circulation or readership. It's not knowing, "We reach 50,000 swimwear buyers." If you'll recall our earlier chapters on marketing, it's knowing the following:

✦ How many swimwear buyers are in the entire swimwear universe.

✦ Which of those buyers are your client's prospects.

♦ Which of those buyers are your readers.

♦ The growth trends, size and future of the swimwear industry.

♦ And, most important, the amount of overlap between your readers and your client's prospects.

Knowing your market is critical. Remember, your clients aren't just buying a magazine page. They're buying the chance to penetrate a market. They need to know they should take advantage of that opportunity.

To demonstrate the value of your magazine's market to your clients, you must first know your magazine's ability to deliver all or particular segments of that market. That means knowing all the marketing points in "Explore the Essentials of Marketing" (Vol. I, Ch. 5). It even means knowing how sensitive the market is to economic barometers, legislation, changes of government leadership and technological advances.

Once you know what goes into your market, you must sell its value. That means telling clients how your title's market fits in with their marketing needs.

SIX CRITICAL ISSUES

Clearly, every magazine has a different marketing story to tell its advertisers. But in most cases, that marketing story will touch on six basic issues of importance to advertisers:

1. *Who's in the market*

2. *Growth of the market*

3. *Current state of the market*

4. *Size of the market*

5. *Buying power in the market*

6. *Future of the market*

Let's see how *Builder* magazine demonstrates the value of each of these marketing issues in its sales-presentation kit.

✦ *Who's in the market.* *Builder* points out that it reaches a market of new-home builders. Those builders, of course, are exactly whom construction-materials advertisers would like to reach.

✦ *Growth of the market.* *Builder* notes that single-family housing starts topped the one million mark four years in a row, that the average single-family home exceeds 2,000 square feet, and that new construction-material sales continue at a near record level. This shows a broader playing field for advertisers.

✦ *State of the market.* In bright graphics, the magazine points out the steady sales of new single-family homes, how mortgage interest rates are dropping, the rising number of new housing starts, and the relative affordability of new homes. This demonstrates that Builder's market maintains relative strength and stability.

✦ *Size of the market.* New construction reached $163.8 billion for 1996, while new construction-material sales reached nearly $75 billion. This spells plenty of financial opportunity for Builder's advertisers. To emphasize this issue, *Builder* outlines how each region of the country remains strong in housing starts.

✦ *Buying power in the market.* *Builder* details how new-home builders are adding more bathrooms, fireplaces, garages, air-conditioning units and other building product into new homes. Clearly, new-home builders wield plenty of purchasing power in those markets.

✦ *Future of the market.* *Builder* predicts that new construction will continue to dominate residential construction. Low mortgage interest rates, strong materials sales and relative affordability will push the housing market for the foreseeable future.

Clearly, *Builder's* combined message to advertisers is simple: "*Builder* provides a stable, lucrative and growing market for products and services." The magazine's media kit (following page) outlines the research, statistics and trends that support the strength of its market picture.

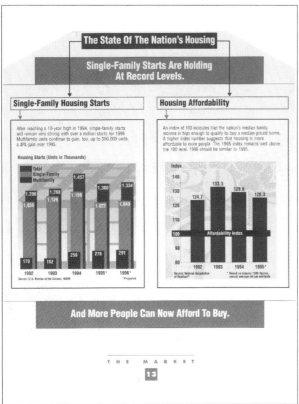

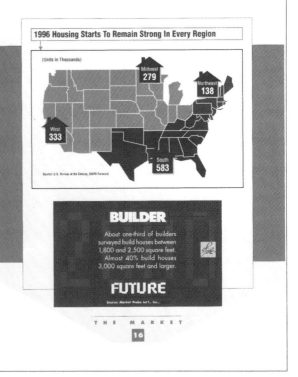

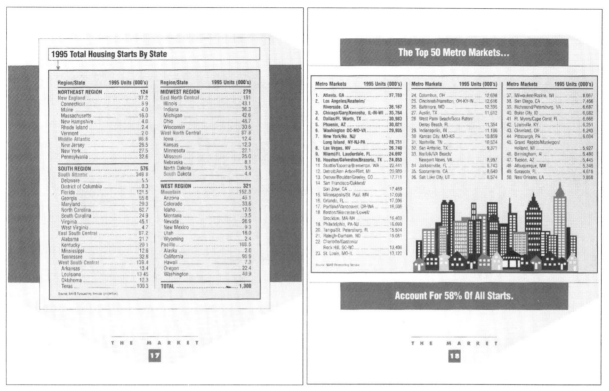

Builder's *media kit outlines the salient points for selling the value of the new-construction markets.*

Carrying it one step further, you can bring in any number of research materials to make your points about your own magazine's market. You can include, for example:

✦ *Market studies*, which indicate who's in the market, as well as the size and buying power.

✦ *Industry studies and reports*, which detail the size and scope of the market, as well as its growth and future.

✦ *Government reports,* such as Census Bureau statistics, which demonstrate geographic distribution and/or demographics.

✦ *News clips and articles*, which show up-to-date information about the state of the market. *Working Mother* magazine, for instance, cited numerous national magazine articles to demonstrate the growing trend of moms in the workforce.

35

Working Mother displays numerous national magazine articles to show the growing trend of moms in the workforce.

FITTING MARKETS TO ADVERTISERS

Of course, in *Builder*'s case, it was relatively easy to connect advertisers to the market message. After all, *Builder*'s advertisers are suppliers for plumbing, electricity, lumber, fixtures, tiles and other products and services needed by new-housing builders. They're satisfied to hear that *Builder* reaches the market they need, and that the market opportunities are stable and growing.

For other magazines, though, it's not always easy to make the market fit the client's market. For example, let's say you sell for a general sports magazine, and your client sells premium golf clubs. How do you convince him that your market, which only *includes* golfers, is a good buy compared to a golf magazine's market, which includes *only* golfers?

Or, if you sell for the golf title, how do you position your golfing market as a better buy for a T-shirt manufacturer than the general sports magazine, your competitor?

36

If you sell for a magaine that reaches a very complex market, like engineering or microcontamination, how easily can you explain the value of *that* market to advertisers?

Perhaps you sell for a magazine that addresses a seasonal marketplace, like skiing. How do you convince advertisers to keep buying space year-'round?

My point is this: To sell the value of your market, you need to understand not only its strengths, but its problems and limitations. Furthermore, you need to turn those challenges into opportunities. Let's look at a few of those issues now.

GOING HORIZONTAL OR VERTICAL?

One of the major guideposts in selling your market, of course, is knowing whether your magazine is *horizontal* or *vertical.*

You might recall these definitions from *Ad Sales*, Volume I. A horizontal book, for instance, might be *Dr. Dobb's Journal,* "targeted at the professional software developer who designs and writes software." The readers, though all software developers, actually work in diverse industries: manufacturing, finance, high-tech businesses, home-based businesses, government, education and so on.

A vertical computer magazine, on the other hand, might be *Government Computer News.* Its 80,000 readers may work in different areas of information management, but they all focus on government-computer work.

The difference is crucial to ad sales. If you work on a *vertical* publication—a golf magazine—and you're selling to a *horizontal* client—a T-shirt manufacturer—you must convince your client that your market is worth targeting.

Conversely, if you sell for a *horizontal* title—the sports magazine—and you're dealing with a *vertical* client—the golf club manufacturer—you have to demonstrate that the value of the market niche outweighs the "waste" factor (those readers who aren't golfers). Or you have to convince your client that the title allows him to test new markets in addition to his target market.

Often, horizontal and vertical titles need to pursue the same advertisers anyway. Let's look at the equestrian-magazine market. One publication reaches both Western- and English-riding enthusiasts. Another reaches only Western riders and a third only English riders. Each publication occupies a different market position, which means each has an advantage with different types of marketers.

Naturally, if you represent the Western-rider magazine, you want to target vertical clients first: horse breeders and equipment advertisers who specialize in the Western market.

If you're a horizontal equestrian magazine, you probably have an advantage with veterinarian suppliers—particularly if your circulation is larger than the English or Western magazine.

But what if the Western rider title wants the business of veterinarian suppliers? The sales rep, in that case, might want to prove that her market is of value to her client, even if it's not as a large as the horizontal magazine's. And if the horizontal title wants Western horse breeders, the salesperson has to show that his market delivers more Western readers than the specialized title.

Once you've determined how your magazine's market matches up with your advertiser's, you're ready to move to the next stage: finding out how goods and services move through the market, and where your advertiser stands in that pattern.

TAKING THE MYSTERY OUT OF THE MARKET

Some market advantages are easy to explain to advertisers. Perhaps your client sells bird food wholesale to pet stores. Your magazine is the market leader among bird owners. Presto! All your client needs to know is that an advertisement can direct readers to her bird food product in their favorite pet store.

But other markets are tougher to evaluate. Let's say you've got the same client, but now you sell for *Avian Specialist*, a magazine directed to bird veterinarians. The question becomes, if bird vets neither buy nor distribute your client's product, why should she advertise?

You can show the value of the avian veterinary market by pointing out that when it comes to buying bird food, 85 percent of bird owners follow their veterinarian's recommendations. Clearly, if vets don't know about your client's product, they can't recommend it to buyers. By not advertising, your client is missing a potent sales opportunity!

The Use of Charts

For markets that are particularly tough to explain, you may find that pictures do the job much better than words. For instance, when I was hired as a consultant for a magazine in the microcontamination market, I didn't know a thing about the market. I sat down with the ad director and said, "Tell me about the microcontamination market." I didn't understand what the ad director told me, so I went to a salesperson, then to the editor. When I still couldn't grasp his explanation, I finally handed him a pen and asked him to chart it out for me: the market, the part his magazine reached, and the part it didn't reach.

It took him a long time to draw the chart. When he finished it, I finally understood what everyone had been saying. We took the chart back to the sales department, where the sales force grabbed it from me, delighted to have a powerful tool for illustrating their market.

If your own market is complex or highly technical, ask your ad director to help you "illustrate" it. If he or she can't do it, get input from your editors. It may be that the entire team needs to sit down. The more complicated the industry, the more critical the task. After all, if you can't explain the market to your advertisers, you can't expect them to know its value!

Let's take a look at how some magazines manage to take the mystery out of their complex markets.

Look at the chart for *Water and Waste Digest* (page 40). Notice how this market divides into three basic sections: the municipal market, the industrial market, and the consulting engineer. This helps to stimulate and streamline presentations to clients: Who are we? Who are you? How can we work together?

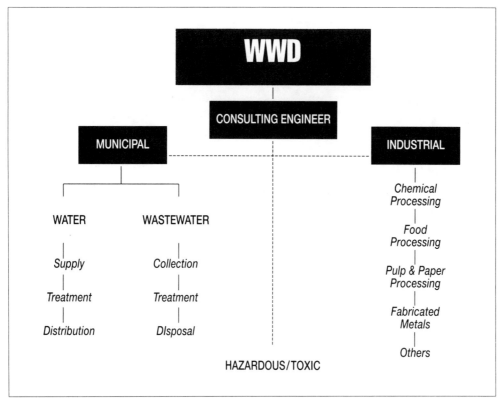

This chart shows the three interrelated markets in the water and waste water treatment industry.

If *WWD* approaches clients who sell management software, for instance, it can tell a sales story about its vertical reach among consulting engineers. If the client produces filters, *WWD* can show its horizontal reach among industrial and municipal waste water facilities.

In a more detailed chart (page 41), the magazine shows how its editorial coverage of water filtration fits into the water treatment process. That would be of interest to clients who perhaps produce water treatment chemicals or provide treatment equipment.

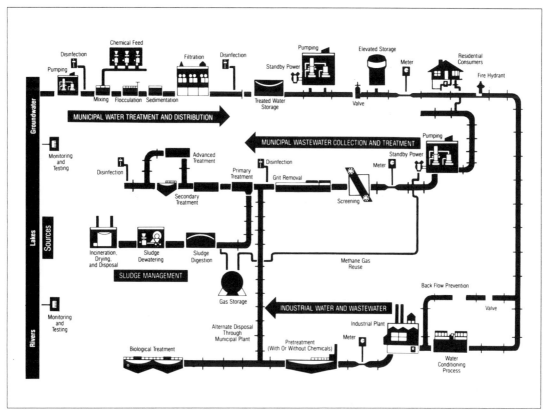

This detailed picture shows how Water and Waste Digest *covers different market segments within the water and waste-water treatment process.*

Other magazines use similar charts. *Computer Reseller News* is a vertical magazine that frequently has to appeal to horizontal clients. As shown in its chart of the computer market, all computer sales begin with an original equipment manufacturer (OEM), like Apple or Hewlett-Packard. Obviously, OEMs can market in any number of ways: directly to middlemen—distributors and wholesalers—or directly to end-users, whether corporate or consumer. Many marketers combine approaches.

What the chart makes clear, though, is that the value-added reseller (which includes both value-added channels and computer retailers) is the "critical link in the chain." The resellers, after all, recommend computer solutions to both businesses and consumers. Resellers are more than a passive distribution link. They're in a position to "advertise" a computer product and make a sale. That's how *Computer Reseller News* sells the value of its reseller market.

41

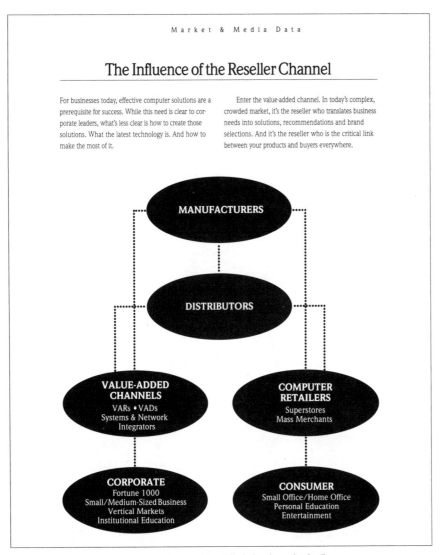

Market & Media Data

The Influence of the Reseller Channel

For businesses today, effective computer solutions are a prerequisite for success. While this need is clear to corporate leaders, what's less clear is how to create those solutions. What the latest technology is. And how to make the most of it.

Enter the value-added channel. In today's complex, crowded market, it's the reseller who translates business needs into solutions, recommendations and brand selections. And it's the reseller who is the critical link between your products and buyers everywhere.

MANUFACTURERS

DISTRIBUTORS

VALUE-ADDED
CHANNELS
VARs • VADs
Systems & Network
Integrators

COMPUTER
RETAILERS
Superstores
Mass Merchants

CORPORATE
Fortune 1000
Small/Medium-Sized Business
Vertical Markets
Institutional Education

CONSUMER
Small Office/Home Office
Personal Education
Entertainment

The value-added reseller is the "critical link in the chain."

Likewise, a chart from the media kit of *Publish* magazine details all the interrelationships of its desktop publishing universe, from input to design to the final product. Again, this shows how each market segment plays an important role in distribution and purchasing. Similarily, a chart from *VA Practitioner* illustrates the buying power of its market using an outline of the human body to make its point.

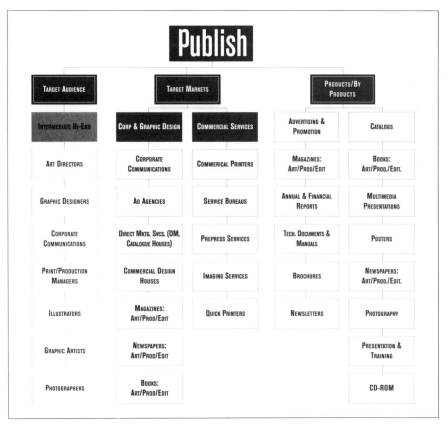

Publish *magazine shows the interrelationships of its target markets.*

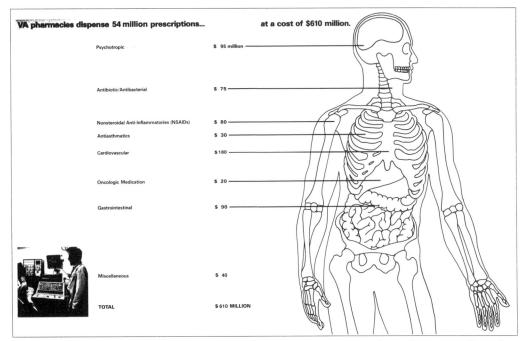

Chart from VA Practitioner *illustrates the buying power of its market using an outline of the human body.*

Finally, the chart below from an architecture business magazine addresses the concerns of building-equipment advertisers who would rather pursue contractors than architects. Although contractors indeed purchase supplies and equipment, most sign for purchases only after receiving detailed specifications from architects. That means architects are a valuable market for advertisers, and the point, of course, is that this magazine delivers that market of architects.

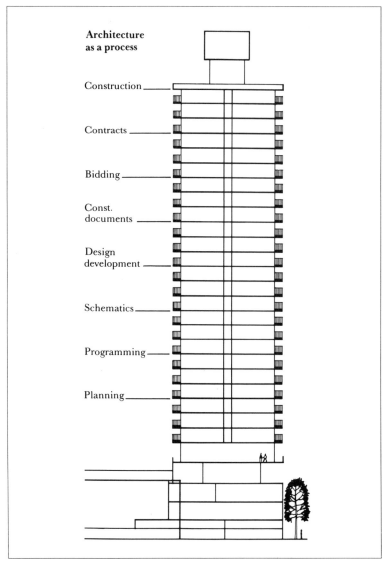

An architecture magazine illustrates how architects are the first link in the building chain.

CHANGING PERCEPTIONS ABOUT YOUR MARKET

Sometimes, your magazine's market doesn't need explaining so much as it does repositioning.

Let's consider the gay consumer market. For years it was seen as a small, peripheral consumer category, only addressed by gay-specific marketers. But in the '90s, many big advertisers—Absolut, Ikea, AT&T—started targeting gays.

Had the market changed? No. But *perceptions* had. Suddenly magazines like *The Advocate* were able to convince clients of the economic and lifestyle clout of its readers.

Perhaps your own market suffers from misperception, whether socio-economic, cultural, ethnic, racial, age, gender or lifestyle-based. Maybe advertisers think of your market as comprising more lower-level managers than top executives. Maybe they believe it's geared more towards females than males. Whatever the market perception, *you* have the ability to change it. Just as you learned in the previous chapter how to position your magazine, you can now learn how to position your market.

Modern Maturity decided to take a new marketing path when it wanted to pursue big consumer categories. The magazine was well aware of advertisers' tendency to think of older people as poor, frail and inactive. Thanks to its widespread marketing campaign, the magazine soon convinced prospects that the "mature" market, age 55 and older, has a higher percentage of discretionary income than any other age group. It also took pains to show that seniors are a lot healthier and more active than stereotypes would grant.

In this case, too, *Modern Maturity* thought it was a good idea to show clients *how* to approach this market. So it created a booklet that told advertisers to give older readers "a test drive" using copy-heavy ads and sample offers. Of course, the booklet also pointed out that while marketers can reach seniors through the mass media, a more effective approach would be to use an editorial vehicle that reached them in their own language, from their own point of view. Namely, to use *Modern Maturity* to sell their product.

T ake off 15 years. At least. They look and act many years younger than their mothers and fathers did at age fifty, sixty or seventy. Proper nutrition, a zest for fitness and a more active life-style have greatly extended the vital years. The lesson to marketers? Talk to a person, not a birth date. Enjoy their continued youth with them. How should you cast them in your advertising? Show them looking and behaving a good fifteen years younger than preceding generations did at the same age. See them as they are.

A page from Modern Maturity*'s booklet demonstrates the vitality of the mature market.*

Some magazines find they also need to challenge market perceptions about seasonality. If you sell for a sports title, your prospect who sells bike clothes might tell you, "I don't need to advertise all year long because sales don't happen all year long."

How might you respond? You can tell advertisers that it's not enough to talk to buyers at the projected moment they take buying action. An advertiser needs to capture *share of mind*—to get the customer's attention beyond the perceived buying season. Thus, bike prospects who advertise through the winter are likely to gain more share of mind than competitors who only show their wares in the spring.

Consider how *Bride's* magazine dealt with a misperception about seasonality. The common notion, of course, is that most people get married in spring or summer. But in fact, as *Bride's* market analysis shows, weddings are almost evenly distributed throughout the year. Moreover, as new brides leave the marketplace after marriage, newly engaged women enter it, giving companies in this industry a continuous opportunity to target new prospects.

THE BRIDAL MARKET IS A POWERFUL
YEAR 'ROUND SALES OPPORTUNITY

Total Marriages per year: 2,362,000

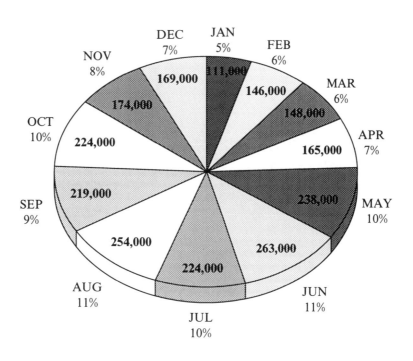

Total number of marriages first six months: 1,071,000 (46%)
Total number of marriages second six months: 1,264,000 (54%)

This chart from Bride's Magazine *targets misperceptions about seasonality in the marketplace.*

Whatever your market's misperceptions—seasonality, age, gender or race—be sure to address them when making your presentation. Your clients need to know that you deliver more than numbers. They need to know that your market delivers *value*.

3

SELLING the VALUE of YOUR CIRCULATION

"No great marketing decisions have been made on quantitative data..."
—Andrew Jackson (1767-1845)
7th President of the U.S. (1829-37)

❖ ❖ ❖

Once upon a time, I'm told, pretty much the only way to talk about circulation value was to carry around subscriber letters. Apparently, in those days before audit statements, waving around letters that said, "I love your magazine!" somehow enticed reluctant advertisers into buying pages.

Well, much as we like them, cheerful letters from readers no longer do much of a job of establishing circulation quality. Today's advertisers demand specific knowledge about circulation quality, and today's sales reps have a far more complicated task in demonstrating it. No longer can the publisher's statement do the whole job of establishing circulation quality.

In fact, the first task in selling the value of circulation actually involves going back a step. You first must establish the value of your *market*. Recall in the last chapter, for instance, how *Builder* magazine used its research and statistics to show the growth and vitality of its marketplace. From there, selling circulation value is just a leap of logic. All *Builder* has to do is show that the people within that marketplace are great advertiser prospects—*and* that they read the magazine.

Let's look at how the magazine does it. Within the media kit, *Builder* not only details who reads the magazine (builders, architects and subcontractors) but points out which percentage of the buying market belongs to each of those categories. Moreover, it outlines the magazine's "tough qualification standards," as well as its circulation growth, sales volume of its readers, and types of construction activity readers engage in.

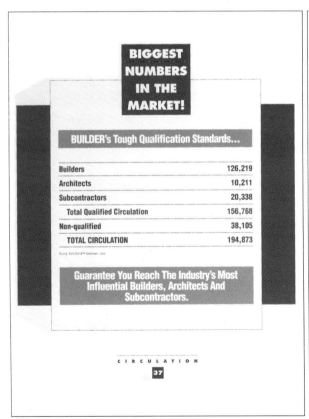

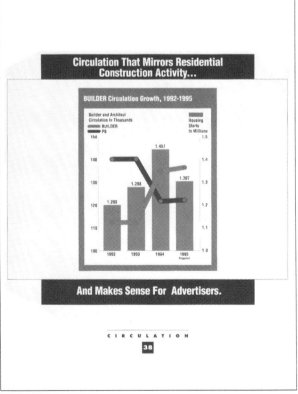

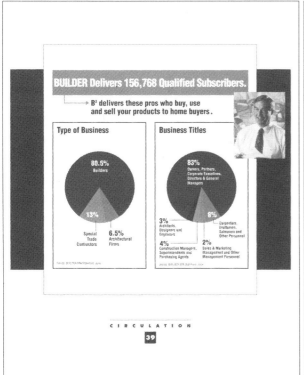

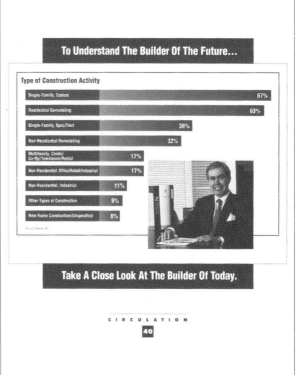

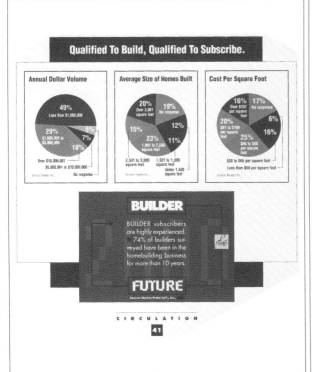

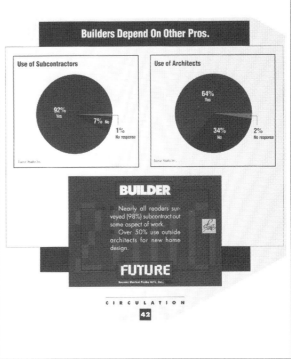

Builder's *media kit details information on who reads the magazine.*

In other words, the magazine relies on a wide range of sources and research to help its advertisers understand the value of its audience. That's what I'll talk about in this chapter.

THE HEART OF THE SALE

As you can see from *Builder*'s media kit, selling the value of circulation gets right to the heart of the Advertising Syllogism: *Your buyers are our readers. You can reach your buyers through our magazine.*

The bottom line in demonstrating circulation value is this: *The circulation must reflect the advertiser's market.* If your advertiser wants to reach mechanics who buy workboots, you must demonstrate that your readership comprises workboot buyers. If your advertiser wants to reach sewing-machine manufacturers, you have to prove that your magazine's readers make buying decisions for sewing-machine companies. In *Builder*'s case, advertisers need to know who buys or subcontracts for plumbing, roofing, and other building supplies. That's why the magazine specifically outlines that "98 percent of readers subcontract out some aspect of work."

Of course, advertisers want to know more about circulation quality as well. They want to know, for instance, that subscribers actually *read* the magazine, and that they are loyal to the title. They want to know if the readership is growing or flat, or if it's keeping on top of market trends. They want to know if circulation accurately reflects the size of their market, or if it's underreaching or overreaching the buying universe.

In addition, advertisers may want to know why they shouldn't go with a competitor whose circulation is bigger, or why one magazine seems to have such a low renewal rate, or why the circulation isn't 100 percent direct request.

To answer all these questions, sales reps need to be armed with as much circulation data as possible. That's what we'll talk about next.

FIRST...THE BASICS

To sell your magazine's circulation quality, you must first take an inventory of its strengths and weaknesses. To do so, refer to your publisher's statement (see "Using the Publisher's Statement to Sell," Vol. I, Ch. 13), talk to your circulation director and look up your reader research. Then, see if you can answer the following:

- ◆ Is your magazine's circulation paid or controlled?

- ◆ If paid, is it mostly newsstand-sold, or subscriber-sold? Does it sell at full price, or at a discount?

- ◆ If controlled, do most subscribers write in to request the magazine? Or are many subscribers attained through directories or compiled lists?

- ◆ Does your title reach top executives in its industry? Top buyers and decision-makers?

- ◆ What's its geographic distribution?

- ◆ What percent of the market does it reach? Is the circulation concentrated in only a certain segment of the market?

- ◆ Does it share readership with a competitor, or does it have exclusive readership?

- ◆ How high is its pass-along rate?

- ◆ How high is its renewal rate?

- ◆ How fast is the readership growing?

- ◆ What's the reader profile? What are the reader demographics?

Once you've collected your circulation facts, you can then use the information not only to present your circulation's strengths, but to anticipate some objections to its weaknesses.

Once you've got all your circulation facts in line, you can then use the information not only to present your circulation's strengths, but to anticipate some objections to its weaknesses. You can also gather the appropriate tools and statistics for presenting to advertisers the full story on your title's circulation values.

The first task, though, is to find your magazine's circulation strengths. As you go through your data, look for the following:

Size. Bigger is not necessarily better in magazine circulation. Yes, some advertisers do prefer mass circulation, particularly those that sell mass-market products like laundry detergent and cosmetics. Other advertisers, though, prefer smaller, targeted audiences. For them, the less waste circulation, the better.

Total market coverage. For most advertisers, this is the critical, number-one area of importance. Magazines that offer complete coverage of an advertiser's market are automatically top-shelf buys, even if their overall circulation is smaller than the competition's.

The closer you can match readers to buyers the greater your ability to demonstrate circulation quality.

The closer your magazine's circulation matches your advertiser's market, the better. So, to determine your circulation value, you must first find out the size and extent of your advertiser's market.

◆ Which buyers does she need to reach?

◆ What are the characteristics of those buyers?

◆ How many of those buyers exist in the marketplace?

◆ What portion of that marketplace does your readership cover?

◆ How closely do your own reader's characteristics match those of your advertiser's buyers?

The closer you can match readers to buyers—the closer you can come to the heart of the Advertising Syllogism—the greater your ability to demonstrate circulation quality.

Buyer and decision-maker penetration. Even if your title is number two in ad pages and number three in circulation, reader quality can give you an advantage. Your advertisers, after all, want to reach buyers, not just numbers. Luxury car advertisers, for instance, would rather reach 30,000 County A homeowners than 300,000 County C renters. Equipment suppliers would prefer 10,000 company executives to 100,000 middle-managers.

Barron's magazine makes this clear in its media advertising analogy: "Reach the right bird and the whole flock will follow." Though its circulation isn't as large as *Newsweek's* or *Time's*, it claims that its readers influence buying decisions and opinions. Get them, and everyone else in the advertiser's market falls in line.

Barron's *shows the advantage of targeting market leaders.*

Growth. In your research, you may find that while your title isn't the circulation leader in its field, it may still be a growth leader. Take a magazine we'll call *Modern Footwear.* Clearly, the chart below shows circulation has boomed over a five-year period. This shows the magazine has energy and relevance among its readers.

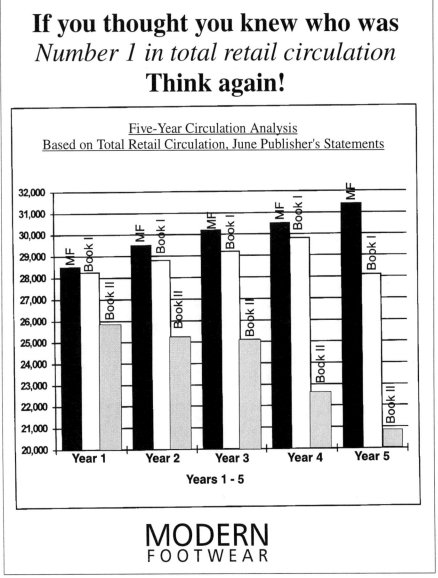

This graph shows that Modern Footwear *has had a healthy growth pattern compared to its competitors.*

Often, large-circulation, slow-growth magazines simply stay that way because of readership inertia. Readers may be buying or subscribing to the magazine more out of habit than of real interest. Magazines with growing circulation, on the other hand, usually attract active, interested readers. Circulation growth means success—in quality of editorial, in vitality, and in the ability to reach the marketplace.

Unduplicated readership. Magazines that reach most of the same readers as their competitors may find it tough to point out circulation advantages. But magazines that delivers unique audiences, or unduplicated segments of the market, offer advertisers a true quality advantage. Advertisers know they can reach buyers in those publications that they can't reach elsewhere.

ANTICIPATING OBJECTIONS

Once you've unearthed some of your title's circulation strengths, take a realistic look at its potential weaknesses. The best way to do that is not only to examine your own data, but to listen carefully to your advertisers during your probing and fact-finding. After all, your advertisers will likely prove sharper-eyed in finding your circulation flaws than you will. See if you can anticipate and answer some of the following common circulation objections:

"Your magazine isn't paid/controlled."

We've addressed this objection in other parts of this book, but it's one of those topics that never seems to exhaust itself. Simply put, some advertisers prefer paid circulation because they believe payment shows active reader interest. On the other hand, controlled-circulation titles often believe they deliver superior market coverage than their paid competitors.

How do you answer this objection? First, let's define "paid" and "controlled" circulation. According to the Business Publications Audit of Circulations (BPAC), "paid" circulation means that copies of the publication have been paid for by the purchaser and sent to the field served. "Controlled" circulation means copies of the publication have been sent free of charge to those subscribers who meet the requirements of "qualified circulation" in the field served. In other words, those readers who don't qualify to receive the magazine—either because they aren't in the industry served by the magazine, or don't meet other circulation requirements—do not receive the magazine.

It is true that *controlled* titles can probably claim greater market penetration than their paid competitors, as well as complete circulation to qualified decision makers. Under most circumstances, a paid publication simply can't provide the same reach as a controlled title.

For instance, let's assume a controlled title called *Potato Growers USA* reaches 25,000 potato farmers, who make up the entire known market. Now let's assume paid competitor *Spuds Today* also reaches the potato-farmer market. For *Spuds Today* to reach the same 25,000 potato farmers, it would have to somehow generate 100 percent paid response from the entire potato farmer market.

For a paid title, that's pretty unlikely. So, *Spuds Today* faces one of two scenarios:

1.   Send subscription solicitations to the 25,000 potato farmers in the market and likely fall short of its goal, or

2.   Send subscription solicitations to a larger universe beyond the potato farmers' market in order to gain a 25,000 circulation.

In other words, *Spuds Today*, as a paid title, would have to choose between *targeting* and *size* when making its circulation choices. Option one, for instance, would likely give the paid title a targeted, but smaller, circulation than *Potato Growers USA*. Option two, on the other hand, would give *Spuds Today* a similar-sized, but less targeted circulation than *Potato Growers USA*. After all, to reach 25,000 circulation, *Spuds Today* would probably have to solicit among beet farmers, suppliers and other non-potato farmers in the universe.

Either way, what happens? The controlled title, *Potato Growers USA*, ends up with the largest possible *targeted* circulation.

On the other hand, a paid title like *Spuds Today* may still claim that it has a higher pass-along circulation among larger farms than

Potato Growers. Moreover, it could argue that because *Potato Growers* reaches *all* the potato farmers, it also reaches those who don't buy advertised products. If the usual 80/20 rule applies, advertisers would need to reach only the top 20 percent of qualified buyers to make 80 percent of their sales. *Spuds Today*, as a paid publication in that industry, would likely have that top 20 percent of qualified buyers.

Moreover, paid titles like *Spuds Today* could also claim they "qualify" their readers through payment. They can argue, in other words, that only motivated readers would spend money to receive the magazine. For that reason, many paid publications that dominate a field often become "must-buys" in the marketplace.

In the end, however, it's important not to get too carried away arguing the merits of paid versus controlled. What's most important is reader quality. In short, if a magazine doesn't deliver the readers advertisers want to reach, it's simply not going to attract those advertisers, regardless of whether its circulation is paid or controlled.

"Your title is too newsstand and/or subscriber-dependent."

Just as many business advertisers differ on the merits of paid versus controlled, many consumer advertisers, likewise, differ on whether they prefer heavy newsstand sales or subscriber sales.

A title that's heavily dependent on newsstand buyers usually has active, interested readers. Because these readers buy the magazine on impulse, with money straight from their pocket, they're more likely to read it thoroughly than those who receive it in the mail.

On the other hand, newsstand circulation is often erratic compared to the more stable subscriber circulation. Subscribers are often more regular, loyal magazine readers. They've made an investment in the magazine and have established a stable relationship with it. They're not buying one issue out of curiosity; they're buying a subscription out of long-term interest.

Once again, the issue of subscribers versus newsstand buyers is not as critical as the issue of reader quality. If an advertiser shows

59

concern over the topic, make sure to bring her back to the main issue: Does the readership match the advertiser's market needs? After all, how a reader buys a magazine is not as important as who the reader is and whether the reader is a good prospect for the advertiser's business.

"You sell too many subscriptions at a discount/with a premium."

This is a tough issue for many consumer titles. Naturally, the more subscriptions a magazine sells at a discount price, the lower the perceived quality of the circulation.

Conversely, many magazines have good reason to sell at a discount price, or with a premium. Some titles, for instance, may be undergoing a start-up or relaunch, and may need to offer low prices in order to build up circulation. Some titles may offer premiums to make the high price of their subscriptions more palatable (which is why weeklies like *Time* and *Sports Illustrated* sell subscriptions with football phone premiums and the like).

Other titles may need to discount in order to stay competitive in the market. Say, for instance, a magazine I'll call *Today's Woman* has a basic price of $12 for 10 issues, and competitor *Women Today* has a basic price of $26 for 10 issues. Obviously, *Women Today* needs to sell at a 50 percent discount to even come close to the basic price of *Today's Woman*.

To answer this objection, you need to discuss your magazine's strategies with your circulation director. What appears as a circulation weakness can sometimes be a competitive necessity, or even strength.

"Your controlled-circulation magazine is not 100% direct request."

Most business advertisers, naturally, want to run with a magazine that carries as much direct-request circulation as possible. The reasons are clear: Those subscribers who specifically request the magazine are naturally more inclined to read it than those who simply

How a reader buys a magazine is not as important as *who* the reader is and whether or not the reader is a good prospect for the advertiser's business.

receive the magazine because their names were pulled from a directory or compiled list.

Here's a good response to that objection: "For total market coverage, many business publications have to rely on a number of sources —directories, association listings and compiled lists—in order to make sure the magazine gets to everyone who qualifies to receive it." Just because a subscriber doesn't send in a form doesn't mean that person isn't a valuable prospect for an advertiser. Many business publications can't afford to shortchange their market coverage by relying exclusively on direct-request subscribers. They need to include other sources as well. What's important is that their advertisers reach all effective buyers the moment their ads appear in the publication.

"You've got too many add/deletes among your subscribers."

Many business advertisers rightly get alarmed when they see huge turnover within a publication's circulation. What they immediately suspect is a) readers are leaving in droves because they don't like the magazine, or b) the title keeps filling its subscriber rosters with barely qualified names.

The truth is, though, that some magazines, especially those in high-tech industries, need to keep turning over their circulation simply to keep up with the pace of the industry. Here's one example from Jim Fischer, circulation expert of *The New York Observer*. During the 1980s, he points out huge consolidations and contractions swept the supermarket industry. At one point, A&P sent all supermarket titles a letter saying that the chain was closing 2,000 stores. Not surprisingly, Fischer's supermarket magazine started ringing up perhaps 8,000 add/deletes in a six-month period.

The only problem was that Fischer's competition was showing only 2,000 add/deletes over the same period. To advertisers, it looked like Fischer's magazine was highly unstable. So, the sales reps at Fischer's magazine began taking the A&P letter on calls with them. Suddenly, by showing advertisers this evidence of industry volatility, the magazine put its competitor in the spot of defending why it had such low reader turnover!

"Your circulation isn't as widespread/diverse as your competitor."

To the uninformed eye, bigger circulation always looks better. But smart advertisers understand that in some markets, the number of people they reach is not as important as where they reach them.

Say you work for a defense contracting magazine. Your competitor has the bigger circulation. But your magazine has the top decision makers in defense. A smart advertiser probably wouldn't look for big circulation because she may already know that the market doesn't hold that many decision makers. In the following promotional piece, *Rotor & Wing International* illustrates how it reaches that type of highly concentrated market.

Rotor & Wing *demonstrates how it reaches the decision makers.*

The same thing holds true for, say, a high fashion advertiser. He might pick Magazine A over the larger Magazine B simply because Magazine A has a better concentration in urban markets, or focuses exclusively on New York and Los Angeles. Specialty magazines that have a relatively small but fervently loyal readership often have the advantage for marketers trying to target these small but powerful markets. After all, any circulation that doesn't consist of advertiser prospects is simply wasted.

"Your renewal rate is too low."

Most circulation managers—not to mention sales reps—dread questions on renewal rates. The reason, simply, is that there really is no such thing as a renewal rate. Every magazine has several renewal rates—conversions from trial subscriptions, first-time renewals, second-time renewals, renewals at "birth," identified renewals and unidentified renewals. Moreover, each renewal rate differs by the source of subscriptions. Direct-mail subscribers, for instance, usually renew better than subscribers who come in through Publishers Clearing House.

Sales reps asked to discuss renewals need to make sure they understand the numbers fully, and can explain them in context. Let's say, for instance, that one sales rep tells his client his magazine's conversion rate (that is, the percentage of new subscribers who renew) is 25 percent. That might sound like the magazine is in serious trouble. But if the rep is working for a bridal magazine, or a high-tech publication where jobs change quickly, that figure might actually look desirable. In fact, an advertiser might see something wrong with a controlled-circulation high-tech book with a high renewal rate. A high number might indicate the magazine isn't keeping up with the industry.

"I don't like your reader demographics."

A magazine's readership profile is pretty much determined by editorial content. The magazine *Mobile Homeowner*, for instance, just isn't going to have the demographic draw of *Architectural Digest*.

Despite what their ad directors may wish to the contrary, some

63

magazines will always have older readers (women's-service titles), or predominantly female readers (health titles). Some circulation departments may try to nudge demographics by selecting different circulation sources or direct-mail lists. But it's almost impossible to budge a readership profile without changing editorial content.

What's important to keep in mind, though, isn't so much whether a magazine's reader demographics are objectively "desirable." The real issue is whether readers buy the advertiser's products. For instance, *Mobil Homeowner* readers might be far bigger purchasers of satellite dishes or certain packaged goods than *Architectural Digest* readers. Lower-income homemakers may prove far more brand-loyal for certain cleaning products or packaged foods than high-income professionals.

So, if an advertiser objects to reader demographics, just go back to the Advertising Syllogism. As long as your readers are your advertiser's buyers, all other considerations are secondary.

"Your circulation is too broad/diverse for our target."

Let's say your advertiser sells sporting goods. Your magazine addresses all retailers, while your competitor covers only sporting-goods merchandisers. Does your title, then, offer wasted circulation? Not necessarily. It may be that many of the large retail readers of your magazine influence buying decisions for sporting-goods departments. Or it may be that some non-sporting goods retailers are considering adding sports equipment to their lines. Or it may be that your title covers the top 35 percent of sporting-goods retailers, and at a lower CPM, than your competitor.

Broad circulation, in other words, doesn't necessarily translate into "wasted." After all, even advertisers themselves may have a tough time deciding whom they need to target. Let's take a high-tech advertiser selling computer equipment. Should the advertiser target the business managers who sign the checks, but don't understand the technology being sold? Or should it target the techies who understand the technology but can't make the purchase?

In cases like those, it may be an advantage to show that a maga-

> As long as your readers are your advertiser's buyers, all other considerations are secondary.

64

zine's circulation reaches both groups of readers. *IEEE Spectrum*, for instance, took this approach in its media advertising. In the following illustration, you can see how the title claimed the ability to hand computer advertisers both the executives and the techies. This helps advertisers know they needn't risk wasted circulation.

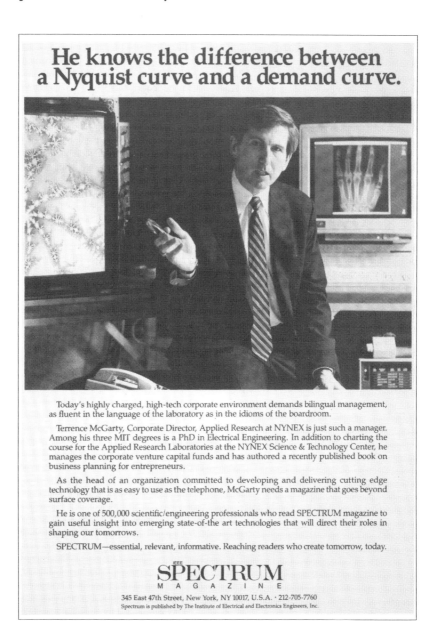

IEEE Spectrum *showed how computer advertisers could reach both the executives and the techies.*

"Your leads are lousy, so your circulation must be, too."

If your advertiser hands you a list of bingo cards and says, "25 percent of your leads are garbage," don't panic. The truth is, the quality of a magazine's circulation isn't always reflected in reader response. Most circulation directors find that when they trace back these "garbage" leads, most, if not all, were not on the magazine's circulation list! Many reader response cards are often submitted by individuals who see the magazine, but who are not regular readers or subscribers.

It's also helpful to remind advertisers that reader-response cards are the advertiser's opportunity to be in touch with small customers. After all, the advertiser's own sales force should already be in touch with large customers and prospects—who are, of course, also your magazine's readers. Bingo cards represent a way of reaching prospects not normally on your advertiser's radar.

THE TOOLS YOU'LL USE

You might think powerful circulation presentations begin and end with your publisher's statement. You'd be wrong. Yes, publisher statements run the whole gamut of circulation topics—from how subscribers qualified to how much circulation has grown. But as we all know, publisher's statements are also filled with often confusing, ambiguous or even trivial information. Moreover, many sales reps are as uncomfortable with this data-filled document as many advertisers are.

That's not to say, though, that you should ignore your publisher's statement! On the contrary, it's the first step for any discussion on circulation (if you need a refresher on it, turn back to "Using Publisher's Statements to Sell," Vol. I, Ch. 13). In the meantime, keep in mind a multitude of other circulation tools that can give your numbers meaning. Consider the following:

Subscriber forms. Not only do many subscriber forms show more specific detail about readers than BPA statements, they can also make specific, compelling points about reader quality.

Once, on a sales call, Fischer found that his magazine's prospect began deriding the title's subscribers, saying, in effect, that "secretaries were not decision makers." By flipping through subscriber forms he'd brought on the call, Fischer was able to show the prospect at least a half-dozen secretaries who'd indicated their buying power on their subscriber forms.

Subscriber forms can also demonstrate other salient points such as sales volume, number of employees or titles. Rather than reading data on a publisher's statement, advertisers can observe subscriber information in a "humanized" form. Subscriber forms show, in a specific, anecdotal way, that the magazine delivers on its promise of total coverage.

Reader service response cards. "Bingo" cards can show advertisers the variety of products and services that interest its readers. That's another demonstration of the magazine's readership value.

Pages from directories, association rosters, and so on. Business magazines that solicit readers from a variety of sources should demonstrate those sources to advertisers. Sales reps can then show that the magazine leaves no stone unturned in finding buyers in the advertiser's market. What ink manufacturer, for instance, wouldn't be impressed that a magazine delivers to top members of the American Printing Association?

Compiled lists. Like directory listings, compiled lists can show advertisers how a magazine finds its readers in particular target groups. Advertisers can discover, for instance, how one magazine reaches all senior-level human-resources managers in Fortune 1000 companies, or how another hits all brick manufacturers with sales volume of $1 million-plus.

Compiled lists can also demonstrate that a magazine is on top of market trends. In the late '70s, for example, when catalog showrooms burst on the scene, Fischer demonstrated to sporting-goods advertisers how his magazine was finding readers in the catalog showroom industry. A compiled list of showrooms showed names of sporting-goods buyers in this brand-new market, proving the magazine could deliver circulation in a market few others had even recognized.

The circulation manager. Sure, media supervisors may be skeptical of a sales rep's pitch on circulation numbers—so why not bring along the circulation manager to back up the information? In the same way that editors on a sales call lend credence to a magazine's editorial quality, so, too, does a circulation director lend credence to a magazine's circulation. Not only can the manager explain the numbers behind the circulation, but he can also explain the magazine's circulation goals and choice of sources. And, since media supervisors work with numbers themselves, they can appreciate a discussion with their counterparts on the magazine side.

A highlighted publisher's statement. Since circulation information is often hidden in dense and difficult text and numbers, why not make it easy on your advertisers? Create a way to highlight the points you want to make in your publisher's statement. For instance, show prospects that your magazine has never missed a rate base, sells at a premium price, and has boosted its rate base 22 percent in seven years. This kind of highlighting brings prospects to the impressive areas of your publisher's statement while simultaneously distracting them from weak areas.

Supplemental reports. Many business magazines analyze numbers beyond the data available in publisher's statements. This analysis can include:

✦ Sales volume breakdowns

✦ Unit breakdowns

✦ Title breakdowns

✦ Function breakdowns

✦ Reader-service response analysis

✦ Universe breakdowns

✦ Circulation growth

All these reports can demonstrate the quality of the coverage the magazine provides. The reports are particularly useful when compared with the competition.

Subscriber or reader research. Pull out any reader data that demonstrates quality demographics, commitment to your magazine, or enthusiasm for advertised products. Let your magazine's research prove that your readers are your advertiser's prospects.

Subscriber samples. Many sales reps learn the value of asking for computer printouts of subscribers to take with them on a sales call. Perhaps you're calling on a large distributor in Philadelphia. Why not bring along a list of Philadelphia subscribers? Chances are good the prospect will love poring over it, recognizing the names of his customers. There's no better way to demonstrate that his buyers are your readers.

Competitive analysis. A competitive analysis can point out the differences between your strengths and your competitor's weaknesses. Your magazine, for instance, can draw comparisons on any number of points, from promotion, growth rate, renewal rate, or the circulation statement itself.

Progressive Grocer ran one ad comparing BPA and ABC circulation statements of three publications in the field. It then highlighted the numbers in its favor, demonstrating its superiority as the most read, highest-quality trade publication at both the headquarters and the store level. (See illustration page 70.)

Some people feel it's not acceptable to take cheap shots at your competitors. And they're right. But it is fair play to compare available public data, particularly when dealing with agencies and sophisticated marketers. After all, that's why magazines choose to be audited in the first place!

Facts to help you evaluate Grocery Trade Media:

Circulation and industry coverage

Comparative Analysis of BPA and ABC Circulation Statements for Major Grocery Trade Media*

	Progressive Grocer BPA	Supermarket Business BPA	Supermarket News ABC
SUPERMARKET INDUSTRY			
Supermarket Headquarters	23,022	23,740	12,900
Supermarket Store Managers	21,124	18,953	11,854
Supermarket Store Personnel	10,953	11,348	627
TOTAL SUPERMARKET INDUSTRY	55,099	54,041	25,381
Wholesale Headquarters	9,203	10,162	7,013
OTHER (SMALL STORE UNITS)			
Superette Headquarters ($1-2 million vol.)	4,123	2,617	—
Convenience Store HQ	—	3,687	—
Other HQ & Store Circulation	—	—	1,722
TOTAL OTHER (SMALL STORE UNITS)	4,123	8,304	1,722
Food Brokers	2,575	3,599	3,338
Rack Jobbers/Service Merchandisers	936	1,460	
NON-RETAIL CIRCULATION	86	325	19,324
TOTAL CIRCULATION	72,022	75,892	56,778

*Latest comparable Statements available from all three publications

Progressive Grocer gives advertisers the most Supermarket Industry circulation where 73% of all retail grocery $-sales are made ($240 billion worth!), representing the advertiser's single most important sales target. In fact, Progressive Grocer reaches an unparalleled 98% of the U.S. Supermarket Universe!

Wholesale Headquarters buy for 96% of Independent Supermarket volume and 29% of Chain Supermarket volume, representing a prime $122 billion retail sales target. Progressive Grocer reaches 100% of all major Wholesale Headquarters and has the highest readership rating among all Independent Headquarters Executives (90.0%) — their biggest customers (1988 McGraw-Hill Research).

While Small Store coverage inflates the Total Circulation figure, it does not represent advertiser sales potential in any way comparable to the Supermarket Industry. For example, the Convenience Store Industry purchases and operates on a distinctly different basis. In effect, Convenience Stores are not in the Supermarket business.

In Progressive Grocer, the advertiser does not need to pay for Small Store Personnel or Convenience Store circulation in order to reach the Supermarket Industry. Fully 89% of Progressive Grocer's Total Circulation goes to the advertiser's primary prospects (Supermarket Industry and Wholesale Headquarters), representing the highest proportion of prime prospect coverage to Total Circulation in the field.

Non-Retail circulation ("Food Associations, Schools, Colleges, Libraries, Government Agencies, Manufacturers, Others Allied To Field and Qualification Not Determined" classifications) is virtually useless for the advertiser who wants to reach the retail grocery industry, and can represent as much as a 34% loss of advertising efficiency right from the start.

Readership (The Supermarket Industry makes *its* choice)

Fact: In every one of the 15 readership studies conducted to date by a variety of research firms and sponsors over the past 20 years, the supermarket industry has consistently rated Progressive Grocer as the most read, highest quality trade publication at both headquarters and store level. The very latest industry-wide study wherein McGraw-Hill Research asked the supermarket industry for its opinion, once again confirms Progressive Grocer's overwhelming media superiority.

Here are three major findings:

SURVEY OF SUPERMARKET PUBLICATION READERSHIP"
(Headquarters & Stores)

	READERSHIP (* Reading at least 1 out of 4 issues)	ADVERTISING READERSHIP	EDITORIAL QUALITY
PROGRESSIVE GROCER	86%	58%	66%
SUPERMARKET BUSINESS	69%	26%	47%
SUPERMARKET NEWS	55%	16%	40%
GROCERY MARKETING	42%	8%	26%

Commissioned May by Progressive Grocer after consultation with advertisers and agencies concerning research criteria. All surveys conducted by McGraw-Hill Research ascribe to the research guidelines and standards established by the American Marketing Association, Association of Business Publishers, Advertising Research Foundation, The Association of American Advertising Agencies and the Association of National Advertisers.

Special category-sections

Advertisers of related products can be positioned in these special sections when they appear.

NON-FOODS

"GM/HBA® Magazine" A complete magazine section in every issue of Progressive Grocer dealing specifically with the retailing and merchandising of General Merchandise and Health & Beauty Aids products serving 9 out of every 10 non-foods headquarters buying influences and store level management who read Progressive Grocer regularly. Standard Progressive Grocer rates.

MANUFACTURER/AGENCY EDITION

"Food Industry Forum" A special, front-of-book section written by and targeted to media, marketing, packaging, research, premium and sales executives of companies (and their advertising agencies) who sell their products through supermarkets. Thus, media, packaging, promotion and other service companies can advertise selectively just to our 16,500 manufacturer/agency readers not included in Progressive Grocer's regular circulation. B&W 1x page rate: $2,950. 4-color page rate: $5,000.

REGIONAL ADVERTISING

Regional advertising, from multi-state regions right down to specific Zip Code areas, is available in every issue of Progressive Grocer, handled as inserts or r.o.p. Minimum space: full page. Regions can be tailored to the advertiser's needs, based on sales districts, broker areas, Nielsen Regions, etc. by State, County or five-digit Zip Code zone blocks. Space reservations should be placed at least 45 days prior to publication date. Rates on request.

FOODSERVICE

"FoodService/Supermarkets" is a separately bound, monthly publication devoted solely to supermarket foodservice and distributed demographically with Progressive Grocer to 47,200 supermarket foodservice executives at headquarters and store level. B&W 1x page rate: $3,950. 4-color 1x page rate: $4,970.

ADVERTISING RECORD

The nation's advertisers invest more total pages and dollars per issue in Progressive Grocer than in any other supermarket publication.

Progressive Grocer *used a comparison of BPA and ABC circulation statements to show superiority in its field.*

Testimonials. Check out the media kit for *GrowerTalks* magazine (page 71). Notice anything interesting? Instead of the usual blow-by-blow on circulation statistics, this piece literally "talks" about the circulation advantages it has over its competitors. It includes quotes from actual readers, as well as examples of subscriber-card data.

This makes a powerful point. First, it shows that the *Grower-Talks* qualification card is thorough—it notes which crops are growing, square footage, etc. Second, it demonstrates without question that its audience comprises loyal readers: "I've read *Grower-Talks* since 1961."

GrowerTalks *displays its circulation with a personal approach.*

Which would you rather read: a laundry list of statistics, or that a certain reader has read the magazine for more than 35 years? That's the beauty of this anecdotal approach. Even if you lack data and statistical analyses, you can still score solid points with marketers about your quality circulation.

Graphics. Even if you're number one in a field, you've still got the challenge of keeping your statistics fresh and interesting. That's when it's helpful to pack your statistics into a strong visual punch.

Let's take this example from *Nursing* magazine. Even though *Nursing* was the leader in its field, it still needed to grow its advertising business. Where would this growth come from? Its competitors. *Nursing* needed to convince advertisers to stop splitting their schedules, so it created a graphic "globe" showing that advertisers gained only 4 percent more reach when they went beyond the *Nursing* universe. The message? That advertisers would be better off concentrating their frequency in the top nursing publication.

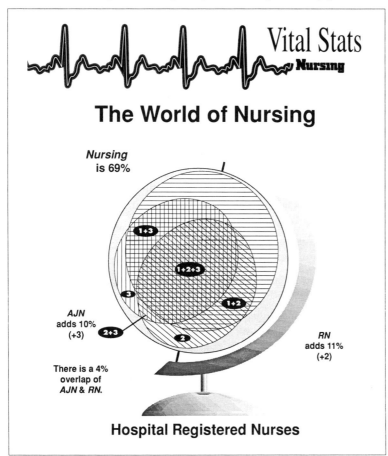

Example from Nursing *magazine shows how advertisers are better off concentrating their ad buys.*

In a face-to-face presentation, you could easily use overheads to demonstrate this particular circulation point. You could simply layer foils that show your magazine's reach and that of your competitors.

Think of other unique and graphic ways to show your circulation. An ad for the Yellow Pages, for instance, plays on the concept of "reach" by bringing to mind the well-known slogan, "Let your fingers do the walking."

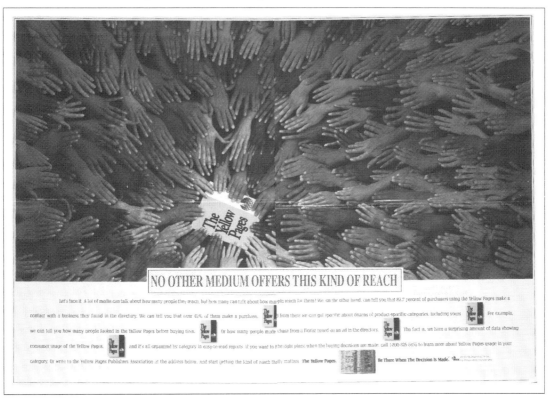

"Let your fingers do the walking" concept from the Yellow Pages.

Try this example. Say I told you that my magazine reached 380,000 chief executive officers every business day and got forty-seven minutes of their undivided attention. Impressive, but not exciting. Now, what if I said this: "Think of the Rose Bowl. Think of all the people in the Rose Bowl. Now, think of three Rose Bowls. How would you like to be able to talk to three Rose Bowls full of people who are your prospects? We can do that for you."

That's a pretty exciting image. And incidentally, that's the image *Wall Street Journal* has used in its media advertising. Prospects, after all, remember visuals a whole lot better than they do numbers.

THREE ROSE BOWLS.
AND IN EVERY SEAT, A CEO.

Imagine reaching 380,000 chief executive officers every business
day and getting 47 minutes of their undivided attention.

Media advertising from the Wall Street Journal *uses a dramatic visual to illustrate the
newspaper's tremendous reach.*

Psychographic profiles. If your title is in a tough circulation battle, you might find it helpful to profile your readers. That's what *Harrowsmith Country Life* did to make a point about its circulation quality and its position in the country market. While it may not have had the numbers or high-income panache of its competitors, it could still prove that its readers were involved, leading-edge consumers.

Harrowsmith's approach was to first determine the percentage of its exclusive readers who don't read other well-known books in the field. It then presented Goldfarb's theory of psychographics to show the quality of this exclusive readership.

<table>
<tr><td colspan="2">

Harrowsmith

READERS ARE EXCLUSIVE

Percentage of Harrowsmith Readers Who Do <u>Not</u> Read:

Financial Post Magazine	97%
City & Country Home	96%
Toronto Life	95%
Select Homes & Food	91%
Canadian Workshop	90%
TV Guide	88%
Outdoor Canada	88%
Canadian House & Home	85%
Canadian Geographic	81%
Equinox	76%
Time	75%
Maclean's	73%
Canadian Living	61%

SOURCE: PMB   English Adults 18+, Total Readership.

</td><td>

Harrowsmith

GOLDFARB...PSYCHOGRAPHICS

An extended outline of some key characteristics for joiner activists goldfarb psychographic segment follows.

<u>Joiner Activists</u>

• The Joiner Activist segment is comprised of leading-edge thinkers. They are non-conformists who help to shape current opinion. Their thinking tends to be global rather than on a short-term or personal level, and involved in issues with a broad social or political impact.

• Some key characteristics of them:

* willing to spend
* eat out most
* shop most for clothes
* convenience-oriented
* will pay more rather than shop around
* concerned about their appearance
* interested in quality
* Day-To-Day Watchers will follow them
* highest incidence of owning an American Express card
* cable converter
* home computer
* least likely to buy lottery tickets
* not "sale" oriented
* heavy pleasure trip takers
* use luxury/resort hotel accommodations
* self-confident
* like new technology

Source: Goldfarb Psychographics, A New Dimension In Data Analysis, July

</td></tr>
</table>

Harrowsmith *demonstrates the percentage and quality of its exclusive readers.*

Goldfarb's theory places consumers in one of six psychographic groups, which Harrowsmith described in detail. The magazine then focused on one category, the "joiner-activist" segment of leading-edge thinkers. According to the theory, joiner-activists are willing to spend, eat out, shop for fashion, pay for convenience, attend to their appearance and purchase quality. More important, joiner-ac-

Harrowsmith

PSYCHOGRAPHIC PROFILE OF THE HARROWSMITH AUDIENCE

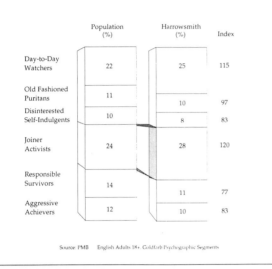

	Population (%)	Harrowsmith (%)	Index
Day-to-Day Watchers	22	25	115
Old Fashioned Puritans	11	10	97
Disinterested Self-Indulgents	10	8	83
Joiner Activists	24	28	120
Responsible Survivors	14	11	77
Aggressive Achievers	12	10	83

Source: PMB   English Adults 18+ Goldfarb Psychographic Segments

Harrowsmith

DELIVERS INTELLIGENT, AFFLUENT READERS

PMB '92 Reader Demographics:	National Composition (%)	Harrowsmith Profile (%)	Index
MARITAL STATUS			
Married/Living Together	66	76	115
AGE			
18-24	14	4	27
25-34	24	26	112
35-49	29	40	141
50-64	18	15	81
25-54	58	71	122
35+	63	70	111
SEX			
Male/Female	49/51	52/48	
HOUSEHOLD INCOME			
$35,000+	56	66	118
$50,000+	36	45	125
$75,000+	15	21	144
HOMEOWNERS			
Own their own dwelling	70	79	111
Own Vacation Home	8	8	104
OCCUPATION			
White Collar	24	36	149
Professional/Business Managers/Owners	16	26	166
SPBM's	11	23	211
EDUCATION			
University Graduate+	14	23	172
College Graduate+	33	48	147

SOURCE: PMB   English Adults 18+. Total Readership.

Harrowsmith

PSYCHOGRAPHIC PROFILES ENGLISH CANADA ADULTS 18+

	Day-to-Day Watchers %	Index	Old-Fashioned Puritans %	Index	Disinterested Self-Indulgents %	Index	Joiner Activists %	Index	Responsible Survivors %	Index	Aggressive Achievers %	Index
Population	21.7	100	10.7	100	10.1	100	23.7	100	14.1	100	11.7	100
Harrowsmith	**24.9**	**115**	**10.3**	**97**	**8.4**	**83**	**28.5**	**120**	**10.9**	**77**	**9.7**	**83**
Cdn. Geographic	23.8	110	7.5	70	12.5	124	27.9	118	13.8	98	10.2	87
City & Country Home	23.7	109	8.2	76	9.0	89	26.4	111	14.7	104	8.8	75
Equinox	23.9	110	7.1	67	8.3	83	34.5	146	9.3	66	11.7	100
Select Homes & Food	26.5	122	9.4	88	10.1	100	25.6	108	13.9	99	9.6	82
Canadian Living	27.4	127	10.5	98	8.5	85	23.1	97	14.8	105	8.8	75
FP Magazine	29.6	137	3.4	32	9.9	98	32.5	137	6.9	49	9.7	83
Outdoor Canada	21.5	99	9.9	93	9.2	91	25.3	106	13.5	96	14.3	122
TV Guide	21.9	101	12.3	115	11.2	112	23.3	99	13.3	94	11.1	95
Maclean's	25.5	118	6.7	62	9.7	97	28.6	121	11.7	83	11.2	96
Time	24.1	111	6.8	64	9.4	93	29.4	124	10.8	76	11.8	101
Toronto Life	25.4	117	3.9	36	5.6	55	36.3	153	11.3	80	8.0	69
Cdn. House & Home	27.2	126	9.0	84	8.5	84	23.8	100	11.3	80	11.6	3.9

SOURCE: PMB   English Adults 18+. Goldfarb Psychographic Segments

Harrowsmith *employs a psychographic profile to illustrate the quality of its readers.*

tivists influence other psychographic groups. That makes them a compelling target audience for advertisers.

Finally, *Harrowsmith* compared its audience with the English Canadian population as a whole. So on a psychographic basis, at least, *Harrowsmith* appeared to have the market wrapped up.

Even if your magazine isn't the circulation market leader, you've still got plenty of ways to show you're number one. You might have the fastest-growing circulation. You might have the cleanest. Find out what your magazine has that no one else has. Use that information to illustrate the value of advertising with you.

Tip: Look through *Advertising Age* and other media magazines to find out how your competitors position themselves to advertising agencies. You can learn a lot about how to shape your own sales story by studying the image other magazines sell.

4

SELLING the VALUE of YOUR EDITORIAL

"There are no facts, only interpretations."
—Friedrich Nietzche (1844-1900)
German philosopher

On its face, nothing could be more obvious than selling the value of your editorial. If you're selling magazine *space*, then you're selling the *magazine*, with all its articles, features, graphics and design. After all, quality editorial is why readers buy the magazine. Why shouldn't advertisers follow suit?

Of course, sales doesn't work that way, and you know it. After all, you've now spent most of your time learning the importance of positioning your market, your readership, your circulation. Who said anything about reading the magazine?

No wonder most salespeople are far better versed in their audit figures and subscriber studies than they are in the latest guest col-

79

umnist. Who can blame them? Audit figures and studies are *hard information* that they can use to paint a pleasing picture of their magazine's ability to deliver a market. The magazine itself, while it may be something they can grasp and flip through, is a far more conceptual sales device. If you're trying to convince a tire advertiser that a 12-page schedule will help him sell more product, it's a lot easier to call on circulation figures than on the article, "Ten Ways to Spot Carburetor Trouble."

Moreover, selling editorial also runs counter to the "church-and-state" issue. Most editors don't want ad salespeople breathing down their necks. They don't want to hear an associate publisher telling them that Client Smith would take out an insert if only Client Smith's gizmo could get just a tiny mention in the "new products" section. And well they shouldn't. Such pandering not only taints editorial, it also stains the magazine's reputation among advertisers.

So how does a sales rep go about "selling" the benefits of editorial? That's what I'll address in this chapter. I'll show you ways to position your editorial to strengthen your sales call. You'll even find in some cases that an editorial sell may be exactly the "push" you need to convince your advertiser of the correctness of his choice.

EDITORS ARE NOT THE ENEMY

Granted, most magazines prefer that ad sales and editorial departments are kept apart—sometimes by a couple of floors. The two worlds reside in separate atmospheres, with editors and sales reps co-mingling only in cafeterias and in conference halls.

In and of itself, separation isn't a bad idea. But what's better than mutual avoidance is for editors and sales reps to come to a mutual understanding of what each department can do for the other. After all, it's the job of editorial departments to serve readers who are, after all, your advertisers' prospects. The better the readers are served, the better the advertiser's response.

Ad sales reps have a lot of critical information to share with editors, just as editors have great ideas they can share with you. Consider the following:

80

1. What you can share with editors

The gossip. Client X just told you his company is going public. Client Y just introduced the hottest-selling leather cleaner in history. Client Z's annual report shows earnings are up 15 percent.

What editor wouldn't want to be privy to the hot gossip in her industry? You might find that once you begin sharing story tips with editors, those editors will share their own leads and information as well.

(Use discretion. No editor wants to be force-fed a story idea from ad people. Keep the conversation light: "Jane, just in case you hadn't heard, they just replaced the CEO at Tyler Industries." On the other hand, you also don't want to betray your client's trust by revealing something he told you in confidence.)

The sources. Editors are often hungry for good sources in top industries. Often forced to cope with packaged information from a company's public relations department, they always appreciate access to a source that can fill them in on background information or breaking news. If you've cultivated a good contact at a top client, why not pass the name along?

2. What the editorial department can share with you

Positioning information. In a previous chapter, I talked about the need to tie together advertising and editorial positioning in your sales story. There's no better way to do that than by talking with editors. Find out how they feel about your magazine's readership and editorial. Discuss their views on who the magazine serves, and learn about the reader response they receive. Any information you glean from your editors will help your advertisers better understand the importance of your magazine's place in the market.

Article information. Do you know anything about your magazine's latest columnist? Do you understand why your title may suddenly be covering environmental issues, or why it's dropping articles on nutrition?

Talking with your editors can help you determine why certain

> Any information you glean from your editors will help your advertisers better understand the importance of your magazine's place in the market.

81

articles have become "must reads" or why others are bowing out. Every time you gather new editorial information, you can use it to target potential new prospects, seek out new advertising categories, or revisit old clients who may have left the magazine.

Warnings. One of a magazine's most precious assets is its editorial integrity. This means that the magazine is free to write whatever information serves its readers, even if that information is distasteful to certain advertisers.

The last thing a publisher wants is to be surprised with a critical article about their biggest advertiser! At some magazines, where the top editor and publisher have a history of working together, an editor can alert the publisher, one-on-one, that a certain article may prove negative to an advertiser. That way, the publisher can handle the potential repercussions.

Consultant Rita Stollman, president of Editorial Management Strategies, tells how one business publication ran a major investigative piece on an advertiser—without warning the publisher. Result: the article appeared just as the advertiser was in the midst of launching a large campaign. Not only did the advertiser scotch the rest of his advertising schedule, he even refused to pay for an ad that had already been run. A simple word to the publisher ahead of time might have worked well to save face, if not the schedule itself.

(Although the top editors may speak with publishers, sales people should not expect that they themselves can review editorial. In fact, *rarely are editors at any magazine expected to give advance articles, or even detailed lists of articles, to sales reps.* Such acts not only violate the rule of "church and state," they can also prove illegal. Magazines like *Business Week*, for instance, routinely embargo their editorial to head off the risk of insider trading.)

Incidentally, a good ad-sales department is rarely bothered by tough articles. Even if one or two advertisers drop out of the magazine, the editorial strength and integrity that results from tough stories will likely draw in other advertisers to replace them. What's more, if the magazine is a "must read" in its field, it's likely that

Editorial is a form of communication between your magazine and your readers—your clients' prospects.

even ticked-off advertisers won't be gone for long. Long term, nothing strengthens a magazine's reputation like fearlessness and accuracy.

GET FAMILIAR WITH EDITORIAL

Editorial is more than the sum of a magazine's articles, features and news content. It's what draws readers into the magazine. It's the connection readers make between their own interests and the information offered in the title. As such, it's a form of communication between your magazine and your readers—your clients' prospects.

What's more, good editorial builds trust. When a magazine offers articles that address the real-world needs of their readers, those readers develop a loyalty to that magazine. They begin to feel that they can turn to every issue for hard-hitting, actionable information. More critical, readers begin to trust the advertising as well. Because they believe in the editorial, they believe in the products they see on its pages.

Consider a computer magazine. If that magazine offered nothing but soft articles on advertisers, coupled with friendly product reviews, readers would quickly catch on that the publication is little more than an advertiser's shill. But if the magazine had built a reputation for tough product reviews and thorough, objective features on industry issues, readers would become convinced of the magazine's high standards. They would more likely to buy software and hardware from its advertisers because they would trust the magazine not to lead them astray.

So it pays, first of all, to know your magazine's editorial. That means not only talking to editors, as I've mentioned, but really *reading* your magazine as well.

Not so hard, in some cases. If you're a motorcycle nut and you're selling for *Dirt Rider Illustrated*, you probably don't have to be convinced to pick up the magazine and look through it. But if you're selling for *Mutual Fund Investor* and still can't balance your checkbook, you may need to spend some time getting to know your title. Read it carefully, read its competitors, and *ask questions*.

83

In some cases, it might be helpful for your department and the editorial department to occasionally gather together as a group to banter about ideas. That way, sales reps can gain a clearer understanding about the magazine's editorial purpose and positioning, and ask questions about the title's competitive edge. During these pow-wows, you might find out that your magazine was first with a huge industry scoop, or learn how reader-mail poured in after an exposé on safety issues.

PUT IT IN IMAGES

Once you're familiar with your title's content, try this exercise I use in sales-training sessions. First, think about what makes your editorial product *special*, *unique* and *different* (SUD again) compared to other publications in your market. Be as objective and as specific as possible. Is your magazine for real car enthusiasts, while your competitors address dreamers? Does your trade title have a features bent while the others in the market are more news- and product-oriented?

Next, draw a picture of your editorial positioning and concept. It may sound silly, but it can help you fully characterize what makes your magazine stand out.

Take a look at this media ad for *Longevity* magazine (following page). It shows a powerful visual of a youthful—but not young—woman shattering an hourglass. The headline reads, "A practical guide to the art and science of staying young." Anyone over 40 can relate to the feeling of wanting to "stop time." They'll be motivated to learn how to live a long and healthy life. This picture tells them that *Longevity* offers them the powerful ability to do just that.

Another potent visual appears in an ad for *Dental Economics* (followng page). Here, a dentist stands among reams of paper, frustration wrinkling his forehead. The caption reads: "Nobody told me it would be like this." Even without reading the accompanying text, the message is obvious: Dentists became dentists to work on teeth, not paper. A magazine like *Dental Economics* helps them take care of the more tedious but financially vital aspects of their job.

A PRACTICAL GUIDE TO THE ART AND SCIENCE OF STAYING YOUNG

Longevity magazine sums up its editorial with a powerful visual.

Nobody Told Me It Would Be Like This.

Meet a non-businessman in the middle of a very demanding business. To him, "investing" is a step in the process of curing a denture. He is prepared to deal with bites, not bytes.

It's a fact, dentists graduate from school with the training necessary to handle a myriad of clinical challenges. But once they are involved in private practice, they discover they have also assumed direct responsibility for activities for which they are largely unprepared – personnel, public relations, finance and marketing.

It doesn't take long for busy dentists to realize that while products and techniques are important, the success of their practices depends on making the right **business** decisions.

That's where *Dental Economics* comes in! It fills the information void by focusing on those issues of dollars and cents importance to dentists. The result is readership from cover to cover, month-in and month-out. This creates the ideal atmosphere for advertising because editorial focus and reader need is the perfect combination for making sales and profits grow.

Dental Economics conveys the frustration of its readers.

Finally, a favorite of mine is this ad from *In-Fisherman*. Using the imagery of fishing equipment (with photos of editors as lures), the magazine ties in editorial as a marketing strength with this powerful tagline: "Editorial is the lure. Advertising is the hook. And in this lake, all 320,000 anglers are trophies."

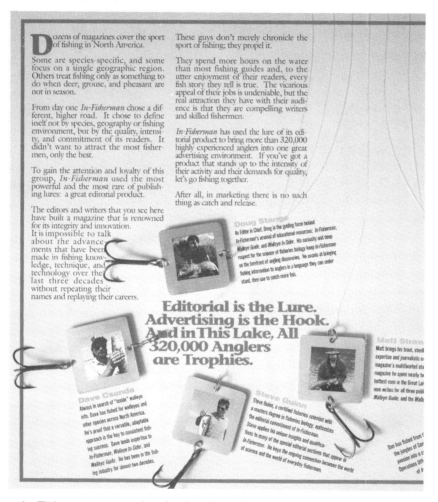

In-Fisherman *magazine ties in editorial as a marketing strength.*

PUT IT IN WORDS

Now that you can visualize your magazine's message, put it in words. First, find out whether your magazine has an editorial mission statement. Read it and see how clearly it states your magazine's objectives. In some cases, you might want to rewrite or modify it so that it conforms to your selling story.

A mission statement isn't merely a statement of *what* the editorial content is about. For your purposes, it needs to be a statement about *why* marketers should advertise in the magazine. It should state concisely your magazine's editorial purpose with a view toward selling advertising.

Look at the mission statement from *Publish* for a good example. Notice how it accomplishes the following sales purposes:

The mission statement from Publish *distinguishes it from other publications.*

1) *Differentiates the magazine from the competition.* The mission statement shows that *Publish* is unique in its focus on case studies of new publishing technology.

2) *Shows reader involvement with advertising.* By stating "*Publish* helps readers determine not only what to buy, but more impor-

tantly, how to use their systems and software," the mission statement shows that readers make buying decisions based on the information from the magazine.

3) *Shows advertisers compatible editorial.* By listing the various editorial sections of the magazine, the mission statement shows that advertisers have a variety of opportunities to speak to readers. It also specifically demonstrates where *Publish* has editorial expertise that the competition may not have.

If your own magazine doesn't have a mission statement, talk with your publisher and editor to try and put one together. As you can see, good mission statements tie together a magazine's editorial and advertising positions nicely. You can use them on your fact sheets, rate cards and media listings to give potential advertisers a precise idea of what you offer.

To write an effective statement, you must look objectively at your editorial. First, decide what your magazine is. Is it news-oriented or loaded with in-depth features? Is it service-oriented? Is it graphically heavy or designed for serious readers? Is it a horizontal publication, covering all aspects of a market, or is it vertical, specializing in one area?

Next, ask yourself some other questions about your magazine's editorial goals. Try these:

✦ How does your publication relate to its readers? Is it friendly? Influential?

✦ Does your title stimulate readers to think? To take action?

✦ Is your editorial exclusive? Is it written by experts in the field?

✦ Does your magazine stand out in its field? Are its editors and publishers spokespeople in the industry?

Once you've thought through your magazine's editorial goals, try again to put it into words. Create a statement that will help advertisers perceive the magazine as the one, unique vehicle that will help them to meet their marketing goals.

TYING IN THE AD PICTURE

You can see how a good visual and mission statement can help you to sum up your title for your advertisers. Now let's go into detail. Let's talk about how you can link your specific editorial to a client's specific needs.

The best way to illustrate this is with an example. Let's say your publication runs an article on an advanced stapling technology for packaging. Your client is a manufacturer of industrial equipment. How might this article garner more ad pages from your client?

Think about it. If your readers are manufacturers who are interested in improving technology, they are motivated to read the article. If they then decide to adopt a new stapling process, they would probably need to purchase new equipment. Here's where your advertiser can benefit.

Use your imagination. A column on child nutrition can be a natural tie-in for food clients. Monthly features on kitchen decor can stimulate readers into looking at home-decorating ads. Even if your magazine's articles don't promote particular products or services, they can still show advertisers that your magazine covers a category in enough depth to generate potential sales.

So whenever you're looking through your own magazine's editorial, keep these questions in mind:

1. *Does the editorial generate a high degree of reader interest?*

2. *If so, does the editorial stimulate interest in purchasing a category of products or services?*

With practice, you may find that *every issue* can yield dramatic selling opportunities!

DEFINE YOUR ADVANTAGES

At this point, you're starting to leverage the sales advantages of your magazine's editorial. But there's still plenty more you can do to reinforce your magazine's special, unique and different qualities. Ask yourself the following questions as you pore over your editorial:

✦ *Are you selling a news publication or a feature publication?* Each type has its advantages to certain advertisers.

For instance, a news/new-product magazine often has many pass-along readers. This can be a big boon to clients looking for mass audience. Feature magazines usually have fewer pass-along readers, but require a longer reading time. That's good news for clients who perhaps want a more select, involved readership.

✦ *Are you selling a horizontal or vertical publication?* The more specialized a magazine, the more compatible its advertising will be with its editorial. Clients selling small dog harnesses, for instance, know they'll find a far more targeted audience with something called *Poodle Owner* than with *Pet Owner's Monthly*. On the other hand, horizontal publications like *Pet Owner's Monthly* can usually attract clients like flea powder manufacturers interested in reaching larger circulations.

✦ *Does your title occupy a special niche?* When a magazine called *FamilyFun* first came on the publishing scene, it capitalized on its unique position between "parent" titles and "women's" titles. Even though both those categories addressed certain parenting issues, neither focused wholly on family activities, like travel, entertainment and education. That's where *FamilyFun* positioned itself, as you can see from the chart it created for its media kit. (See following page.)

FamilyFun's media kit makes clear that its activity-focused editorial appeals to families with more kids and bigger households than other parenting titles. That, of course, becomes an important marketing point for ad sales.

See if your own title meets a need that other magazines don't. Use that information to leverage your own sales effort.

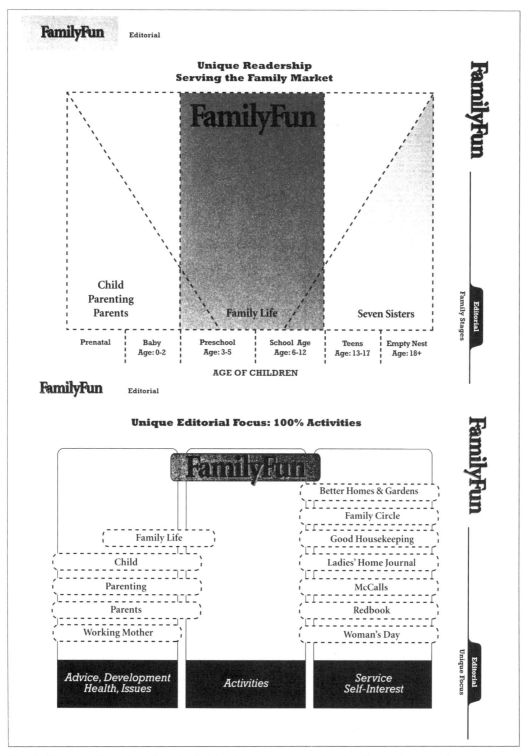

FamilyFun positions itself as the bridge between parenting books and women's magazines.

✦ *Does your title have longevity? GrowerTalks* magazine emphasized its editorial leadership by highlighting its long-term commitment to the farming market. The ad below, tagged "A Tradition of Leadership," illustrates the magazine's seven decades of service to its readers and advertisers.

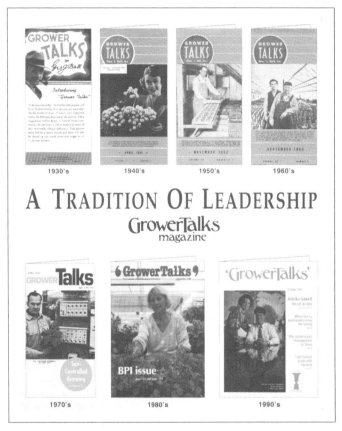

GrowerTalks *magazine emphasized its editorial leadership by highlighting its long-term commitment to the farming market.*

✦ *Is your title a leader?* Editorially, leadership can be defined in many ways, and that can create just as many selling opportunities. Perhaps your news title, for instance, regularly beats out the competition on scoops. Perhaps your editors are considered opinion leaders, widely quoted in other media. Maybe you've just won a coveted design or editorial award worth mentioning in your media kits.

You can find lots of ways to get your leadership position across. This example from *Forbes*, for instance, shows that *Forbes* identified the Iraqi government as a danger in its news analysis long before the Gulf War. Given that *Forbes* is not as frequently published as newspapers or news weeklies, this focus on foresight and accuracy works well in establishing the magazine's leadership qualities.

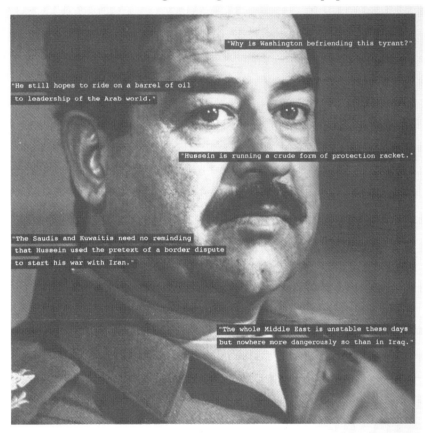

Forbes attacked Saddam Hussein 10 months ago.

Last year, when Washington was trying to befriend the Iraqi dictator, Forbes saw him as a dangerous foe. One whose power comes from the barrel of a pistol. And as we reported in our December '89 article, this power, backed by a battle-hardened, million-man army posed a real threat to Saudi Arabia and Kuwait.

Our assessment of Hussein was right on target. In fact, we called Washington's tilt toward Iraq "one of the least sensible twists in U.S. foreign policy." What were the decision-makers thinking of then? And what were they thinking of in 1980 when, just weeks before he attacked Iran, we warned that the "most brutally repressive ruler in recent history" was suffering from delusions of grandeur?

Forbes not only reports events, we anticipate them. With tough, insightful reporting. That's what lies at the heart—or more precisely, the guts—of every Forbes story.

In fact, in survey after survey, top executives say Forbes' gutsy reporting gives them better information than either Business Week or Fortune.

What's more, it's the most efficient way to reach them.

So if you really want your ads to make an impact, run them in the magazine that reveals history before it even unfolds. Forbes.

No guts. No story.

Forbes
Capitalist Tool

Forbes *demonstrates leadership position through its prescient editorial.*

93

Other magazines embellish their media ads with outside testimonials, mention of awards, or quotes from outside media mentioning their editorial. *International Business*, for example, ran an ad showing how the American Stock Exchange made mention of the title in its annual report. Some titles, like *Men's Health* and *Esquire*, have pulled quotes from their *own* editorial in media ads, trusting that prospects have taste and discrimination enough to recognize quality editorial when they see it.

International Business *ran an ad showing how the American Stock Exchange mentioned the title in its annual report.*

Incidentally, perhaps the best demonstrations of leadership are testimonials from your advertisers—particularly if they're well known. Choose testimonials carefully so they reflect your main sales points. One outdoors magazine, for instance, pitched its buyer's guide not only with reader testimonials, but with advertiser feedback. No one can argue with the value of claims like, "Your program has generated more business for us than any other form of advertising," or "Thanks for helping us boost our sales!"

TRY A SELF-AUDIT

Perhaps the most thorough—albeit, the most labor intensive—way to promote editorial is with an *editorial audit*. Like an advertising audit or circulation audit, an editorial audit precisely measures the *quantity* of editorial in your magazine. (Incidentally, editors undertake their own editorial audits to find out how in-depth, overwritten or dense their own articles are. The ad-sales editorial audit, however, accomplishes different goals.)

With an audit, you can show advertisers how thorough and comprehensive your coverage is. You can demonstrate precisely how much color your magazine uses or how many column inches ran on new product categories, features, fashion spreads or new-company profiles. This demonstration can pay off in changing advertiser perceptions of your magazine. Often enough, it can also change your own perceptions, and even win you new accounts you may not have previously considered.

Here's how it worked for one publisher of a food-business magazine. According to an article in *Folio:*, the publisher first created two broad editorial categories that corresponded to ad categories: food products and food-processing equipment. The publisher then measured separate categories within those categories: frozen food, cereals, candy, meats, and so on, in the food products category; refrigeration, materials handling, and the like in the food-processing category.

The publisher then marked up each issue with a felt-tip pen, measured the results, and created a report and worksheet that defined how much editorial the magazine devoted to each category. Salespeople were given copies of the report to use on calls. Results? Several new accounts, in ethnic foods and waste-processing equipment, came into the book, and the publisher could attribute a significant increase in new pages directly to the editorial audit!

DON'T NEGLECT READER RESEARCH

So far, you've seen how you can evaluate and position your editorial. But what about your readers? After all, they're your clients' prospects—and they're your best editorial cheerleaders. No one can create a more convincing case for your magazine than the people who buy it and read it.

So the next time you consider a subscriber study, make sure you include questions about editorial. You can then use the information to make a potent case in your sales presentation. Consider the following questions to pose to readers:

✦ How many recent issues have you read?

✦ How much interest do you have in the following topics?

✦ How much time do you spend with each issue?

✦ How long do you keep an issue?

✦ What other magazines do you read?

✦ Have you taken any action as a result of reading certain articles or editorial?

✦ Why do you like this magazine?

Questions like these undoubtedly help you unearth ad-sales benefits you may not have known or considered. You may find, for instance, that your readers spend more time than you think with the magazine, or that they respond very favorably to a new column or design change.

Even better, you can use this information to demonstrate how *effectively* your magazine brings together readers and advertisers. Clients are much more willing to listen to your sales story when they're convinced that readers "connect" with the magazine.

Consider this example from *Discipleship Journal*. The magazine emphasized its readership strength by letting readers testify as to how they "used" *DJ*—cutting out articles, asking for reprints, saving back issues for reference. When a reader says that he requested 50 copies of a magazine, that's a terrific illustration of loyalty and commitment.

HOW I USE *DJ*
Notes from our readers

I have come to recognize DJ as a magazine that reaches committed Christians, people who are very sincere about perfecting their faith. DJ's strength is its emphasis on practical Christianity. It is rare because it contains no fluff everything it offers is geared to helping Christians grow and mature.
George Barna
Marketing researcher and author of
The Frog in the Kettle

I chose money as the theme for a family week at Woodland Bible Camp last winter. After reading your issue on money [Issue 53], I called and requested fifty copies. We gave each family a copy of DJ to study. During the week we discussed the articles plus other lessons I'd prepared. Some families were changed!
Tooger Smith
Lyons, Indiana

A great magazine! Discipleship is more than beginning with Christ: it is going on with Christ. Maturing. Being completed in Him. For as long as I live, I know I must keep a passion for discipleship. To strengthen that passion, I intend to keep reading DJ.
Calvin Miller
Pastor and author of The Singer trilogy

I mark portions of each article that I may want to recall later with a highlighter pen. When I'm preparing a Bible study, a devotional, or a workshop, I can pull the important points or illustrations from articles I've highlighted. I also use some of the questions from the "On Your Own" sections for my own research or to stimulate discussion in small group Bible study.
I keep all my DJs readily accessible and I often refer to articles when I counsel young women. The powerful testimonies of others encourage and challenge them.
Dianne Doty
Garden City, Kansas

As I make my way through DJ, I have my trusty Exacto knife at the ready. I carve articles out of each issue and stash them safely in my files for sermon material. DJ has been a rich source of sermon support for me. On more than one occasion I needed an idea to prime my pulpit pump and I reached for an old DJ article.
Youth Pastor William Westafer
Lemon Grove, California

What do I like best about DJ? When I flip the last page I can always say, "I learned something new . . . I can, by God's grace, apply that to my life." The articles in DJ always help me to better understand the Word of God.
Joni Eareckson Tada
Author, speaker, and artist

I file cards with specific topic headings in a recipe box and refer to them when I teach a Sunday school class, or when a friend needs help with a problem. I list each article under all the topic headings that apply. When I need help on a specific subject, I can look through the file and pull out the magazines that will help me.
Lorraine Fling
Harleysville, Pennsylvania

Every magazine is worth sharing. I give an issue to one of our pastors if it covers a subject of particular interest to him. I loan copies to friends for articles that meet a need in their lives. I gave a subscription to our senior pastor, because he had expressed how helpful the copies I gave him had been. I also sent a subscription to a young minister just starting a new church who was having difficulty finding good sermon material.
Shirley Ryan
Phoenix, Arizona

Discipleship Journal *demonstrates its reader strength with testimonials.*

Reader research also assures advertisers that readers spend time with ads. As consultant David Orlow states in *Folio:*, "Documentation of editorial readership is clearly a direct and important way to imply the effectiveness of advertising."

DRAWING COMPARISONS

Once you're well-versed in your own magazine's editorial benefits, you might find it useful to study your competition. To find what's special, unique and different about your own magazine, it's naturally a big help to know precisely how it differs from its competitors. So try these approaches:

An editorial audit of your competitor. Using the same categories you created for your own editorial audit, see how your competitors measure up in magazine content. Perhaps you'll find your magazine treats certain subjects in-depth while your competitors treat them lightly. Maybe your magazine runs more editorial pages overall, or more color, or more news content.

Once, I consulted on a health magazine called *Let's Live.* Its primary problem was distinguishing its editorial from others in the health field. Other titles seemed to give more in-depth coverage to certain topics such as preventative medicine, cosmetics, herbs and other natural-health areas.

In an editorial audit, though, we found that *Let's Live* was the *only* title to cover *all* these health areas. That gave it a tremendous advantage, as well as a great positioning statement: "A balanced editorial for a balanced life." That "balance" was especially appealing to advertisers seeking to recruit shoppers on the holistic path. (See illustration on following page.)

A comparison of subscriber studies. By checking your own studies against your competition, you may find your readers have a deeper connection to your own magazine, or spend more time with it, or believe it to be more trustworthy than your competitor's.

A masthead comparison. Does your title have an editorial board? That's an asset your competition may not have. Perhaps your magazine also has a greater number of experienced staffers, or industry experts, or a larger overall editorial staff.

A story-by-story comparison. Pick a topic your magazine has covered well, like industrial safety. Now see what your competition has done with the same subject. You might find that this kind of anecdotal approach can demonstrate your own magazine's editorial superiority, particularly in topics of interest to advertisers.

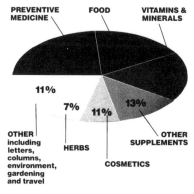

LET'S LIVE Magazine

A balanced editorial for a balanced life.

When a reader purchases **LET'S LIVE** magazine, he or she is choosing the largest available package of information on health and natural living. There are more health-related articles and more health-related advertisements. As such, there is more space devoted to both editorial and advertising.

Our size, together with our editorial philosophy, results in the most balanced editorial package in the health industry. We treat our readers as we hope they will treat their own lives—as a whole.

LET'S LIVE also appeals to more people. Our editorial environment captures the attention of your prospects and customers at a time when their interest in health and well-being is at a peak. This is the perfect place, *each month*, to speak to our audience about the benefits of your products. And our editorial mix ensures that all appropriate categories— including yours—will be covered during the year.

The accompanying chart demonstrates **LET'S LIVE'S** balance, showing the amount of editorial space devoted to various aspects of natural living. It also shows how we lead the health industry in these important areas.*

- SUPPLEMENTS (45% more editorial coverage than our nearest competitor)
- PREVENTIVE MEDICINE (128% more editorial coverage)
- COSMETICS (110% more editorial coverage)
- HERBS (8% more editorial coverage)
- BOOKS (we are the only health magazine to devote editorial coverage to book reviews)
- NEW PRODUCT NEWS (33% more than our nearest competitor)
- HEALTH FOOD INDUSTRY NEWS (only **LET'S LIVE** covers the health food industry from a consumer's point of view)

*Based on a six-month (March-August, editorial study of **LET'S LIVE**, American Health, Bestways, Delicious!, East-West, New Age Journal, Prevention and Total Health.

LET'S LIVE averages 52% advertising per issue.

Let's Live*'s positioning statement: "A balanced editorial for a balanced life."*

You might also try comparing columns and departments. How well does your coverage of new trends and products stack up against your competition?

A meeting with your editors. Once again, editors can be invaluable in helping you define your magazine's editorial strengths. After all, editors are on the front lines of editorial competition! See if they can tell you whether the competition has been lowering its editorial stand-

99

ards, perhaps by laying off staff or eliminating important coverage. Editors are usually well-versed in the strengths and weaknesses of the "enemy."

OTHER TOOLS YOU CAN USE

You can call on any number of other promotional tools to demonstrate your magazine's editorial excellence. Don't neglect the following:

Editorial calendars/advance schedules. Every magazine schedules special features, articles or columns, and each presents a selling opportunity. Retailers, for instance, always respond to a city magazine's annual back-to-school or fashion issue. A food-trade title featuring a special report on waste management might open up new accounts. A trade-show issue for a professional home-decor title always attracts gift manufacturers.

Most business magazines produce quite detailed editorial calendars for their advertisers, depicting every feature over the course of an entire year or more. However, while I'm an advocate of thorough editorial calendars (after all, nothing helps sales like a good editorial hook), it's my belief that these calendars shouldn't be *too* detailed.

Here's why. First of all, overly detailed editorial calendars can give you an editorial disadvantage. One magazine I know, for instance, not only listed every story to come, but listed sources as well. Since this was a computer title, the magazine was at a hopeless editorial disadvantage. There was no way the editors could stay on top of a fast-moving industry with every feature pre-sold and pre-digested.

Secondly, detailed calendars open you up to competitive swiping. If your competitors know your magazine will conduct an annual salary survey of insurance adjusters (and believe me, they'll find out), they can beat you to the punch with their own survey. That no longer gives your title an advantage.

Also, rigid editorial calendars invariably disappoint advertisers.

100

By publicizing editorial deadlines and content, they make it much easier for magazines to fail in the eyes of their advertisers.

It's better, then, to list editorial categories rather than specific stories in editorial calendars. There's no harm in saying "September is our back-to-school issue." You open a can of worms, though, by saying, "September is when we profile Mr. Evens, senior vice president of marketing at The Children's Clothing Outlet." Who knows how the store, or Mr. Evens, will be doing by then?

> It's better to list editorial *categories* rather than *specific stories* in editorial calendars.

Reader letters. One teen magazine I know regularly gets *thousands* of letters each month from readers. You can bet advertisers are interested in that kind of reader involvement! Reader letters demonstrate that readers pay close attention to editorial—enough to actually respond.

Bobbit Publishing publishes a baseball-card magazine with a large adult *and* child readership. One day I walked into the office through the circulation department and saw a piece of paper sitting on a desk. It was torn from a three-ring school binder and written in pencil: "Dear Mr. Bobbit, I have a Don Drysdale card from 1964. Can you tell me how much it's worth? Your friend, Tony."

I asked the publisher how many of these kinds of letters the magazine receives. "Hundreds," he told me. Though it's not an audited statistic, it makes a great promotional piece!

Editorial reprints. Requests for editorial reprints not only show reader involvement but also demonstrate your magazine's expertise and leadership. For instance, if your pharmaceutical client wants to reach migraine sufferers, she knows her prospects could probably get headache information from almost any medium, from brochures to TV shows. But if you can show how migraine sufferers have been requesting reprints of your article, "Minimize your migraines," you can prove that these readers *trust* your magazine's expertise. Chances are excellent that that trust would extend to her advertised product as well.

Awards/citations. Naturally, national journalism awards are the best testimony of your magazine's editorial excellence. Tops are the Jesse

H. Neal Awards (business press) and National Magazine Awards (consumer press). Advertisers, though, are also impressed with awards given by experts in the magazine's industry. Any soybean-farming title that wins kudos from a national farming institute, for instance, would likely convey expert status. Such market expertise often proves to be more impressive to advertisers than straight, un-recognized journalism.

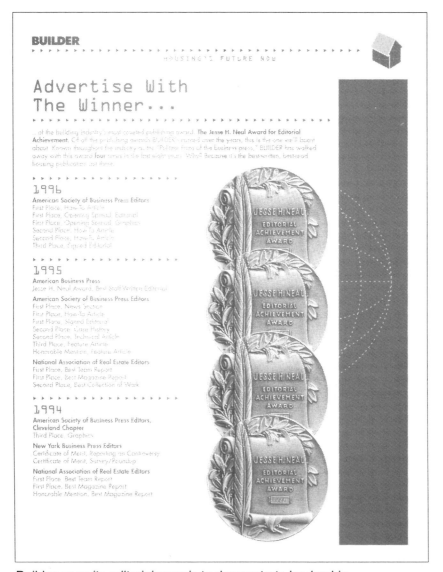

Builder *uses its editorial awards to demonstrate leadership.*

THAT FINAL SALES CLINCHER

So, when you put together your final client presentation, make sure you do what you can to make your editorial stand out. Remember, you can't assume your prospects have already read your publication, or even that they know what it's about! After all, they likely receive dozens of different magazines weekly and can't possibly be familiar with all of them. But when *you are the expert* in your magazine's editorial, you can educate your clients.

As Orlow puts it in *Folio:*, "Whenever you confront an ad-marketing problem or opportunity and you need that final sales clincher, look to your magazine itself." Look to editorial. It's the one thing that *consistently* makes your magazine different from the rest.

5

SELLING the VALUE of ADVERTISING

"The meek shall inherit the world, but they'll never increase market share."
—William G. McGowan (1927-)
American communications executive

The "power" of advertising, as you may recall from Volume I, lies in the ability of advertising to help your clients through their Seven Steps to a Sale, from "establishing contact" to "keeping the customer sold." In this chapter, we'll take the concept even further. I'll show you how to demonstrate to your clients not merely the benefits of advertising, but the benefits of advertising *in your magazine.*

First, let's recall just what advertising does for your client. Here's an example from our earlier chapter in Vol. I:

Say your client is a shoe manufacturer who's invented a new posture-improving support cushion built into his new "PosturEase" line of shoes. He decides to run a monthly ad page in your magazine, the *Dress for Success Digest*.

After a few months, he finds out the following:

✦ *Advertising creates brand awareness.* Readers who have seen ads about "PosturEase" recognize the name when they go to their shoe store. They understand the shoe's features and what make them different from other shoes they might buy.

✦ *Advertising creates interest.* Now potential customers want to sample the product to see if it really works.

✦ *Advertising creates conversion.* They wear the "PosturEase" shoe and form a positive opinion about it. Some of the shoe's new customers may have switched to "PosturEase" from another shoe brand.

✦ *Advertising enhances loyalty.* Now that they have bought the shoe, they continue to see advertising for it. This increases the likelihood that they will buy the shoe again, or buy a different version, or that they will recommend it to friends.

✦ *Advertising enhances perceived value.* By now, lots of people are wearing the shoe, so the product gains a perceived value of quality and reliability reinforced by continued advertising.

✦ *Advertising creates increased market share.* By the time other copycat manufacturers join the "posture-improving" shoe market, your client is already ahead of the game because of the awareness created by "PosturEase" ads. This gives him substantial market share or allows him to set a premium price for the shoe. Either way, he gets the ultimate payoff: *A bigger bottom line.*

MAKING THE POINT

It's pretty tough to squeeze all those points into a 20-minute presentation. For most sales reps, what works is tailoring your presentation to your magazine and your client by finding a shorthand way to convey the potential value of advertising. In other words, you must (once again) anticipate your client's needs and match your presentation to it.

First find out what your clients want from advertising. Second, ask yourself: *what does advertising in my magazine offer?* Take a look at some ways certain magazines have looked at both questions and found solutions.

✦ *Advertising offers impact.* Ask most clients what they want from advertising, and they will most likely tell you this: immediate impact and immediate response. They want to justify their advertising investment quickly. For many advertisers, the payoff of long-term benefits may pale next to the allure of short-term impact.

Although it's important to sell for the long term, don't forget to demonstrate to clients how the right ad can create immediate impact as well. Notice how *Parade* makes the point in its trade advertising.

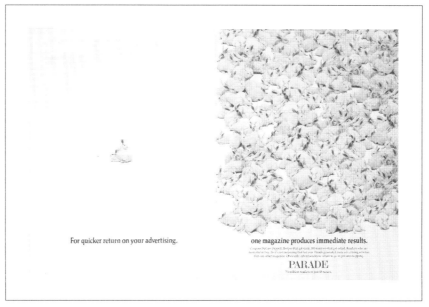

For quicker return on your advertising.

one magazine produces immediate results.

PARADE

Parade *magazine emphasizes both the size and responsiveness of its readership.*

✦ *Advertising offers results.* Here's another example that anticipates a common client need. As you know, most clients would like to see *measurable* results from an advertising buy. This ad from *Baking Buyer* (following page) speaks to that point with the headline "You need measurable results."

107

Under a strong visual of a measuring cup, the copy goes on to reassure advertisers: "In a world of subjective opinions and qualitative surveys, every successful business has its own quantitative scoreboard: measurable results." The following page then encourages buyers to look at the value of their current marketing. The headline asks, "Do you know if your advertising is working?" Such a high-impact head lures prospects into exploring the value of advertising in *Baking Buyer*.

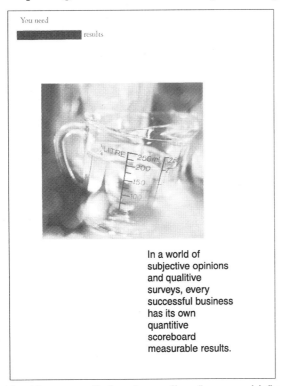

You need

results

In a world of subjective opinions and qualitive surveys, every successful business has its own quantitive scoreboard measurable results.

Baking Buyer *media brochure offers "measurable" advertising results.*

◆ *Advertising generates new business.* Obviously, another client concern involves finding new business—and in this example, *Baking Buyer* shows just how the magazine's advertising pulls in customers. The title's brochure comprises copies of original responses from *Baking Buyer*'s reader inquiry service. By flipping through the pages, clients can see how in one instance, a reader requested information on basket trays, muffin brushes and Italian pastries; another wanted information on desserts, chocolates

108

and cakes. As *Baking Buyer* points out, "each circled number represents a potential sale!"

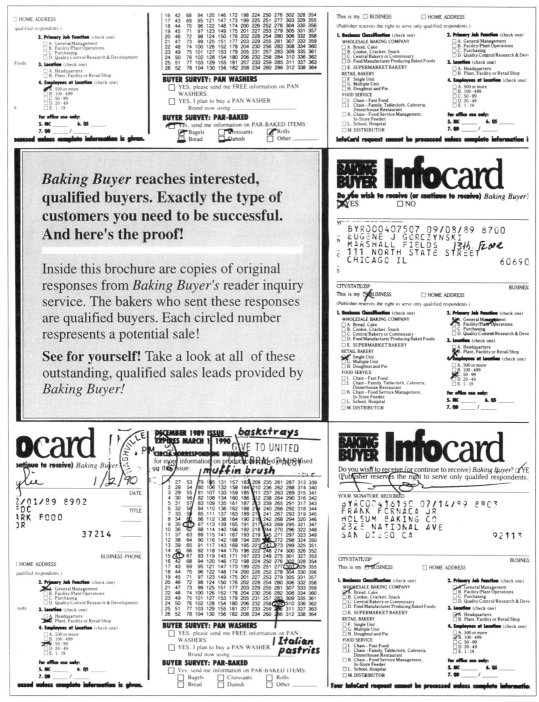

Baking Buyer demonstrates impact by showing the advertiser exactly who has responded to its bingo cards.

This works well in a presentation simply because it makes something abstract become concrete. It's one thing to tell clients the numbers of inquiries you had last month; it's another to display the bingo cards and show who has responded to what. Any time you can say, "Ms. Client, here are 25 inquiries in your product category," you can bet you will command attention. You will have shown the literal value of advertising in your publication.

◆ *Advertising leads to profits.* The business magazine *Water & Waste Digest* has done a beautiful job of pulling all these client concerns together to demonstrate a return on investment.

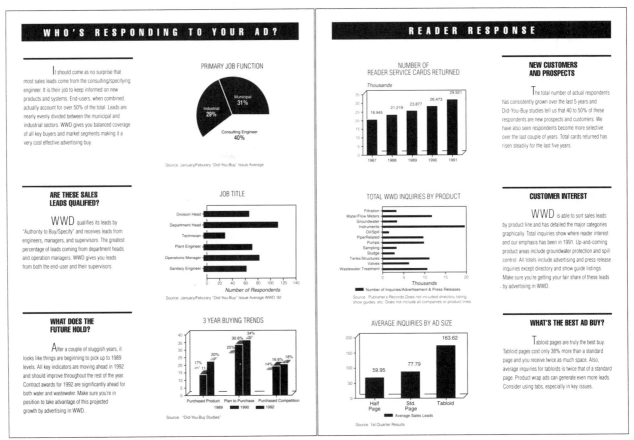

WWD *uses its research to demonstrate the strength of its reader inquiries.*

Step by step, *WWD* has outlined in its sales materials three critical concerns: who responds to its advertising, the amount and types of inquiries, and what kind of return on investment advertisers can expect. All this information undoubtedly comes from the magazine's own research on advertising effectiveness, and it's laid out in a sensible, easily-grasped format.

For instance, under the headline "Who's responding to your ad?" *WWD* displays respondents' job functions, job titles, and even buying trends that prove they are ready to buy for the future. Its "Reader Response" segment charts the magazine's growth in inquiries over five years, and indicates that most readers show an interest in "instruments," "meters" and "structures" in their inquiries. Even better, this page dramatically illustrates that tabloid pages pull almost twice as many inquiries as standard-page ads.

Finally, the heart of the presentation is in the section "Return on Investment," which details the average order sizes, the products

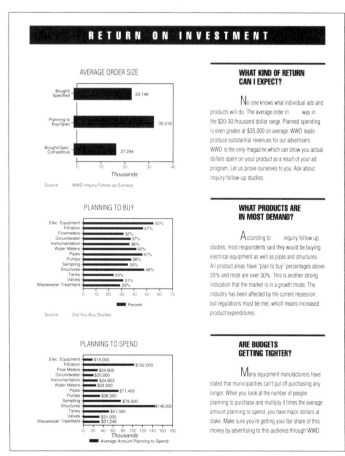

WWD *shows who is planning to buy and how much they plan to spend.*

111

most in demand, and the amount of money readers plan to spend on various equipment purchases. All together, *WWD* clients can find out who's planning to buy and how much they're planning to spend. *WWD* concretely and succinctly shows advertisers how much value they can expect from an ad page.

Notice that the real value of this information is that it comes from readers who actually responded to advertising in *WWD*. This can be much more meaningful than a subscriber or readership poll. Readers may say they love the magazine—but only advertiser inquiries prove it!

If You Don't Solicit Inquiries...

Most consumer magazines, of course, can't rely on inquiries to measure the value of their advertising. So, how can they demonstrate the value of advertising?

Here's how. First, recall these Seven Steps to a Sale:

1. *Establishing contact*

2. *Generating awareness*

3. *Arousing interest*

4. *Building preferences*

5. *Making specific proposals*

6. *Closing the sale*

7. *Keeping the customer sold*

In most cases, image and consumer advertising are most effective in the early steps, such as in generating awareness and building preferences. These ads are designed to woo and win new customers.

And what is a new customer worth? Plenty. You may recall from Vol I, Ch. 9, for instance, how just one new customer can lead to sales many times greater than the original sale. A woman persuaded to try a new lipstick, for instance, may be so taken with the product that she will try a foundation and eye shadow in the same brand. Another customer who enjoys a brand of shoes may add hiking boots to his next order. That's not even counting the recommendations these customers will make to friends. The power of *brand awareness*—as consumer advertisers well know—is such that a powerful name can sell just about anything. Consider, for instance, how both the Gap and Banana Republic successfully launched popular lines of bath products, solely based on their names and reputations.

The point? While you may not be able to show an advertiser a dollars-and-cents return, you may be able to show that advertising is crucial in gaining a potential customer's *share of mind*. And a customer won means profits.

Consider this chart from a McGraw-Hill study. In the study of more than 2,500 product lines, McGraw-Hill found that advertised products score 250 times higher in brand awareness than non-advertised products. The more pages of advertising, the greater the increase in awareness. Even modestly advertised products enjoyed substantially more awareness than non-advertised products.

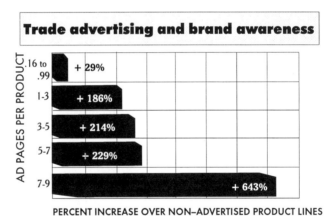

Trade advertising and brand awareness

AD PAGES PER PRODUCT	
.16 to .99	+ 29%
1-3	+ 186%
3-5	+ 214%
5-7	+ 229%
7-9	+ 643%

PERCENT INCREASE OVER NON–ADVERTISED PRODUCT LINES

A McGraw-Hill study shows advertised products score substantially higher in brand awareness than non-advertised products.

Furthermore, the higher the awareness, the stronger the alliance to the product. A study by the University of Massachusetts at Lowell, for example, shows that once customers have a minimal threshold of brand awareness, brand preference follows closely. In a separate study, the school found that advertised products were preferred three times as often as non-advertised items.

113

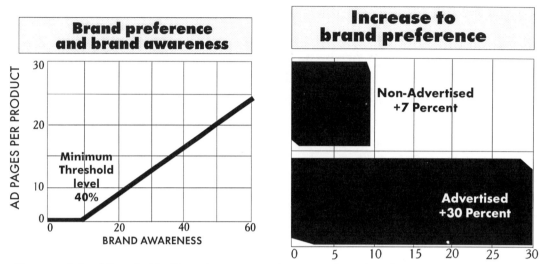

Even a minimal threshold of brand awareness increases brand preference. (Source: University of Massachusetts at Lowell.)

Make sure you can use your magazine's own brand awareness studies to demonstrate the power of your advertising.

OTHER POINTS TO BRING UP

What else can you tell clients about the value of advertising in your publication? Plenty. Aside from reviewing the information in "The Power of Advertising" (Vol. I, Ch. 9), take note of the following suggestions:

What's your ad growth? Maybe your title has more ad pages than your competition, or it can boast the hottest growth rate, or the most impressive slate of clients. All of these statements reflect the value of advertising in your magazine. By illustrating, as *Athletic Business* does below, that you are number one in ad pages, you confirm that more clients trust your publication for results than they do any other magazine.

THE MAGAZINE

Athletic Business leads the industry in readership & advertising pages. It is rated the #1 "Best Read", "Most Useful" magazine in the market. If you want proven results, go with the magazine that's a proven winner! — **Athletic Business**

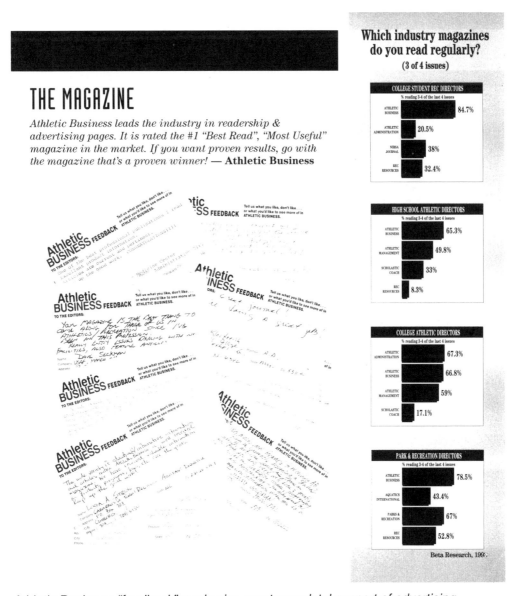

Athletic Business *"feedback" cards give great anecdotal support of advertising.*

How long have your advertisers stayed with you? Maybe some of your clients have been with your magazine for a decade or more. You might not think twice about these older standbys, but the fact that you have able to consistantly meet their needs in changing times (and even fickle markets) exemplifies your title's advertising effectiveness.

115

Here's an example: One of my clients, *Trade a Plane,* had little hard data backing up its marketing power and sales effectiveness. But what we did have were clients who had stayed with the magazine from Day One—more than 50 years ago. You can be sure of this: People do not advertise for 40 or 50 years if they do not believe that they are getting something worthwhile in return.

Are your advertisers exclusive? Let's say your magazine reaches the ceramics industry. If the *top* glaziers, clay manufacturers and kiln-equipment makers are in your magazine—and your magazine alone—that's terrific testimony to the value of advertising in your magazine. It's like owning a hot nightclub. The best advertisers come to *you,* not to the others. Let's face it: Everybody likes to follow the market leaders. If prospects know that bigger and better companies currently run in your title, they will be that much more inclined to line up at the "velvet rope" in hopes of joining in.

TESTIMONIALS ARE GOLDEN

Maybe one of your advertisers recently told you she had received a record-breaking number of inquiries from her last ad. Perhaps another just confided that your value-added programs far exceeded his expectations. Don't just acknowledge it—get it in writing! Testimonials like these are golden coin for buying confidence among clients and prospects.

Of course, you can't just passively wait for advertisers to send in their wonderful anecdotes. Be proactive. When someone tells you a good story, or details a great response to his last ad buy, ask for permission to quote him for a promotional piece. Better yet, try to collect testimonials with a particular strategy in mind. Perhaps you would like testimonials on your magazine's value pricing, or market penetration, or inquiry response rate. See if you can collect particular examples to specifically boost the strong points of your magazine.

For best results, make sure your testimonials cover all the bases in your magazine. You don't want a menu of testimonials from only small companies, or from companies in one or two product areas. Try to collect testimonials from each of your major categories, and from companies both small and large. Make sure you also include industry leaders in your testimonials, and that you pursue a range of quotes from clients throughout the country.

Once you have all your bases covered, your collection of testimonials should essentially tell your entire sales story! From that point on, you should be able to provide targeted testimony to the value of advertising in your magazine, no matter which new prospect you may be trying to reach.

Best of all, people do not give testimonials unless they mean them. They gain nothing by publicly stating to the industry and to all their competitors how successful they have been with your magazine. So if you want testimonials—and you should—be sure to go for them! It's more important than you may think.

In the end, testimonials are just a few of the many opportunities available to demonstrate the value of advertising in your magazine. Use your magazine's advertiser studies, brand awareness studies, and your own imagination to put together compelling reasons why an ad in your magazine pays off, both in dollars and in sense.

6

PUTTING it TOGETHER: SELLING the VALUE MESSAGE

"It is impossible for ideas to compete in the marketplace if no forum for their presentation is provided or available."
—Thomas Mann (1875-1955)
novelist and critic, Nobel prize winner 1929

Okay, pop quiz: Now that you've learned how to sell the value of your market, editorial, circulation *and* magazine advertising, can you find a simple and effective way to convey it to your clients?

If you're hesitating—or more likely, ready to throw the book on the floor—relax. Selling the full "value" message really isn't as tough as it sounds.

Granted, the last few chapters gave you a lot to chew on. You've learned to examine the strengths and weaknesses of your readership, marketplace, editorial and competition. You've learned what constitutes "value" in each of those areas, and you've got a sense of what it takes to position your title in the marketplace.

At this point, though, you probably need some help digesting all that material and putting it together to create a powerful selling message. That's what I'm going to talk about in this chapter.

First, let me get the bad news out of the way. There's no magic pill to replace your own thinking and creativity

But here's the good news: What this chapter does offer is inspiration and examples. In my career, I've collected samples of how various magazines pulled together their value messages into terrific presentation materials and media kits. Each of those magazines beautifully defined what is *special, unique* and *different* about their market, editorial, readership and advertising power. I've learned a lot from them, and you can, too.

CUSTOM HOME'S SIMPLE SALES MESSAGE

Let's look, for instance, at this media kit presentation from *Custom Home*.

In the very simplest way, this kit highlights the value of the magazine's *market, circulation, editorial* and *advertising,* using research, statistics, subscriber and advertiser studies. Let's see how *Custom Home* puts it together.

The value of market:

◆ 20 percent of new single-family homes are built by custom builders (and in all sizes and styles).

◆ 26 percent of building materials sold for new construction go into custom homes.

◆ Custom homes have grown progressively bigger over the past five years.

◆ Aging baby boomers are driving the growth of custom housing.

What's all that tell an advertiser? *That* Custom Home *reaches a significant and growing part of the market for new construction.*

120

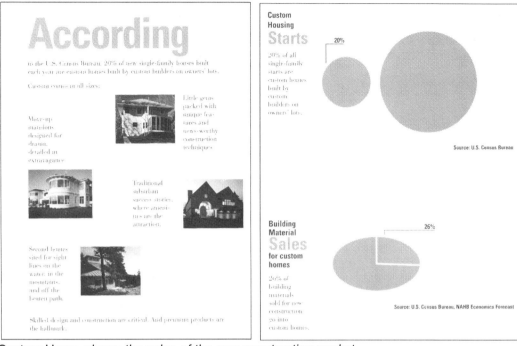

Custom Home *shows the value of the new-construction market.*

The Value of Circulation:

✦ All circulation is direct request.

✦ The vast majority of its builder and architect readers do not read the competitor, *Builder.*

✦ Readers are small specialized builders and residential architects, the drivers of the custom-home market.

✦ *Custom Home*'s readers—builders and architects—build larger and far more expensive homes than typical single-family home builders.

✦ Up to 95 percent of readers are also buyers in such categories as windows, doors and roofing.

✦ *Custom Home*'s circulation is larger than its competitor, and it includes architects as well as builders.

What does all that tell advertisers? *That* Custom Home*'s read-ers are also its advertisers' customers, and that advertisers can find more buyers in* Custom Home *than in* Builder.

121

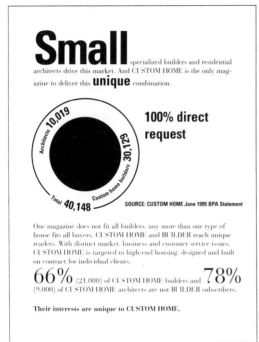

Custom Home *uses reader research to demonstrate the value of its circulation.*

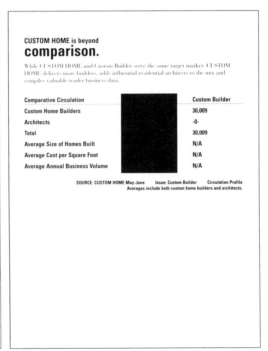

Custom Home *demonstrates that up to 95 percent of its readers are also buyers of* windows, doors and roofing. Moreover, Custom Home's *circulation is larger than its competitor and includes architects as well as builders.*

If you recall, that sales point comes right from the Advertising Syllogism:

1. *This is your prospect.*

2. *This is our reader.*

3. *Your prospect is our reader.*

4. *Your prospect—our reader—reads this magazine.*

5. *Your prospect's buying behavior is affected by reading this magazine.*

6. *Therefore, you can sell your prospect—our reader—by advertising in the pages of our magazine.*

7. *Here are our advertising recommendations.*

8. *Close the sale.*

The value of advertising:

+ *Custom Home* is the fastest growing magazine in the industry, and the biggest ad-page gainer among residential-construction publications.

+ The magazine sponsors the annual trade show, "Custom Builder Symposium."

+ The title offers custom publishing, custom production and direct mail as special services to advertisers.

+ Trade magazines are the premier way custom home architects can gather information about products.

The message to advertisers is that *readers pay attention to* Custom Home*'s ads, and that the magazine has inspired enough advertising confidence to become the fastest-growing in the industry.*

Growing market share.

CUSTOM HOME is **the** fastest-growing magazine in the custom housing industry and the biggest advertising page gainer among all residential construction publications. CUSTOM HOME expanded by 55 pages in   and is up another 31% year-to-date

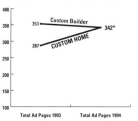

*Comparing CUSTOM HOME's 6 issues in   to Custom Builder's 7.

SOURCE: The Auditor/TAP

CUSTOM HOME connects
advertisers and readers.

The annual Custom Builder Symposium, co-sponsored by CUSTOM HOME and NAHB's Custom Builder Committee, unites leading custom builders for two days of networking and education. It's the year's premier event for the custom market. Advertising and sponsorship packages make it an outstanding place to raise a product profile.

CUSTOM HOME's Pacesetter Awards and Design Awards are exclusive programs recognizing America's finest custom home builders and projects. Sponsorship investment reaps conspicuous dividends in publicity and prestige.

Ask your CUSTOM HOME district manager for more information on sponsorship opportunities.

More Ways CUSTOM HOME Helps you Reach the Market

Direct Mail
Rent CUSTOM HOME's list and deliver your message to your customers—directly. Our BPA-audited circulation list consists of custom builders (30,129) and architects (10,019) that can be selected to fit the following profiles:

  Job Title
  Primary Business Activity
  Sales Volume
  Products Specified
  Size of Home Built
  Average Square Footage of Home Built

As part of the Hanley-Wood magazine family, CUSTOM HOME advertisers can also take advantage of our Master File. The Hanley-Wood network includes more than 400,000 building, remodeling and retail professionals. Hanley-Wood direct mail consultants can help you to define your market and then create a custom list from specific demographic information.

Custom Production
Beginning in   Hanley-Wood offers advertisers the opportunity to reach key targeted segments of the market. Our circulation database and print production capabilities allow you to create customized demographic versions. We can also provide customized ink-jet printing on advertising pages to reach specific segments of your customer database.

Custom Publishing
Custom publishing is a cost-effective way to deliver your product and company information professionally. Projects can include newsletters, magazines, books, videos, CD-ROMs, advertorials, inserts, audio tapes and more. In   Hanley-Wood acquired a custom publisher, The Wells Group. Now called Wells, Hanley-Wood, this 30-person division provides custom publishing services to Hanley-Wood advertisers.

By demonstrating its fast ad growth, Custom Home *shows the value of advertising in its title.*

Why advertise in CUSTOM HOME?

Reach an important market.
Custom housing represents 20% of all new homes built and 26% of all new construction building material sales. NAHB predicts 208,000 custom home starts in

Target custom builders' and architects' unique information needs.
CUSTOM HOME is focused on providing the latest business, design, selling, marketing, customer service and product information with specific relevance to these professionals.

Sell high-end products. Lots of them.
The bigger the home, the larger the purchases, the more luxurious the products. CUSTOM HOME readers build homes that average 3,429 square feet, at almost $94 per square foot. These readers buy your high-margin products to satisfy the needs of the most discriminating homeowners.

Talk to the team that specifies your products.
CUSTOM HOME reaches the team that makes purchasing decisions on major building products: 30,129 builders and 10,019 architects. 90% of subscribers make purchasing decisions.

Be where the readers are.
Trade magazine ads are the top choice in the mix professionals use to get product information, according to the   Architect Survey. The top three ways that custom home architects use to gather information about products are: ads in trade magazines (88%); catalog files (84%); and articles in trade magazines (82%).

Influence the leaders.
Sponsoring a CUSTOM HOME award program or the Custom Builder Symposium reinforces your advertising and puts you in touch with the industry's top talents. And leadership is contagious.

Play with a winning team.
With a network of publications serving the residential construction industry, Hanley-Wood has an unparalleled understanding of the market and its niches. CUSTOM HOME is custom-crafted to the high-end market, which influences all other types of housing. It offers exceptional opportunities for up-market advertisers.

Custom Home *readers pay attention to its ads.*

The value of editorial:

A brief letter from the editor touches on more selling points:

◆ The January new-product issue is used by readers all year long.

◆ The magazine is preparing research on affluent baby boomers, the drivers of the custom-home market.

◆ The magazine has expanded coverage of various building topics, in addition to "sharing secrets" of top architects and designers in a special series.

Advertisers thus learn that Custom Home *stays on top of market trends and provides unique information readers won't find elsewhere.*

Put together, that's a powerful four-part selling message. And all of it, as you've probably noticed, addresses the heart of the Advertising Syllogism: *Your buyer is our reader.*

THE "RIGHT" MESSAGE FROM *DIY RETAILING*

Now let's look at how the magazine *Do-It-Yourself Retailing* tells a similar story about the various strengths of its own publication.

First of all, the magazine creates a selling message based on the Advertising Syllogism. Here's how:

With a section called "Right Market," *DIY Retailing* demonstrates the value of the market, telling advertisers, in other words, *This is your prospect.* By creating a section called "Right People," *DIY Retailing* follows up with the message, *This is our reader* and *Your prospect is our reader.* With its third section, "Right Magazine," *DIY Retailing* tells advertisers, *Your prospect—our reader—reads this magazine.* And finally, with the section "Right Message," the title finishes the Syllogism: *Your prospect's buying behavior is affected by reading this magazine. You can sell your prospects by advertising.*

Take a look how *DIY Retailing* spells out each part of its sales story:

"Right Market"

◆ *DIY Retailing* has a greater focus on the $113.4 billion do-it-yourself consumer market than any other magazine in the industry.

✦ The primary group of retailers reached by the magazine will grow almost 20 percent in sales during the next few years.

"Right People"

✦ The magazine reaches 100 percent of the hardware-store, home-center and wholesaler universe.

✦ *DIY Retailer* audits its readership by outlets, wholesalers, title, product category and key buyers.

✦ *DIY Retailer* reaches the small mom-and-pop stores, which comprise 93.5 percent of the stores and 68.1 percent of industry sales.

"Right Magazine"

✦ *DIY Retailing* is the only magazine addressing the management needs of home-center, hardware and building-material outlet stores.

✦ The magazine was rated "most preferred" and "most useful" over three competitors in a reader survey.

✦ *DIY Retailing* focuses on how-to management and merchandising issues to help its readers sell more product and manage more productively.

"Right Message"

✦ *DIY Retailing* runs more editorial pages than two of its competitors.

✦ The magazine features more pages in various product categories, like tools, plumbing and hardware, than each of its competitors.

✦ *DIY Retailing* also features more pages on operational and management issues, like advertising/promotion and market trends, than each of its competitors.

In the final analysis, this four-part message focuses primarily on the editorial and market strengths of *DIY Retailing*, especially compared to the competition. The message to advertisers: *In* DIY Retailing, *you can talk to your buyers through a magazine that better addresses their needs than any other advertising vehicle.*

SELLING POWER IN THE GOLF MARKET

Finally, let's take a look at how *Golf Product News* puts together its selling story. Its goal is to show advertisers that the publication is "the common denominator that unites the market for your ad campaign."

What does that mean? Essentially, that advertisers can use *GPN* to "control the sales channels in a competitive market." It means they can reach all the distribution channels, all the decision makers and all the potential sales leads in the market for golf products.

The magazine sells this message by connecting the publication's features to a host of benefits. Here's how they match up:

Editorial: *Golf Product News* unites the market with comprehensive editorial crucial to all sales channels.

Market Coverage: *Golf Product News* enables advertisers to contact all distribution channels in the market.

Audience (Circulation): *Golf Product News* enables advertisers to contact all decision makers who control the buying power in the market.

Sales Leads: *Golf Product News* identifies all potential buyers entering the purchase process.

Let's look at each of these in more detail.

Value of Editorial

The magazine's primary editorial feature is product news. Benefits of that editorial include:

✦ High interest among retail decision makers, who prefer product news to other editorial, such as merchandising tips. Also, 90 percent of readers read at least 75 percent of each issue.

127

✦ Trustworthiness among retailers, who rate *Golf Product News* their primary source for news on products and suppliers.

✦ Essential reading among retailers, who say that staying current with product news is part of their "basic job responsibilities."

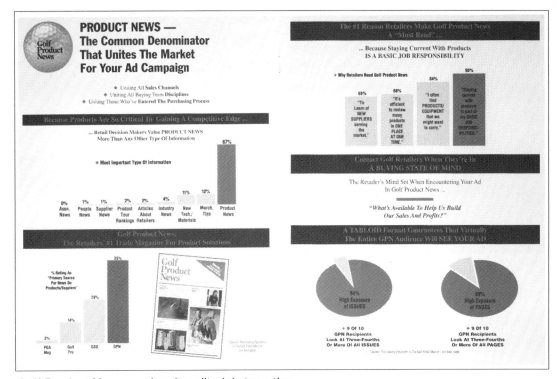

Golf Product News *pushes its editorial strengths.*

The message to advertisers: *Your buyers need, read and trust Golf Product News as part of their basic job responsibilities.*

Value of Market Coverage

Under the headline, "Penetrate more of the FACILITIES representing your greatest sales opportunities," *Golf Product News* details the following benefits:

✦ Advertisers reach a growing market. More than 75 percent of readers have increased golf product sales in recent years (32 percent of them significantly).

✦ Advertisers receive targeted coverage. Up to 98 percent of readers carry product lines ranging from golf gloves to balls.

128

✦ Advertisers can penetrate a growing women's market. More than half of *GPN* facilities have increased purchases from the women's golf market—and one of every four customers of *Golf Product News* retailers is female.

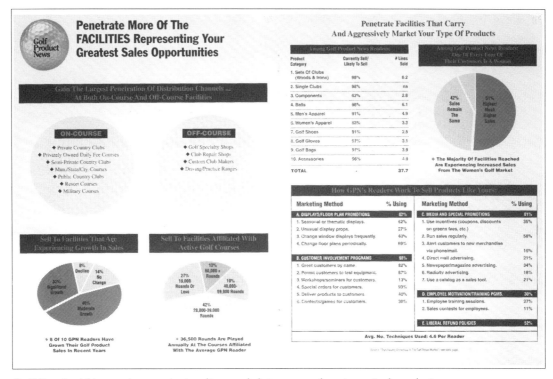

Golf Product News *demonstrates its reach into a growing, targeted market.*

The message to advertisers: Golf Product News *reaches successful, growing retailers who stock the very products advertisers sell.*

Value of Audience/Circulation

This section, headlined "Contact ALL of the DISCIPLINES controlling today's purchasing power," addresses the following benefits:

✦ Advertisers can reach buyers, not lookers. More than 90 percent of readers are involved in final purchasing decisions.

✦ Advertisers can reach people who can aggressively market their product. Nearly 90 percent of readers are responsible for all merchandising/display decisions (an important consideration for golf-product manufacturers).

129

✦ Advertisers can reach the largest penetration of distribution channels. Seventy percent of all readers are members of teams that buy products. The average reader makes purchases for multiple golf shops.

✦ Advertisers can contact all the disciplines controlling purchasing power. Seventy-two percent of readers are sought out for opinions on golf products, merchandising and retailing.

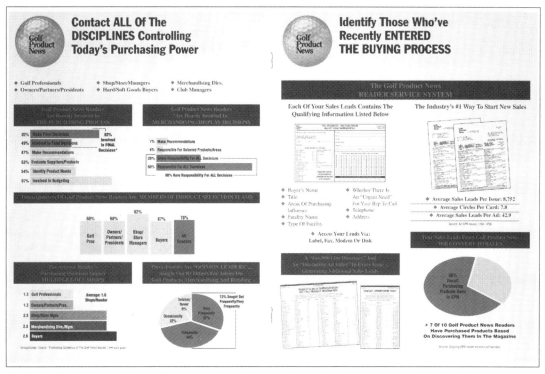

Golf Product News *shows its range of readers and number of average sales leads.*

The message to advertisers: *The readers of* Golf Product News *are important buyers; decision makers, not just influencers.*

Value of Sales Leads

Finally, to confirm the importance of the sales leads that emerge from *Golf Product News*, the magazine indicates the following benefits:

✦ Sales leads from *GPN* convert to sales. Sixty-eight percent of readers purchased products after finding them featured in the magazine.

130

✦ Advertisers reach only targeted leads, with no waste. Each reader—or sales lead—is qualified by title, area of purchasing interest, type of facility and so on.

✦ Advertisers get tangible results from their investment. The number of average sales leads per issue is 8,752, and the average number of sales leads per ad is nearly 43.

The message to advertisers: *Readers of* Golf Product News *are active buyers who respond to your advertising.*

THE MESSAGE IS CLEAR

In all these cases, each magazine stated its selling message clearly and specifically. No advertiser reading these media kits would have to guess at the value of the magazine's circulation or market, nor would the advertiser need to read the magazine itself to get a sense of the quality of its editorial. Each media kit contained a solid sales message forged from its reams of research.

Unfortunately, many other publishers still seem to take the lazy route to sales. Recently, for instance, I came across a media kit for a national parenting title that contained more than 40 pages of information about the magazine. It had facts aplenty, ranging from MRI's demographic readship profiles to lists of awards and honors to details about special issues, circulation increases and audience quality.

The only thing it lacked was a selling message! Sure, every piece of information in the media kit essentially said something positive about the magazine's circulation or editorial quality. However, no one at the magazine took the trouble to spell it out to advertisers. The media kit was no more than a laundry list of *features*, without a single *benefit* in sight.

Of course, any experienced sales rep can take media-kit information and turn it into a selling message. Tell a good sales rep that 69 percent of readers are ages 18-24, and she'll find a way to turn that into an advertiser benefit.

But why not let your media kit tell the story? By creating a solid selling message and positioning statement in your magazine's media kit, you've established a big selling opportunity. Your advertisers won't have to pore over sheets of material trying to figure out what benefits are in it for them.

The point I'm making is that it's critical to take collected data and interpret it to the benefit of the advertiser. That's what I'll talk about next.

STEPS TO THE SELLING MESSAGE

To jump-start your creative process, I'll give you a few guidelines.

1. Keep the message simple. Go back to your magazine's mission statement and positioning statement. Ask yourself what it is you most want advertisers to know about your magazine.

Each of the three examples above, for instance, clearly derived their selling messages from their positioning statements. Here's how those positioning statements came across in their media kits:

For *Custom Home*: Our magazine is foremost in reaching and influencing the buyers in a growing, affluent industry.

For *Do-It-Yourself Retailing*: Our magazine has a stronger focus than any other on the critical issues facing retailers who serve this growing do-it-yourself consumer market.

For *Golf Product News*: Our magazine is a trusted source of crucial information that affects the primary buyers in the golf-product marketplace.

As you can see, each of these positioning statements clearly helped the magazines refine and define their selling messages. By knowing which messages to convey, each magazine could choose the statistics and research that would best support them.

Golf Product News, for instance, chose information that focused on reader expertise and editorial trust. *Custom Home* focused on information that spoke about the growing marketplace.

2. Look for the highlights. You probably recall all too well the

132

difficulty in defining the value of your magazine's editorial, circulation and market. In each case, you had ask umpteen questions about your magazine's features and benefits: What percentage of the buying universe did you reach? Did your magazine address a horizontal or vertical marketplace? How qualified were your readers? How did your editorial audit measure up to your competitor's?

At the end of working through the last four chapters, you probably came away with scores of pages and lots of information about your magazine. Now comes the tough part: How do your arrange all of it into a well-defined selling message?

For the best results, go through each of those categories (market, editorial, circulation) one by one, looking for the best, *most important* or *most surprising* information. Don't try to create a selling message just yet; just look for the highlights.

Let's take an example. Say, for instance, you work for a cosmetics-industry magazine we'll call *Beauty Report*. In conducting your research and asking questions about your market, editorial and circulation, you brainstorm and come up with the following notes:

◆ Six awards from Beauty Buyers Industry Association over the past five years

◆ Three times the coverage of skin creams, hair remover, bleaches and waxes than the leading competitor

◆ Fourty percent more color used throughout than the top competitor

◆ Beauty products industry growing 15 percent annually over next five years

◆ *Beauty Report* only publication to reach cosmeticians and dermatologists as well as wholesalers and retailers

◆ Hundred percent market coverage among independent beauty suppliers with sales of $1 million or more

◆ Ninety-six percent of sales in beauty industry pass through large independent beauty suppliers

◆ 100 percent direct request

◆ Seventy percent of readers have buying authority; remaining 30 percent (cosmeticians and dermatologists) are buying influencers

◆ Complete penetration in West and East Coast, where 78 percent of beauty industry products are sold

◆ Eighty-six percent of subscribers renew annually

◆ Circulation grew 44 percent over past two years, outpacing all others in market

◆ Advertisers can reach leading independent suppliers at lower CPM than competitor

◆ Sixty-four percent of readers have responded to *Beauty Report* advertising over last 12 issues

◆ Readers cite *Beauty Report* advertising as the number one source of information about new products

◆ Ad pages grew 26 percent over past year

◆ Sixteen pages of testimonials from pleased advertisers available

Now that you've noted some of the critical information from your publication, you can pull together the material to create a powerful selling message.

3. Compile and edit your information. Use your positioning statement as a guide to structure your information.

For *Beauty Report* you might work with the following positioning statement: *Our magazine is the most trusted publication among the cosmetics buyers who are responsible for 75 percent of beauty-products sales today.* Notice again how this statement works right from the Advertising Syllogism: *Your buyers are our readers. You can reach your buyers from the pages of our magazine.*

Now you can sort out your information. Instead of throwing random facts at your advertiser, you can state the following points:

134

Market selling points

✦ The beauty products industry will grow 15 percent annually over the next five years.

✦ *Beauty Report* has 100 percent market coverage among independent beauty suppliers with sales of $1 million or more.

✦ Ninety-six percent of the sales in the beauty industry pass through large, independent beauty suppliers.

Circulation selling points

✦ Seventy percent of *Beauty Report's* readers have buying authority; the remaining 30 percent (cosmeticians and dermatologists) are buying influencers.

✦ *Beauty Report* has complete penetration in the West and East Coast, where 78 percent of beauty-industry products are sold.

✦ Eighty-six percent of subscribers renew annually.

Editorial selling points

✦ Readers spend 20 percent more time with *Beauty Report* than with its leading competitor.

✦ Editorial is cited as "the most reliable" in an independent survey of cosmeticians.

Advertising selling points

✦ Advertisers can reach leading independent suppliers at a lower CPM than *Beauty Report's* competitor.

✦ Sixty-four percent of readers have responded to *Beauty Report* advertising over last 12 issues.

✦ Readers cite *Beauty Report* advertising as their number one source of information about new products.

✦ Sixteen pages of testimonials from pleased advertisers are available.

4. Create the selling package. Now that you have your selling points in line, you can pull together a presentation package that translates the whole value of your publication.

Like *Custom Home,* you might simply divide your media kit into various segments that address different selling points, such as "editorial," "circulation" and "market." Or, like *DIY Retailer,* you might want to tie the selling messages together under a banner.

Another option is to build the selling message gradually. First, you can decide which selling point you'd like most to stress in your presentation. Then as you walk through your categories (market, circulation and so on), you can tie every piece of information to that main selling point. (That was the strategy behind *Golf Product News.*)

It's now up to you to sort through your materials, recall everything you've learned, poll your peers, and create your own selling masterpiece. And for further inspiration, don't forget to turn to the the "masters" who have preceded you. Look through as many media kits and sales materials as you can. Each one can be a selling textbook for you!

7

USING the RATE CARD as a SELLING TOOL

"What is a cynic? A man who knows the price of everything and the value of nothing."
— Oscar Wilde (1856-1900)
playwright and novelist

❖ ❖ ❖

"I've been in this business ten years," says one associate publisher I know at a business magazine, "and I still hear the same questions and confusion from customers on rate cards."

Given the length, breadth and depth of data on rate cards, confusion is understandable. The typical rate card contains more than 200 separate price "cells," covering purchasing options ranging from, say, the 6X rate for a half-page full-color ad to the 3X rate for a full-bleed page, third cover, with a fifth color added. And those cells don't even take into account the scores of other buying options generally available on most titles, such as rates for classified ads, special issues, digest inserts, gatefolds and so on.

To the untrained eye, rate cards, like the mumbo-jumbo price stickers on new cars, frequently seem overly vague or complex, full

137

of fine print and the suggestion of hidden charges. That's why using your rate card to sell may sound rather ineffective at first, even oxymoronic. It may be hard at first to guide your rate-card discussion to the meat of the issue, the question that every client wants to know: *What is the bottom line? What is advertising going to cost me?*

You need a skill set to talk about rate cards, and that's what I'll discuss in this chapter. With knowledge and practice, you can train yourself to understand the competitive strengths of your magazine's rates, as well as your competitor's weaknesses.

For suggestions on rate-card analysis, I turned to David Orlow, a rate-card expert and president of Periodical Studies Service.

THE "OPEN RATE" FALLACY

For most agencies and individual clients, the "open" rate—the one-time, black-and-white page rate—stands out on a rate card like a neon light. The open rate is the price yardstick by which most clients compare magazines. Simply put, if Magazine A has an open rate of $4,500 per page and Magazine B has an open rate of $5,250 per page, it will appear to the client that Magazine A looks a whole lot cheaper.

The problem is, of course, that while the open rate acts as a yardstick, it's a pretty inaccurate one. The open rate seldom, if ever, tells buyers the actual out-of-pocket advertising cost. In fact, the open rate generally overstates the "real" price of advertising, and makes most magazines look far more expensive than they are. With the whole range of frequency discounts, page discounts and other advertising incentives available to them, most magazine advertisers usually end up with a per-page cost that's considerably lower than the open rate—even when running color pages.

Moreover, the real issue for most advertisers isn't open rates. It's CPM. Advertisers want to know how to reach their prospects—your readers—at the lowest cost per thousand. If a magazine doesn't offer the right *audience* at an acceptable price, it makes no difference if its page rate is 25 percent lower than another's.

138

It's your job to *focus your client on the actual out-of-pocket advertising cost to reach the buyers he needs*—particularly if your magazine has the competitive disadvantage of a high open rate. Don't be distracted if a client begins harping on the fact that your open rate is $750 higher than a competitor's. Instead, have the facts at hand. Find out your client's advertising needs, *and* your competitor's full rate schedule, before engaging in price debates.

THE RATE CARD COMPARISON

By now, of course, you already know plenty about determining advertiser needs. You also know a lot about selling the value of advertising in your magazine, and you can demonstrate to your clients the payoff of an advertising investment.

In rate-card discussions, however, you have to arm yourself with new information. You have to know specifically how your rate schedule measures up against the competition.

This is not as easy to do as logic would dictate. Buying magazine advertising is not like hiring a moving van or purchasing an airplane ticket, where you can make more of an apples-to-apples price comparison. As Orlow states in *Folio:* magazine, "Each magazine carries a unique message (graphics and language) to its unique audience, and with a unique effect (information, pleasure, etc.). Even when two magazines compete closely in the same market, it is not unusual to find significant differences in price structures. Unlike transportation companies or savings banks, the particular unique physical characteristics and aesthetic services which each magazine provides make comparison of price structures far less obvious."

The truth of this statement makes selling magazine advertising both easier and harder than selling other, more tangible goods. If two stores next to each other sell the same Frank Sinatra CD, for instance, most buyers would simply buy where the CD is cheaper. For those stores, the only effective marketing option would be to keep the price as competitive as possible.

Magazines, however, have far more selling options. They can sell a magazine's editorial quality, or its readership power, or its marketing reach. They can sell its production quality or its circulation demographics. After all, an advertiser weighing the merits of two magazines would rarely consider price alone. She would have to consider magazine readership, reputation, editorial quality, reach and a whole host of other factors that would affect the value of her investment.

It would be naive to suggest, though, that price doesn't figure into her decision as well. In fact, price is a major factor in any advertising buy, and rate-card discussions and comparisons are inevitable. And even though two magazines in a market may appear to have very different open rates and price structures, you can still find ways to make comparisons between your rates and your competitor's.

LOOKING AT YOUR OWN RATES

Most publishers use a complex formula for determining their rates. As I noted in "Mastering Your Rate Card" (Vol. I, Ch. 12.), rates are derived not only from looking at the competition and the advertising marketplace, but from many other variables as well, such as the magazine's profit structure and production costs.

So, to get the most knowledge from your magazine's rate card, you're going to have to break it down. The first step is to look at the four principle areas of interest to your advertisers: CPM, frequency, page size and color. Speak with your sales manager or publisher and see if you can find out the following information.

CPM

✦ What is the current "open rate" (1X b/w page rate)? What was it the previous two to three years?

✦ How much has the open rate increased over that period? By what percentage?

✦ What is the current circulation?

✦ How much did circulation/readership increase or decrease over that period? By what percentage?

✦ What is the current CPM?

140

✦ How much did CPM increase/decrease over that period? By what percentage?

This information gives you a general sense of how your magazine has determined its value to advertisers over the past few years. Let's assume you found out the following information:

	Current	Previous Year 1	Previous Year 2
1X b/w page rate	$3,900	$3,800	$3,600
% increase	2.6%	5.6%	
Circulation	230,000	215,000	190,000
% increase	7.0%	13%	
CPM	$16.95	$17.67	$18.95

What would this tell you? That while your open rate has been going up over the past few years, circulation has increased even more. This information helps you to sell *overall value*. From this chart, you can see your advertisers have been receiving an increasingly better bang for their bucks. In fact, your CPM has actually *decreased* nearly 10 percent over that time!

I'm not saying you'll always find this kind of selling message in the numbers (especially since most publishers generally raise rates in tandem with circulation increases). But you can at least explore your numbers a bit to find their true value. That way, you're equipped to deal with advertisers who might only point out how expensive your title is, or how much your open rate has increased.

Frequency/page discounts

✦ What percentage discount (from the 1X page rate) does your title offer for 3X, 6X, 9X, and 12X schedules?

141

✦ What discounts are offered for 12-page, 18-page or 24-page buys?

You'll need to construct a grid chart, like this:

1X b/w rate	1p. $3,900	2/3 p. $2,760	1/2 p. $2,400	1/3 p. $1,990
% Discount				
3X	4.0	5.2	5.2	5.5
6X	8.0	7.9	7.9	10.0
9X	12.0	11.5	11.5	15.0
12X	15.0	15.0	15.1	18.0
12 pages	15.0	0	0	0
18 pages	18.0	0	0	0
24 pages	20.0	0	0	0

Having this information at hand obviously helps you sell the *value of frequency*. Instead of simply giving dollar figures to your advertisers, you can point out, for example, how your title's 12X rate carries nearly twice the discount of a 6X rate, and nearly four times the discount of a 3X rate. By running an ad every month, an advertiser would effectively double the per-page savings of running every other month!

Remember: frequency itself is a potent sales tool. Maybe your client feels she only needs six pages annually to get her message across—but you might show her that just a few extra pages, purchased for an incremental price, could substantially increase her reach and exposure. The extra page may not add substantially to your own commission or to the magazine's revenues, but "the benefit is the goodwill," as one publisher puts it. You've shown the client the right way to advertise. The goal is to help her get as much exposure as possible for the budget she has.

Fractional premiums

✦ What does your magazine charge for fractional ads, such as 2/3 page, 1/2 page and so on?

✦ What percent of the 1X b/w page rate is that price?

✦ What is the "fractional premium" of that price—meaning the percent of the page rate divided by the percent of space?

Here's how that grid chart might look:

	1X rate	% page rate	% fractional premium
1 page	$5,250	100.0	0
2/3 page	3,970	75.6	+13.3
1/2 page	3,150	60.0	+20.0
1/3 page	2,365	45.0	+35.1
1/6 page	1,315	25.0	+50.0

Again, you can use this information to sell the *value of larger page buys*. You can see that the smaller the page your advertiser buys, the larger the premium she must pay as well. For instance, while a 1/6 page ad takes up only 16.7 percent of the page space, it sells for a full 25 percent of the price of a full page. If the price corresponded directly to space, the 1/6 page would sell for $875, not $1,315. Your magazine, in other words, charges a 50 percent premium to sell that spot.

Conversely, those numbers also mean that your advertiser can double the size of her ad without paying double the price. If she bumped from a 1/6 page ad to a 1/3 page ad, for instance, she would pay 80 percent more for 100 percent more space. If she bumped from a 1/3 page to a 2/3 page, she would pay less than 70 percent more for 100 percent more space! That's far greater exposure for less money than she might think.

Combine these savings with frequency and page discounts, and you can come up with even more of a value message for your advertiser. Play with the numbers, and talk to your advertiser about her needs. If she's on the fence about testing a larger buy, show her that the investment may be less risky than she might have believed.

Four-color premiums

♦ What does your magazine charge for a 1X 4/c page?

♦ How does that compare to a 1X b/w page, in percentages and in dollars?

Here's how that comparison might look:

	1 p.	2/3 p.	1/2 p.	1/3 p.
1X, b/w	$5,250	$3,970	$3,150	$2,365
1X, 4/c	$7,875	$5,955	$5,135	$4,350
Premium, in $	$2,625	$1,985	$1,985	$1,985
Premium, %	+50.0	+50.0	+83.0	+83.0

When viewed this way, it may be surprising how much four-color can add to the cost of a page. From this perspective, it's clear that adding color to a 1/3 page nearly doubles its price, thanks to a premium of nearly twice that of a full page. Therefore, advertisers who want color in their ads would likely find it much more cost effective to purchase bigger ads. Not only would the price be to their advantage, but so would the relative impact of the larger size combined with color.

OTHER RATE CARD ISSUES

Now that you've looked at the four major categories of interest for advertisers, check your rate card for other values. Consider these areas:

Network buys

Magazines that belong to a multi-title stable almost automatically have a rate card advantage over single-title publishers. Consider, for instance, *Folio:, Catalog Age* and *Direct,* all owned by Cowles Business Media. Each addresses a different audience: magazine publishers, catalogers and direct marketers, respectively. But all carry similar advertising from list companies, paper manufacturers, printers, envelope companies, and just about any supplier that caters to all three industries.

All of that gives each title two levels of rate-card advantage. First, the combined titles offer big CPM savings. Most likely, it would cost far less per thousand to reach three different audiences in a combination buy than to reach these same audiences separately through three different publishing companies. After all, multiple-magazine companies have inherent overhead and cost efficiencies that they can pass along to advertisers.

Second, these combined titles tend to offer bigger frequency discounts. If an advertiser wants to run a three-page schedule, a one-magazine company might offer him a 3X frequency discount. However, at a two-title company, a three-page buy for two titles would likely earn a 6X frequency discount, and perhaps other bonuses or price advantages as well.

But what happens if your single magazine competes against a multi-title publisher? Are you at a rate-card disadvantage? Not always. Once again, you have to take into account your client's marketing goals and your own circulation and rates. It may be that your client needs to focus only on the specific audience offered by your magazine. For him, placing a variety of ads in three magazines at a multi-title company would result in a great deal of waste circulation. This could mean that a six-page buy in your magazine would prove less expensive and more targeted than two three-page buys in your competitor's network.

Once you've explored all the angles in your own rate card and your competitor's, it's likely you'll find advantages lurking in discounts, CPMs or circulation value.

The fine print

It may not make or break a sale, but the esoterica of your rate card might yield some insightful sales points. Consider these:

Special issues and supplements. Although most publishers price their special issues at the regular rate, your magazine might yield some significant savings here, particularly for certain ad categories. A pharmaceuticals publication, for instance, might have special rates for travel advertisers in its annual summer special issue. A food title might offer special buys for its kitchen spectacular. Annual supplements might be published with their own special rates. Make sure you explore all the opportunities for giving advertisers a bargain.

Special position. Most advertisers want preferential positions, and most magazines make them available—at a price. It may be that your magazine charges less for special positions than your competitor, or that it would waive the position charge on a large space buy. Find out your policy, and your competitor's, and use it to your advantage.

Color costs. Your advertisers would be grateful for any color savings you might pass on. Say, for instance, your client wants to add spot green to an ad. Choosing her own spot color would likely add production costs to her ad buy. But allowing the magazine to choose the green color would likely keep her costs down. Find out how to assure your clients of the production choices they prefer at the lowest expense possible.

Spreads. What does your magazine charge for spreads? How do they compare with full pages? In *Folio:*, Orlow notes how one men's consumer magazine gives a whopping 38.5 percent discount for full-color spreads, enabling advertisers to upgrade their ads for a rather minimal cost.

Inserts. How do insert costs compare with full-page ads? Does your magazine offer a good value relative to the impact?

Bleeds. Does your magazine charge for bleeds? Would charges be waived for new or long-term accounts?

146

Renewal discounts. Can you offer an incentive to induce advertisers to increase page buys from the previous year?

Odd sizes. Does your magazine offer gatefolds, digest-size inserts, "islands," junior pages in tabloids or other odd-sized ads? Some advertisers appreciate the impact potential of unusual-sized ads.

Merchandising possibilities. Does your magazine offer free classified ads, marketplace listings or postcard-deck inclusions in exchange for certain ad buys? Would your production department help out with advertising production or design? Does the title offer directories or special issues as additional advertising opportunities? Be sure to read "The Big Plus: Selling Ancillary Products" (Vol. I, Ch. 18), for more information on value-added sales.

In short, you'll find almost no end to the selling possibilities you can pull from your rate card. Emphasizing your own rate-card strengths, however, is only half the selling story. The other half lies in comparing your pricing to your competition.

MAKING THE COMPARISONS

Comparing magazine rates, of course, isn't like comparing the costs of paper plates or vacuum cleaners. Everyone knows you shouldn't pay more than $4 or so for a box of cereal, but who knows what you "should" pay to reach 10,000 electrical engineers, or 100,000 married women with an average of 2.4 kids?

As a marketing consultant, of course, your job is to show value in your magazine's pricing structure. One way to show that value, obviously, is to compare it to the competition's. So, just as you did with your own magazine's rate card, find out what you can about your competitor's. Consider the following guidelines:

CPM

✦ What is the current open rate (1X b/w page rate)? What was it the previous two to three years?

✦ How much has the open rate increased over that period? By what percentage?

◆ What is the current circulation?

◆ How much did circulation/readership increase or decrease over that period? By what percentage?

◆ What is the current CPM?

◆ How much did CPM increase/decrease over that period? By what percentage?

As with your own magazine, this information will tell you how your competitor has determined its value to advertisers over the past few years. Once you've constructed that information, find out:

◆ *The difference between the competitor's CPM and your own.* Sometimes the difference is obvious, sometimes not. If your CPM is 10 percent higher than your competitor's, for instance, find out why. Do you have a more affluent audience? Does your title reach more decision makers in the industry? Does it have more authority in the marketplace? Do its readers have more affinity to the magazine? Does the magazine have an overall lower page rate? *Be sure to balance any increased cost to the advertiser with increased benefits.*

◆ *The difference between effective CPMs.* Assume you and your competitor both publish titles in the small-appliance manufacturing industry. You're both courting an advertiser that produces aluminum parts for toaster ovens. Your competitor has a higher circulation than your own, as well as a lower overall CPM. Where's your advantage?

Most times, it's in the effective CPM. Say your competitor's CPM to reach 35,000 readers is $18.50 and half those readers are in the business of making toaster ovens. Now let's say your CPM to reach 26,000 readers is $19.75 and three-quarters of your readers are in the toaster-oven field. For your competitor, the effective CPM of reaching 17,500 prospects would be $37.00. The effective CPM of reaching 19,500 prospects in your own title, by contrast, would be $26.00. Clearly, you can show this advertiser that you deliver more benefit for the investment dollar than your competitor.

Few CPMs are created equal because few audiences are created equal. The only way for advertisers to make accurate CPM comparisons is to compare apples to apples—like audiences to like audiences.

Frequency/page discounts

✦ What percentage discount (from the 1X page rate) does your competitor offer for 3X, 6X, 9X, and 12X schedules?

✦ What discounts are offered for 12-page, 18-page or 24-page buys?

✦ What other discount policies does your competitor offer? How do they compare with your own?

Once again, you might find it helpful to construct a grid chart for your competitor, as you did with your own. Then, comb through the numbers and make your own comparisons.

Let's say you find out the following:

	1p. $4,200	2/3 p. $3,050	1/2 p. $2,700	1/3 p. $2,330
1X b/w rate				
% Discount				
3X	0	0	0	0
6X	6.0	5.9	7.9	10.0
9X	0	0	0	0
12X	17.0	17.5	19.1	19.0
12 pages	17.0	0	0	0
18 pages	18.0	0	0	0
24 pages	22.0	0	0	0

Now you've got some interesting selling points. For one thing, your competitor offers no 3X or 9X discounts; your own magazine, by contrast, has more flexibility. Moreover, while your competitor's 12X discount is steeper than your own, its 6X discount is less. That means your advertisers would get a much better deal from your magazine by running anything less than a 12X schedule.

Remember, many times rates are negotiated as special deals that you may not find on your competitor's rate card. Many titles, for example, grant free pages to advertisers as rewards for new or increased business; or they may give favored clients a 6X buy at a 9X rate.

So let's say that your prospect, Goodwell Glass Works, currently runs a six-page schedule in your competitor, *Glass Monthly*. First, you want to find out from Mr. Goodwell exactly what kind of frequency discount he's getting from *Glass Monthly*. He may tell you he's paying the 7X rate for his six-page ad buy.

Now compare that discount to your own. A quick run-through might tell you that Goodwell Glass could run seven pages in your magazine for the nearly the same price as six in *Glass Monthly*. What client wouldn't want greater exposure for the same amount of money?

Now let's say a second prospect, Shriner Equipment, has a 13-page schedule in the same competitor. You find out that Shriner is buying each page at the 12X rate, and you know your magazine's 12X rate is higher than *Glass Monthly*'s. Are you at a disadvantage? Not necessarily. It might be that your magazine's 12X rate entitles first-time clients to an extra 10 percent discount. Or it may be that your title offers a free page to clients who buy a 12X schedule.

> You can often find competitive advantages in your frequency discount schedule. Find out your client's needs, and then compare your competitor's rates and options with your own.

The point is, you can often find competitive advantages in your frequency discount schedule. Find out your client's needs, and then compare your competitor's rates and options with your own.

Next take a look at your competition's fractional premiums.

Fractional premiums

◆ What does your competitor charge for fractional ads, such as 2/3 page, 1/2 page and so on?

◆ What percent of the 1X b/w page rate is that price?

◆ What is the "fractional premium" of that price—meaning the percent of the page rate divided by the percent of space?

Compare your competitor's fractional-premium grid to your own. How much more would the competition's advertisers pay to upgrade from a 2/3 page to a full page? What would it cost them to bump up from a 1/3 page to 2/3 page?

You may find that while your competitor has sharply discounted certain page sizes, it may also be charging significantly more than your own title for other page sizes. Do any of its premium charges seem unusually high? Perhaps the magazine uses a high premium to discourage any page buys smaller than 1/3 page. Such information might give you a selling edge for certain clients.

Play with the numbers, and talk to your advertiser about his needs. You might be able to show that an investment with your title could yield greater exposure for the money.

Look at these numbers in tandem with frequency and page discounts. How does the competition's rate for a 6X half-page schedule compare with your own? Would this same advertiser be able to run a 6X, 2/3 page schedule in your own book for a comparable price?

Once again, play with the numbers, and talk to your advertiser about his needs. You might be able to show that an investment with your title could yield greater exposure for the money.

Four-color premiums

✦ What does your competitor charge for a 1X 4/c page?

✦ How does that compare to a 1X b/w page, in percentages and in dollars?

✦ How do those numbers compare with your own?

Once you know your competitor's premium for color charges, you might find your own title at an advantage. It may be that your competitor adds an ultra-high color premium in order to keep its open rate low. Or it may be that your competitor has a high open rate and practically gives its color away, which might make your title a better draw for black-and-white advertisers.

Other rate-card issues

Now that you've looked at the four major categories of interest for advertisers, check your competitor's rate card for other selling points. Consider these areas:

Spreads. What does the competition charge for spreads? How do they compare with full pages? Does the magazine discourage or encourage upgrades?

Inserts. How do insert costs compare with full page ads? Does your own title offer a better value?

Special positions. What's the charge for placing an ad on the second, third or fourth covers? What about charges for ad adjacencies? Do new advertisers or favored accounts receive special positions as an incentive? How do your own position charges compare?

Bleeds. Does your competitor charge for bleeds? Would its charges be waived for new or long-term accounts? How do its charges compare with your own?

Renewal discounts. Does your competitor offer an incentive to induce advertisers to increase page buys from the previous year? Which title offers the better discount: yours or your competitor's?

Odd sizes. Does your competitor offer gatefolds, digest-size inserts, "islands," junior pages in tabloids or other odd-sized ads? Or does it discourage unusual ads resulting in a selling edge for your own publication?

Merchandising possibilities. Does your competitor offer free classified ads, marketplace listings or postcard-deck inclusions in exchange for certain ad buys? Does its production department help out with advertising production or design? Does the title offer directories or special issues as additional advertising opportunities? If the same advertiser were to approach both your title and your competition with the same 12X color schedule, which book would offer the more enticing merchandising package?

Clearly, it takes some practice to play all these angles in your rate card. Time and experience will eventually make clear the price advantages and disadvantages of both your rate card and your competitor's. Just make sure you tie your rates to your customer's individual needs. No rate (particularly your competitor's) is a bargain if it doesn't yield the audience and market that your advertiser needs.

> No rate (particularly your competitor's) is a bargain if it doesn't yield the audience and market that your advertiser needs.

8

ADDING VALUE to YOUR SALE: INNOVATIVE MERCHANDIZING

"Anyone can cut prices, but it takes brains to make a better article."
—Philip D. Armour (1832-1901)
American industrialist

As long as the world has had sales, it has had sales incentives. Thirty years ago it was glasses packed in boxes of laundry detergent. A century ago, it was trading cards on cigarette packs. A millenium ago, Ghengis Khan probably got a free spice rack for every camel he bought.

Ad sales, of course, is no different. But since selling magazine space is somewhat more complicated than your average retail sale, you can expect sales incentives to be more complicated.

Remember, an ad buy is an investment your client makes to increase her sales and profits. By giving her an incentive, you *add value* to that investment by improving its chances of payoff. In short, you're not just telling your client, "If you buy a page we'll

153

give you a pair of free movie tickets." You're saying, "If you buy a schedule, we can create a special program for you—a sweepstakes, a trade-show event, a coupon device—something that will enhance your exposure and customer contact."

Such programs are called *value-added* or *merchandising* programs. In these times of heavy media choice, you can't sell without them. A perfectly-crafted sweepstakes, postcard deck, online or direct-mail promotion not only gives your clients a sales edge, it gives your magazine an edge in a crowd of competitors.

Value-added programs can run the gamut of product possibilities, restricted only by your magazine's assets and your own imagination. As a sales incentive, one client could simply receive a free mention in a reader-service guide. Another may get a favored exhibit spot at your magazine's trade show. A third may rate a whole promotional program, complete with brochures, coupons and custom publishing. Your magazine's policies, and your own experience, eventually dictate the right value-added program for your client. I'll show you where to begin.

> Remember, an ad sale is an *investment* your client makes to increase her sales and profit.

THE VALUE-ADDED BASICS

Perhaps you sell for a magazine in the industrial-packaging industry. Client Jones of Jones Gluing Supply is ready to close on a 12-time one-page schedule, but you believe that the right extra sales push can bump it up to a monthly spread.

What can you offer? The only right answer is whatever will benefit both your title and your client. Here's a rundown of some typical—and atypical—value-added devices your magazine might offer as incentives. (And you don't have to stop at merely offering a "free" value-added. You can always *sell* any merchandising opportunity that might give Jones Gluing Supply an extra marketing push!)

Prepare yourself. It's a long list of options.

1. Advertising/Marketing Options

✦ *Ads or listings in buyers guides.* If your magazine distributes a guide as a reader service, you could offer Jones the chance to appear.

♦ *Direct mail.* Jones could send product samples directly to core prospects culled from your subscriber list. Ads in the magazine could instruct readers to "watch for the mail!"

♦ *Merchandising displays, sweepstakes and contests.* If Jones Chemical Adhesive is sold at retail, your title might help to create "shelf talkers" (which promote the new glue on the store shelf), or store displays of the product, or your title could sponsor a contest or sweepstakes in the store or in your pages.

Incidentally, the beauty of sweepstakes is that the contests are flexible and long term—you can run the same sweepstakes for months and continue to get response. Sometimes you can fund a sweepstakes jointly with your client; other times, you might choose to use the same sweepstakes for more than one client at a time.

♦ *Reader service.* You might offer Jones the chance to be listed in your magazine's reader service guide or bingo card listing. As readers respond to the listing, you could send the names and addresses of potential sales leads to Jones for follow-up.

♦ *Ad packages in supplemental marketplaces.* Perhaps you could join forces with, for example, a consumer-crafts magazine to run joint ads for Jones Chemical Adhesive. Or you could run ads in sister publications that address the food-packaging industry.

♦ *Postcard decks.* If your magazine creates a postcard deck of services direct-mailed to subscribers, you might include a coupon, product sample or mini-brochure from Jones.

2. Survey/Research Options

♦ *Focus and exchange groups.* Perhaps Jones wants direct customer feedback on the new Chemical Adhesive. Your title could arrange a focus group of industrial packaging managers to meet and discuss the new material.

♦ *Effectiveness testing.* If your title has access to a lab, you could offer to have your magazine's own experts test the Jones Chemical Adhesive against other adhesives. The results could be published in your magazine.

✦ *Product-tracking services.* If your magazine regularly tracks reader response to ads, or mails out subscriber surveys, you could offer Jones the ability to track reader response to its ads or to survey readers on their use of chemical adhesives.

✦ *Research on brand awareness, purchasing, and advertising effectiveness.* Your magazine's research department could send surveys to readers to determine which adhesion products they buy, whether they might be interested in testing a new adhesive, or whether they took action after seeing a Jones ad. Surveys might also indicate how readers deal with adhesion problems in the plant, or how they feel about other Jones brand products they might use.

✦ *Reports on marketplace opinions and reactions.* After sending product samples to selected readers, your title could solicit feedback from users of the chemical adhesive. Perhaps your title could survey a variety of packaging manufacturers to find out whether they have tried the new adhesive, or whether they would be willing to try.

3. Editorial Options

✦ *Index of articles.* A prominent mention of Client Jones on a floppy disk, CD-ROM, or printed index will keep the Jones name in front of readers indefinitely.

✦ *Press releases.* You might create a joint announcment of the new Jones Chemical Adhesive, with samples or photos, and send it to a list of business and consumer magazines.

✦ *Complimentary subscriptions.* Copies of your magazine could be sent free to top Jones clients and prospects, or to Jones management.

✦ *Videotapes.* Your title could sponsor and produce a video of the new Jones Adhesive being used on the plant-packaging line, complete with user testimonials. It's great publicity to send to top Jones prospects—and to your readers.

✦ *Newsletters.* Jones might be interested in sponsoring a special packaging newsletter to be mailed to top prospects and readers.

✦ *Advertorials, reprints, and other types of custom publishing.* Maybe Jones Chemical Adhesive could sponsor a special magazine section on "Gluing Problems in the Plant" (an advertiser-sponsored section is called an *advertorial*). You could reprint the special section and send it to non-subscribers who are top Jones prospects. Or you could custom-publish a brochure or flyer on adhesion facts to send to subscribers and prospects.

✦ *Educational materials.* Your title could create special brochures on gluing problems, sponsored by Jones. Or you could put together Jones-sponsored fact books or reports on adhesion issues.

✦ *Profiles of corporations in the target market.* Your title might include a special advertorial or supplement which features descriptions of top packaging manufacturers, perhaps focusing on their gluing issues.

4. Trade-Show Options

✦ *Convention and trade show services.* You might spotlight the new Jones Chemical Adhesive in a showcase of new bonding products. Or you could create a special insert for a show daily. You could also distribute samples of the glue product during the show, or distribute literature and promotional items.

✦ *Sponsorship of seminars.* Perhaps your magazine hosts a regional packaging convention each year, or is a key player in the annual Packaging Association Educational Series. Jones could be offered a key role in sponsoring workshops, coffee hours or cocktail parties.

✦ *Speakers bureau.* Jones's own chemical experts might be featured in a seminar or workshop about adhesion problems in packaging.

5. Miscellaneous Options

✦ *Creative services.* Since you've got access to printing and design help, you might offer to design brochures or sales materials for Jones.

✦ *Meetings with selected market targets.* Because your magazine reaches plant operators and other Jones prospects, you might arrange a special invitation-only get-together to discuss gluing problems in the workplace.

You get the idea. There's virtually no end to the ways in which you can enhance your client's ability to reach his marketplace and add value to his ad schedule.

REAL-LIFE EXAMPLES

Of course, talking with your publisher can give you a good idea of what your own advertisers can expect as incentives. In addition, be sure to look at what other magazines, particularly your competitors, offer their clients.

Avionics Magazine *offers reports any advertiser would appreciate.*

You'll find some titles offer only a few, but choice, value-added services. Consider *Avionics Magazine* (page 158), which offers two reports any advertiser would appreciate. The Buyers Access Report (B.A.R.) lists buyers in the advertiser's market, including company names, addresses, phone numbers, and even purchasing intentions and budgets. *Avionics* also offers the Reader Response Analysis Exclusive (R.R.A.E.), which every month summarizes reader survey information, including budgets and buying intentions.

Similarly, *Athletic Business* drives advertiser interest with its Sales Lead Quality Analysis report. Each year, the magazine tells its frequent advertisers the titles and markets of customers most interested in their products and services.

3x-5x ADVERTISERS

3-5x advertisers receive all of the preceding, plus:

Sales Lead Quality Analysis

Every Fall, Athletic Business will run a report based on all your sales leads to date. What markets are you getting the most response from? What are the titles of the people most interested in your product? Get this detailed report free of charge with at least a 3x program in Athletic Business!

6x-8x ADVERTISERS

6-8x advertisers receive all of the preceding, plus:

10,000 Free Names

Choose up to 10,000 names from Athletic Business' mailing list, free of charge, for your next direct mail campaign. If you're using direct mail to complement your advertising program, take advantage of this offer to put one of the industry's most powerful lists to work for you. (List rental is free, advertisers pay all postage, labels sent to 3rd-party mailing house.)

Competitive Ad Tracking

How often are your competitors advertising in Athletic Business? Instead of searching through past issues one by one, Athletic Business will provide you with a report that tracks your competitors' advertising in AB over the last 12 months. (Future schedules, as proprietary information, are not included.)

9x-12x ADVERTISERS

9-12x advertisers receive all of the preceding, plus:

Free Ad Space

If you run a 9x-12x schedule, and have increased or maintained your schedule over the previous year, you are entitled to additional free ad support in Athletic Business' Buyers Guide issue. You can run either another ad (same size), or double the size of your space in this issue (ie: a 1/2 to a one-page ad)!

Please talk to your Athletic Business Account Executive about customizing a marketing program for your company.

Athletic Business *tells advertisers the titles and markets of customers most interested in their products and services.*

Other titles, though, prefer a wide menu of incentives—particularly when the title is part of a larger publishing group. *Convenience Store News,* for example, offers no fewer than 29 value-added services. Everything from focus groups to a speakers bureau are made available to the magazine's print advertisers.

VIP SERVICES

Convenience Store News is more than the No. 1 publication serving the American c-store industry. It's the No. 1 marketing resource for suppliers who want to expand their sales to this important market. Here is a partial list of special merchandising services and marketing opportunities available to our advertising partners. To find out how to qualify, call your Convenience Store News account executive or 1 800 223-9638.

1. **Ad-Q ad effectiveness testing.**
2. **Article index on computer disk.**
3. **Buyer's Guide, with free company and product listings.**
4. **Buyer's Mart press releases, with b&w photos.**
5. **Complimentary subscriptions.**
6. **Consumer, retailer and distributor focus groups.**
7. **Convenience Store News & Insights video publishing.**
8. **Convention marketing packages, including extras such as Product Showcase and Gold Rush.**
9. ***C-Notes* supplier newsletter.**
10. **Creative services.**
11. **CSNews University seminar sponsorship.**
12. **CSNews Speakers Bureau.**
13. **C*Star product tracking services.**
14. **Custom publishing, including advertorials.**
15. **Custom research, including brand awareness, purchasing, and advertising effectiveness surveys.**
16. **Customer meetings with selected retailers and distributors.**
17. **Direct mailings of your literature.**
18. **Educational materials, including Industry Report data.**
19. **Flash field reports on market opinion and reaction.**
20. **Industry Report *Fact Book*.**
21. **Inserts of your literature in show copies of *CSNews*.**
22. **Merchandising Magic display contest and ad package.**
23. **Reader service inquiries.**
24. **Retailer and distributor corporate profiles.**
25. **Reprints of editorial features.**
26. **Sampler Sack at NACS; sample and literature distribution at selected industry events.**
27. **Speaking Out Sessions (retailer-supplier exchange groups).**
28. **Supplemental Marketplace advertising packages.**
29. **Technology Forum.**

Convenience Store News

The whole story. The whole industry.

Seven Penn Plaza · New York, NY 10001-3900 · 212 594-4120 Fax 212 714-0514

Convenience Store News *provides scores of services to enhance ad sales.*

Likewise, advertisers in *R&D* magazine can select among the following:

♦ *Plan-to-buy studies.* *R&D* publishes monthly surveys in various product categories, such as microscopy and computers/software. Advertisers in those categories would clearly be interested in finding out the reader results.

♦ *Marketing services.* Because *R&D* is owned by a large company, it can help advertisers reach their marketing goals through custom research, list rentals, database management, custom publishing and instant inquiry fulfillment. Such strategies can help an advertiser "increase brand awareness, introduce a product, penetrate a new market, target key accounts, increase share of market or ROI..." The list of advantages goes on and on.

R&D's marketing strategies help advertisers increase brand awareness, introduce a product, penetrate a new market and increase market share.

✦ *Product showcase.* Called "*R&D*'s Product Center," the magazine's showcase of advertiser product "reaches 100,000 *R&D* buyers/specifiers in over 52,000 locations."

✦ *Literature showcase.* A polybagged, bimonthly editorial supplement showcases brochures and literature for the scientists and researchers that *R&D* advertisers need to reach.

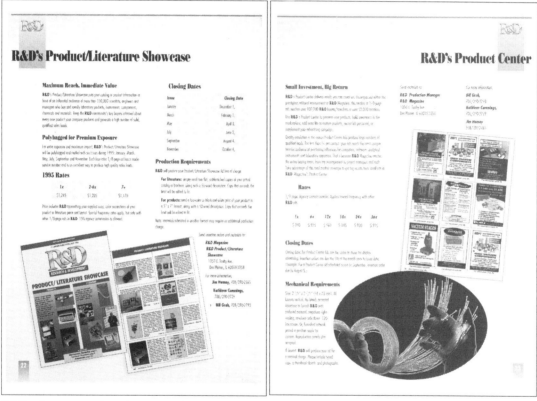

R&D *showcases brochures and literature for the scientists and researchers that its advertisers need to reach.*

✦ *Postcards.* *R&D*'s "direct-response ad cards" help advertisers "introduce new products, build awareness in the marketplace, promote catalogs, literature and price sheets, refresh interest in older products, test an advertising message and generate quality sales leads."

✦ *Tech-spec ads.* These specially designed ads sell highly technical products with an editorial approach. Instead of merely running a display ad, advertisers can choose to have their technical products explained and displayed in a reader-friendly format. Such ads provide the information of a product brochure without the expense.

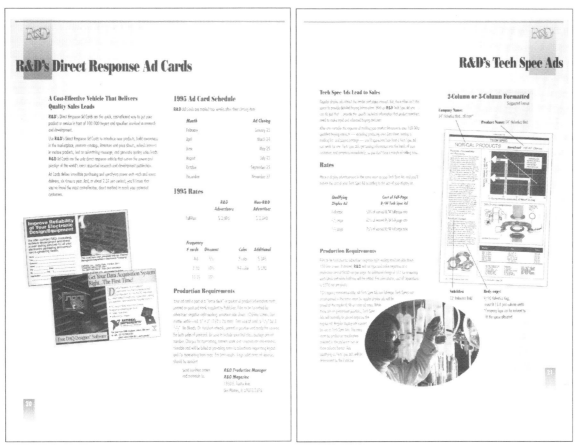

R&D's response cards offer a great sales advantage to advertisers. "Tech-Spec" ads sell high-tech products with an editorial approach.

THE ONLINE POSSIBILITIES

Given that just about every print magazine today has a Web page counterpart, the value-added asset of the moment (as of this 1997 printing, at least) is the online-advertising package. To date, hundreds of advertisers and publishers have found the costs of online ads low, and the advantages numerous.

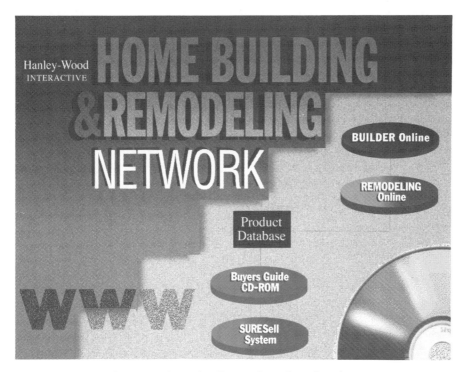

Hanley-Wood *offers a variety of online options for advertisers.*

Here's how it works. Let's say a bathroom-fixtures supplier decides to advertise on a Web site for a publication we'll call *Great Homes Today*. For a simple promotion it could choose a *hyperlink*. A banner on *Great Homes*'s home page, stating, "Click here for 21st century bathroom designs presented by Bath Emporium," could link viewers directly to Bath Emporium's home page. From there, viewers could flip through Bath Emporium's Web site to see its new designs, company information and price lists.

If Bath Emporiums wanted more oomph! for its promotion, it might also co-sponsor an online trivia quiz or contest with *Great Homes*, thus gathering the names and addresses of participants. It might also ask viewers to register names, addresses and demographic information in order to view a special site or download blueprints or other information. Bath Emporiums could then send special e-mail messages or regular direct mail to registered viewers.

164

Using another approach, Bath Emporiums could change its online promotion at a moment's notice, advertising "21st century designs" one week and, "50% off sale" the next. It could even participate in *Great Homes*'s special CD-ROM, "Great Bed and Bath Designs." Best of all, Bath Emporiums could collect any online response information immediately, as opposed to waiting for the slow trickle of bingo cards.

That's not to say, however, that online promotions are perfect value-added merchandising. For one thing, the online audience is still small. In 1996, only 11 percent of households included regular Web surfers, and most of those surfers were adult males, not exactly the audience for bed and bath. For another, Web publishers have no knowledge of who's viewing their site. Most times, they don't even know if those 500 daily "hits" they receive represent 500 separate viewers, or one viewer visiting 500 times. That makes the Web a nice place for attracting attention, but a fairly poor place for gathering truly qualified leads.

Moreover, attracting online direct sales from customers is still a tough business. At this point, only a tiny fraction of online users have actually shopped online. Most are too wary of cyberspace piracy to input their credit card numbers, or even telephone numbers. That limits an advertiser's ability to sell electronically.

Of course, all that is bound to change as Internet technology and security improve. In the meantime, while online advertising can't possibly replace the value of print advertising, it can at least create great promotional attention for preferred advertisers.

A big plus is that the Internet can only improve as a value-added medium. Consider this *Builder* promotion on the following page. It stresses that 69 percent of its readers will use the Internet, and 83 percent will have CD-ROM drives, by the year 2000. That means advertisers will soon have a substantive place to promote their custom-home materials and building plans.

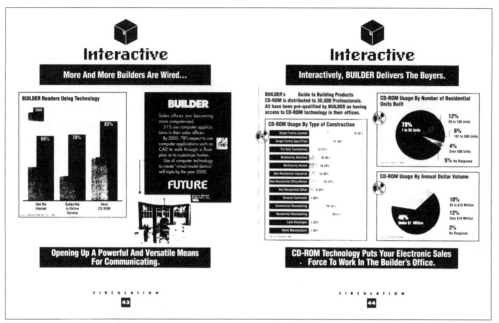

The Builder *promotion stresses that 69 percent of its readers will be online by the year 2000.*

WHAT'S THE RIGHT OFFER?

Many publishers attach incentives to their ad pages the way retailers put prizes in cereal boxes: Buy X number of pages, and you receive X value-added program. *R&D* magazine, for instance, notes how advertisers in its February show issue receive free directory displays, 50 percent discounts on postcards, 50 percent discounts on direct-mail lists, and bonus show distribution. That's terrific incentive to run in the special issue.

But for optimal sales, it's important for publishers to be flexible with value-added offers. Suppose an *R&D* show-issue advertiser had no interest in the direct-mail list incentive. Could that advertiser "trade in" that incentive for a free postcard, a bigger directory display or a marketplace listing? As an ad sales rep, it's important to not only find out the limits and boundaries of your magazine's incentive program, but to keep an open mind to alternatives.

It's also critical, of course, to keep an open mind to your advertiser's needs. One advertiser may have no interest in any ancillary products, but instead may want discounts on pages. What's your magazine's policy on this? Another advertiser may not like any of

166

your usual incentives, but instead may want a specially designed coupon program. Is your magazine set up to help her out? As a marketing consultant, your job isn't so much to meet your magazine's guidelines as to *meet your advertiser's needs.*

It also takes imagination, common sense and often restraint to know just what kind of value-added program makes sense for your advertiser. You probably can't afford to create a whole direct-mail program for a three-page buy—even though your client would love it. And you don't want to reward a two-year contract with a mere listing in the buyers guide.

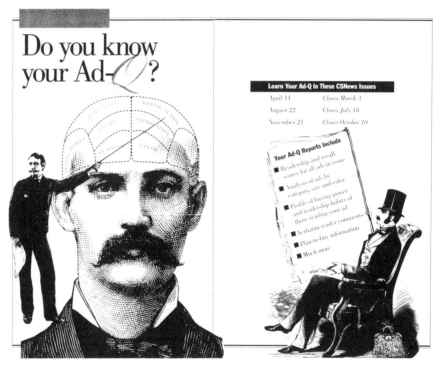

Ad-tracking reports, as in these from Convenience Store News, *make for popular value-added programs.*

As you can see, the whole process is really a *negotiation* with your client: he wants the biggest bang for his buck, and you want to hold his interest without giving away the store. We'll go over the finer points of negotiation in a later chapter titled "If You're Asked to Cut Rates." But for now, keep these points in mind when considering value-added offers.

167

✦ *Know what you can afford to give away.* Don't start off with grand plans that you know won't ever get approved by your ad manager. You'll risk disappointing the client and displeasing your higher-ups. But don't risk looking cheap or disrespectful by offering small gratuities to a large and respected client. Match your assets to your client's needs.

✦ *Know what's valuable to your client.* You don't need to "spend" lots of your magazine's time and money on a client if it isn't necessary. You may have an asset your client values that costs you nothing!

For instance, *Marvel Comics* ran a promotion for Combos snacks, creating a "Combo Man" contest. "Combo Man" was a superhero designed with parts of actual Marvel superheroes. Kids had to guess which superheroes made up "Combo Man" to win a prize. For the client, the real value wasn't in the prize giveaway. It was in the use of the Marvel superheroes—an asset that cost Marvel nothing to "give away." Without that super-hero tie-in, it's not likely Combos would have had the big value-added push it needed to draw kids to its two-page spread.

✦ *Begin on common ground.* Don't start off talking about shelf talkers if your client is more interested in a trade-show promo-tion. Get a feeling for your client's marketing needs and inter-ests *before* you sit down to talk about value-added. If you've done your marketing-consulting homework on your cli-ent—and you must—you should have no problem constructing a program that will anticipate and meet his needs.

✦ *Don't get in a rut.* At first, you might be tempted to offer the same kinds of value-added deals to everybody: "If you increase from a six-month to a 12-month schedule, you get a free listing in our buyers guide and inclusion in our postcard deck." Many publishers, in fact, even list such offers on their rate cards.

It's not a bad idea, since it gives clients some guidelines as to what your magazine considers value-added. Also, a lot of clients

168

need and appreciate that free listing! But don't be afraid to use your imagination. Clients are much more enthused about programs developed for their needs. (The "Combo Man" promotion, for instance, was clearly tailor-made for Combos snacks!)

When thinking value-added, think about what's important to *this* client alone. If he's advertising a new overnight delivery service, perhaps he'd be interested in a free rental of your mailing list to drop promotional brochures. If he's launching a new product, maybe he'd like to survey readers through your subscriber surveys. Match the program to his unique needs.

Don't let clients lose sight of the benefits of advertising in their haste to get freebies.

♦ *And keep selling value.* Consider for a moment that your advertiser wants to increase his schedule just to get that great ad-tracking report. Sounds good to you, right? Well, not necessarily. The last thing you want is an advertiser who values your magazine by the goodies it brings him. If your advertiser wants more pages, that's great—but *make sure he understands the real benefits of increased advertising.* The value of advertising is in the way your magazine can help your advertisers meet their marketing goals. Don't let clients lose sight of those benefits in their haste to get freebies. You need to sell for the long term, not for some short-term value-added program.

TO GIVE AWAY, "EARN" OR SELL?

If you recall my earlier chapter on ancillary products (Vol. I, Ch. 18), most of these value-added sales incentives I've mentioned probably sound familiar. Often these programs—postcard decks, directory listings, mailing lists—are *sold* to advertisers as ancillary products, as well as given away as sales incentives.

The question, then, is understanding when to offer that "extra" to an advertiser, and when to sell it. For that, you can of course rely on your magazine's policy and on your own common sense. If your magazine specifies that you give ad-tracking reports only to six-time advertisers, you don't offer it free to someone who's considering a three-page schedule.

On the other hand, you shouldn't make the mistake of keeping those ad-tracking reports to yourself. Your three-time advertiser may not have a right to free reports, but she may be able to buy them.

Perhaps you have an outerwear advertiser buying a six-page schedule. Your magazine's policy might include free directory listings with this minimal page buy. But suppose this advertiser additionally wants a place in your postcard deck, as well as the chance to join a sweepstakes program. What's the policy? As long as he's willing to pay for these ancillary products, why not? Part of your job as a sales rep is to know the whole menu of merchandising programs available to your advertisers—not only for sales, but for sales incentives.

Incidentally, you can also let certain advertisers "earn" their way toward a special program. Consider this example. An athletic-business magazine has no trouble attracting footwear advertisers, but has trouble getting those advertisers to increase their page buys. To solve this problem, it decides to have each advertiser accumulate points with each ad page buy. Advertisers can then use those points to "buy" a space in the postcard deck, or a free booth at a trade show.

Earning points works particularly well when advertisers literally can't afford either to buy a merchandising program or a big schedule. By accumulating points over months, a small advertiser can earn the same value-added deal that the big advertisers enjoy.

LEARN TO TRADE ASSETS

Often, small, single-title publishing companies feel they don't have the clout to spring big merchandising ideas on clients. After all, how can they offer directory listings, big-money sweepstakes or trade-show space if they don't have those assets in the first place?

The fact is, hoever, that sales reps don't have to rely on their publishers for value-added goodies. They can look to their own clients.

Take the case of *Minnesota Parent,* a small regional magazine. To create a value-added merchandising program, *Minnesota Parent* pulled together the assets of its advertisers and developed a multi-tiered promotion called the "Minnesota Parents Pass." Multiple re-

170

gional advertisers, including restaurants, clothing stores and other businesses, were invited to join by offering special deals for participating readers. Readers could call the "Parent Pass Line" to find out how to obtain a pass from the magazine.

The title also sponsored a "Baby Fair" with more than 50 exhibitors, co-sponsored by a food advertiser. *Minnesota Parent* even used its relationships with area businesses to create value-added programs it couldn't otherwise afford. In one case, advertisers were offered the chance to give away 100 pairs of complimentary movie tickets. The giveaway gave exposure both to the area theaters and to the advertisers sponsoring the contest.

Scholastic's *Instructor* magazine, likewise, created teachers guides sponsored by Universal Studios, Warner Brothers and Dixie Kids Paperware. Each guide utilized the unique assets of its sponsor. The Universal Kids Magazine, for instance, gave monster makeup tips and offered the chance to win a Universal Kids T-shirt. Warner's sponsored magazine contained a movie guide. And the Dixie-sponsored guide discussed trees and reforestation.

Added-value merchandising can turn two negatives into a positive. A health title, for example, might create a nutrition brochure that's printed and sponsored by one advertiser and features products from several others. A beauty magazine might create a product-sample kit, featuring items from several clients, to give away to attendees at a consumer trade show.

If you've got two reluctant advertisers looking for an incentive, trading assets can not only create a great merchandising program, but a great sale as well!

In short, publishers need more imagination than financial clout to create great merchandising programs. When it comes to value-added, the list of possibilities never ends. Look at your own clients and discover what you can do to combine assets and create opportunities. Don't view merchandising as a freebie or giveaway, something that costs you. Instead, consider it a way to *make the most of what you have* to add value to your client's ad buy.

Multiple advertisers can join forces to create a sweepstakes, as in this example from Parenting.

SECTION II

THE DYNAMICS
OF RESEARCH

9

The ROLE of RESEARCH

"There are two types of knowledge: One is knowing a thing; the other is knowing where to find it."
— Samuel Johnson (1709-1784)
English lexicographer and author

❖ ❖ ❖

Assume for a moment that you're on the best sales call ever. Moments after shaking hands, you and your client are talking like old friends, swapping jokes, sharing stories. Your client looks your magazine over as if she's never seen anything like it. Great pictures! Wonderful articles! You walk out beaming, sure of a sale.

Wrong. It goes to your competitor. It goes to the sales rep who says his magazine delivers 32 percent more of your client's target readers, has a pass-along rate that exceeds your pass-along rate 2:1, circulates among 45 percent more professionals earning $50,000+, and has newsstand sales that outsell yours by 100,000 copies a month.

True, your competitor didn't mention that his total circulation was smaller than your magazine's—or that his book spends less on art and editorial, and that it's had three editors in a year. He didn't have to. He did his research. He knew that his magazine could deliver her target better than yours, and he proved it.

That's why you need to know about research. No matter what kind of book you sell, small or large, consumer or business, you can find the research to bolster its advertising value. And that can only spell more sales.

It doesn't matter whether you fell asleep during statistics classes or would rather peel potatoes than add up a column of numbers. If you're at all curious, and in this job you should be, you'll find after reading this chapter that research is actually fun. It's a kind of detective work for unearthing hidden treasures about your magazine.

HOW RESEARCH APPLIES

First, understand that you *need* research. It's basic to developing your marketing strategy.

Perhaps your magazine covers the industrial-laundry market. You're visiting a new client who makes supersized washtub parts. You have two choices: You can hand him the magazine and hope for the best, or you can build a case that gives him almost no option than to run in your magazine.

What kind of case? Here's where research comes in. The right research can do the following:

Position the magazine. "We're number one in the industrial-laundry market in circulation. We've received six editorial awards and have the industry's top executives on our editorial board."

Describe the magazine's impact. "For four years in a row, we've been voted 'Most Informative Title' by the Industrial Launderers of America. Six out of 10 readers do not read any other industrial-laundry magazine."

Document use of product or services. "Eight out of 10 of our readers use supersized washtubs, and five of 10 replace them yearly. Seventy-five percent of our readers are empowered to buy for their companies, and 67 percent of them make recommendations specifically on washtubs."

Describe readers. "We reach 95 percent of the top executives in the industrial-laundry market. Seventy-five percent of our readers manage businesses with sales of $1 million or more, and have an average of 75 washtubs on site."

Describe unique position in the field. "We cover the entire laundry market, while our competitors home in on only the washing or drying aspects. Moreover, our focus is on top businesses. Rather than targeting mom-and-pop operations, we target only those businesses that depend on your product."

Show reader involvement. "Seventy percent of our readers read every issue cover to cover. The average time spent with our title is more than an hour. For every subscriber we have five pass-along readers, all of whom are professionals in the industrial-laundry business. Eighty percent of our subscribers will make an inquiry from our advertisers at least once during the year."

Of course, much of this sounds familiar, since you've already learned about positioning. However, in this chapter, you'll see how research lays the groundwork for positioning. It helps you gather and weave together all the information you'll need to fill in the gaps in your sales story.

You'll also find that research can do much more for both you and your client. You can use research to untangle sales problems. Perhaps one client complains that your magazine no longer reaches his target market. Another says that inquiries to her ads seem to be dropping off. Can you fix the situation? Not without research.

In short, research becomes the foundation that holds up your presentation. In a mud-slinging magazine market, research helps you stand above the fray, proving in hard, measurable facts the value of your magazine.

WHO DOES RESEARCH?

Your magazine may have a research department set up to survey subscribers, conduct market studies and determine how well readers remember your clients' ads. In many cases, magazines also hire outside firms to conduct reader studies, largely because in-house surveys often lack credibility among advertisers. Outside firms usually also handle sophisticated or intensive research, including studies on reader pass-along and advertising recall. Many publishers also use outside firms to conduct in-depth information-gathering through telephone research and focus groups.

WHAT'S AVAILABLE?

Let's take a look at some of the more common forms of research:

1. Reader Studies and Profiles

This information, which can take many different forms, includes hard numbers about your magazine's subscribers and newsstand buyers.

Your magazine's *publisher's statement*, for instance, tells you where your readers live, how much they paid for the magazine, and whether they're first-time buyers or loyal renewers. You might recall that information from "Using Publisher's Statements to Sell" (Vol. I, Ch. 9).

Your magazine's *reader profile* adds meat to those circulation numbers. This profile, often gathered from subscriber studies and questionnaires, tells you the following:

✦ *Reader habits,* which include how much time readers spend with the magazine, as well as how many read each issue cover to cover. You might also learn the number of pass-along readers, as well as the names of other publications your readers may read.

✦ *Demographic information*, which includes household income, age, gender, education and professional status.

✦ *Lifestyle information,* which describes your readers' leisure, travel and recreational habits. You can find out how often your readers eat out or go to movies or concerts; which memberships they may hold or civic activities they may join.

178

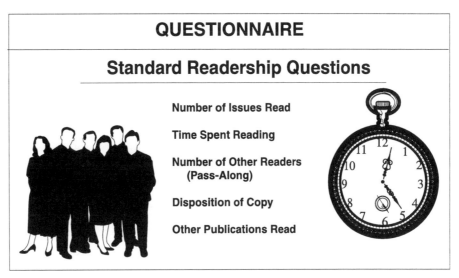

Reader habits. Source: Simmons Market Research Bureau.

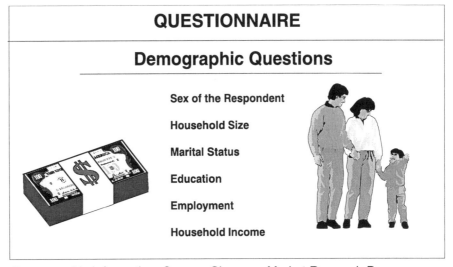

Demographic information. Source: Simmons Market Research Bureau.

✦ *Purchase/usage information*, which tells you whether readers own cars and homes; or whether they purchase alcoholic beverages, own credit cards, or invest in stocks, bonds or other investments. Trade titles may also find out which plant equipment readers use, or how much they spend each year in building supplies, office equipment or other relevant products.

179

This research can indicate which readers plan to buy new software for a fulfillment system, which own tennis racquets, which eat out twice or more a week, or which will spend more than $250,000 this year on factory improvements. All this can give advertisers a sharp focus on whether these readers are indeed in the market for his product.

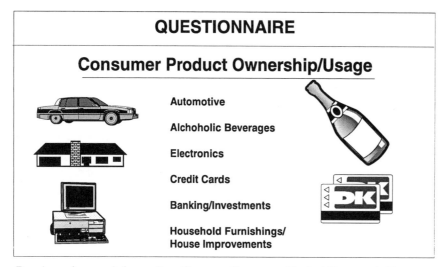

Purchase/usage information. Source: Simmons Market Research Bureau.

2. Advertising-Perception Data

Generally, this is a two-step research process. First, the magazine or research company asks readers whether they knew about a particular company prior to its ad campaign. Several months later, those same readers are asked the same questions following the ad campaign. With this data, publishers can show that advertising makes a difference in the readers' awareness and opinions.

By the way, this kind of research can make for a good merchandising tool. If you're having trouble selling a client, offer the opportunity to present his product in a reader survey. It's a great way to generate interest in the magazine!

Advertising research can make a great value-added merchandizing tool.

3. Inquiry Follow-up Research

As another kind of advertising survey, this research applies to magazines that have some kind of direct-response vehicle, such as a

180

Follow-up on "bingo cards" can help your advertising client.

"bingo card." Your magazine can contact respondents and ask what they bought, what they might be thinking of buying, and whether the advertiser followed up with them.

This is great material to have on hand when advertisers complain that their leads haven't turned into sales. It may be that readers *are* interested in the product, but the client missed an opportunity to contact prospects or to close a sale.

Similar research includes *campaign tracking*, which determines whether a particular campaign boosted reader awareness of a product and service. *Advertising recall and effectiveness* studies ask readers if they saw an ad, remember its message, and changed their behavior after seeing it.

4. Affinity Studies

These surveys reveal how readers see themselves and their relationship to your magazine. Clearly, readers who identify with and relate to a magazine will be inclined to spend more time with it. A survey or questionnaire might ask readers: Does this magazine provide you with up-to-date information? Do you clip and save articles? Do you spend more than one hour reading it per month?

Naturally, the higher readers score in their "affinity" to a magazine, the more advertisers like them. The assumption is that readers who love the magazine will be more inclined to feel positively about its advertisers.

5. Consumer/Market Studies

This type of study looks at the whole market or buying universe. For instance, if you sell for a golfing title, your magazine might want to know how much its readers spend on golf equipment compared to the U.S. population at large. For the answer, the magazine would turn to consumer and market studies, which would measure buying and recreation habits among U.S. adults. Or, the title could conduct a study of U.S. golfers, and compare their equipment spending to the spending of its own readers.

6. Syndicated Research

This research is conducted by independent firms, including Simmons Market Research Bureau and Mediamark Research Inc. Both measure reader demographics, readership and purchasing habits across the population. Normally, agencies use this research to make apples-to-apples comparisons of high-circulation magazines. If *Woman's Day* claims its readers buy more Tide than *Ladies' Home Journal* readers, syndicated research would supply the data to back up (or knock down) the claim.

Here's how Simmons works. Researchers conduct personal in-home interviews to gather data on magazine-reading habits. Later, the representatives send the interviewees a booklet of products and services to determine which products and services they buy and use. Such data may indicate, for instance, that one newsweekly has a far younger demographic than another, but that the competitor's readers have a far higher average-income level and buy more home products.

It's expensive research, but trustworthy. Agencies prefer syndicated research because it's conducted by independent firms. In fact, many agencies won't even consider running national advertising in magazines that are not part of syndicated research studies.

Small magazines sometimes emulate syndicated research with a method called *prototyping*. Here, the magazine hires a firm to match areas of its own readership study with its competitors' syndicated studies.

For instance, say a non-syndicated magazine I'll call *Home Digest* decides to compete against a syndicated title like *Better Homes*. Prototyping could accurately compare *Home Digest's* readership numbers and demographics with its competitors. Prototyping works much like appraising a house: you assess your home's value against the value of the neighborhood-at-large.

WHAT *v.* WHY

In its simplest form, most magazine research really boils down to *what* and *why*. Your advertisers want first of all to know the hard

182

Agencies prefer syndicated research because it's conducted by independent firms.

facts about readers—their ages, incomes, how much time they spend with the magazine. But they also want to know the open-ended, more touchy-feely information: Why do they prefer Competitor A over Competitor B? Why do they care about price or quality? How passionate are they about their interests?

Finding out *why* is the job of *psychographic* research, a topic that's still relatively new to publishing. According to Rita Stollman, president of Editorial Management Strategies, psychographic research really emerged from the packaged-goods industry. Instead of selling the fact that one cigarette tasted better than another, or that one car had more headroom than another, advertisers began associating behavior and personalities with brand. In other words, smoking this cigarette would make you a rugged individualist; driving this car would show your status and good taste.

Applied to publishing, psychographic research works like this: Assume two magazines both claim to reach married female readers in their late 30s with average $60,000 household income. Demographically, the two readerships are identical. Psychographically, however, one magazine's readership is among church-going, stay-at-home moms; the other reaches politically-active entrepreneurs. Clearly, the two groups would have a different relationship to their individual magazines—and to advertiser products.

Why do psychographics matter? Because they illustrate affinity and passion for a magazine. If readers love and trust a magazine because it speaks to their own passions and interests, then by extension, they trust that magazine's advertisers as well.

Consider this positioning statement from *Mother Jones*: "Our subscribers are passionately involved with *Mother Jones*. The key to their consumer hearts is in the causes they espouse. Their passions fill their lives, and the best way to sell them products and services they need is through the magazine they passionately believe in."

In this instance, *Mother Jones* used psychographic research to show how its own readers' passions translated into purchasing behavior. *Mother Jones* readers had indicated willingness to invest in

183

socially responsible companies. So, the magazine pursued such companies as advertisers, even though those companies perhaps before hadn't seen *Mother Jones* as an investment book.

Similarly, *Walking* magazine's independent survey indentified four types of walking enthusiasts: impassioned walkers, enlightened health and fitness walkers, recreational walkers and functional walkers. This survey showed that the enlightened health walkers made up 33 percent of the market.

Because most people walk, the magazine needed to show that to many people walking is a hobby, a sport, or their passion. Far from the *functional* walker who walks from the parking lot to the mall, *enlightened health and fitness* walkers want and need the kind of editorial and product information only a special interest magazine on walking can provide.

That became powerful data when properly combined with other demographic data, like age and income. With its subscriber overlay, *Walking* found that the greatest percentage of its readers were enlightened health walkers. That became a persuasive point for advertisers.

The point is, reader psychographics can not only position a magazine editorially, but in sales as well. Advertisers can discover how readers identify with and are loyal to a magazine, and by extension, to their own advertised products.

TYPES OF RESEARCH METHODS

Now let's look at how research is accomplished. You'll find that your magazine can use many different methods to get readers to talk about themselves.

Mail surveys. Almost all magazines conduct at least some research through the mail. It's relatively inexpensive, and it's relatively easy. Your magazine simply pulls a sample from the subscriber file (usually 1,000 names) and sends out questionnaires.

Usually surveys begin with questions that readers can easily answer and that help them relate to the magazine. Most readers of a

Valid results from a
survey require at
least half of the
contacts to respond.

pet magazine, for instance, would be very motivated to talk about the kinds of pets they have. Subsequent questions might ask about how readers house their pets, what kinds of pet toys they buy, and what kinds of food and treats they might be interested in purchasing. Readers might also be asked whether they have children, or whether they live in an apartment or single-family home.

For mail surveys, though, the biggest challenge is getting enough readers to respond. In order for survey results to be meaningful to advertisers, the responses must be *statistically valid*. In other words, the magazine must be able to project the results onto the rest of the readership.

Let's say a magazine sends out 1,000 surveys and gets only 50 back. Twenty-five of those 50 indicate that respondents like to play tennis. Does that mean the title can claim that half of the 1,000 people surveyed are tennis players? No! The survey doesn't have enough response for statistical validity.

How much is enough? Experts agree that at least half the people surveyed must send back the questionnaire for valid results. So, if a magazine receives only 30 percent response on its first mailing, it has to mail again and again until it pulls in the remaining 20 percent. Sometimes magazines will include a dollar bill or some other incentive to pump up the response rate.

Telephone surveys. While more expensive than mail, the telephone clearly generates a better response rate, and it's particularly useful if the magazine needs results in a hurry. To ensure that the responses are statistically valid, magazines need to conduct telephone surveys *consistently*, asking each person the same close-ended questions each time: *Did you receive the subscription as a gift? Have you recommended this magazine to others?* Because telephone surveys require such expertise, most magazines prefer to have them conducted by outside firms.

Focus groups. Focus groups bring together a half-dozen or more magazine readers to talk about interests, likes and dislikes. Focus groups don't produce statistically valid data—which means they

185

can't tell you that 25 percent of readers buy cold cream or that 43 percent of subscribers eat out twice a week. What they do provide is a lot of useful feedback and anecdotal data. Magazines use them both to strengthen their advertising presentations and to improve their own magazine content.

Assume you sell for a doll-collecting magazine. Generally, you wouldn't want to ask your focus group members any "survey" questions, such as how much time or money they spend on dolls, because you can't project that information onto the readership. Instead, you can use the focus group to talk about how people *think* and *feel* about doll-collecting. That can give you valuable information about how readers relate emotionally to the magazine and to its advertisers.

You can also use focus groups simply to find out which questions to ask in your subscriber studies. You can discover what people like and don't like about your competitors, and how you might distinguish your magazine. That can help you refocus the next survey conducted with your readers.

Another variation of the focus group is *in-person interviewing,* which gathers the same kind of information, but uses a one-on-one approach. You might also pick up some interviewing tips from *intercept studies,* which are those "man-in-the-street" surveys you often see in shopping malls. Although most magazines don't use these methods for information-gathering, they can give a flavor for what kinds of questions people can answer comfortably. The more you understand how researchers gather data, the more creative you can become in your own surveys and presentations!

Light-bulb research. This relatively inexpensive survey method involves binding a reader-survey card into the magazine itself. Why "light bulb"? Because it's a simple way to get bright ideas.

You can ask anything in this kind of survey and vary the questions each issue. A cooking magazine, for instance, might survey food preferences one month and cookware ownership the next. A beauty magazine might publish a special questionnaire insert every six months on makeup use.

186

All this yields good, timely information, useful not only for developing editorial coverage, but for selling advertising. After all, surveys like this demonstrate the reader's interest in the magazine. The only drawback is that the results aren't statistically valid, since the respondents are self-selecting.

Still, this kind of research can be the dessert for your sales presentation. After you've served up your last piece of persuasive information, you can drop in the latest "light-bulb" survey to add something fresh, like the fact that 80 percent of your survey respondents prefer French cooking to any other kind. Very often, it's this kind of up-to-date research that your advertisers appreciate, even if it's not product-specific. It's another way to strengthen your relationship with your client.

Other market research. It's relatively easy for magazines to survey their readers for hard data, such as age and income. Few readers are turned off by the simplicity of a multi-choice questionnaire! But open-ended information, such as why readers prefer one magazine to another, can be a lot trickier to gather and interpret. Why does one female cosmetics buyer with a $75,000 income buy Chanel products, while another with the same income buys Avon?

Gathering such answers is the task of market research firms. Companies like Gallup, Opinion Research, Audits & Surveys, Facts Consolidated and countless others conduct the kinds of complex surveys and research necessary for figuring out lifestyle and behavior information. That information then guides advertisers—particularly consumer advertisers—in their marketing techniques. Obviously, cosmetics companies would love to know why a magazine's high-income readers prefer Avon products to Chanel.

READING YOUR RESEARCH

Okay, time to talk numbers. Don't worry if you can barely figure out a 15 percent tip. By the end of this section you'll know enough about statistical data to put far more energy and depth into your sales presentation.

Basically, we'll look here at what goes into putting together a clean survey and what you can expect to get out of it. It's important to understand that if a survey isn't done exactly right, the results are worthless. A botched survey, no matter how expensive or involved, means you've got nothing to take to your client.

Samples and Response Rates

Conducting a survey doesn't mean sending questionnaires to every reader. But it does mean selecting a large enough sample to represent the entire readership.

The higher your survey response, the better the confidence level.

In general, a good sample size is 1,000 readers, regardless of the number of readers over all. However, some magazines survey up to 10 percent of the readership. Your magazine can pick the sample in one of a few ways. One might be to draw randomly each sixth or tenth name, whatever works for the size of the list. Another would involve drawing samples from distinct reader groups. For a dog magazine, for instance, you might want samples from multi-dog households, from readers with pedigreed pets, and from small-dog and large-dog owners.

The *response rate* is the percentage of people in the sample who *completed* the survey, not simply the number of those who sent it back. Here's an example of how it's determined:

Total readership:	20,000
Surveys sent:	2,000
Returned by post office:	35
Surveys delivered:	1,965
Completed surveys:	1,120
Response rate:	57%

As we noted earlier, surveys with response rates below 50 percent require some kind of follow-up, whether that means additional mailings, a reminder card or a phone call. In some cases, magazines in a highly competitive marketplace need to aim for an even higher response rate. A 55 percent response rate won't do if your competitor's survey results are based on a 75 percent response.

You'll find you can use response rate information as a competitive edge. If you can show that your competitor's study earned a 38 percent response while yours earned 57 percent, you can make a persuasive point about your readership. Or, if you know your competitor had 500 surveys returned by the post office, you might surmise that magazine is working from an outdated list.

Margin of Error

Margin of error is the percentage difference you can expect between your sample responses and those of your readership. Generally, the margin of error shouldn't exceed 5 percent.

Here's how the margin of error might appear in a survey:

Universe of readers	50,000
Sample size	2,000
Respondents	1,000
Margin of error	+/- 3%

Therefore, if 60 percent of respondents say they spend 20 minutes or more with a publication, the true response percentage for the entire readership would be 60 percent plus or minus 3 percent, or between 57 percent and 63 percent.

The higher the margin of error, the more questionable the data. If a competitor, for instance, claims 19 percent to 31 percent of respondents read every issue, that 6 percent margin of error (6 percentage points on either side) would make the information basically worthless. Advertisers could not use the data as a basis for an effective marketing decision.

Generally, the margin of error shouldn't exceed 5 percent.

Confidence Level

Used in tandem with margin of error, the *confidence level* spells out how well you can project the findings of your sample onto the entire universe of readers. In other words, if 25 percent of the readers in your sample said they earned more than $100,000 annually, the confidence level would tell you whether the rest of the readership would respond in the same way.

Ideally, any survey's confidence level should be 95 percent or better (which is not the same as saying you need 95 percent response!). Such a level would means that in 95 out of 100 surveys, 25 percent of your readers sampled would state that they earn $100,000.

The higher your survey response, the better the confidence level. If you get a 75 percent response rate to a survey while your competitor gets a 48 percent response, you can be confident that your sample more accurately reflects your readership. The confidence level is what allows you to take a sample of 1,000 readers and project that data over the entire 100,000 readers.

Banner Points

Banner points let you identify elite subgroups within your subscriber base. Generally, banner points, which run across the top of a survey report, cross-tabulate a survey's responses by a number of categories, such as gender, age and household income. (See chart on next page.)

So in a survey of golfing women, for instance, the banner points might tell you that 45 percent of women who belong to a country club take at least one golfing vacation a year. Another survey's banner points might indicate that 23 percent of people over age 50 spend $100 a year or more on cold cereal.

Any of this survey data gives you an opportunity to present to your client either the big picture of your readership or its most alluring parts.

Are You A Member of a Board of Directors?

	Top Manager	Middle Manager	General Manager	500+ Employees	Less than 500 Employees
Total %	25 100.0	50 100.0	50 100.0	75 100.0	25 100.0
No answer	3	10	5	12	3
Yes %	20 75.0	25 50.0	10 20.0	25 33.0	5 20.0
No %	2 8.0	15 30.0	35 70.0	38 50.7	17 68.0

In this chart, banner points summarize data for a specific group of respondents. For instance, 75 percent of top managers are on boards of directors; 70 percent of general managers are not.

Incidentally, all this information is spelled out for you in the reports that accompany your magazine's surveys. Each report not only includes survey results, but also information on who conducted the research and how (mail, telephone and so on), as well as who tabulated the results, the margin of error, the confidence level and the banner points.

If you can, compare your competitor's reports to your own. Once you know how to read your own research numbers, you'll be able to tell rather quickly whether your competitor is using shaky data or drawing weak conclusions from its own surveys. All this can be wisely utilized when making your case before your client.

INTERPRETING THE NUMBERS

Often when presenting research, you'll find it's not *what* you say about your readership that will make the difference to your client. It's *how* you say it.

Ask yourself, for instance, which sounds more impressive:

"Ten percent of Americans are gardeners—compared to 20 percent of our readers," or "Our readers are twice as likely to garden as the average American!"

In this section, we'll talk about the various ways numbers appear in research reports. We'll also show you how to interpret them in the best way possible for your clients.

Indexing

Let's say your research shows 9.7 percent of U.S. adults bought vegetable-garden fertilizer in the past year. At the same time, 19 percent of your own subscriber base also bought fertilizer in the same annual period.

	Lawn and Garden Equipment Digest			
Amount spent in last 12 months on vegetable-garden fertilizer				
	U.S. Population	**Index**	**Subscribers**	**Index**
Bought $5-$9	2.8	100	1.0	35.7
Bought $10-$19	4.3	100	7.5	134.4
Bought $20-$29	1.1	100	4.7	427.3
Bought any amount	9.7	100	19.0	195.9

Indexing shows how reader buying habits compare to those of the general population.

Comparing your readership with the entire U.S. population is done through indexing. You'll find it a very useful selling tool. Indexing expresses the behavior of the U.S. population using the number 100. That way, when you compare your own readers' behavior to the U.S. average, you end up with a number that's greater or less than the average—a number at which you arrive by dividing your reader responses by the total population and multiplying by 100.

In this case, you'd divide 19 percent by 9.7. That would give you 1.959. If you multiplied 1.959 by 100, you would find your readers have an index of 195.9. Essentially, that says your readers spend nearly twice as much as the average household on fertilizer.

You can see that it's often much more impressive to describe your readers with an index than with straight percentages. Comparing 9.7 percent to 19 percent doesn't say much; but illustrating with an index clearly shows that your readers are well "above average" when it comes to consumer behavior.

The Mean and the Median

You probably remember these basics from high school: Within a set of numbers, the *mean* is the average, the *median* is the middle. So if you've got nine readers aged 12, 22, 34, 46, 52, 67, 72, 75, and 89, you can see that both the mean and median age of your reader would be the same: 52. But if your readers are aged 12, 22, 34, 35, 40, 67, 72, 75 and 89, the mean would become 49, while the median would actually be 40.

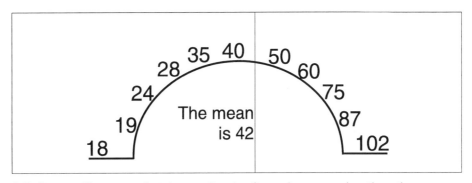

A Bell curve illustrates that the median is often a lower number than the mean.

In most cases the median is lower than the mean. Look at the bulge in the Bell curve. Among the sample ages, 18, 19, 24, 28, 35, 40, 50, 60, 75, 87 and 102, the mean is 42. That number, however, isn't even on the chart. In fact, 40 is the median—the number found at the top of the Bell curve.

That the median is lower than the mean may be good if you're talking about readership age; not so good if you're talking income. (Agencies usually prefer you to use the median when you're making a presentation because they feel it's a more accurate reflection of the readership.)

Whether you decide to use the median or the mean for your presentation, make sure you're consistent. That's particularly important if you're comparing your subscriber numbers to your competitor's. If you use the median to talk about reader income while your competitor uses the mean, you might just end up handicapping yourself.

Here's another example of how to obtain a median:

How many minutes do you spend reading this magazine each month?

No. of minutes	No. of respondents
10	16
15	22
20	32
25	41
30	56
35	45
40	30
45	21
More than 45	15

Median= 30 minutes (sum of respondents above=111; sum of respondents below=111)

Collapsing data means combining totals from several responses to create a single response.

Collapsing Data

Here's a neat trick that's often used to hide information or strengthen weak data (watch out for it from your competitors!) *Collapsing* data means adding the percentages from two or more answers to get a larger percentage.

Here's an example:

How do you rate the editorial in our latest issue?		
Response	No. of respondents	Percentage
Very Poor	20	10.5%
Poor	20	10.5%
Fair	30	15.8%
Good	50	26.3%
Very Good	40	21.1%
Excellent	20	10.5%
Outstanding	10	5.3%

By collapsing data, this publication could claim "More than 60 percent of our readers rate our magazine from good to outstanding"—even though 26.3 percent rated it "good," while a mere 5.3 percent called it "outstanding."

How can you tell if someone is collapsing data? Learn to read the numbers and watch out when you see very large categories of responses. You might even want to seek out the original data to find out what's being masked under the "collapsing" technique.

Net Numbers

At times, *net numbers* help ensure that advertisers don't miss the readership forest for the trees. Here's what I mean by that. Let's say, for instance, that your magazine's reader survey picks up the following buying information:

Reader purchases of camera-related items:	
35mm cameras	72.3%
Medium format cameras	12.9%
Large format cameras	2.7%
Instant cameras	30.2%
Lenses	28.1%
Electronic flash	13.4%
Slide projectors	41.6%

Your research further shows that 90.4 percent readers bought *some* kind of camera equipment. Even though the largest category of buyer was 72.3 percent, you can legitimately claim a "net" buying figure that sums all the research like this: "Nine out of 10 of our subscribers (90.4 percent) bought photographic equipment."

Same Number, Four Ways

Now, knowing what you do about research and numbers interpretation, let's look at four different ways you can express the same information about your subscribers.

Let's say you work for a sports-car title. You know that 22.2 percent of your readers enjoy a household income of $100,000-plus, while in the general population, only 6.3 percent of households have that income. How can you use this data to impress advertisers?

Total household income: $100,000-plus	
U.S. population:	6.3% (Index=100)
Sports Car Digest readers	22.2% (Index=352)

Example 1: "Nearly one in four of *Sports Car Digest* readers enjoy an annual household income of $100,000 or more, compared to only one in 16 for the United States."

Example 2: "*Sports Car Digest* readers are more than three times as

196

likely to have $100,000-plus incomes as the typical U.S. house-holder."

Example 3: *"Sports Car Digest* readers index at 352 against the U.S. population in terms of $100,000-plus household income. That means our readers are 252 percent more likely to have household incomes of $100,000 or more (*SCD* index minus 100="percent more likely").

Example 4: "Out of every 1,000 *Sports Car Digest* households, you'll find 222 with incomes of $100,000 or more. But out of every 1,000 U.S. households, you'll find only 63 with that level of income. That's 159 more households per thousand!"

PUTTING IT TOGETHER

In the next chapter, we'll discuss how to pick and use the research that will best support your presentation. Remember, research is useless if it doesn't address your magazine's benefits and your client's needs. It's also useless if your client doesn't understand it or can't find the value in it. Once you learn what research is, you can then learn to make it work for you.

10

UNDERSTANDING
and
USING RESEARCH

"Research is to see what everybody else has seen, and
to think what nobody else has thought."
—Albert Szent-Gyorgyi (1893-1986)
American biochemist

❖ ❖ ❖

Once you understand the research basics, you need to look at what you really want to get out of your research. In the end, there's just the bottom line. You want to document the relationship between your magazine's readership and your advertiser's prospects. In other words, you want to tell your client: *"Your* prospect is *our* reader—and we've got the research to prove it."

The question is, where do you start? For the answer, look to your client.

Since you're out to prove that her prospect is your reader, you need to first know just who her prospect is. That gets back to the marketing basics we've talked about in earlier chapters. Remember, as your client's marketing consultant, you now know how to look at your client's marketing goals and target market. You know how to find out what she sells, how her product fits into the marketing universe, who's buying her products, and who fits her customer profile.

Once you're able to describe her prospects and marketing goals, you can then sift through your own research data and find out what fits.

It's like buying a sweater for someone: You first find out the person's size and taste. You make some judgments based on his coloring, physical shape and personality. You find out a little history about how he normally dresses; whether he's a cotton-sweater sports-minded guy or someone who wants a cardigan to keep warm around the house. And then you sort through the rack to see what would look right.

Like buying a sweater for a stranger, though, presenting research can be a difficult and iffy proposition—*if* you haven't done the right homework.

Here's an example. Let's assume you sell for a doll-collector's magazine. You can use research to define the prospect universe—that is, all the people who collect dolls around the country. You can then use reader surveys and circulation data to show that your magazine reaches 65 percent of these people who collect dolls. From there, you can present additional readership studies to show that these people are loyal to the magazine and buy an average of $250 worth of doll items yearly from advertisers. Given all that, it's easy to see that an advertiser's message can reach core buyers.

Rarely, though, are research presentations all that simple. Often you must use research creatively to solve an advertiser's sales problems, or to turn what looks like a problem into an asset.

Let's go back to the doll magazine. Say your advertiser says to you: "I can see that I'll reach my core market with your book. But your competitor has ad rates that are half of yours, and still reaches 50 percent of my buying universe."

Solution? Go back to your subscriber studies. You might find

Remember that your *advertiser's* interests come first. In other words, make sure you talk about the *market* first, then the *magazine*.

that your competitor's readers are in the *bottom* half of the buying universe, and have only 70 percent of the household income of your readers. You might find that they own fewer dolls, or buy less frequently. If you look at your CPM in terms of "cost-per-thousand doll buyers," your magazine's ad rates might actually be less than your competitors!

In short, there's no end to the ways you can present and interpret data. All you need is a curious mind and a little forethought.

Here's a tip on presenting your research so that it will have maximum impact on your advertiser. Always remember that your *advertiser's* interests come first. In other words, make sure you talk about the market first, then the magazine. Tell your advertisers about your readers. Describe what your readers do, what they buy, how they can be reached. *Then* tell your magazine's story. Follow this logic, and you'll have a much better chance of pointing your client's attention in the direction of a sale.

SHOW AND TELL

Now let's look at a few practical ways that you can put the best possible face on your research and numbers. As we stated earlier, it's often not *what* you tell your advertisers, but *how* you tell your story. Following are a few tips and examples on how to wring the best impressions from your survey data.

Be Specific

Let's say you're about to approach a client that sells pasta-making equipment. From your subscriber study you learn that 50 percent of your respondents spent $100 on pasta makers last year.

Which statement, then, do you make to your advertiser? *Our subscribers spent an average of $50 apiece last year on pasta makers,* or *Half our subscribers bought pasta equipment last year, and they spent $100 apiece.*

You know why the second one is more impressive? For one, it specifies a target market; it shows your advertiser that a large group of your readers are *his buyers*. And secondly, it shows that these buyers are also big spenders. To your advertiser's ears, the first statement sounds like a stereotyping of the whole readership, which, in fact, it is.

Remember: Know what your numbers mean and know how to present them. Don't just say "X, Y and Z subscribers are your best customers." Supply the interpretation. Find the way to make the strongest sales point.

Express Important Relationships

Let's get back to that photography reader survey I outlined in Chapter 6. Assume that out of a sample of 1,000 readers, you found that 400, or 40 percent, own a 35mm camera. Now let's say that 250, or 25 percent, bought a 35mm lens.

Either of these statistics might be impressive to a camera-lens advertiser. But let's make the case stronger. In this case, it would be logical to deduce that the 250 readers who bought 35mm lenses must already be camera owners. So how about if you express that 250 as a percentage of the 400 who own a camera? What you can then tell advertisers is this: "62.5 percent of all 35mm camera owners bought auxiliary lenses in the past 12 months."

Clearly, 62.5 percent makes a bigger impact than 25 percent. If you learn to look for these connections when reading your reader data, you'll get far more sales mileage out of your research.

Learn to Project

When I consulted with a title called *Trade A Plane*, we used research to dig up the following sales point, which proved invaluable to our advertisers. We learned that our readers planned to spend almost $6 billion in the coming year to purchase aircraft.

Here's how we found that out. The magazine had 142,742 subscribers. The subscriber survey showed 64 percent planned to buy aircraft in the coming year, and they were planning to spend an average of $63,900 per airplane.

What we did was *project* those results onto the full subscriber base. Sixty-four percent would equal 91,355 readers spending nearly $64,000 apiece. That added up to $5,755,365,000 that would be spent on aircraft. We could then say to our advertiser: "I'm sure you don't want to give up a $6 billion market." Who could pass up an opportunity like that?

Think creatively, and you'll find lots of ways to use projections. Once, for instance, *Country Journal* found out that its acreage per reader was higher than that of its competitor. When we worked out ad rates at a cost-per-thousand acre, we made a compelling case for advertisers. But then we strengthened it by projecting the average acreage onto the entire subscriber base and then comparing that with the amount of privately owned acreage in the country. The result? *Country Journal* could justify a claim that its subscribers owned one-thirtieth of all the privately owned land in the United States!

Know Whom You're Up Against

Depending on your client, you might sometimes find that your competition isn't actually what you think it is. And that will change the kind of research you'll need to show your client.

Take the case of *ABA Journal*, a business magazine for the legal profession. The title was seeking investment advertising. But to get it, the magazine had to compare itself with other magazines that normally attract investor advertisers. In other words, even though it was a professional journal, it was going to be looked at as a consumer magazine.

So *ABA Journal* compared its household income data against syndicated research data from top consumer titles. The results were surprising. *ABA*'s readers had a 33 percent income advantage over *Fortune*, a 28 percent increase over *Forbes*, and 23 percent over the *Wall Street Journal*.

ABA Journal Readers Are Not Reached By Traditional Titles

	% ABA Journal readers not reading
Worth	99
Investor's Business	97
Barron's	95
Financial World	94
Business Week	82
Fortune	82
Money	81
Forbes	80

To attract investor advertisers, ABA *compared itself to investor magazines.*

ABA Journal Has Income Advantage Over Other Publications

	ABA Advantage
Fortune	33.3%
Forbes	28.6%
Wall Street Journal	23.0%

ABA *proves the superiority of its readers' affluence.*

Using indexing, the *ABA Journal* also demonstrated that its readers were more likely to invest than the average American. And the magazine's reader survey showed that the readers also indexed high on the number of investment transactions. This was an important point for investor advertisers, since they make commission on each trade.

The Value of ABA Journal Readers' Portfolios is Well Above the Affluent Average

	Total Affluent	ABA Readers	Index
Any Securities	$59,700	$134,500	225
Funds	$31,900	$51,000	157
Bonds	$13,400	$28,400	212

ABA Journal *readers have larger portfolios than the average affluent household.*

Notice that the *ABA Journal* was prepared to say the same thing about its readers in many different ways. Why? Each angle added weight to the total presentation.

Moreover, each angle prepared the magazine to combat inevitable skepticism. A potential advertiser, for instance, might say, "If your readers are big investors, I could get to them through other investment journals, in addition to getting all those other investment readers." To which *ABA* could respond with information about how its readers are more active traders, and that most of them are not reached by traditional titles. Advertisers would have a hard time arguing with that.

ABA Journal Readers Are More Active Traders

	Median # Securities Transactions/Year
Investor's Business	11.4
Barron's	10.2
ABA Journal	8.4l
Worth	7.7
Financial World	7.1
Forbes	7.0
Wall Street Journal	6.4
Fortune	5.8
Money	5.6

ABA *shows more active traders than most investment titles.*

Find the Elites

Even a start-up magazine can make a compelling case for it-self—even without the mass circulation of its competing titles. The secret is in finding the elite target audience—the one your client desperately wants—and showing your prospect how efficiently you reach it.

Let's look at how *Newsweek Woman* did it. Basically, the title painted a compelling picture of its reader demographics that made other, bigger competitors look like so much wasted circulation.

The magazine, a demographic edition of *Newsweek*, targeted 700,000 high-income female professionals. Its promotional brochure positioned it right away: "Today's affluent working woman may be hard to catch, but she's easy to reach. Maybe you can reach her with us." Basically, the magazine defined a subgroup that may exist within big titles like *Ladies' Home Journal*, but was much tougher to target.

The promotion also showed that 53.2 percent of readers were professional managers earning $40,000-plus. Thus the magazine claimed to have the lowest CPM reaching this target group. The reasoning was this: While a similar readership may exist in *McCall's*, it would only comprise, say, 8.9 percent of the total. That meant an advertiser trying to target the cream could do so more efficiently with *Newsweek Woman*.

Finally, the promotion stressed that *Newsweek Woman* had the "editorial to support that [affluent, professional] interest." Along with pages reproduced from the magazine, the piece highlighted whom the magazine reached, when it reached them and what an advertiser could do to take advantage of the market.

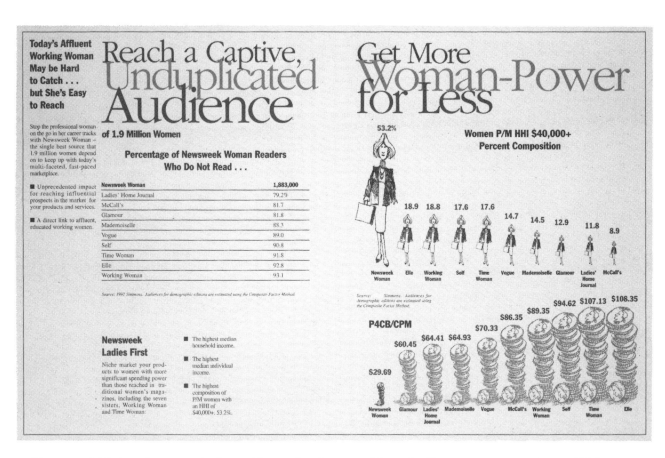

Newsweek Woman*'s research showed how advertisers could reach affluent women at a lower CPM than traditional women's titles.*

That's a nicely sewn-up positioning statement for a magazine that hadn't even had its first subscriber survey. What it showed was that you can still make a case for your title as long as your data—whatever data you can get—shows that *your* reader is your *advertiser's* prospect.

PUTTING IT TOGETHER: CASE STUDIES

No doubt you'll have advertisers throw lots of curve balls at you in your career. With enough research, you'll not only be ready, but you'll occasionally hit one out of the park.

How do I know? Here are a few real-life examples of how research helped *me* pull presentations together.

Solving the Sales Problem

I once was a rep for an antiques magazine that had a sales problem: Antiques dealers felt the magazine was no longer supportive; that its ad rates were too high, and that it could no longer sell effectively in volume.

We decided to tackle the problem with research. First, we needed to know what percentage of readers were buyers, and whether those readers would like to see more ads from dealers. What would it take to get people to buy antiques? Were they not interested? Were prices too high? Was the readership too young?

To find answers, we turned to reader surveys. From there, we found that collectors were dropping subscriptions because of the the magazine's increased focus on newer items. So now we had two problems: the loss in readers would mean losing advertisers.

After conducting editorial audits and focus groups, we learned that readers didn't distinguish between editorial and advertising. They were even reluctant to tear out a page because advertising was so valuable to them! That was a surprise to the publisher, and good news we could pass on to advertisers.

As a result, we could explain to advertisers that the solution wasn't less advertising—it was more informative advertising. We showed them that if they ran larger ads with more product, they could sell a variety of goods more effectively, and that it would take fewer ads for them to make more profit.

Moreover, we told them that the high reader interest in advertiser information enabled them to follow up any reader inquiries by sending brochures about similar antiques of the same period.

In this way, we fulfilled our roles as marketing consultants. We developed a closer relationship with advertisers and distanced ourselves from the competition.

Finding Circulation Opportunities

You've heard it said that statistics can prove anything? Well, here's an instance from the woodworking universe that proves how solid yet contrary presentations can be created from the very same research.

After an extensive reader study, *American Woodworker* claimed to advertisers that it "targets America's most active woodworkers—the intermediate and advanced enthusiast, who accounts for 84 percent of the $10 billion woodworking market."

It was a pretty heady claim, and it was based on a study of how woodworkers see themselves. Results showed these enthusiasts distinguished themselves by four categories: beginners, low intermediates, upper intermediates and experts. In terms of spending time on woodworking, beginners made up 12 percent of the market; lower intermediates were 29 percent; upper intermediates were 37 percent, and experts were 18 percent.

As woodworkers moved from beginner to expert, the demographics changed (and in most cases improved). The age of the reader increased; the percentage of male over female increased, the number of projects completed each year increased, and so did the number of hours spent per week and the number of years of experience.

Moreover, the greater the expertise, the more money spent on woodworking. So in the end, that justified *American Woodworker*'s

208

potent claim: Because the magazine reached the experts, it reached the money-spenders as well.

But now consider a magazine selling against *American Wood-worker*. It may have a larger circulation, but because of its editorial thrust, it attracts fewer experts and more beginners.

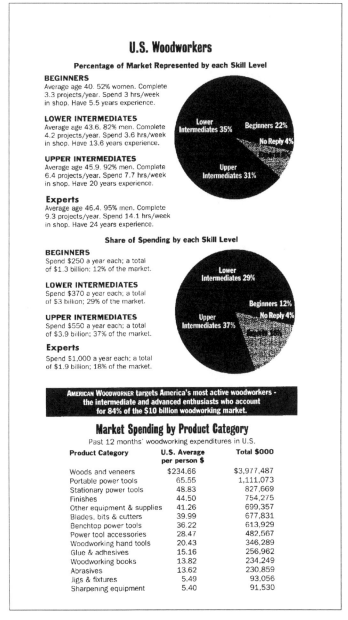

U.S. Woodworkers

Percentage of Market Represented by each Skill Level

BEGINNERS
Average age 40. 52% women. Complete 3.3 projects/year. Spend 3 hrs/week in shop. Have 5.5 years experience.

LOWER INTERMEDIATES
Average age 43.6. 82% men. Complete 4.2 projects/year. Spend 3.6 hrs/week in shop. Have 13.6 years experience.

UPPER INTERMEDIATES
Average age 45.9. 92% men. Complete 6.4 projects/year. Spend 7.7 hrs/week in shop. Have 20 years experience.

Experts
Average age 46.4. 95% men. Complete 9.3 projects/year. Spend 14.1 hrs/week in shop. Have 24 years experience.

Lower Intermediates 35% · Beginners 22% · No Reply 4% · Upper Intermediates 31%

Share of Spending by each Skill Level

BEGINNERS
Spend $250 a year each; a total of $1.3 billion; 12% of the market.

LOWER INTERMEDIATES
Spend $370 a year each; a total of $3 billion; 29% of the market.

UPPER INTERMEDIATES
Spend $550 a year each; a total of $3.9 billion; 37% of the market.

Experts
Spend $1,000 a year each; a total of $1.9 billion; 18% of the market.

Lower Intermediates 29% · Beginners 12% · No Reply 4% · Upper Intermediates 37%

AMERICAN WOODWORKER targets America's most active woodworkers - the intermediate and advanced enthusiasts who account for 84% of the $10 billion woodworking market.

Market Spending by Product Category

Past 12 months' woodworking expenditures in U.S.

Product Category	U.S. Average per person $	Total $000
Woods and veneers	$234.66	$3,977,487
Portable power tools	65.55	1,111,073
Stationary power tools	48.83	827,669
Finishes	44.50	754,275
Other equipment & supplies	41.26	699,357
Blades, bits & cutters	39.99	677,831
Benchtop power tools	36.22	613,929
Power tool accessories	28.47	482,567
Woodworking hand tools	20.43	346,289
Glue & adhesives	15.16	256,962
Woodworking books	13.82	234,249
Abrasives	13.62	230,859
Jigs & fixtures	5.49	93,056
Sharpening equipment	5.40	91,530

American Woodworker *claims its target audience accounts for 84 percent of the market.*

So what would its sales reps tell advertisers? Simple: "You don't want to concentrate only on the experts. If you do, where will your new customers come from? Our prospects are open to being sold. Here's a chance to build loyal buyers and keep them as they gain experience."

Both magazines, then, can serve the industry in slightly different ways. And both can look at the same research—the same universe—and tell a compelling story to advertisers.

Measuring the Universe

The magazine *Early American Life* wanted to show that its readers were not only intensely interested in Early American living, but also high-income, well-educated and willing to spend on their interest.

For this, an ordinary reader survey wouldn't do. The magazine instead decided to measure the entire *universe* of Early American enthusiasts. It sampled not only readers, but living history museum visitors, American history book buyers, historic travel-tour participants and handmade-basket buyers.

First, the magazine used its information to define the "Early American Market Consumer." The magazine then asked these consumers which sources they turned to for information about their interest.

After determining how much time these readers spend with their favorite magazines on Early American living (28 percent spent one to two hours per week), the magazine further divided these history buffs into two groups: "heritage seekers" and "heirloom collectors."

It was clear that heirloom collectors, who made up 24 percent of the sample, were generally older, less well educated and had smaller households and lower incomes than others in the sample.

But heritage seekers, who represented 76 percent of the total sample, were on the whole better educated, younger, had more children living at home and resided in larger households. They were more likely to be interested in home restoration and to have traveled in the past 12 months.

In short, they were the hot buyers. Which meant *EAL*'s final task was to prove that its readers were heritage seekers. By combining its own reader information with this universe market study, *EAL* was able to show advertisers it reached a potent group of prospects.

The Early American Market: A Passion for the Past		Consumer Clusters

Demographics:

Heritage seekers and Heirlooms represent two distinct demographic clusters within the Early American Market Consumer profile.

	Heritage Seekers	Heirlooms
Percent of Market	78%	24%
Female	64%	71%
Median age	47	57
College graduate	72%	38%
Median household size	2.8	21.9
No children in household	63%	87%
Employed full-time	88%	65%
Professional/managerial position	66%	31%
Median household income	$67,500	$27,500

Early American Life *market survey shows heritage seekers are the hot audience.*

211

So, before you step into your next client meeting, make sure you've done your homework. If you've got the right data in hand, you can sell just about anything.

SECTION III

THE CHALLENGE OF OBJECTIONS

11

The PSYCHOLOGY of OBJECTIONS

"You can discover what your enemy fears most by observing the means he uses to frighten you."
—Eric Hoffer (1902-83)
American longshoreman and philosopher

Think for a moment about the best day of your career. It probably *wasn't* that day when every client cheerfully said "yes" to those six full pages, and by the way, make them full color (although I agree, that is always a good day!). More likely it was that day you were met by scowls in that client's office, challenged at every turn, and still able to walk out an hour later with a full schedule.

Granted, handling objections is probably the hardest part of your sales job. But think of it this way: *overcoming* objections can be the most satisfying part of your job. To a seasoned sales rep, objections can be a valuable source of feedback, and even an opportunity to ferret out a client's interests and *sell*. Once you've got the skills and the attitude to handle objections, you just might feel the same way.

Chances are, though, if you're inexperienced, you probably see objections as more of a minefield than a field of opportunity. That's okay; in fact, that's smart. Objections *are* minefields, and new or cocky sales reps who rush into them risk blowing out a sale.

But even if you're new to sales, you don't have to be afraid of objections. You can learn negotiate them with confidence, caution and skill. That's what I'll talk about here. Think of this chapter as a map through the minefield, complete with tools to defuse the explosives.

HANDLING OBJECTIONS: THREE VIEWPOINTS

In this chapter and the next, we'll look at objections from three points of view:

1. *Psychology*, which means understanding how you and your client feel about obstacles to the sale. It means knowing who you are, what people skills you have, and what motivates you in selling.

2. *Structure*, which means understanding how the Advertising Syllogism and the Steps to a Sale can help you answer objections.

3. *Content*, which means understanding the specific tactics that can help defuse the landmines in the sale.

I've found that each sales rep approaches objections with different strengths and weaknesses. Some are great *psychologically*. They're risk-taking, courageous and confident. They have great ability to read people, but they might not apply structure to their selling technique, or know the right tactics to use in different situations. Others are terrific with *structure* and *content,* but they're too uncertain to apply what they know. Without all three elements in place, sales reps are all too likely to walk away without overcoming objections, closing, or without even understanding what went wrong.

Incidentally, the three elements apply to the client as well. In some sales, your client may simply need to feel psychologically at ease. In other cases, you'll win your client by demonstrating the logic behind making an advertising buy. Other sales will rely on your quick thinking and ability to answer pointed objections and demands.

216

In the end, what's needed is an integration of all three points of view. You can't walk confidently through an objection unless you know what you're talking about, and have the ability to structure and use your insight.

In this chapter, we'll talk about how to integrate psychology, structure and content. In the following chapter, "Overcoming Objections: The Nitty-Gritty," I'll present specific tactics.

THE PSYCHOLOGY OF OBJECTIONS

When you deal with objections, you naturally deal with the psyche. After all, this is the one point in the sale where tensions run high, personalities assert themselves and defenses go up or down. The rest of the sale may be all logic and discussion, but once objections enter the scene, a distinct shift in the mood is palpable.

That's why many salespeople dread handling objections. It's not necessarily because they don't know how to answer them; it's that they're not comfortable that the straight line to the sale has taken a sharp turn. Instead of agreement, there's questioning. Instead of being on the same side, there's opposition.

IT'S ABOUT FEAR

Let's face it. It doesn't feel good when people say "no" to us. Everyone wants to be liked; nobody likes rejection.

So there you are, walking into Ms. Bigshot Client's office. Immediately you know it doesn't feel right. She's smiling, but her eyes are hard. Her arms are crossed in a "let's get this over with" attitude. Five minutes into your presentation, she sighs and says, "Look, we really don't have the budget for this. Let's not waste any more time."

How are you feeling about all this? Anxious? Rushed? *Fearful?*

Right. Most of the time, when it comes to handling objections, you're dealing with fear. *Your* fear, of course: *I'm looking bad. I'm no good at this.* And *her* fear: *I might get ripped off. I don't know this magazine. I don't want to change how we do things.*

The truth is, sale resistance and objections are common, almost

217

natural. Think about the last time you were browsing in a store and a clerk said, "May I help you." How did you feel? Maybe you colored a little, felt a prickle of tension, wanted to withdraw. How did you react? "No, thanks. Just looking." That's knee-jerk sales resistance, something that helps you to avoid being influenced or seriously involved. Resistance helps the prospect keep control.

Often, it's the same with your own prospects. "I'm not interested in advertising," or "Our budget is closed," are typical knee-jerk reactions. They come from a visceral response to a sales query.

Even though this fear is expected, it doesn't have to take over. Fear crushes the teamwork that's essential to a good sale. Instead of working for a common interest—improving the prospect's ability to market her goods and services—you and your client become at odds. She throws an objection, you hit back an answer. She throws another, you respond with defense. This tit-for-tat goes on until the one with the least stamina gives up. Whatever the outcome, everybody loses.

So, if you're going to handle objections, you've got to handle fear—both yours and your client's. You've got to change the visceral response and show that both you and your client are on the same side. That means you've got to change your way of thinking about objections. I'll talk about that next.

Your Client's Fears

If you're new to sales, you might think your client holds all the trump cards. After all, *he's* the one with the power to say yes or no to you. *He's* the one with budget—the one who listens and decides while you try to convince him to buy.

In fact, many clients expect you to feel this way. Those are the ones you'll find testing you. They'll look into your eyes and study your body language to see if you really believe in your magazine and in what you're saying. After all, if *you* don't, why should they? These clients might even try to bait you with objections to see how you might react.

218

The truth is, though, that clients often have their own emotional reactions and fears in a sales situation. They'll usually cover up those fears with objections. Don't be fooled. You need to expect and understand those fears as they arise. Only then can you calmly and thoroughly defuse them.

Do the following client fears ring familiar?

1. *Fear of making the wrong decision:* "I need to get back to you on this after I've checked it more thoroughly."

2. *Fear of making any decision (the procrastinator):* "Let me think about it."

3. *Fear of change:* "We'll just keep the same program as last year." (In your competitor's publication.)

4. *Fear of being cheated:* "Will your publication deliver what it claims?"

5. *Fear of looking bad to associates/peers/superiors:* "Let me speak with my associates."

6. *Fear of acting without sufficient thought or knowledge:* "Send me more information."

In a sense, all these fears amount to the same thing: *I'm not convinced.* Your task is not to get defensive or call your clients on their fears. Your goal is to make sure your clients have and understand all the information they need to make an informed, confident decision.

Your Own Fears

To do that, you've got to also have an understanding of your own fears. See if these sound familiar:

I'm not confident about my magazine.

The client doesn't look like he'll like me.

I had a horrible rejection last time.

My presentation isn't good enough.

The key to handling fear is to override it with logic and intellect. Let's look at each of these worries and see what's really at stake.

My magazine isn't good enough. In this instance, you're *too* aware of your magazine's shortcomings and limitations. Maybe it doesn't have the circulation of its competitor—or maybe it's not as slick or glossy. Maybe it's trying to overcome a poor editorial reputation.

It's important to *know* your magazine's Achilles heel, but it's just as important to shield it. Don't let your title's imperfections hinder your success. If you believe your magazine must be perfect to produce results, you'll overreact to objections.

> If you believe your magazine must be perfect to produce results, you'll overreact to objections.

The truth is, almost *every* magazine is a sales opportunity. Magazines reach prospects, and therefore have the wherewithal to help their clients do a better job of marketing. As a marketing consultant for your client, it's up to you to understand and believe in the strengths and capabilities your title may have. This way, your client will understand them, too.

The client doesn't like me. It's natural to want to be liked, and it's crucial that you express empathy with your client. But you must guard against the *need* to be liked. You and your client are in a business relationship. If you give in to the need to be "nice," you'll likely find yourself nodding in agreement as your prospect ticks off reasons as to why he shouldn't advertise.

Do that, and you'll be short-changing your prospects, your company and yourself. Stick to the knowledge of what your magazine can offer your prospect. Take the focus off yourself.

That last client objected—why shouldn't this one? Objections can be intimidating. Consider what happens when a single drop of black ink falls into a glass of water. The water turns dark. Likewise, salespeople often allow a single objection to darken the entire sale. Some may become apologetic and beg for a sale. That's both ineffective and unattractive.

The fact is, if you're afraid of objections, you won't look at them clearly—and you'll lose the sale for sure. Some objections might signal "Tell me more." Some might mean "maybe." Some might even be a buying signal: "I'd like to buy, but I just need to vent one thing."

Remember, the prospect buys because of *his* needs and desires, not because of yours. Instead of cringing at objections, pay attention to your prospect's expressions, body language, tone and gestures. Use your people-reading skills to interpret what his specific objections really mean. Then use those objections to relieve his fears and doubts, not to compound your own fears and doubts. Negative emotions can kill the sale.

My case isn't strong enough. It's a given: The effectiveness of magazine advertising is intangible. You know this. Despite your media kit full of circulation numbers, readership facts and response results, you can't "show" your readers your magazine's effectiveness. You can't assemble all your readers into a sports arena and hand your prospect a microphone to deliver his sales message.

But you can offer your clients confidence. If you've built your presentation carefully, you can give them enough logic and proof to indicate that advertising in your magazine is a low-risk expense that will result in significant sales. You can convince them that advertising is less risky than *not* advertising. You can build up their trust in the publication, and in yourself. Ultimately, that's why they'll buy!

Your job as a salesperson is to provide your clients, and yourself, with the information, proof and the rationale that your publication will help your prospects achieve their goals. This information will give you and your client confidence. It will override the emotional or knee-jerk decision not to buy.

YOU NEED INSIGHT

If you're going to deal with people's psychology, it helps to think like a psychologist. Here's a very basic tip: if you sense resistance, don't push your point of view. Lead your clients to it gently.

Here's how. You might recall from "Power Presentations" (Vol I,

Ch. 22) how a psychologist friend of mine uses a counseling technique called "insight therapy." In it, the patient works through all the emotional and intellectual steps to reach a full understanding of a problem or idea.

For instance, a good marriage counselor would never tell a couple, "Well, after hearing you talk about your problems, it's absolutely clear to me that you need a divorce. Thanks for coming in. My secretary will refer you to a good attorney."

Why not? Because patients, on some level, need to go through a discovery process of their own in order to explore possible solutions or make changes. It's not enough to get feedback or advice; what's needed is the patient's own conviction of the need to change.

THE STRUCTURE TO HANDLING OBJECTIONS

Let's say somebody blindfolds you and puts you in an unfamiliar room full of furniture. What's the first thing you do? You figure out where you are. To move blindly through a room full of obstacles is plain terrifying, unless you take specific action immediately to figure out where the furniture is and how to get around it.

It's the same with handling objections. Let's say you walk into a client meeting and the first thing you hear is, "We absolutely hate your magazine's liberal news bias. Frankly, we no longer wish to be associated with it."

Unless you know specifically what to do with that objection, you're as good as blindfolded. You need to know how to figure out your way around the obstacles to your sale, no matter how unfamiliar they may seem. And for that, it's best to rely on my two favorite tools: the Advertising Syllogism, and the Eight Steps to a Sale.

The Advertising Syllogism. Whenever you hear any objection, first try to determine how it fits into the Advertising Syllogism. Here's how it goes:

1. *This is your prospect.*

2. *This is our reader.*

3. *Your prospect is our reader.*

4. *Your prospect—our reader—reads this magazine.*

5. *Your prospect's buying behavior is affected by reading this magazine.*

6. *Therefore, you can sell your prospect—our reader—by advertising in the pages of this magazine.*

7. *Here are our advertising recommendations.*

8. *Close the sale.*

So let's take that objection above: "I don't like your magazine's liberal news bias." This is not the time to argue political points of view, no matter how tempting. Remember, you can hardly control your client's belief system, so why try? Instead, get to the logic in the Syllogism. Why should this client buy an ad? Not because your magazine is liberal, conservative, Tory, Labor or Whig. It's because the client's prospect reads the magazine.

So, based on the logic of the Syllogism, here's what you can say: "I hear your concerns, Mr. Belle, and understand them. Just as I know you understand that 30,000 environmental professionals subscribe to this magazine for the very reason you cite, and are passionately involved in its editorial. Frankly, it doesn't matter what you think of the magazine's editorial approach, or even what I think.

"What matters is what the readers think, and our readers love this magazine! These 30,000 professionals are the largest, most targeted market for your software product that you can find anywhere. I hope you won't pass up an opportunity to reach them."

Remember this Advertising Syllogism whenever you hear an objection. When a prospect says your rates are too high, or that he doesn't like your editorial, just return to the logic: *Your prospect is our reader. You can sell your prospect in the pages of this magazine.* Once you come back to the steps of the Syllogism, you can follow through to the close.

The Eight Steps to a Sale

The logic of the eight selling steps also saves you from getting tossed around by objections. Here's how they go:

1. *Make your opening.*

2. *State benefits of advertising.*

3. *Qualify your prospect; find out her needs and concerns.*

4. *Get agreement on needs.*

5. *Make your sales presentation.*

6. *Get agreement on points in your presentation—how your magazine meets her marketing needs.*

7. *Get commitment.*

8. *Follow through on the sale.*

The Eight Steps, like the Advertising Syllogism, guide you toward establishing rapport with your clients and prospects. Once you qualify your prospect, find out her needs and get her agreement on the benefits of advertising, you're in great position to head off or defuse her objections.

Keep in mind, too, that objections usually don't enter a sales presentation until about Step 6, when you're seeking agreement on sales points. If you've led your prospect through the first five steps without a problem, you'll likely find it easy to defuse objections here. All you need to do is figure out where the objection fits into the step. For instance:

Prospect: *I don't see why I need to advertise with you. I want a national distribution, and your magazine has primarily a Northeast circulation.*

You: *I know we've talked about how you feel your ski product has far more awareness in the West than in the Northeast (Step 3—Qualify your prospect). The Northeast represents the biggest untapped market for your product, and a schedule in our publication will bring your name to 300,000 active skiers. Isn't your money better spent reaching those* *who want to know you than on those who already do?*

What happens, though, when an objection pops up where you least expect it? What do you do when you're hit at the start of a sale, or right when you're ready to close? Well, that's a bit of a longer discussion. I've saved it for the end of this chapter.

DEFUSING OBJECTIONS

Now let's talk about specific ways you can meet objections head on.

Plan Ahead

The best way to defuse sales objections is to head them off before they start—before you even speak to your client. Make objections part of your precall planning.

We've already talked about this topic in "Discover the Payoff of Precall Planning" (Vol. I, Ch. 19). The fact is, if you've done your homework on your client—your fact-finding, probing, trust-building, and reaching agreement on needs—you should easily be able to forecast any potential objections.

Maybe you've found that your client prefers to use broadcast to magazines. Or that her company has been hit hard in the recession. Whatever you've found, you can use that information to construct a presentation that will meet her needs and anticipate any problems she may have advertising in your publication.

Pace Yourself

During the presentation, you must pace yourself so that your prospect hears and understands you fully and completely. Organize your presentation so that your client agrees with each point you make every step of the way. Ask questions to be sure she's following your points, and make sure you get an agreement from her at each step. If you're not sure how to do it, see "The Power Presentation" (Vol. I, Ch. 13).

This approach removes your client's fear of making a mistake. Once she truly understands the value of advertising in your magazine, any objections she might raise would likely be real, not merely excuses or smokescreens.

Head Them Off

If you anticipate specific objections from your client, why not bring them up yourself before she does? That can often take the steam off your client's worries before she even raises them.

You might say, for instance, "Some people are concerned about our publication's editorial repositioning, and I imagine that you may have that concern too." Broaching the subject yourself demonstrates your confidence in handling the issue, gives you more control over the discussion and allows you to turn a disadvantage into a strength.

Use your judgment, though. Be sure of your client's objections before bringing them up yourself. If your client hadn't been wary of your editorial repositioning, you might be opening a can of worms.

Stay on Your Client's Side

Sometimes you'll find yourself in a friendly, chatty sales call, feeling great as your client nods in agreement with everything you've presented. Then she starts hitting you with the objections: Your readership's too small; your CPM is higher than your competitor's; I don't like your design.

What happens then? Once again, you end up in that objection/reaction tennis match. Instead of working together, you're at opposite sides of the court.

The way to stay on the same side is to change your strategy and expectations. There's a simple trick to doing it. Instead of thinking of your prospect's "objections," think in terms of her "considerations."

The very word "objection" tends to create opposition. It means "a feeling or expression of opposition, disapproval, dislike or reproach." Not too effective in a sales discussion! Consideration, though, means "careful thought or attention; deliberation or mediation; something that should be considered in making a decision." One expects a business person to have considerations before reaching an important decision.

For example, say you're shopping for pants that will make you look slimmer. The salesperson pulls a pair off the rack. Your con-

226

cern as to whether the pants are slimming are her *considerations*. She *considers* your concern to help you make a good buying decision.

"Objections" invite defense; "considerations" invite information. Think in terms of "considerations" and you'll be able to take a lot of the heat out of your sales negotiations.

Let Go of the "Suck"

Tim Gallway, author of *Inner Game of Tennis*, describes what he calls "the suck of the game." In tennis, the "suck" is the need to win the match.

Gallway instructs championship tennis players to ignore the accuracy of their stroke and instead focus on the way the ball spins as it flies toward them over the net. At first, their game falls apart as they try this. But with practice, the players can consistently announce the direction of the spin and, without any further instruction, find their stroke improving. That's because they have let go of the suck of the game. They've let go of the need to win long enough to be in closer relationship to the ball.

To best overcome objections, salespeople must let go of the suck of the ad-sales game—making the sale—long enough to be 100 percent engaged with the prospect. This gains them time to work *with* prospects rather than against them.

I'll now show, step by step, the best ways for you to work *with* your prospects in handling their "considerations."

STEPS TO HANDLING OBJECTIONS

Let's say you're making a presentation to Mr. Taylor of Taylor Industries, a cold-cream manufacturer. He stops you to say, "Your magazine seems very nice, but really, we prefer to use broadcast for our marketing."

How to handle it? Try these steps:

1. *Hear him out.* It may seem to you that you've heard Taylor's objection 100 times already from other cosmetics clients. But don't *assume* you know exactly where Taylor's going with his thought. Let him elaborate. You may hear something new, like, "I used to use your magazine until Jones took over our marketing."

Handling objections requires your grace, skill and *patience*. Don't make the mistake of riding roughshod over the process, forming your rebuttal before he's even finished his sentence. You must completely focus on your prospect to hear the real significance of his objection.

Believe me, prospects know when you're only pretending to listen, and they don't take it well if you interrupt them to refute their point. Don't say to Taylor, "Oh yeah, we hear about broadcast a lot." Such behavior is disrespectful and weak. Be confident, maintain direct eye contact and show your concern for his feelings.

2. *Consider your options.* After you've heard Taylor's objection, pause and decide whether to minimize, ignore or handle the objection.

If Taylor had given a knee-jerk objection—"I don't see the need to advertise"—your best strategy might have been to ignore it and keep selling. If he had given an objection you couldn't overcome—"Your magazine gives me waste circulation"—you could have minimized it by agreeing, and then pointing out that the targeted circulation you deliver outweighs the problem.

Since Taylor told you that he prefers broadcast, your best strategy would be to handle the objection. You might decide to show, for instance, how advertising in your magazine can actually enhance his television marketing.

3. *Restate the objection.* You don't have to echo Taylor's words, but you must paraphrase his objection. "If I understand you correctly, you're concerned that our magazine won't deliver your target market as effectively as broadcast?"

When you do this, you're showing Taylor your concern, clarifying his point, and buying yourself useful thinking time. You might

228

even find some clients withdraw their objections once they hear them restated!

Note: Paraphrasing the objection can also provide you with a platform to answer it. If Taylor tells you, "Your rates are too high," you can respond by saying, "If I understand you correctly, you're concerned about receiving sufficient value on your investment?" Now instead of dealing with the issue of price, you can sell the value and benefits of the publication.

4. *Question the objection.* You might ask Taylor to elaborate on his point: "Could you explain what it is broadcast delivers that works for you?"

Questioning not only gains you valuable time, but may give you a strategic direction. Taylor might answer, for instance, that he's satisfied with the CPM of television advertising, but he's concerned that he's got too much wasted reach. That gives you an opening to talk about your targeted audience.

Many times you may also find that the prospect didn't understand a point or that you didn't communicate properly. By asking questions, you open up a useful dialogue with your client. If instead you launch into a monologue about your magazine, you're cutting off your client's ability to communicate with you. Do that, and you will practically hear your client's ears snapping shut.

5. *Answer the objection.* Once you've started a dialogue about Taylor's objection, you can then form your answer by choosing the most meaningful information from your conversation. Since you now know Taylor's concerns about CPM and targeting, for instance, you can address them thoroughly and effectively. And since you've demonstrated that you're willing to listen to Taylor, you can expect that Taylor, at this point, is more likely to listen to you.

6. *Confirm the answer.* Once you've handled Taylor's objection, check to make sure he's satisfied that his concerns have been met. Say, "That clarifies the point, doesn't it?" or "With that question answered, we can go ahead, don't you agree?"

If Taylor says yes, you can lead to the close. If he's still hesitant—"I'd really like to think about this"—determine what else is on his mind. Maybe he's fearful of a change in marketing direction. Maybe he feels he needs to check it out with other associates. Find out what else he needs to know to feel reassured.

You might ask a "what if" question, such as "If I could show you that 85 percent of our circulation is in your primary market, would you consider an advertising schedule?" That would open up a new, positive direction for you to address his concerns.

7. *Ask for the order.* Once you've handled all of Taylor's concerns, step back and review the major benefits of advertising for the Taylor cold-cream product.

If you've done your job, you've uncovered Taylor's needs, presented the value of advertising in your publication, demonstrated how your publication can meet his needs, and alleviated any objections or concerns. Closing the sale, at this point, should be a natural outcome, a *fait accompli*. Ask for the order simply and clearly.

HELP! I'M NOT READY!

Let's face it. One of the big problems with objections is that they emerge when you're least prepared to handle them. Say you've just dialed Ms. Wiggins of Wiggins Chemical, a prospect you've been trying to reach for weeks. It's your lucky day, as you've made it past the Secretarial Palace Guard and actually have Wiggins on the line. You state your name, your publication, and begin your well-rehearsed opening, when she cuts in with this zinger: "We have investigated your magazine already and found that it does not reach the kind of audience we require. Thank you anyway."

Once you've brushed off your ego, remember to ask yourself: wouldn't it be nice if every sales presentation could actually adhere to the Eight Steps to a Sale?

1. *Opening*

2. *Statement of benefits*

3. *Qualification and fact-finding*

4. *Agreement on needs*

5. *Presentation*

6. *Agreement*

7. *Commitment*

8. *Follow-through*

In this scenario, objections would pop up in Steps Five and Six, just as you and your client are agreeing on your sales points. That would make your job pretty easy. It's not hard to handle objections at a point when you've already discussed your prospect's marketing needs and the features and benefits of your own publication.

Client: *I don't believe your magazine has enough national reach.*

You: *As you can see, Mr. Client, we do in fact reach 95 percent of the top buyers in your marketplace...*

But what happens when things don't go according to schedule? Wiggins, for instance, leaped right past your Opening, Statement of Benefits, Qualification and Fact-finding, Agreement on Needs, and Presentation—all the way down to Step Six. She hit you with an objection right out the gate!

In this instance, you've basically got three choices. You can hang up the phone and hope for a better day. You can answer the objection immediately and cross your fingers that you'll make it back to Step One at some point. Or you can find a way to deflect the objection—for now—and try to reestablish the natural sales structure.

Let's take a look at the risks and rewards of those options.

At times, it may simply be appropriate to just handle the objection as soon as it comes up. To illustrate, let's assume that you and Wiggins have a long history. You've already had many discussions about the kind of market she needs to reach for her product, and you previously established that she is not reaching the markets she desires through her current media choices. If you handle her present objection now, chances are good that you can come back safely to your Step One. After all, you've already done the work to establish trust and an intellectual foundation.

You: *Ms. Wiggins, I understand your concerns about reaching the top buyers in the flouride-chemicals industries. May I show you that you can reach 70 percent more buyers than you currently reach with your media buy?*

Now let's assume you and Wiggins have actually never spoken. Sure, you may have sent her a sales letter and media kit, but you have no real idea if she's given them any attention. Moreover, you sense from her tone that she's not about to give up control of the conversation.

In this case, don't be tempted to take the bait and go straight to handling the objection. Sometimes, these tossed-out comments—"Look, we just don't have the budget" or "Listen, magazines just don't work for us"—are nothing more than bullying techniques or brush-offs. They're designed to make you feel defensive.

More importantly, such techniques are also designed to put the cart before the horse. By shooting you with objections, your client is setting it up so that you can't understand her particular market needs. And if you don't know or don't have a chance to discuss those needs, how can you know which benefits and features to present to her? Handling her objection now would be like trying to close before you've sold.

In that case, you want to get permission from the client to get back to her objections in a few moments.

You: *I hear and understand your concerns about our publication's audience. I'd really like to answer those concerns for you. But to make sure I can address your needs in a way that has the most meaning for you, would it be all right if I simply asked you a couple of brief questions first?*

If Wiggins gives you the okay, take this opportunity to do some probing, just as we'd discussed in "Master the Art of Strategic

Questioning" (Vol. I, Ch. 21). With probing, you're neither challenging her objection nor presenting your sales story to closed ears. Instead, you're engaging her in a discussion about her marketing needs! Even better, because she's already told you her objections, you have a clear idea that you need to probe for specific information about her buyers. You can later work that information into your Eight Steps to a Sale.

Of course, if Wiggins refuses to engage in probing, you must handle the objection more directly. But at least at that point, you can lower your expectations about the kind of sale you may expect.

Don't Play To Lose

Let's consider another example. Say prospect Mr. Gump greets you with this: "I don't like controlled circulation." If you take the bait and start discussing the relative merits of controlled magazines versus paid, what are the odds of your winning this discussion? About the same as if you started defending your rights when your spouse tells you she doesn't like your socks on the floor. You won't win because your spouse has already given you the message that she wants a clean floor—just as your prospect has decided that all he wants is paid circulation.

Why play a game you're going to lose? The truth is, most people find that if they handle objections right out the door, they never regain the control of the sale. The only way for them to "win" is to try and change the game.

So if Gump insists on paid circulation, ask him to explain his preference, just a little, so you can get a handle on his marketing needs and desires. Hear him out! Maybe he'll tell you, for instance, that he believes paid circulation delivers better quality readers. You can then politely acknowledge his need for quality prospects, and with his permission, ask additional fact-finding questions about his buyers and his marketing needs.

Later, you can work this into your presentation so that Gump hears you without resistance. You can indicate to him that a magazine either delivers quality readers or it doesn't, regardless of

233

whether it's paid or controlled. You can point out that the fundamental task of any marketing vehicle is to deliver buyers. And you can show, by following your Advertising Syllogism, that your magazine delivers exactly what he needs.

Whenever you find objections blocking you from your Steps to a Sale, don't panic. And don't be tempted to answer objections in a vacuum. Instead, show that you hear your prospect's concerns, and get permission to ask questions. As long as you don't rush yourself or your client, you should be able to get back to the Steps where your sale belongs.

If the Objection Comes at the End...

Now let's say your client hits you with her objection right at the end of the sale. Too hesitant to speak up earlier, she might say, "Really, your circulation is too small for our needs. I'm sorry."

Of course, your job was to have flushed out all your client's concerns previously; to make sure that nothing remained clouding the waters. But if an objection remains, with no way to overcome it, take the time to review that objection against the benefits on which you've already agreed with your client. Answer her objection to the best of your ability, and remind her of the advantages she'd gain by running with your publication. Then go ahead and close.

12

OVERCOMING OBJECTIONS: The NITTY-GRITTY

"Whoever said, 'It's not whether you win or lose that counts...' probably lost."
—Martina Navratilova (1956-)
American tennis champion

❖ ❖ ❖

Congratulations! You've just taken care of one of the biggest obstacles to sales success. You've learned how to interpret the psyche of your client.

Now that you're psychologically groomed on how to do it, it's time to learn what to say. Believe me, there are just about as many ways for clients to say "no," "not yet," or "let me think about it" as there are pages in your annual double issue. Each objection requires its own type of handling, and I'll talk about many of them in this chapter.

If you think about it, this entire two-volume set on ad sales is really about handling objections. Let's face it: the act of sales is really the act of defusing objections and making clients feel comfortable and secure in their buying decisions. Objections aren't merely a step in the sales process. They *are* the sales process. As a marketing consultant, your entire job depends on your ability to understand your client's needs and respond to their concerns.

In this chapter, I'll reiterate some key points and show how you can apply them to specific objections. You can learn to think fast on your feet with the knowledge that you already have.

TYPES OF OBJECTIONS

Objections usually fall into general *types*. Take a look below at some of the major categories of objections you can expect to hear from clients. As you'll see, handling each requires a slightly different level of expertise.

Asking for More Information

This "request" often appears as an objection. When an advertiser tells you, for instance, "I don't think you reach my prospects," what he might actually be saying is, "Tell me more about your circulation."

Don't be wary of prospects who want information. Questions express *interest*. Sales reps should be (and most are) delighted to work with prospects who delve into the issues. In fact, given an opportunity, these prospects may answer their own objections and even sell you on why they should advertise.

Remember, the prospects who don't ask questions before placing an order are often the ones who will cancel later.

Tell Me It's OK

If a prospect keeps raising objections even after she's given you buying signals, she's probably asking for reassurance. She needs to assure herself she's making the right decision. What she's really saying is, "I'm going to buy from you, but I'll tell you everything on my 'no' list and you, as the expert, tell me why I can scratch it off. Then I'll feel I've been responsible and won't have any lingering doubts."

As a marketing consultant, your entire job depends on your ability to understand your client's needs and respond to their concerns.

236

Don't fail your prospect now. Review all the benefits of advertising in your publication and illustrate how your publication meets her needs. Provide her with the positive reassurance she's asking for.

Rumors

If you hear prospects telling you, "Sorry, but I hear your magazine's for sale," or other such rumors, pay attention. They might be giving you an opportunity to lay hearsay or misinformation to rest. They might also prompt you that your competitor has been coaching the prospect on how best to object to you. Don't be disheartened or catty about rumors, or appear that you take them too seriously. The best way to defuse gossip is to answer it, and to draw attention to your magazine's strengths. (Incidentally, if a rumor *is* true, make sure you've got your publisher's guidance on how to handle the information!)

Excuses

Prospects who have no intention of buying think excuses are the most polite way of saying no. "I want to think it over" and "I don't have the budget" are often excuses. I've met people whose excuse for not buying is that they don't have enough business and, therefore, no money. A year later, their plea is that they don't need to buy advertising because they have too much business already!

Your challenge with excuse-givers is to shake out the truth. Be direct. "I'd really be interested in knowing the reasons you think we can't help you reach your marketing goals." Let them know you're interested in knowing the truth! Excuses sometimes indicate this prospect isn't sold yet, or that you're not speaking with the true decision maker. If you suspect the latter, do what you can to talk to that decision maker yourself.

The Smokescreen

"Smokescreen" objections camouflage the real issue. They crop up when the prospect has a hidden agenda—saying one thing and meaning another. You'll recognize the smokescreen when you hear an objection you've already addressed: "You don't reach our target market," for instance, when you've shown beyond question that in fact, you do. Or, "You don't address our industry," when your editorial audits show otherwise.

What's maddening about the smokescreen is that you can't answer the objection until you find out what it really is. One salesperson on a national publication that had once been regional continued to hear objections that this nationally audited publication reached only the regional market. The real issue was a lack of faith in the publication's editorial and its ability to do the job on a national level.

If you suspect a smokescreen, ask the prospect if, in addition to this concern, he has any other thoughts that would prevent him from making an advertising commitment at this time. You may unearth the real objection.

The Brush-Off

Here's an objection that kills a sale before it even begins. If you're phoning a prospect to set up an appointment and she starts telling you, "I don't believe in advertising" or "Our budget is closed," you're getting the brush-off.

Take heart. You may simply be calling at an inconvenient time, and may need to reschedule. Or this prospect may have learned such remarks are powerful enough to demoralize most salespeople and keep them off her back.

If that's the case, begin by giving the prospect a reason to speak with you—an initial benefit: "Ms. George, I have a way to help you reach 50 percent more of your top prospects than you currently reach with your current media buy." Assure her that you need only a few moments of her time: "Within five minutes, I can share some market insights with you." Then stick to your time limit.

There is one benefit to handling the brush-off client. Only the strongest and most confident salespeople will engage this tough prospect in discussion. You'll have few competitors.

The Valid Objection

These objections raise logical and sometimes well-founded points about the limits of your publication. Specific concerns, like "Your circulation doesn't cover the market" or "Your rates are higher than your competitors" must be addressed directly with substantial data and/or proof. While answering these objections, you may need to acknowledge shortcomings, but you can still make a strong case about the overall effectiveness of advertising in your publication.

When the Answer Is "No"

In this case, your prospect has considered your presentation and has decided not to buy. The sale is over—but the learning process isn't. Review your sales call. Was this a qualified prospect? Did you clearly present the benefits and features of your publication? Did you respond to each concern? One part of the sales game is knowing when to take a strategic retreat and return another day.

If you anticipate specific objections from your client, why not bring them up yourself before she does?

HANDLING SOME COMMON OBJECTIONS

Having sorted through some types of objections, let's examine some of the actual concerns you'll be hearing from clients. Before you look ahead for the solutions, take a minute to think about how you could respond to each of these objections and turn them into selling opportunities.

Agency-client communication

+ I don't handle advertising decisions. Talk to my agency.
+ I don't decide where to place the space. Talk to the client.
+ Our agency didn't recommend your publication.
+ The client rejected our recommendation of your publication.

Price objections

+ Your rates/CPM are too high.
+ Your rates/CPM are too high, given your magazine's effective reach.

Media objections

◆ We prefer using direct mail, newspapers, TV, radio, passenger pigeons.

◆ Our salespeople already cover the market.

◆ I'd rather invest in more salespeople.

Marketing objections

◆ Everybody in the industry already knows us.

◆ We don't need more sales—we can't deliver more product/service.

◆ We're not interested in your market this year.

Competitive objections

◆ We're completely happy with our current media buy.

◆ We can only afford one publication—your competitor's.

Sales-lead objections

◆ You don't produce enough quantity/high-quality leads.

◆ Your leads don't turn into sales.

◆ We can't measure any results.

Delaying tactics

◆ Let me think it over. Call me next week/month/century.

◆ I don't have time to see you/handle this issue/make any changes.

◆ Our ad copy isn't ready/we don't like our ad.

Brush-offs

◆ I don't believe in advertising.

◆ I don't believe in your magazine.

Editorial objections

✦ You don't give us enough editorial support.

✦ I don't like your magazine.

Budget objections

✦ We're cutting our ad budget. Business is down.

✦ We like your magazine but we don't have the budget.

Circulation objections

✦ Your circulation is too big/small/regional/national.

✦ Your publication isn't audited.

✦ You're not paid/controlled.

✦ You're too horizontal/vertical.

The ultimate objection

✦ Your competitor gave me a deal.

Now let's see how you might handle some of these real-life objections.

1. Agency-client communication

Talk to my agency. It's your job to find out the real relationship between the ad agency and the client. Is the agency truly in charge of these decisions? Or does the client contact simply want to avoid responsibility? It may be that someone at your client's business can and would handle advertising decisions, but you haven't found that person yet.

If the agency does handle advertising decisions, it's still useful to stay in touch with your client. Give him a reason to speak to you. If he doesn't want to talk about ad space, talk about marketing. Find out what's new in his business. Share market information. Ask questions about the state of the industry. In short, serve as a marketing consultant—someone whose input your client would value.

> It's your job to find out the real relationship between the ad agency and the client.

241

You might find that once you've demonstrated your expertise and interest, people who weren't interested in talking about ad space may change their minds. They may even be more inclined to speak favorably of your title with their agency.

In short, it's important that you maintain a relationship with your client, even when the agency makes the advertising decisions. Make sure you look over the earlier chapters on marketing consulting and agency relationships (Vol. I, Chs. 5 and 15) to be clear on how to do it right.

Talk to the client. If you hear this from the agency—after you've been sent there from the client—you're probably getting the runaround. No one is taking responsibility for advertising decision-making. Your job in this case is to create "action steps" so your contact at the client or agency starts getting involved in the sales process.

"Action steps" are ways to prod your contacts into decision-making. You may want to set up a conference call or meeting with your client and agency contacts. You may want to ask your agency contact for sales literature she's pulling together for the client's next trade show. You may want to engage each contact in market discussions. In short, you want to get your contacts interested in learning about the marketing benefits of advertising in your publication.

The agency/client didn't recommend your publication. Here's where you need to probe for the real issue. How was this decision made? What criteria was used to dismiss your publication? Does the agency believe your readership is too small? Does the client have a budget concern? You can't address the real objection until you know what it is. Find out!

Of course, you can usually avoid this situation by unearthing potential objections *before* they cause problems. The trick is not to receive brush-offs like this after the fact, where you're left in a defensive selling position. The trick is to head off objections during your probing. Knowing *ahead of time* your client's criteria for creating an ad schedule helps you to position your magazine at its optimal strength. You might want to review the chapters on probing

> It's important that you maintain a relationship with your client, even when the agency makes the advertising decisions.

(Vol. I, Chs. 19 and 21). Don't let yourself get caught by surprise!

2. Pricing objections

Your rates are too high. Think about what your prospect means. Does she think the rate is too high for the financial investment she's been asked to make? If so, go back and restate the value of advertising in your magazine.

> Instead of dealing with the issue of price, you can sell the value and benefits of the publication.

Does she mean that your rates are higher than those of your competitor? If so, see if your *effective reach* matches the rates. It could be that your competitor has a lower CPM, but more wasted circulation. That might mean that your magazine's CPM *per qualified reader* (also known as CPQR) is actually lower than your competitor's.

Look for advantages in your BPA or ABC statements. Your magazine might simply have a better readership, with more first-year qualified readers, for instance, than your competitor. Or it may be that your readers have a higher demographic, or more buying power. Show your client whatever she needs to see to understand the *value* of your rates.

Also, try to find out "how much is too much" in your prospect's mind. Maybe she'll tell you she'd buy at $1,000 less if you can show her that she would gain more than that $1,000 in value. You might be able to turn the objection into a sale. It all comes back to selling the value of the publication rather than getting into a price war.

If you need to know more about rates, check the index and look over "Using the Rate Card as a Selling Tool" (Vol. II, Ch. 7).

3. Media objections.

We prefer direct mail, TV, radio, etc. As you may recall from earlier chapters, just about every client uses a variety of marketing tools to reach his market. If your client prefers TV advertising for his gardening tools, that's fine—*as long as you understand his reasons for choosing that medium.* Many salespeople at larger consumer books don't sell directly against TV. After all, these clients obviously feel that TV offers benefits and meets some of their sales challenges!

What you can do, however, is find out what your client likes about TV. Maybe he prefers its low CPM. Maybe he likes mass exposure. Maybe he just likes to watch TV! Whatever the reason, you can use it to show how your magazine can strengthen and complement his current media buy. Show that your magazine offers many benefits that TV, radio, newspapers and other media can't offer. To review those benefits, go back to "Where Advertising Fits into the Marketing Mix" (Vol. I, Ch. 7) and rediscover how magazines can fit into your client's marketing mix.

Our salespeople already cover the market. I'd rather invest in more salespeople. Once again, you probably know by now that magazine advertising can help salespeople create more sales. Advertising can cover gaps in the market, create leads and generate awareness of your client's product or service. All of that stimulates your client's prospects in their buying choices. If your client insists on black-and-white thinking ("Either we use salespeople or nothing"), make sure you point out how advertising will help her get the most from her reps. You may also want to review the chapter on budgeting (Vol. I, Ch. 10) to find out how you can help your client embrace advertising as a worthwhile "investment" in her sales process.

4. Marketing objections.

Everybody in the industry already knows us. Find out what your client really means by this. If everyone in their market knows his company, shouldn't "everybody" be buying from it? What is the company's current market share—and what *could* it be if the market really understood the value of your client's product?

You see the point. As a marketing consultant, part of your job is to show how you can help your client change and improve market perceptions about the company.

If your prospect tells you that his business comes through word-of-mouth, congratulate him—after all, third-party testimonials are the best kind of advertising anyone could have. But then ask your prospect, "If someone buys from you, what is the worth of that customer in terms of repeat buying?" Then ask if he's content to rely on word-of-mouth, or would like to take a more proactive approach. (See "The Power of Advertising," Vol. I Ch. 9, for steps on demonstrating customer value.)

That's the "ripple in a pond" approach. By advertising in your magazine, your client can obtain more "pebbles"—that is, customers—to maintain the ripple effect of repeat sales.

We don't need more sales—we can't deliver more product/service. To answer this objection, review the client's Seven Steps to a Sale:

1. *Establishing contact*

2. *Generating awareness*

3. *Arousing interest*

4. *Building preferences*

5. *Making specific proposals*

6. *Closing the sale*

7. *Keeping customers sold*

Advertising doesn't always have to be about closing sales. It can address any marketing issue your client has!

It's possible that your client is telling you she doesn't need to work on the first six steps at the moment. But no matter what, she does need to keep the customers she has. Maybe your client doesn't need any more leads at the moment, but she would certainly benefit from reinforcing her position in the industry. She might need to run image ads or corporate ads to ensure her customers continue to buy.

Advertising isn't always about closing immediate sales. It can address any marketing issue your client has! Maybe your client needs to ride the wave to future customers. Advertising can generate awareness so that new customers come aboard when the current crop starts to disappear.

See if you can shift your client's thinking on what advertising can do for her business. Advertising can address both short-term and long-term marketing issues, and keep customers sold. (Besides, if the client has a full slate of customers, she's probably got the money to advertise!)

We're not interested in your market. Go back to the Advertising Syllogism for a moment. Are your readers indeed your client's prospects? You might be surprised at the answer, and so might your client.

Perhaps you're selling for an architects' magazine, and your client is a building supplier. Your client may feel architects aren't his market; after all, they're not the ones making decisions on what building materials to buy. But you can point out that architects *influence* those decision makers who purchase building materials. What building contractor wouldn't listen to her architect's recommendations? Now you can show that your client *can* reach decision influencers by advertising in your magazine.

To sell the value of your market, you have to understand who's in your market, who's in your client's market, who's in the entire buying universe, and how those three markets intersect. Review "Selling the Value of Your Market" (Vol. II, Ch. 2) for tips on understanding and dealing with this objection.

5. Competitive objections

We're completely happy with our current media buy. We're only going with your competitor. I won't kid you. These are tough objections, and ones you'll probably face a lot.

To deal with them, first formulate an honest answer as to why your client prefers the competition. This, of course, goes back to probing and strategic questioning—knowing about your client's prospects and markets and how you can best position your own magazine. What does your magazine have—in market penetration, cost, benefits, editorial—that your competitor doesn't? What can you find that's *special, unique* and *different* about your own magazine?

If your magazine is indeed the number two buy in a market, see if you can justify the importance of frequency and exposure for your client. Or point out how you approach the market in a way that's different from your competitor. Look at what your magazine can offer, and help your client understand the importance of adding on to his current media buy, if not displacing it.

246

Compare your magazine's rates, circulation, editorial and positioning to your competitor's.

Compare your magazine's rates, circulation, editorial and positioning to your competitor's. Find out what your client gains—and loses!—by choosing your competitor over your magazine. Acknowledge his preference, but be sure to point out what he might also gain by advertising with you.

6. Sales leads objections

You don't produce enough quantity/high quality leads. Your leads don't turn into sales. First, make sure that your client's main advertising goal is producing leads. That may sound obvious, but unless you've done your pre-call planning, you might not realize, for instance, that your client's real intent is to generate awareness for a new product line, or to reinforce his company's position in the marketplace. In that case, lead-generating would be a secondary goal.

If, however, your client's primary goal is to produce leads, don't automatically assume your magazine falls down on the job. Check out your client's process for dealing with leads. Are the leads handled properly? Are they answered promptly? (Once again, your probing should clue you in ahead of time as to how your client distributes and follows up leads. It may be that he has the same complaint for *every* magazine in which he runs advertising—or that he just wants to pit your magazine against another!)

Whatever you find out, don't blame your client for "losing" his leads. You'll just lose credibility, even if you're right. Instead, investigate. Once one of my clients complained none of his leads had turned into sales. So, my sales reps and I called up a dozen or so respondents to his ad. We soon found out that several of these people had not been contacted by our client, and of those who had, some were already in discussions to make purchases. Our client contact, of course, had no idea that good things were happening in the field with his leads!

Even if your magazine does *not* perform well as a lead generator, make sure your client hasn't evaluated your publication solely on the basis of lead generation. It may be that your magazine works well in leading prospects through earlier, less visible sales steps,

247

such as generating awareness or making preferences. Or it may be that your client is using the wrong response device. Perhaps he should try a bind-in business reply-card, or offer a sweepstakes, or test a postcard deck. It's possible a lead-generation program simply isn't the right approach for his market! Maybe your client is trying to address busy executives, like physicians, who simply don't have the time to follow up directly on advertising they like.

Keep probing and problem-solving. Be sure to review "The Power of Advertising" (Vol. I, Ch. 9) for further help in proving your magazine's worth. It is better to work from the selling *offensive* than *defensive.*

We can't measure any results. This objection goes right to the heart of knowing the value of advertising. Let me paraphrase what publishing kingpin Bill Ziff once said: 'The value of advertising is sometimes less akin to statistics than to literary criticism." In other words, not all advertising is directly measurable, but that doesn't mean it's not valuable. Advertisers intent on measurable results may be passing up a valuable chance to communicate with their customers and prospects.

7. Delaying tactics

Let me think it over. Sounds fine, right? Certainly, "let me think about it" doesn't sound much like an objection. But be careful. This tactic may mask a hidden objection. It may indicate that the client isn't fully sold yet. It may show that you've failed to create an urgency about your sales message.

If your client wants to think it over, find out what it is she needs to think about. What concerns is she weighing? Is she not convinced of advertising's benefits? Spend some time flushing out the real objection.

If you can't pinpoint anything more than a vague sense of disinterest, it may be that she simply doesn't buy into the value of what you're offering, or that she's not feeling a need to take immediate action. If so, create a sense of urgency. Offer special ancillary products or special events to enhance the sales package, provided she acts *now.*

> It is better to work from the selling *offensive* than *defensive.*

248

Further, get her to state the benefits of advertising with you. If she mentions, for instance, that she likes your readership demographics and CPM, but still needs to think about it, tell her you'd be happy to call her back. But then add this: "Since we've both agreed on the benefits of advertising, why miss out on those benefits by delaying? Why pass up getting those new customers for another week or month?" Let your client know what she risks, or may lose, by continuing to postpone her decision.

I haven't had time to see you/handle this issue/make any changes. In most cases, what you're really hearing from your client is this: "You're only getting my business if you make it easy for me." Your job, then, is to make it easier for him. Give him an "action step" that gets the ball rolling. For instance, don't start off by telling your client that you need 90 minutes of his time to re-evaluate his marketing practices. That's scary! Instead, break it down. Sell him an ad in the next issue. Sell him an ancillary product. Buy him lunch!

In cases like this, your worst competition is your client's "To Do" list. So don't try to sell a busy client on a 12-time schedule. Just do what you can to get on his "To Do" list! Many salespeople I meet don't understand the importance of my own "To Do" list. Those who aren't on my list don't have a chance of selling me, no matter how pleasing their presentation. Those who do make my list— those who make it easy for me to sit down with them—at least have a shot.

We don't like our ad/our ad isn't ready. First of all, you need to explore whether this is a real concern or a mere brush-off. If your client truly doesn't have time to put together an ad she likes, find out how you can help her speed the process. If she says she doesn't like her ad, find out what it is she *does* like. Ask her to clarify what she'd like changed. Take her through the next action step. Do what you can to get her on the path to committing to a schedule.

Once again, it's also possible that your client isn't feeling a sense of urgency to proceed. Let her know that you don't want to see her missing out on the benefits of reaching new customers. Help her along! Don't assume, as many sales reps do, that your clients have

249

thought through everything. It's your job to help them with their thinking. Half the task of selling is to simply get in the client's office; the other half is to act as a valued marketing consultant, assisting them in their job (getting more sales) every step of the way.

8. Brush-offs

I don't believe in advertising. This is a nice, general objection that lets your client sweep you right under the rug. Be careful! Though you might be tempted, don't ask your client straight out why he doesn't believe in advertising. Instead, rephrase the question positively. Which of the Seven Steps to the Sale does he need to achieve? Does he believe in reaching and selling to his prospects? Does he believe in communicating with his customers and reinforcing their relationship with him? If your client doesn't want to talk about advertising, fine. Don't talk about advertising. Talk about how to sell his product.

If your client says he believes in selling, the door is open for you to talk about your magazine as the conduit between him and his prospects (remember the Advertising Syllogism). You can then follow up with a discussion on the value of magazine advertising. To refresh your knowledge, review "The Power of Advertising" (Vol I, Ch. 9).

I don't believe in your magazine. This objection gets back to probing. Exactly what does your client mean by this? Does she not believe in the market your publication reaches? Does she doubt its circulation quality? Is she put off by its reputation? Use your probing techniques to flush out the real objection here. Then circle back to the Advertising Syllogism and steps to a sale to show your client how your readers comprise her market.

9. Editorial objections

You don't give me editorial support. Ask your client to define what he means by this. Let's say that you sell for a fast-food magazine, and your client manufactures hot dogs. Does your client believe that he deserves tit for tat: hot dog editorial coverage for advertising? Does he want a fluff piece on his new plant? Is he miffed that

> Half the task of selling is to simply get in the client's office; the other half is to act as a valued marketing consultant.

250

the magazine didn't mention his foot-long wiener, or that the editors gave it a bad review? Does he feel your magazine gives better coverage to pizzas?

In handling whatever objection he has, remember that the principle issue here lies in the Advertising Syllogism. You need to assure your client that editorial "support," however he defines it, isn't the real issue. The real issue is whether *the client reaches his prospects and customers with his advertising.* Maybe your magazine doesn't write all that much about hot dogs, or maybe it does skew toward pizza coverage. But look at it this way: Fast food restaurants—your client's prospects—are your readers. These readers buy both pizza and hot dogs. Your magazine may "hook" readers with pizza editorial instead of hot dog editorial, but it's still pulling in the people your client needs to reach.

You might also suggest that your client call the editor to discuss his concerns. Let him know that editorial coverage is the editor's decision, not yours, which accounts for your magazine's editorial integrity. Any potential news source should always be a welcome call on the editorial side.

I don't like your magazine. You might hear this objection in one of many forms: "I don't read your magazine." "Your editorial is too technical." "Your magazine is too controversial."

You might be tempted to explain or defend your magazine's editorial. Chances are good that your client may simply misunderstand your magazine. But in the end, your client's opinions about the editorial need to be put into perspective. What *really* matters (back to the Advertising Syllogism) is that the magazine reaches your client's prospects—and that those *prospects* like the editorial.

In fact, the very reason advertisers may not like your magazine could be why readers *do.* Your magazine may well be too technical for advertisers—if it's written for technicians. Your golf magazine may be of no interest to T-shirt makers—but golfers buy T-shirts. Your magazine may be controversial, but maybe controversy is what hooks your readers. Try to focus your advertiser's attention less on the quality of the bait you use, and more on the fact that it hooks the prospects they need. After all, more auto executives probably read *U. S. News & World Report* than *People* magazine, but that doesn't stop them from advertising in *People*!

10. Budget concerns

We're cutting our ad budget. Budget-cutting objections are a chicken-and-egg dilemma. What comes first: the investment to gain sales or the sales to pay for the investment? The trick to handling budget cutting is to find out what's involved. Which part of the budget is being cut? What's left? What criteria has been used? Which marketing goals is the company letting go, and which has it retained?

Naturally, your client has to make certain marketing decisions in cutting a budget. By finding the answers to those questions, you can position your magazine as fundamental in meeting her remaining goals.

Remember, your magazine is a tactic in a marketing strategy. It's a tool that your client uses to accomplish certain goals. Consider this example: your client has decided to stop fishing for prospects this year in order to focus on serving current customers. That's her *strategy*. Therefore she wants to stop using the *tactic* of direct-response magazine advertising.

It isn't your job to argue against your client's strategy. But you can help her see the wisdom of investing in your magazine as a tactic. You can show her that magazine advertising can reinforce customer relationships, either with image campaigns, discount coupons, special-event tie-ins or other techniques.

In order to have this discussion at all, however, you should already have an established relationship with your client. To be involved in your client's budget matters, you must act as her marketing consultant. Don't let her down! And be sure to review "Ad Budgets" (Vol. I, Ch. 10) to refresh your memory about budget-setting.

252

To be involved in your client's budget matters, you must act as her marketing consultant.

I like your magazine, but I don't have the budget right now. It's always nice to hear that the prospect likes your publication. Ask what it is she likes about it, and you may find her selling herself.

After you've established the value of the magazine, ask when her company reevaluates its budget. This might be an opportunity to get a future commitment.

If your advertiser revises her budget throughout the year, you'll have frequent opportunities to make a sale. Find out how to take advantage of that process. And don't wait too long to get a commitment. Otherwise, you'll lose the advantage of dealing with prospects who like your publication. Get your prospect to commit while she's intellectually and emotionally hooked.

Be aware that sometimes a budget issue is a smokescreen or excuse.

Be aware, though, that sometimes a budget issue is a smokescreen or excuse. You might ask the prospect, "If it weren't for the budget consideration, is there any other reason you wouldn't be working with me now?" At this point, a new objection, or the real one, may emerge.

When advertisers assure me that the budget is the only stopping point, I explain that other advertisers with similar problems have been sufficiently convinced of the value of advertising in my publication. Many of them chose to reallocate their funds from less profitable marketing methods. Advertisers often find this a persuasive suggestion.

11. Circulation objections

Your circulation is too big, too small, too anything. Of course, any circulation objection is a big one. Your job is to determine what's really at stake. In other words, *is your reader your client's prospect?*

Let's say your client sells rivets, bolts and screws. Your magazine addresses the bolts audience. If your client argues that your circulation is too small, it's your job to show that the bolts audience is important to his interests. It may be that bolts buyers are heavy consumers of rivets and screws, or that they influence buyers of rivets and screws. By advertising, your client may be the only rivets-

253

and-screws advertiser to reach this exclusive audience.

Now, let's say your magazine addresses the rivets, bolts and screws market, and that your client is a bolts manufacturer. This client may argue that your circulation has too much waste. Here, you need to return to the Advertising Syllogism to demonstrate the effective reach of your magazine.

It may be that your magazine offers more bolts buyers than the leading bolts magazine. Or that your bolts buyers work for bigger companies and have more spending power than your competitor's readers. You could explain that rivets, bolts and screws are the three legs holding up the market, and to reach the best bolts prospects, your advertiser must include your magazine in his ad schedule.

The point is, you must make your client see the value of the readership and what it is about your audience that's important to him. Whether your client complains that your circulation is too regional, too national, too big or too small, you must return to the Advertising Syllogism. (See "Selling the Value of Circulation" Vol. II, Ch. 3, for more ideas on dealing with these objections.)

Your publication isn't audited. For an objection like this, you need to get agreement on the real issue at hand. Does your client want to see a piece of paper? Or does your client want proof that your magazine delivers the audience you say it does?

The traditional way to deliver that proof is through a magazine audit. Find out from your client, though, what the audit would tell her that's important to her. Does she want to know whether your readers have requested the magazine? Does she want to know that you're not discounting subscriptions to the bone? Your job is to offer proof of whatever it is she may question about your readership. You may want to have available subscriber studies, printing bills, postage receipts or other evidence of readership value.

Of course, you might show your client all the subscriber data at hand, only to hear her say, "...yeah, and you *still* don't have an audit." Many advertisers simply want to see that piece of paper, particularly when making apples-to-apples comparisons with other

Show your advertisers how you can still offer a quality audience without an audit.

magazines. For the most part, though, many clients will accept the proof of your readers' worth. Talk to your publisher and circulation director to find out how to explain to advertisers why your magazine isn't audited. Show your advertisers how you can still offer a quality audience without an audit.

You're not paid/controlled. We've talked elsewhere about the debate between paid- and controlled-circulation quality. The truth is, whether a book is paid or controlled isn't, in and of itself, an indication of whether it performs well for a client.

Ultimately, your client's concern—whatever the publication—are the title's *readers.* If they're making the buying decisions, are well-qualified and have high renewal rates, they're the ones your client would want.

Check the index for more information about paid versus controlled titles.

You're not horizontal/vertical. As you might recall from "Explore the Essentials of Marketing" (Vol. I, Ch. 5), most magazines reach either horizontal or vertical audiences. However, horizontal advertisers don't always pair up with horizontal audiences, nor do vertical advertisers with vertical audiences.

What counts is whether the audience is in the advertiser's market. For example, a sports-car manufacturer might want to advertise in a general business magazine to reach high-income readers. At the same time, he might want a vertical title, like *Auto News,* to reach real car buffs. Likewise, a mutual fund investment company may want to advertise both in investment titles and in titles like *Atlantic Monthly,* where serious, well-educated readers might want to learn more about where to put their money.

At the risk of sounding a broken record, I'll say it again—it is all anchored to the Advertising Syllogism. If the readers are the client's prospects, it doesn't matter whether they're found in horizontal or vertical titles. What matters is whether they meet his marketing needs.

12. The ultimate objection

Your competitor cut me a deal. This gets into the area of rate cutting, which we'll discuss at length in "If You're Asked to Cut Rates" (Vol. II, Ch.17). For now, I've found the following analogy helpful when dealing with a client who wants to start cutting deals. You might find it useful too.

Anyone who's been to the beach may have experienced something called a riptide, a flow of water moving along the coast that can carry you far from where you started without your awareness. When you're standing at the waterline and looking out over the water, everything looks peaceful and serene. But underneath the water, something menacing is happening.

I believe that rate-cutting is the riptide of publishing. When you cut deals, you're taking the profits out of the company. This can hurt the long-term health of the magazine, from circulation development to research to editorial quality. Some publications even intentionally set high rates for the purpose of allowing for rate negotiating. That's dangerous because it undermines the value of the publication.

It's better to emphasize your publication's concern for delivering the market, with the best editorial environment and most on-target circulation, than to spend the rest of your relationship apologizing for poor performance. Make it clear that your publication's ad rates have been set as fairly as possible so that all clients know what they're paying for. Everyone buys the same quality at the same price. You may even want to tell your clients that you'd prefer to address the issue now rather than spend the next few months or years apologizing for poor quality.

Objections create *resistance,* both in you and the advertiser.

CONVERSATIONAL POINTERS

Keep in mind that objections create *resistance,* both in you and the advertiser. It's like any disagreement: both parties stiffen, get entrenched, find it harder and harder to move around and see the other's viewpoint.

But there's a big difference between a *sales* disagreement and, say, an argument with your spouse. In sales, *you* are the one responsible for smoothing the discussion, for gently tugging your client back to the points of your presentation. Your prospect, on the other hand, has no vested interested in finding common ground. It's up to you to soften the tension.

Here are some techniques that can help you smooth rough spots into agreement. Practice them enough, and they'll work naturally into your presentation.

✦ **Pacing for the future:** "If you keep an open mind, you might think of that point from another angle after we finish our discussion."

✦ **Heading off a "no":** "Before you make up your mind, consider that your views could change once you have had a chance to hear our proposal."

✦ **Changing the subject:** "Let's talk about how we can increase your leads for your new product." If you sense resistance, shift the topic to an area of more interest to the client.

✦ **Offering a benefit**: "In five minutes, I can show you how your qualified leads can increase 25 percent." Show how compliance with your viewpoint will pay dividends.

✦ **Drawing out resistance**: "Let's look at what's really at issue." Get your clients to discuss every aspect of their objections. After they've talked themselves out, you are more informed as to their real resistence and can perhaps better resolve their concern.

✦ **Comparing:** "Let's talk about where you get more value: from your direct mail, or from the schedule I'm proposing." Engage your client in comparing his preferred investment, media choice or marketing plans to your magazine. Or, show how using advertising in tandem with his media choice produces much greater results.

✦ **Using "and," not "but."** "I can respect your desire to pay less than our published rate, and..." continue with your own point of view. The word "and" removes opposition and communicates your desire to be agreeable. It enables you to speak to the issue without attacking your client's view. In turn, this helps your client to be more receptive to what *you* have to say. You can empathize without agreement.

Try several variations for blending your client's viewpoints with your own. If you agree with the client's point of view: "I understand your point of view, and..." then continue with your own views. If you cannot agree: "I can understand why you see it that way, and..." If your client's emotions are strong: "I can respect your feelings, and..."

◆ **Asking "how" instead of "why"**: Think of something from the client's side of the conversation that might bring you closer in agreement, and ask a "how" question. "Let's discuss the new overnight service you've established." Your client tells you how much it has helped build his business. "How can you use advertising to sell the value of your new service and help build sales?"

This technique works well when the issue, individual, or situation is particularly sensitive. Keep in mind that "yes" or "no" questions don't establish discussion, and "why" questions can sound confrontational.

IT'S ALL ABOUT VALUE

When you sell, you need to prove, again and again, that the *value* of your publication outweighs any doubts your prospects may have about *investing* in advertising. Think carefully about how you must move through *each step* of the sale in order to gain commitment. Build your case carefully at each point, and you'll surmount most potential objections long before they have a chance to grow.

In the end, handling objections of any size and shape will determine your success as a salesperson. Prepare yourself. Know your publication's strengths and limitations. Armed with the confidence that preparation brings, you can welcome objections as your greatest opportunity to sell.

258

SECTION IV

CLOSING THE SALE

13

DEVELOPING the RIGHT CLOSING ATTITUDE

"The word 'impossible' is not in my dictionary."
—Napoleon (1761-1821)

❖ ❖ ❖

I once knew a sales rep who had just had a terrific sales call. Her prospect had nodded at every point she'd made and showed promising enthusiasm about the magazine.

Flushed with confidence, this rep decided not to waste another moment. She went back to the office, drew up a contract, and messengered it right over, ready to sign.

Her prospect called back immediately. But instead of saying, "Where do I sign?" he thanked her very much, but said he was going to "pass on advertising for a few months."

Was this a sales fluke? Did this prospect possess some kind of bizarre amnesia that made him forget all those great sales points he'd just heard during the presentation?

261

Not at all. The problem lay with the sales rep. *She never uncovered hidden objections to close the sale.* An assumption of a sale is not a close!

We'd all like to think that none of us really need to *ask* for the order. We'd like to believe that if we show our client we understand his needs and concerns, and that if we impress him enough with charts and visuals and statistics, he'll just walk over, shake our hand, and write us a big check.

Too bad it doesn't work that way—not most of the time, anyway. You've got to close the sale. Selling without closing is like planting the seeds, watering, tending and weeding your crop, and then failing to harvest the fruit of your labor.

And yet—how tempting it is to skip over it. Closing takes guts! Closing quite literally means inviting your client to *commit* to a sale. It means asking for a "yes" or "no." By forcing the client into a decision, closing speeds the sales transaction.

Because closing is so critical to the sale, I've devoted four chapters to instruct you in just that. You'll find that closing isn't a matter of just getting up your nerve and asking for the order. Nor is it a matter of perfecting your presentation technique or learning to tackle objections. All those things may be a part of a good close, but they won't seal the sale for you.

To close well, you need three skills:

1. *Attitude*

2. *Timing*

3. *Technique*

In this chapter, we'll deal with the first key to closing—your attitude. You'll find that mentally preparing for the close will bring you a long way toward the result you want. After all, your attitude may be the one thing that keeps you from asking for the sale to begin with.

262

STEPS TO A NEW ATTITUDE

Think for a moment of how you feel when you're at that critical junction in the sale. That's when you've just wrapped up your last point in your sales discussion, you've fended off three major objections, your client is studying the rate card, and a pregnant silence hangs in the room.

Do you feel confident about just stepping up to the plate and saying, "So, now that you know how our magazine can help you meet your market-share goals, may we count on your business?"

Or do you feel like running out of the room, and hedging your uncertainties with vague, hopeful remarks, like, "You'll see our rates are very reasonable for the value we offer," or "I hope you'll give us serious consideration?"

You see my point. It's not easy to count on your gut at these moments. It feels better to play it safe, to not risk offense, to not push your client—to not hear the dreaded "No!"

So where do you get the guts to close? Simple. You take care of three critical areas:

1. *Enthusiasm about your magazine.*

2. *Thorough presentation.*

3. *Knowledge of your own fears and doubts.*

Let's take a look at each area.

STEP ONE: BE ENTHUSIASTIC

Here's the real secret to a good close: *the first person you must close in any sale is yourself.*

In other words, you have to step back and ask yourself some hard questions about your own attitude toward your magazine:

◆ *Do you believe in what your magazine has to offer?*

◆ *Do you feel your magazine will really help your client's business?*

263

◆ *Do you like and enjoy your magazine?*

◆ *If you were a qualified prospect, would you invest in advertising with your publication?*

If you're not sold on the merits of your own magazine, you're in trouble. Believe me, your shrugging attitude will not be lost on your client. Worse, you'll balk, hesitate or avoid closing altogether.

On the other hand, if you believe that no qualified prospect could possibly pass up this advertising opportunity, you're in excellent shape. When you're excited, you're client is excited. You can enter the sale with *action expectancy*. To *expect* a positive outcome is a pretty good sign that you'll get it.

Attitudes are contagious. Just think, for instance, of going to your doctor with a pain in your stomach. Which statement from your doctor would make you feel more confident:

> "Well, we think this medication will work for you. Give it a shot. It costs a lot of money, but try it."
> Or:
> "We've had great success with this medication. You'll be well in no time."

You get the point. Professional counselors and consultants must be poised, self-assured and confident about the solutions they suggest. We expect this. If they waver, why should we listen? The truth is, most people don't like to make decisions. They want to be convinced that certain decisions are in their best interests.

In other words, your client needs you to be a confident, bold sales professional. Don't let him down. Take the time to understand what makes your magazine special, unique and different. Go over the qualities your magazine offers that no one else's does. Know why your magazine will help your client's business. Talk with people who like the magazine, and take a whiff of their own enthusiasm.

Then go close your sale. You can't convince your client to buy if you can't convince yourself to sell.

> Professional counselors and consultants must be poised, self-assured and confident about the solutions they suggest.

264

STEP TWO: BE THOROUGH

I can't stress this enough. You must pay attention *to each step* of the sale before closing. (Unless, of course, your client gives you clear signals earlier in the sale. Take the hint and close!)

That means preparing each of the Eight Steps to a Sale and presenting them in order:

1. *Opening*

2. *Statement of benefits*

3. *Qualification and fact-finding*

4. *Agreement on needs*

5. *Presentation*

6. *Agreement*

7. *Commitment*

8. *Follow-through*

Closing without the Eight Steps is putting the cart before the horse. You must qualify your client, get agreement on needs, make your presentation and uncover his objections. Only when you've answered *all* your client's concerns does the close itself become simple; the natural outcome of all that has occurred.

Don't ever assume that the sale is "in the bag." Think about that sales rep I mentioned at the beginning of the chapter. She'd assumed her sale was a done deal; that the prospect's enthusiasm was conviction. Wrong! Judging from her prospect's questions, she not only failed to close, she had even failed to address his needs and concerns!

Recall, for instance, the Seven Steps to a Sale:

> Only when you've answered *all* your client's concerns does the close itself become simple; the natural outcome of all that has occurred.

THE STEPS OF A SALE

Keep Customers Sold

Close the Sale

Make Specific Proposals

Build Preference

Arouse Interest

Generate Awareness

Establish Contact

In this instance, it may have been that the sales rep had only reached Step 3 of her sale, "Arousing interest." It may have been that the client had not fully established a preference for print over direct response, or for her magazine over her competitor's. In other words, the sales rep mistook "liking" for "buying" and skipped over some of the critical steps that lead to keeping the client sold.

On the other hand, if the salesperson's presentation had been more thorough, her client would have been not merely interested but *confident*. He wouldn't have stepped back after the presentation and said, "Now wait a minute. Everything this rep told me sounded good, but what about this point? And what about that point?" Without the client's confidence, there can be no sale.

Enthusiasm alone isn't evidence of buying behavior. Think about it. When was the last time you "oohed" and "aahed" over a great piece of stereo equipment, or a loaded laptop, or a gorgeous pair of shoes? You may have expressed great enthusiasm to the sales rep (after all, we all like to make people feel good), but did you back it up with the cash? I wonder.

Some salespeople who consider themselves poor closers simply move too fast in the process.

Never forget that the professional salesperson sells solutions to specific problems. When you act as a marketing consultant, you analyze your prospect's problems and propose an advertising schedule to fit your client's needs. And you make sure your client agrees with your analysis *every step of the way*.

Some salespeople who consider themselves poor closers simply move too fast in the process. They mistake a suspect for a prospect and a prospect for a client. They try too soon to move someone from suspect to customer. But those who do their homework, and move at the proper pace, move naturally to the close. (In fact, the best way to do this is through "mini-closes" or "test closes," which I'll discuss in the next chapter.)

By the way, did you wonder what became of our sales rep's sale? I'll tell you what happened: A week after he called, the prospect called again to say he wasn't interested in using her magazine at all.

STEP THREE: KNOW THY FEARS

If you're thorough and believe in your magazine, and you're *still* having trouble closing, perhaps what's stopping you is that old bogeyman—*fear*.

That's not so hard to understand. One of the hardest things we do in sales is risk hearing "no." None of us like to make all this effort preparing for a "yes" only to have it shot down in the end.

But you can understand and turn around your fears. Once you do, you'll automatically start closing with more enthusiasm and confidence. To start, all you have to do is know what's at the hollow heart of these common obstacles:

1. *Fear of rejection or failure*

2. *The "professional visitor syndrome"*

3. *Fear of hucksterism*

4. *Fear of pushiness*

5. *Undeveloped closing instinct*

Let's look at each one in turn.

OBSTACLE #1: Fear of rejection or failure. A business refusal is not a personal rejection. You know this, but do you truly feel it?

Fear of rejection kills sales. When you're focused on yourself and on your feelings, you can't focus on your prospect. You can't truly listen. As a result, you may miss the other person's closing signals. You may even forget your best ideas, or cloud up your intuition!

Closing, of course, means facing the possibility of rejection. But you don't have to fear it. Unless you can risk hearing "no," you'll never hear "yes."

To deal with this fear, keep three techniques in mind:

- *Face it*

- *Turn it around*

- *Close in increments*

Here's how they work.

1. *Face it.* When I learned to ski, the first thing my instructor showed me was how to fall down. First, I had to learn to fall deliberately and correctly. Then he had me fall again and again. That way I lost my fear of falling. The instructor knew that if I tried to ski with fear, my body would be too stiff and self-conscious to move properly and freely. Ironically, by "learning" to fall, I could focus on skiing, not falling.

You, too, can face your fear of rejection in the same way. I'm not suggesting you should go out and court "nos"—after all, you should always do your best in a sale (besides, your ad manager wouldn't be too thrilled). But when the "nos" come—and they will—expect them. Don't dwell on them. Look objectively at what you learned from them. Did you prepare thoroughly? Was this prospect properly qualified? Did you understand her needs?

Once you've done that, move on. Forgive yourself. Stay positive. In fact, you might want to give yourself a mini pep talk the next time you dial. Keep a favorite positive reminder right on the phone, where you can be sure to see it.

Remember, too, that the key to motivation is *learning* and *experience.* Each call you make feeds your knowledge and skill, whatever the outcome. At the end of each call, ask yourself what you've learned about your client, about the sales process, or about yourself. In the end, you'll find this learning provides the internal push to improving your performance.

And be sure to congratulate yourself for having tried. After all, sales reps who hear nothing but "yesses" are likely playing it too safe. They're probably going for the easy closes, the smaller schedules. Only those sales reps who go the extra mile, who stretch for the sale they think they can't get, are the real winners—and those are the ones who are bound to hear "no."

2. *Turn it around.* Here's an easy tip. Think of each rejection as moving you closer to a sale.

It sounds silly, but it works. First, calculate your closing ratio. If you make 100 calls each issue and close 20 accounts, your closing ratio is 20 percent, or five calls per close. Once you know that every fifth call has the odds of being a "yes," you can rest easy during those first four "nos." In fact, you can thank each of those rejections for improving your chances of getting a "yes."

Or, you could do it this way: Say you sell $70,000 in advertising per month. That means each of your 100 prospects is worth $700, whether they buy from you or not. In your mind, then, you could thank each prospect for the $700 you gained on the call, regardless of the outcome. You might even prefer to calculate your commission on each call rather than on each close.

3. *Close in increments.* If you want to improve your closing ratio, just set smaller goals. Don't feel you have to bag a 12-time schedule or nothing!

Instead, start each call with a *written* list of three goals: your primary, secondary and tertiary. For example, your primary goal may be a six-time schedule, your secondary goal may be an insertion in the next issue, and your tertiary goal may be turning around a difficult objection.

If you successfully close on several of these goals, you'll be less likely to leave your presentation empty-handed. Remember, closing does not necessarily mean immediate landing an ad sale. You may want to close a contract, or a single insertion. You may want to close on the next appointment or on an ad agency's recommendations to your client. You may simply want to close on agreement of a major sales point, such as editorial leadership or the value of your market.

Each close, each "yes," brings you one step closer to a sale with one prospect or another. By achieving each success, you feed your self-confidence and build that attitude of "action expectancy." You make yourself a winner on almost every call. That way, you're likely to go for the close more often.

OBSTACLE #2: The Professional Visitor Syndrome. Maybe you're one of those salespeople who love to go on sales calls, but just hate to ask for a "yes" or "no." You drop by your client's office, pretend all is well, and act like a helpful pal, checking in to make sure she's having a good day.

It's a good act and can you make lots of friends, but it isn't likely to make anybody much money. As I said before, closing takes guts! Don't hide from taking responsibility for the outcome. Professional visitors don't succeed financially. Remember, you don't get paid commissions on sales you've *almost* made.

So, if you're tempted to drop by your client's office to say "hi," add some purpose to the call. Talk about a new issue you're sure she'd like to be in. Show her the new card decks you're producing, or the expanded circulation list. Give her a chance to nab a favored booth spot at the trade show. Bring something that will give your client a buying opportunity, and will give you a chance to close!

OBSTACLE #3: Fear of hucksterism. Some salespeople believe closing is pressure and manipulation. They're terrified of becoming

270

Once you truly believe in the benefits your publication offers, you'll understand that closing helps your client.

one of those obnoxious stereotypes who's all phony smile and slick hair. They don't want to feel like hucksters, so they don't press for the sale. They take their "marketing consulting" role so literally that they should be earning per diems instead of commissions!

What they don't know is this: closing is part of marketing consulting. It is not something you do *to* a prospect. Rather, it's something you do *for* and *with* a prospect.

After all, why are you selling your prospect? So that she'll have the opportunity to increase her own business. Once you truly believe in the benefits your publication offers, you'll understand that closing helps your client. It's not a selfish act at all.

OBSTACLE #4: Fear of pushiness. Some salespeople believe persistence means pushiness. They're wrong, but not by much.

The truth is, it's better to err on the side of being too persistent. It's better to be overly enthusiastic and overly committed to your goals than to step back out of fear of pushiness.

If you don't cross the line from time to time, you probably aren't playing close enough. It's not hard for clients to forgive over-eagerness. After all, it's a great thing to get carried away by your own excitement about your magazine!

In my first job as an advertising salesperson, I asked the sales manager why he hired me. During the hiring interview, of course, I'd been my usual assertive self, asking questions, pressing for answers, wanting to know everything about the job, and wanting him to know everything about me. Know what the sales manager said? "You closed me six times in the first interview." I'm sure I hadn't yet developed my closing skills, but I was enthusiastic, persistent and lucky to possess a closing instinct.

Persistence pays off, but only if it doesn't lead to pushiness. Just watch any four-year-old go for the close on, say, an ice-cream sandwich. If he gets a "no," he'll simply wait a few minutes and ask again. Or he'll back off and try again in another way. That's pushiness and it's not likely to result in any ice cream.

271

But let's say this four-year-old understands that the major objection to the ice-cream sandwich is that it would ruin his dinner. Let's say he even establishes that, given his unique metabolism and appetite (features), an ice-cream sandwich would not only *enhance* his appetite for broccoli at dinner, but also get him out of mom's hair for an hour (benefits). That's persistence. It's not merely chipping away at mom's resistance (which leads to resentment and buyer's remorse). This persistence makes mom feel good about saying yes—and perhaps even may lead to a full schedule of ice-cream sandwiches!

Persistence simply means finding the correct route to a close. We've all met, for example, the qualified and excited prospect who then fails to return our calls. He may be signaling a "no," or he might simply be distracted by more pressing matters. As far as I'm concerned, once a qualified prospect has indicated sincere interest, I won't let go until I get a "yes" or a "no." A dangling prospect grates against my need for completion.

You may have also experienced a prospect who ditched your several dozen calls only to phone unexpectedly and book a schedule. Just when you were about to give up, you're suddenly shown the truth of closing: *Gentle persistence*, with a dash of patience, pays off!

OBSTACLE #5: Underdeveloped closing instinct. Most of us know a lot about when to back off a prospect. We might see her frowning at the table, paging through the media kit with an arched brow and critical eye. Nobody needs to tell us that the time isn't right to close! We know enough to hold back.

It's good to listen to those internal cues. But now, consider your other closing instinct. That's the one that tells you that yes, the time has come to close. Just how well developed is that instinct?

If you're like most budding sales reps, you probably need to work on it. Many salespeople go by the book and don't recognize whether they've really connected with their prospect. Some salespeople think they've closed when in fact they've only thought about it. They're like

To improve your closing instincts, try audiotaping or videotaping several role-playing sessions.

the sale rep at the beginning of the chapter who didn't act on her client's enthusiasm. Remember, an assumption of a sale is not a close.

To improve your closing instincts, try audiotaping or videotaping several role-playing sessions. Chances are you'll be surprised, during the playback, by the closing opportunities you may have missed. Expressions of interest—"That sounds great," "I didn't know I could get an extra page," "I like what you're telling me"—are clear closing signals. They indicate that it's time to make a move.

Keep in mind that closing attitude is the first step in accomplishing the close. Once you're mentally prepared to close, you've done much of the battle in gaining the sale. You're ready to use timing and technique effectively to finish out the job.

14

TIMING the CLOSE

"I never lost a game. I just ran out of time."
Bobby Layne (1926-1986)
quarterback for Detroit Lions

❖ ❖ ❖

Like a good joke, a trapeze act or a perfect soufflé, the secret of a good close is *timing*.

On your sales call, picture yourself as a juggler. One by one, with skill and grace, you toss each of your balls into the air, the brightest ones being the benefits of advertising in your publication. When your timing is good, your balls sail through the air while your audience applauds. When your timing is off you lose your focus and the balls fall to the ground.

With juggling, it's very easy to know whether your timing is good or bad. It's a bit tougher in sales. How do you *know* all your balls are in the air? How do you *know* your audience is in the palm of your hand, ready to buy?

For closing, the rule of thumb is this: a prospect is ready to buy when she's *excited* about what advertising in your publication can do for her company. Your job is to get her to that stage of excitement, to get her so involved with your "act" that she's ready to move, *now*. You want her so convinced of the value of what you offer that price becomes a detail, or at worst, an obstacle she'll find a way to overcome.

Think about how *you* feel when you're ready to buy. When you go shopping, do you ask the salesperson, "Show me the least expensive item you have?" Not usually. You look for what you need and want, and only then compare items for the best value and price. And if you're really excited about an item, price becomes secondary.

That's how you want your client to feel. When the value of advertising for your client exceeds the price, she is ready to buy. The key is to close when *your client* is ready—and that may be earlier or later than you expect.

> When the value of advertising for your client exceeds the price, she is ready to buy.

DON'T HESITATE

If you're selling correctly, your selling process will be one of continually moving forward. Your presentation should be thorough and each piece must pull your client along.

Again, timing is critical. Don't rush your client or burden her with an overload of unnecessary information. And don't risk becoming all talked out—running short on sales points while your client is still unconvinced. Hold back some gems that you can use later. Like a good encore at a concert, a well-mentioned benefit after your presentation can re-ignite your prospect.

That enthusiasm is important, because you must have it to close. Closing must be accomplished while the client's excitement is at a peak. Think of the sale as a symphony. When your listener is enchanted and enraptured by the music—close! Close at the height of the music's crescendo. If you wait until the denouement, you'll lose the momentum. If you wait until your follow-up call, you'll have lost the edge.

Whenever possible, don't let your client leave to "think it over." Close first—while you're with her—while she's focused and listening. By the time you follow up, your prospect will be in a whole new phase of distractions and business plans. It's a rare prospect who, once out of your presence, will maintain a level of motivation and excitement to buy. If you can't close the contract, get as many agreements from your prospect as possible, and obtain a "next action step." You might even ask your prospect, "What do we need to do now to make this happen for you?"

LISTEN FOR CUES

You might be worried that you won't "know" when your prospect is actually ready to buy. Someone who's been smiling and nodding during the whole presentation may prove a no-sale in the end. Another who's done nothing but pose objections could be cueing you that he's ready to buy.

Listening for buying cues is like learning a racquet sport. If you wait for the ball to get to you before you make your move, you'll never be in position to make a powerful return. I doubt that you'll ever hear a prospect say, "Excuse me, could you wrap this up? I'm just about ready to buy." *You're* the one who has to watch for cues. Your prospect may not even be aware of her cues, and she might give them when you'd least expect them. But if you know what to look for, you'll be ready.

Listen for these buying signals from your prospect.

♦ **An offer to reinforce or expand on the benefits you've presented**. Whenever a prospect brings up a positive point about why she should buy, ask her to elaborate. Ask how advertising is going to help her business. Build on her point. If you offer encouragement, you'll understand that your prospect often sells herself, so let her keep selling! Accept her gift—tell her she's made an important point, and close.

♦ **A "ready to buy" question**. Your prospect might, for instance, ask about your closing dates, when you'll have special issues and sections, or what kind of merchandising tie-ins and frequency discounts to expect. Prospects usually delve into these matters when they're ready to advertise.

(The possible exception: an ad-rate question that comes up

277

too early in the sale. It may be a brush off or an excuse not to buy your magazine. Try not to mistake it for a buying signal.)

✦ **A sudden shift in tone or body posture.** Your prospect may start talking quickly as she gets excited, or may slow down as she becomes more focused and deliberate about the points you're making. That's usually a good moment for you to take the plunge.

✦ **A sudden shift in attentiveness.** If your prospect suddenly leans forward while talking to you, or gives you more eye contact, she's starting to connect. The moment to go for the close is when your prospect becomes caught up in doing business with you.

✦ **An action that indicates involvement.** If, for instance, your prospect calls in a second decision-maker or pulls out her ad materials to see how they might look in your publication, consider it a good time to close.

TRY THESE GENTLE CLOSES

It's easy to think that closing takes place at the end of the sales process. But if you close only at the end of the process, you add tension and pressure to the sale. What's best is to close throughout the sales process with "mini closes" or "test closes."

A mini close essentially reinforces the links you make between your client's needs and the features and benefits of your publication. First, visualize this triangular relationship:

Trial closes prepare you and your prospect, intellectually and emotionally, for the final close.

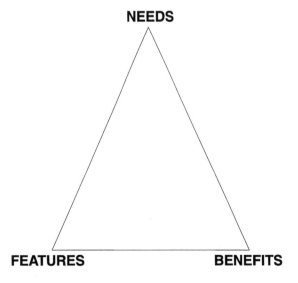

NEEDS

FEATURES   **BENEFITS**

278

Now, start verbalizing this relationship to your client. When speaking of editorial quality (*feature*), for instance, you might say, "Editorial quality is what enables us to attract the high-income readers (*benefit*) that you're looking to reach with your product (*need*)." Once you have connected those three points, you can go for the mini close, or "tie-down": "You can see how this makes sense in your market, don't you agree?"

In other words, start your mini close with statements like, "Why this is important to your needs, number one, is...." Or, "What this means to you is...." Or, "How our publication can help you is...."

Then tie down your sales agreement: "Doesn't this make sense to you?" "Can you see how this helps your marketing needs?" Or, "This is important, don't you agree?"

Think of each mini close as a building block for your sale. Each agreement to your sales points prepares your client for the final close.

A test close works in similar fashion. Unlike a mini close, a test close (or trial close) doesn't ask for agreement to specific sales points. Rather, it's a type of closing question that tests your client's willingness to buy.

You might, for instance, ask how your prospect thinks advertising will affect winter-inventory needs. Or you could ask which trade shows she might be interested in promoting in your publication. A positive response or willingness to talk about specific advertising possibilities shows she might be ready for the next step.

Using a trial close is a lot like fishing. You throw out some bait, and if your prospect bites and starts tugging, you pull her in. You may be surprised to find that your prospect is ready to "bite" sooner than you thought.

Trial closes also prepare you and your prospect, intellectually and emotionally, for the final close. For you, the trial close is a bit like a weather balloon. It lets you check the lay of the land to determine what excites your prospect and what makes her hesitate.

279

More important, a trial close enables your prospect to get used to hearing closing-like questions. In fact, if you're doing your job well, you'll be closing your prospect a bit at a time, actually weaving the closing process together throughout the sale. All you would need with the final close is a confirmation and tying-up of loose ends.

In the end, trust your instincts. If you think your prospect is ready to buy but you can't say *why* you think so, give it a gentle close. Remember, you can't afford to create more resistance in the sales process. Use statements like, "Do you feel comfortable discussing a possible schedule?" Or, "Shall we move forward?" If your prospect reacts well, great. If you don't hear a "yes," don't be discouraged. You've lost nothing; just keep selling.

TAKING THE HEEBIE-JEEBIES OUT OF CLOSING

In the last chapter, we talked about the fear of closing, of how you may flinch as you prepare to pop the "Big Question." Now I'll show you how good timing goes a long way in reducing those heebie-jeebies. When you time things well, the Big Question doesn't become quite so threatening any more. By the time you ask it, you *know* your client ought to be ready to buy.

Don't make the mistake of thinking that the close is something that happens only at the end of the sales presentation. If you sell that way, you're putting yourself at a disadvantage and your client in a tense position. An eleventh-hour climax isn't exactly a comforting end to your sales story!

As I've said before, you want your close to be the natural outcome of your presentation. Here's how to get there.

1. Move Your Prospect From "IF" To "HOW"

The best way to make the close smooth is to guide your prospect from talking "ifs" to talking "hows." Here's how it works:

When you sit down and tell your prospect all the reasons why she should advertise, the assumption is that she has not yet made a decision. The implication is that she can take advantage of all these benefits *if* only she would advertise with you.

280

Talk to your prospect about *how* she might advertise her new "strawberry-scented Band-Aids:" "In February, you might want to run the new-product ad since the Band-Aids are going to be introduced into 132 stores nationwide. That ad can tie into your direct-mail campaign. Now in March..." Instead of wondering *if* she's going to advertise, you're talking about the nitty-gritty—about *how* her ad campaign will shape up in your magazine.

The process works much like a trial close. When you've moved your prospect from "if" to "how," the final close is not far away. By discussing specific advertising ideas and schedules, you can turn a concept into a concrete plan.

2. Involve Your Prospect in Joint Ownership

I learned the effectiveness of joint planning in graduate school. Before writing a paper, I would meet with the professor to discuss the concept. We would then discuss specific ideas. By the time I had submitted the paper, my teacher was deeply involved with it—after all, many of the ideas were his. He already "shared ownership" of the paper.

I'm not sure that this technique would be considered excellent scholarship, but it was great salesmanship. See how joint planning can work for you. In any good presentation, you should involve your client in discussing his needs and in reaching agreement on solutions. If you've done your precall planning and you've got a real dialogue going with your client, the close is but steps away.

3. Ask for Slightly More than You Expect

We often subject our clients' use of our publication to our own low expectations. If a six-time contract has helped her increase sales, perhaps it's appropriate to suggest she run nine or 12 times. Of course, you need to believe in and justify your recommendation to your client.

And sure, you might get knocked down. Many prospects, as a matter of course, look for ways to cut back on your recommendations. If you're assertive, perhaps the worst that could happen is

> In any good presentation, you should involve your client in discussing his needs and in reaching agreement on solutions.

that your client would go for the schedule you expected she would take anyway.

Most important, however, such recommendations move the discussion from "if" to "how." When you say, "A six-time schedule would do the job, but a 12-time schedule would put you strongly ahead of the competition," you've changed the tone of the discussion from *whether* she should advertise to *how often*.

4. Respond to Objections

Objections at the close? Granted, the close is not the time to explain why your CPM is higher than your competitor's, nor is it the time to analyze the merits of magazine advertising.

But not every sale goes according to schedule. Your task, when arriving at the close, is to flush out any final objections you think your client might be harboring. Make sure nothing is clouding the waters. If you rush into the close while your client still looks puzzled or undecided, you risk stumbling on objections just at the point when you should be finalizing the sale. Nothing kills your timing like hearing, "I'm sorry, we don't have the budget" at the very moment your client should be excited about advertising with you.

So how do you cope?

✦ **Make sure you have dealt with *all* of your client's objections ahead of time.** In other words, let's say you know, from your fact-finding and pre-call planning, that your client prefers the mass readership of your competition. However, during your "agreement on needs" stage of the sale, your client never brings up any concerns about readership. Should you just go forward and assume all is well?

Not necessarily. Instead, you might find it better to address the unstated objection. You might say, for instance, "Some of our clients have concerns that we can't provide the mass readership of our competition. I'd like to show you how our own circulation will give you the effective penetration you need without the waste circulation of our competitor." That way,

282

your client can't surprise you with a readership objection when you should be closing. Let your intuition be your guide as to whether or not to verbalize a potential objection at this point. Weigh the risks carefully.

✦ **Ask about potential problems.** If your client seems reluctant to move forward, simply ask: "Is there any reason why we should not proceed?" You may have thought that you covered all the necessary ground, but your client may still have doubts and you might need to return to the objection-handling stage. Or you can say, "I understand that you see a limitation in our publication. However, if you weigh that against the benefits that we have agreed upon, I know you'll be more than satisfied with the value you'll receive when advertising with us." Then go ahead and close.

In other words, don't ever assume that objections won't pop up at the close, or that you've handled every point in the sale to your client's satisfaction. At the same time, don't blithely pass by objections in your hurry to close. Take the time to hear your client's concerns, which are sure to come up when you least expect them.

5. Summarize Your Benefits

Once you've made your presentation and recommended an advertising program, you may want to summarize the benefits before you get to the Big Question. It will help you lead your prospect through the decision-making process and to a buying decision.

Here's why a summary of benefits works:

✦ It's an easy and comfortable transition. You don't have to be clever or come up with a new idea.

✦ It reinforces the prospect's positive attitudes by reiterating major benefits and points of agreement.

✦ It reminds your prospect of how your magazine meets her needs.

✦ It gives you a few moments of breathing room. Critical point! You need to collect yourself so that you close with confidence.

283

In leading to the close, check in one last time with your prospect. Ask, "Have I covered these points to your satisfaction?" Or, "Does this program make sense to you?" Or, "It's clear that we have a match here between your target market and our readers, don't you think?" If you see nods of agreement, close.

If you hear a negative response, ask another question to isolate the remaining objection. Maybe your client is fine with the price, but still concerned about editorial quality. Circle back to that phase of the presentation and lead to a close again later.

Closing the sale is like shooting a basket. It takes strategy and court sense. You've used your presentation to move into a strong position and set up the shot. You've demonstrated controlled yet spontaneous skill. You've come across as confident and powerful, and you've practiced your shots over and over. You know you're in control. But until you shoot, you have nothing. If you lose possession of the ball, you lose your advantage. Take the risk.

In Chapters 15 and 16, I'll present some proven basic and advanced techniques for closing sales.

15

BASIC CLOSING TECHNIQUES

"If I had six hours to chop down a tree, I'd spend five-and-a-half hours sharpening my ax."
—Abraham Lincoln (1809-1865)

❖ ❖ ❖

Once you've learned *when* to ask for the close, the question then becomes *how*.

When you sell as a marketing consultant, you're naturally focused on the *whole sales process,* not on some artificial final moment. That means by the time you get to the close, you shouldn't be springing something unexpected on your prospect. You should simply be acknowledging and confirming the agreements you've arrived at together.

That being the case, you want your close to be natural and effective. You don't want to sound as if your final statements are out of *101 Magic Closing Phrases*. You want to segue into the close as easily as one scene to the next in a movie.

Having said that, though, you still need to be *prepared* to say just the right thing to your client to ensure you'll get the sale. That's what this chapter is about.

CLOSING GIMMICKS DON'T WORK

Granted, book stores are filled with manuals of closing phrases and gimmicks. The only problem is that most are designed to trick your prospect into buying. Don't think your prospects won't recognize tricks when they hear them. If you try a sneaky close, you'll lose the sale.

Besides, trying to memorize a series of closing gimmicks is wasted energy. You won't remember them at crucial moments, and worse, you'll lose focus on your client. It's better to rely on a substantive sales presentation than on a hat full of closing tricks.

Still, you do need to master a few *natural* closes so that you can choose the most appropriate and effective closing technique at any given time. You can sound out different techniques ahead of time and see which ones sound right to you, and which fit naturally into your presentation. If you fail with any one technique during the sales process, you might succeed with another.

> Remember, what's most important is that you *do* close, and that you're comfortable with the closing technique you choose.

It's okay to try out several different closes in one sales call. Persistence pays. Many prospects need gentle prodding and time to think about their final agreement. If you vary your approach and ask for the order in different, natural ways, you'll create more impact while respecting your client's need to hear your proposal and mull it over.

Remember, what's most important is that you *do* close, and that you're comfortable with the closing technique you choose. Look over this chapter with care. Practice what you read. If a voice inside you tells you that a particular technique sounds false or manipulative, trust yourself and drop that technique. Unless *you're* comfortable with what you say, you can bet you're client won't be.

A FEW POINTERS...

Before we talk about specific techniques, keep these tips in mind:

✦ *The fewer words, the better.* Closing is a time for you to *choose words carefully*—more so here than at any other time. Don't rush into a stream of sentences and risk confusing your client.

✦ *Use positive words.* Stick to selling terms like "investment" and "benefit" rather than negative words like "cost" and "problem." Don't give your client an opportunity to lose the positive momentum you've made in your presentation.

✦ *Assert yourself.* Your pace and tone are critical. You must inspire confidence in your client. Pay close attention to your eye contact and body language. Don't hunker over or look away when you make your close.

EIGHT SIMPLE TECHNIQUES

Years of experience in closing means I can now save you a lot of time. I've outlined for you eight of the most effective and natural ad sales closes.

Some of these closes may seem a bit abrupt, but don't worry. Remember, you're reading them out of context of the sales process. If your timing and pacing are correct—if your prospect is primed and ready to close—any of these will sound completely natural in your sales call.

I suggest you practice these closes aloud and write out different uses for each. If you practice now, you'll be able to deliver them naturally to your prospect. In closing, your delivery style will mean just as much as your choice of words.

The Direct-Request Close

This is the simplest and most straightforward close. When the moment's right, ask for the order. For example:

✦ "May I reserve this space for you?"

✦ "Let's run this next month, OK?"

✦ "May we schedule this ad for the January issue?"

✦ "May we count on your business?" (Don't ask your client to "give you" the business. That sounds as if she's doing you a favor rather than making a sales investment.)

Many salespeople are afraid to use a direct close. They think being explicit leaves them no room for discussion. But at this point, you ought to know if your prospect is ready. Have courage.

The Assumptive Close

If you sense your prospect is really ready to do business, use a close that assumes a sale is at hand. Instead of asking, *talk* to your prospect in terms of how effective his advertising program will be.

✦ "I know, Jim, that this program we've been discussing is going to fulfill your objective of launching your new-product line. Let's move ahead and start with the next issue."

You assume that unless he says no, all is well.

A word of caution: don't use an assumptive close unless you're sure the client is ready to buy. If you're off base with your assumption, you'll sound manipulative. Your client will feel trapped, and your sale will disappear.

The Alternative-Choice Close

Like an assumptive close, an *alternative* close (also called an *either/or* close) assumes that the prospect is ready to buy. So, instead of giving her a yes/no option, you offer your prospect instead a *positive choice* that takes "no" out of the picture. For instance:

✦ "Will you run this spread in the February issue, Mary, or should we schedule it for March?"

Or,

✦ "Do you want to run the corporate-image ad this month, or would you rather go with the new-product ad?"

Again, don't use this close if you're not certain of your client's willingness to buy. To "unready" clients, an "either/or" close can

288

sound like a sneaky way to get trapped into a contract.

The Physical-Action Close

With *physical action,* you literally demonstrate to your prospect that the close is at hand. You might get him, for example, to fill out the insertion order with you. Or you could spread the particular ad materials on the table. You could even ask to use the telephone to call someone back at your office, such as the production manager. "May I use your telephone? I'd like to call our production department to reserve this special position for you in the May issue."

The Concession/Inducement Close

Here's a good close for magazines that offer value-added merchandising services to advertisers. With a concession close, you offer the prospect something special in return for deciding to buy now. For example: "If you decide to place your ad in this issue, Linda, we can arrange to do a special survey for you across a targeted list of readers."

The Urgency/Impending Event Close

Like the concession/inducement close, an *urgency* close uses selling points to create a sense of urgency about the sale. You might, for instance, suggest impending price changes, availability of special positions, trade show issues, sponsorships or research studies. For example: "If you act now, we can place your ad in our special section on corporate travel."

The Testimonial/Narrative Close

With a *testimonial* close, you can tell your prospect about other advertisers who've already had success using your magazine. It helps if your prospect knows and can identify with those companies. You can point out how her marketing and sales needs are similar to other advertisers' needs. And you can demonstrate how advertising in your magazine has helped them.

A strong written testimonial can be very powerful. Or you can tell your prospect to feel free to call anyone on your list of other successful advertisers. For example: "Ms. Cobert's company was experiencing the same problems that you are in opening up this new market. She said that within six months of advertising with our title her sales have increased 15 percent." Now you can combine this narrative close with a direct, assumptive or alternative-choice close.

One word of caution: remember not to promise the *same* results. Let your prospect draw her own conclusions from the comparisons you've made.

The Call-Back Close

If your client insists you call back for an answer, handle your call with care. You may be tempted to open the conversation by asking her if she's thought over your proposal. Don't. You'll hear "no" more times than you'd like, and then you'll find yourself in a defensive-selling position.

Instead, start your conversation by offering new information or by reviewing your magazine's major advertising benefits. Now is the time to break out those little gems you may have held back during your sales presentation. For example:

✦ "The last time we talked, I forgot to mention the increase in circulation that our magazine has experienced in the last three months."

Or,

✦ "As you may remember, when we last met, we discussed how..."

then summarize the major points of agreements that you reached, and move right to the close.

MOVING TO THE NEXT LEVEL

It may take some time to master the eight closing techniques above. Try role-playing them with your colleagues. Listen to yourself to see what seems natural to you, and what seems uncomfortable.

Notice how your clients respond to you. You might find that

certain techniques, like physical action, work well with clients who like to participate in your presentation. Other techniques, like assumptive closes, might work well with long-term clients who enjoy doing business with you. Keep experimenting with different techniques until you feel you've hit your stride.

Check the next chapter when you're ready for more of a challenge.

16

ADVANCED CLOSING TECHNIQUES

"Even if you're on the right track, you'll get run over if you just sit there."
—Will Rogers (1879-1935)
actor and humorist

Basic closing techniques are a bit like three-speed bicycles. They're fine for getting you most places you'd like to go. But when you want to stretch your skills and take on more challenges, you need more sophisticated equipment. To add finesse to your selling process, you need advanced closing techniques.

Advanced closing techniques help you push your selling skills. They require more thinking on your feet, more grace in delivery, more preparation. They are what I call "quietly assertive."

With advanced closing techniques, you take bigger risks for bigger gain. You begin to push for the "maybe" six-time schedule instead of merely the "sure-thing" three-time schedule. You display more confidence and authority at the critical moment of closing.

Let's look at some of these techniques.

"Feel, Felt, Found" Close

Like the testimonial close, the *feel, felt, found* close lets your prospects know about successful experiences other advertisers have had with your title. The difference here, though, is that your prospect, rather than being primed to close, is *fearful* of making a mistake. That means you'll want to use testimonials to reassure and empathize with him. You'll want to demonstrate that other advertisers, despite their anxiety, realized that every good business decision involved courage and calculated risk. Despite some concerns, they went ahead anyway, made the right decision, and are now reaping the benefits.

Let's say that your prospect expresses some concern that your magazine reaches too limited a market. You can respond this way: "I hear exactly how you 'feel.' I had a tire client recently who 'felt' the same way you do and was concerned that we didn't reach enough independent truck owners. However, he went ahead with a six-time schedule just like the one we're discussing and last week he told me he 'found' that he has already seen a 10 percent increase in sales to independent truck owners. I'd like to see you have the same kind of experience. Let's go ahead and schedule this program."

The Sharp-Angle Close

This close works something like a *quid pro quo*. What happens is that your prospect expresses a desire for something you know your magazine can offer, like a special position in a trade-show issue, an extended due date, or sponsorship of a special event. She might, however, be making the request to get off the fence, or to rationalize her decision to buy or not to buy. You can use that request to move the decision in your favor. (You might even want to list possible requests ahead of time so that you can try out this close.)

Suppose you're meeting with a bank advertiser you've been trying to upsell for months into a full schedule. She's hinting that she wants to be adjacent to the lead column in your special monthly finance section. You're prepared for her request, and you're prepared to grant it. You know she wouldn't ask for this special position unless she had reached a turning point in her decision-making process.

With the sharp-angle close, you answer her question with your own question. Pin down her commitment *first*, before you grant your own.

Prospect: *Can I get a special position in the finance section?*

You: *Let me check on that for you. If I can get you a special position, can I count on you to approve the schedule today?*

Less experienced salespeople would probably answer, "I'm sure I can arrange that." Notice how the latter reply would bypass the opportunity to close.

The Boomerang Close

This close works by turning around your prospect's main objection. Although we've talked about answering objections in previous chapters, this close takes the process a step further and actually turns the objection into a reason to buy.

Prospect: *You don't have any advertisers in our product category.*

You: *The fact that you will be the first advertiser in your product category is the very reason you should advertise now. It's the perfect time. While I expect other furniture manufacturers will at some point join the magazine, you now have a limited window of time to be the only office furniture manufacturer getting hot leads from our magazine. Plus, you have the added benefit of reaching open-minded prospects who have not yet developed brand loyalty. This is a rare opportunity to grab the leadership position by being first in your category, to be first in our readers' minds. Shall we begin with the next issue?*

Before meeting with a client, you might want to catalog every major objection you might encounter in a sales discussion. If your prospect claims your competitor has a bigger circulation, you can point out, "Yes, but given our targeted and more affluent readership, you'll be able to reach twice as many prospects for your product, without wasting your important message on readers who won't

295

buy." If you can, practice boomeranging every potential objection so that a perceived deficiency becomes an asset.

The Set-and-Spike Close

Like the boomerang, the *set-and-spike* close is also based on a client's objection. You'll find this particular close takes some skill to do correctly—but it can be a powerhouse move.

If you've ever played volleyball, you understand how "set" and "spike" work. One player sets the ball with precision close to the net. His teammate then spikes the ball with a powerful overhand straight into the opponent court. It's a killer move.

In sales, you make your set early in the conversation by first deciding which objections your client might raise. You then engage your client in a small-talk discussion that will become analogous to your sales presentation.

Here's how it might work. Assume that early in your sales meeting, you mention how much you admire your prospect's new BMW. He starts talking about the car's high performance and quality. You might comment at this point about how expensive BMWs are. He'll likely defend his buying decision, while the two of you agree that quality performance is, after all, worth more money.

That's the set. Later, when your prospect voices price objections about advertising in your publication, you can hit the spike: "You were telling me earlier, Joe, about your new BMW and explaining to me the importance of high quality and performance. Our magazine is a lot like your BMW—you're investing in the highest performer in the market. You're someone who appreciates that quality is more important than price. Why don't we lock up this 12-time advertising schedule."

As you can see, the set-and-spike technique takes some care to do correctly. If your client begins to suspect he's been manipulated, you've lost the sale.

That's why it's very important that you use the set-and-spike

296

only in areas where you *truly believe* what you're saying. Many times a set-and-spike isn't appropriate. But if during your conversation, an analogy presents itself to you, use it.

Tip: The more natural the conversation, and the more time that passes between the set and the spike, the more powerful the spike will be.

The Balance-Sheet Close

Were you ever so troubled by a decision that you listed the pros and cons on a piece of paper? Most everyone has at one time. A comparison list, or a balance sheet, is a very helpful way to settle a decision—particularly for a prospect who's on the fence about advertising.

With this technique, you ask your prospect to list with you all the reasons she should begin advertising now. You then write these reasons in the right-hand column on a sheet of paper. That helps the prospect reinforce all the reasons she should buy.

Now you write your prospect's objections on the left side. Most prospects have only one or two reasons why they feel they shouldn't buy. Concerns lose their magnitude when listed side by side with benefits. Let's see how it might work for a furniture-store prospect for a city business journal.

CONCERNS	BENEFITS
1. Less direct response than newspaper	1. Reaches top business executives
2. Higher CPM than newspaper	2. Businesses buy multiple units at high end
	3. Executives have high incomes
	4. Lower page rate
	5. Highly targeted: No waste circulation
	6. Glossy 4-color stock: can show quality of products

Concerns lose their magnitude when listed side by side with benefits.

Now you can review your balance sheet with your prospect: "As you can see, Ms. Booth, when we balance your objections against what you would get, it's clear that there are more reasons for you to advertise in our business journal than not. Obviously, few decisions in life are made without some element of indecision and risk. And no publication, including ours, can claim to be perfect. While we might have a slightly higher CPM and deliver fewer direct leads than the city newspaper, we do deliver the cream of the crop—this city's affluent business community. On reviewing the balance sheet, it's apparent we can do the job for you."

Once you get your client to agree with you, you can move toward the close. "I think it's the right time to go ahead with this advertising schedule. Don't you agree?"

The Reduction-to-the-Ridiculous Close

I find this close works best with price objections. What you're doing is effectively reducing the prospect's concerns to their logical, and minimal, conclusion.

Lets assume your prospect says, "It costs too much." Ask how much he considers "too much." Then work with the difference instead of the total investment.

For instance, your prospect might say your magazine page is $500 more than your competitor's. You know you have 8,000 more potential buyers—which works out to six cents per additional prospect. You also know your client's profit on an equipment sale is $2,000.

So here's what you can say: "I'm sure, Mr. Kraft, that you want to capture every sales opportunity possible with those additional 8,000 buyers that would see your equipment advertisement. A single sale would pay for the difference and think how much more equipment you have the potential of selling."

Get his agreement that this line of thinking makes sense. Now, you can ask for the order.

298

The Quality/Price Close

This closing technique works well if your magazine is a quality buy and your prospect is looking for quality, but may still be clinging on to price concerns.

You might, for instance, begin with, "Ms. Hayes, as a publishing company, we had to decide whether to produce a quality publication or to go for the low end. I'm sure that you're glad that we decided to go for quality or you wouldn't be interested in advertising in our magazine."

You might add, "We decided that it would be easier to explain price one time than it would be to apologize for poor quality forever [slight pause] and knowing how quality-minded you and your company are that makes sense, doesn't it?"

Then close: "So let's go ahead and start getting you the new business you're looking for."

The Columbo Close

If the best your client can say is, "Let me think about it," muster up your courage and try the *Columbo* close. (I named this one after the TV police detective who spins around with an "Oh, by the way" zinger just as he's shuffling out the door.) It's important to hold off on your Columbo close until your prospect feels safe that this meeting or call is winding down.

Prospect: *Let me think about everything we've talked about, and we can talk sometime next month.*

You: *Sure, and it's been really great having this opportunity to talk with you about your business.*

[You shake hands and walk toward the door. Then you pause and turn back toward your client.]

You: *Oh, by the way, there's just one more thing. I meant to ask if you would be promoting that new second-day shipping service now that your competitor is thinking of placing a schedule.*

If you've done this correctly, you might find you've hit a hot button that opens up the conversation up again.

The Columbo close can often power a slow mover into a buying frame of mind. It's also great for dropping in a key sales point you may have held back for just this purpose.

AVOID THE CLOSE-KILLERS

Once you're practiced in the right way to close, you'll probably have no problem steering past what's wrong. Here are 10 points to keep in mind to prevent shooting down your good work.

1. *Don't oversell.* As salespeople, our gift of gab serves us, but *listening* serves us better. Overselling can alienate the prospect and even undo the sale by triggering additional objections. Learn to be comfortable with silence.

2. *Don't move in too fast.* Make sure you've established value in the prospect's mind. A high-pressure premature close sets up resistance.

3. *Don't wait too long, either.* Many salespeople keep talking, as if waiting for the prospect to jump up and yell, "OK, I'm ready now!" If you don't take responsibility and initiate the close, you'll have one bored and frustrated prospect.

4. *Don't ask manipulative questions.* Some salespeople like to pounce on prospects they've set up with trick questions. For example:

   You: *Do you want your business to grow?*

   Prospect: *Of course I do.*

   You: *Then you'll advertise in our publication, won't you?*

   Your prospect recognizes a set-up. Don't give her a chance to lose her trust in you.

5. *Don't cower.* Many salespeople seem embarrassed to go for the close, as if the prospect is about to hit them. If you're not confident, you can't expect your prospect to be.

300

6. *Don't stop selling until you get to "yes."* I see this closing error all the time. Just because a prospect smiles and nods when you say, "I know you'll want to begin advertising in our upcoming special issue," you shouldn't be fooled. A smile is a good sign, but it's not a "yes." Only a "yes" is a "yes."

7. *Don't burn your bridges.* Even if you feel the sale is gone for good, be careful not to say or do anything that will prevent your return. Keep the lines of communication open. Someday you may get a "yes" instead of a "no."

8. *Don't close without the decision maker.* You may have a terrific time "selling" someone at the company who doesn't have the wherewithal to buy. While this person may be a wonderful ally, don't stop with her. Make sure that when you close, you're closing with the right person.

9. *Don't take nosedives.* Remember that fine line between playing it safe and taking a risk? Don't get so caught up in being assertive that you're undercutting rates or promising deals you can't keep. Make sure you respect your publication's bottom line.

10. *Don't miss the buying window.* Keep alert to your prospect's closing cues. Don't insist on completing the presentation if your prospect looks like he's ready to buy *now*. Your prospect's interest is a tough thing to capture, and an easy thing to lose.

AND AFTER YOU'VE CLOSED...

Once you've closed the sale, don't just walk away in triumph. Reinforce your client's decision by complimenting him on his insight and by inviting him to broaden his reach by buying ancillary products. Assure him of satisfaction and personal service.

Send a thank you card, and be sure to follow up soon with a service call.

17

IF YOU'RE ASKED to CUT RATES...

"Let us not negotiate out of fear. But let us never fear to negotiate."
—John F. Kennedy (1917-1963)

I f it hasn't happened yet, it will. A client will say to you "give me a deal." Translated, she'll want you to cut rates—to offer a price below the one printed on the rate card.

In today's ad market, there's a lot of pressure to cut rates. How you and your sales manager handle the pressure will determine your sales success.

I believe rate-cutting is extremely tricky. How can a client trust your word if she thinks her competitor might be getting a "better deal?" And once you start handing out deals willy-nilly, you'll find it's tough to stop.

Moreover, sloppy rate-cutting can hurt your magazine's business. Often, what you give away in price has to be made up in the number of pages. And please note, publishers and ad directors: reckless slashing can also confuse your salespeople as to how to conduct business and how far to go with deals. Instead of educating clients on the unique value of the book, sales reps may feel compelled to play up the price. Ultimately, that means rate-cutting can lower your value of the publication as it becomes a commodity rather than a solution to the client's marketing problems.

Handled improperly, rate-cutting can also hurt your relationship with your clients. Instead of treating them as marketing partners, you might find you're treating them as adversaries. Each party in a rate-cutting deal might be out to "win" over the other. That's hardly conducive to good business. Plus, once your clients get used to buying on price alone, they'll quickly desert you for the next (cheaper) passing ship.

In short, it's best to stick to your published rates. But let's be real. Times are far from ideal. And when it's not possible to hold your line on rates, *you must know how to negotiate deals with caution.* It's critical to keep up your publication's value in an increasingly price-wary environment.

That's what this chapter is about. You'll learn how to negotiate successfully, to examine other options you may have, and to preserve the integrity of your publication and your job.

RATE-CUTTING, DEFINED

When we talk about rate-cutting, we're not talking about innovative discounts, like pages for volume buys, or rewards for renewal business. Those types of incentives are standard practice for reinforcing business relationships. and are often printed on the rate card itself.

What rate-cutting does mean is that Advertiser A and Advertiser B pay different prices for the same spot in an issue, even though both A and B have the same advertiser status. In other words, like advertisers pay *different* rates for the *same* space.

Rate-cutting might mean giving an advertiser a page unit at a price that's below what's printed on the card, such as a one-page buy at a three-page rate, or a flat 15 percent discount for any sched-

304

ule at all. Rate-cutting might also mean giving away services that wouldn't normally be offered, such as bonus pages for advertisers who haven't met the formal requirements for earning a bonus.

In some magazine companies, selling off the rate card is grounds for dismissal. Others don't cut the page price, but throw in unearned frequency discounts, free color, rate protection, waived production costs, you name it. Still other magazines provide discount mailing-list privileges, inserts or postcard decks. Fewer and fewer, however, resist the pressure to cut deals at all.

Publishers started aggressively cutting rates during the mid-'80s, and the practice hasn't abated since. Increased competition is one reason. Not only have magazines proliferated, but so have all kinds of other media, from classroom TV to online services, all of which give advertisers more choices. And more choices allow advertisers to simply follow the laws of supply and demand: When supply is plentiful—as it is with media—the buyers can call the shots.

Rate negotiation has been business as usual in radio and television, which often sell space as a commodity. And in retail, of course, commodity- and discount-selling is entirely appropriate. For instance, say I've researched new office-computer equipment and have decided on the company brand and model number for a laptop I'd like to buy. Now, I can negotiate the price with different dealers, playing one against the other. One dealer may drop the price, another may throw in some software I need. Regardless, the computer is the same make, model and quality.

Magazines, however, are not analogous. The phrase "all things being equal" is often unfairly applied to magazines because each magazine has its own personality and its own value. That allows publishers leeway in setting different CPMs.

At the same time, magazines are a conceptual buy, which often makes them difficult to "value," at least from an advertiser's perspective. The resulting ambiguity contributes to the pressure to negotiate rates.

Publishers who make deals often operate without any rules or

305

guidelines. Those that do need to negotiate the best packages for themselves and their advertisers must learn how to see clearly through the fog. They must preserve the value of their magazines—and their relationships with their clients. That's what we'll talk about next.

SELLING IS NOT NEGOTIATING

First, selling and negotiating are different skills. Both require a mutually beneficial agreement. Both demand that the salesperson understand the prospect's needs, present solutions to meet those needs, answer concerns and objections, and confirm a commitment.

Negotiating goes one step further. It involves *differences* between two parties. Both parties start out with different needs and positions, and through the bargaining process, reach an agreement. Client Taylor, for instance, starts out with a request: "Your competitor is willing to come down 20 percent in price. We'll go with you if you can match their price." It's your job to respond.

> Remember, the most successful sales/negotiation attitude and posture is, *I want your business, but I don't need your business.*

This is shaky ground for many salespeople. They're trained to be on the *offensive*—to sell benefits. But now, instead of working as marketing consultants, they're asked to become deal makers. Instead of ensuring long-term commitments, they're creating short-term arrangements. Instead of building the value of the publication, they're worrying about how much to give away.

Once put on the defensive in a price war, a salesperson's confidence in himself and his magazine often falters.

When that happens, the game is lost. No one can be convincing as a salesperson, let alone as a negotiator, if he is insecure about himself and his product. Remember, the most successful sales/negotiation stance is, "*I want your business, but I don't need your business.*"

Even if your magazine isn't rate-cutting, you can certainly benefit from knowing how to negotiate. Negotiation can give you the confidence to travel down other avenues first before even entering discussions of lowering price.

306

MAKE IT WIN-WIN

The overall goal in negotiations shouldn't be to beat the other guy. What you *don't* want is for the client to walk away thinking he got something over on you—and you don't want to saunter out pleased that you bluffed him. Once you make negotiations a contest, you'll end up with one-shot, resentful clients. Remember, if the client leaves the table unhappy, he may cancel later or choose not to renew.

So whenever you're negotiating, keep in mind the psychological needs of your client. *How will it make him look if he accepts your offer?* Be sensitive to his need to save face every step of the way.

Second, remember that negotiations aren't just a matter of winging it, the way you would haggle with a souvenir vendor in Tijuana. I recently asked a salesperson, "How much are you willing to negotiate?" "That depends," he replied. On what? "Oh, I'm not sure," he said. "I guess I play it by ear." A prescription for disaster.

To negotiate successfully, you must be prepared *psychologically* and *intellectually*. You must have a game plan and stick to it (or at least know when it's best to stick to it and best not to). A plan lets you control what you're doing when you sit down with your negotiating partner.

Let's look at some methods for preparing yourself.

Have a game plan. First, ask yourself a simple question: *What do you want from the negotiation, and why do you want it?* Brainstorm: Make a list of objectives and prioritize them. For one client, you may want a three-page increase. For a more difficult client, you may simply want a renewal.

What's at stake? A modified schedule? The client relationship? Your sales quota? You need to know what you're willing to give and what it will cost you. Not every page is worth getting.

When you know what you want, develop a step-by-step strategy. Have Plan A, and backup plans B and C. You don't know that your client will respond to your original idea.

Let's say Client Taylor, who asked for 20 percent off, is an important prospect who represents a new ad category you're trying to break.

In that case, Plan A might be to demonstrate how your magazine offers more value for his money than your competitor. Plan B, if needed, might be to add value to the page rate by offering discounted or free space in the magazine's postcard deck. Plan C might be to give Taylor the six-page rate if he agrees to buy four pages.

Trade, don't yield. Consultant Anne Miller, president of New York-based Chiron Associates, says she sees salespeople make the same negotiating mistake again and again: They don't trade; they collapse. A client says, "I want to be in the first 25% of the book," or "I want you to waive bleed charges," or "I want a special pavilion at the trade show." What does the rep say? More than likely, a nervous "okay" and "I'll see what I can do." Fearful of losing the client altogether, most salespeople prefer to give in. What's the harm in yielding on something as benign as bleed charges?

The problem, though, is that once salespeople start giving, clients keep asking. Every "okay" signals advertisers to press for more. Instead of giving away the store, sales reps need to learn that no "freebie," even a small one, comes without its price.

Example:

> **Client:** *I want to be in the first 25 percent of the book.*
>
> **You:** *To be in the first 25 percent of the book, you would have to increase your commitment by a page.*
>
> **Client:** *I want you to waive the bleed charges.*
>
> **You:** *I'll try to waive the bleed charges if you can give us flexibility on position.*
>
> **Client:** *I want to be in a special pavilion at your trade show.*
>
> **You:** *For a special pavilion, you would have to increase your commitment in our show daily.*

Instead of giving away the store, sales reps need to learn that no "freebie," even a small one, comes without its price.

Notice how each "trade" gives advertisers the message that *the magazine has value.* It's not a commodity product to be discounted or given away. Each time a sales rep gives in to a request, no matter how small, it eats away at the magazine's value in the eyes of its advertisers.

Look out for your client. As you put together your strategy, always make sure you know what's in it for your client. Try to imagine what *his* first offer might be. Imagine how he might react to yours. What will he object to? What might he accept?

This is where your people-reading skills come into play. Know the kind of person you're dealing with. Does he like to be in charge? Does he thrive on agreement, or on conflict?

Client Taylor, from your encounter so far, seems to be a driven personality, someone who likes to be in control. Even though you have Plans B and C in reserve, you might want to phrase your offers so that he has maximum input in deciding what's valuable. You don't want to say, for instance, "Let me show you why we can give you more value for your money than our competitor." Instead, you might want to say, "Let's talk about what's at stake here. How much value would you be getting for your money?" Let *him* reach the conclusion that your magazine is a better buy.

Have information. When it comes to negotiating, information is power. Through your probing and pre-call planning, you should know exactly what your client's goals are and how your magazine can help him to achieve them. That knowledge can give you the confidence to negotiate successfully.

Let's say, for instance, that Client Taylor's goal is to increase market share 2 percent, which would be worth $10 million to his business. If he starts haggling you about the fact that a two-page spread will cost him $1,500 more in your book than in your competitor's, you can point out that *your* book is the one that can help him better achieve his business goals. "And after all," you can say, "we're talking about $10 million here. Why risk your potential gain for only $1,500?"

Let your prospect reach the conclusion that your magazine is a better buy.

309

Know who should negotiate. Before you walk into negotiations, make sure you're right for the job. Perhaps you need more expertise. Maybe you're too emotionally involved, or you don't believe in the negotiation. Maybe you feel outnumbered.

If Client Taylor has a reputation for playing hardball, you might not want to go in alone. Bring a colleague, the ad director or the publisher into the room with you.

Know your own needs. Perhaps you've got the skills to negotiate, but you're lacking confidence. Maybe you feel you'll be intimidated in the process. That's a dangerous signal. If you feel insecure, you may become passive or overcompensate with aggression. Either way, you risk blowing the deal.

To gain confidence, prepare. And you can prepare psychologically and intellectually with techniques like *visualization, role-playing* and even *self-hypnosis*.

Visualization allows you to walk through the sales process in your mind. You're the script writer, actor and director; you can play out different scenarios in your thoughts. If you suggest Plan A, what might Taylor's response be? How would you counter his potential objections?

If you think you're up against a particularly tough session, try *role-playing* it first with your colleague, ad director or publisher. That's especially useful if your role-playing partner already knows Taylor's history and personality.

And try *self-hypnosis* to give yourself an extra boost. It may sound a little spooky, but self-hypnosis is simply is a powerful form of self-talk. You can take a few minutes before you walk in the meeting to give yourself positive suggestions about your self-confidence and ability to do the job. Trust me: Repeating "I'm confident and successful" may sound hokey, but the message sinks in, and bubbles up just when you need that extra surge of strength.

ONCE YOU'RE IN THE ROOM...

Now let's talk about the finer points of actually making the deal.

Pick the time and place. Many books on negotiating recommend negotiating on your own turf. That's not always practical for salespeople, but you still can have some control over the the physical layout of the negotiation area. For instance, you won't feel much control if you sit on a spindly chair while Taylor sits royally behind his desk, leaning back (with his feet up!). Suggest moving to a conference table or coffee table instead.

Moreover, allow plenty of time. Often in negotiation, patience is a virtue—the longer you can spend discussing the issue, the more likely both parties will come to an understanding.

In some cases, you may want to create a sense of urgency as a way of pressuring the client to take action. Maybe you've already given him right of first refusal or special position. In that case, stick to a time limit. You may even have a client in the wings who would gladly take the same offer.

Set an agenda. Once you sit down, it helps to review the points and plans you'd pondered during your research stage. Write down a few reminder notes and take them with you to ensure that you cover all your points.

Be discreet. If your inside cover dropped out the day before closing, you might want to use that fact in your negotiation, but don't be in a hurry to say so. That only sets you up for distress selling, which gives your client a decided advantage.

Learn what's valuable—to you and your client. I like to tell this story to make an important point about negotiation.

Two sisters wanted the last orange in the refrigerator. After arguing, they decided to compromise. Each would take half.

As it turned out, one sister wanted the orange for juice. She squeezed her half, threw out the rind, and had half a glass of juice. The other sister wanted the orange for a cake. She scraped off the

311

rind, threw out the fruit, and baked half a cake.

Each sister saw a different value in the orange. If they'd explored their needs further, they could have had a full glass of juice and a whole cake.

This demonstrates that value is relative. What may be of value to your client may not necessarily be important to you. That's why it's also important to ask "why" questions during your negotiations. If your client, for instance, says he only wants the second cover or nothing, ask *why* he feels the second cover is critical to his strategy. Depending on his answer, you might be able to give him another position or value-added strategy that would give him the visibility he seeks.

Don't get trapped into believing that your client *only* wants price, or free pages. Maybe your client would actually be more interested in using your publisher's "800" number in ads for reader response. You could offer such a service and still hold a firm line on rates.

Begin on common ground. Look for areas of mutual benefit and shared interest. That may sound simplistic, but the truth is, negotiations often go the way of family arguments, where one party says, "I want," and the other says, "I can't" or "I won't."

Perhaps you know that you and Client Taylor already disagree over price. Instead of battling it out, think of what you know Taylor *likes* about the magazine. Perhaps he's been very impressed with your title's direct response performance. Maybe he feels your graphics and editorial are superior to your competitor's.

If you can start off by selling the *benefits* of your proposal—that Taylor can, for example, get special positioning next to a well-read column in your magazine—you can begin your discussions with feelings of goodwill. Then, if disputes arise, Taylor would be much less likely to sabotage the deal.

If you do find yourself in a controversial area, move on to other points. You could say, "Clearly we've reached an impasse. Let's set this issue aside for a moment and work on other issues. We'll return

> Remember, when people want to do business, the details rarely get in the way. When they don't want to do business, the details *always* get in the way.

312

When you make a concession, ask for something in return.

to this later." Don't let negotiations stall. If you can agree on everything else, you can clear up that last niggling point more easily.

Remember, when people want to do business, the details rarely get in the way. When they don't want to do business, the details *always* get in the way.

Make concessions carefully. The *manner* in which you concede can matter far more than *what* you concede. Try to concede in small increments; giving a little at a time, and slowly. Make your client *earn* that concession from you.

Moreover, when you make a concession, ask for something in return. You should already have in front of you a list of several things you can ask of your client: a promise to renew, an increased schedule, a bigger ad.

Don't merely trade for the concession; *create value for what you're trading*. Don't allow your advertisers to believe they're walking away with something for nothing. As an example, you might say, "I understand you want a position opposite the table of contents. Right now I've got five other advertisers who want that as well." Or, "I see you want a special position, but you're at a minimum page level. I'll really have to fight my sales manager to get that for you." To simply say, "Okay, you've got it," is to acknowledge that your magazine lacks value.

Have a panic strategy. Let's face it. In particularly tough negotiating sessions panic is often lurking beneath our composure. At some point, your client might start steeling up on you, shooting you with threats like, "If we don't get the second cover of the book, the deal's off."

What *don't* you do? *Don't* react. Instead, play for time. When you're backed into a corner, keep quiet, let your client pour it on, and when he's done, be still and summarize: "Okay. Let's step back for a minute and see where we are. So far, we've agreed on these points, and we still need to resolve..." By summarizing, you take the heat out of the negotiation and give yourself time to regroup and present your Plan B.

313

Panic strategies also work well on the phone. If your client is pushing you, don't feel you have to give a knee-jerk response. Just tell him, "Thank you. Let me think about this issue and I'll get right back to you." That gives both of you a chance to regroup.

Here's where negotiation differs from sales. A sales situation requires you to think fast on your feet, to counter objections and to keep selling while your client is excited. In a negotiating situation, you need to slow down and *consider* every point being made. The last thing you want is to give in just to get the ad. Make sure your client feels you're working, and thinking, as hard as you can to ensure all parties get what they need.

Know your bottom line. Be prepared to walk if you sense concessions are cutting too deep. Know when you'll end the discussion and take your losses. A "no" today could be a "yes" tomorrow.

As one negotiation expert put it, "...the big secret in cutting a good deal is to care, but not to care too much." In other words, if you're prepared to walk, you can be a tougher negotiator. You know you won't have to give away the store to meet client demands.

Furthermore, it helps to know your client's alternatives beforehand. If you know, for example, that Magazine Y has a reputation for undercutting every competitor, that might affect what you're willing to accept as your own bottom line.

Get it in writing. After memories fade and emotions flare, it's a good idea to put your agreement to paper, written plainly and explicitly. Written agreements prevent misunderstanding. If any problems are still lurking, written documentation will force them to the surface before any major damage is done.

THE PSYCHOLOGY OF NEGOTIATIONS

Good negotiations aren't just a matter of professional performance. The best negotiators are those who understand the psychological rules of the game. Here are a few to remember:

Know what you're willing to risk. Successful negotiators understand that risk is the underpinning of the whole process. Power often

> "...the big secret in cutting a good deal is to care, but not to care too much."

314

goes to the greater risk-taker, not the compromiser. That's because the risk-taker is more likely to determine strategy and follow through with it than make crippling concessions in fear of blowing the deal.

You need to know your own strengths and weaknesses as a negotiator. Are you a good poker player, or does your face give you away? Could you and would you risk bluffing? What would you do if a client calls your bluff? Like poker, the negotiation game involves risks. If you're not willing to take them, you may lose.

This may sound counter to everything I've said about attending to your client's needs. It isn't—as long as you know you're always acting in the best interest of your magazine *and* your client. Your client gains nothing by watching you devalue your magazine for the sake of making a sale. Take calculated and careful risks, but *never* risk the dignity of either your magazine, your client or yourself.

Listen. We know careful listening is important in selling. It's doubly so in negotiating because you must learn what isn't being talked about. Does your client have a hidden agenda? Perhaps Taylor says he'll go to Magazine Y if you don't concede—but maybe your listening instincts tell you that he has no such plans.

A hidden agenda casts a shadow on your negotiations. It interferes with the issues being discussed. You may need to flush that agenda out and ensure that both of you are clear on the real issues. Once again, be sure you ask your client "why" questions. For instance, "You say you have plans to go to Magazine Y. Can you explain to me what you believe Magazine Y can do for you that we can't do for you?"

Don't get emotional. If your client is pushing your buttons, don't let him see it. Negotiators who get angry or upset are at a tremendous psychological disadvantage.

Early in my career, I watched an otherwise savvy executive get snagged by a skillful negotiator. She'd arranged several weeks prior to an association dinner for a speaker to address the subject of negotiation. Despite several calls, her secretary was unable to reconfirm the speaker. The executive herself, in a panic, finally reached him the morning of the dinner meeting.

At this point, he reminded her to bring his $1,000 honorarium check. She exploded, knowing money hadn't been discussed and that the association had no speaker budget. Finally, she agreed to pay him—out of her own pocket.

That night when he got up to speak, he used her negotiating mistakes to illustrate several fundamental negotiating strategies. First, he told his audience, she assumed he would speak for free because they hadn't discussed money. Second, she waited too long to reconfirm the date. He had time on his side, knowing she had no alternative. Third, when he mentioned the fee, she became angry and didn't get off the phone to regain composure and devise a strategy. He concluded his talk by tearing up the check.

The moral: *Remember to pause.* When you feel your blood pressure rising, it's a sure sign you should keep quiet, sit back and *think*.

Watch out for the other guy. I've watched lots of salespeople trip up because they take their client's tactics personally. Although every negotiating session is unique, you'll find many times that psychological tactics are part of the game. Here's a list of some of the ones you might encounter, and how to handle them if you do.

◆ **Good guy/Bad guy.** You've seen it on dozens of cop shows. Two negotiating partners show up; in this case, the client and his agency representative. The agency guy rants and raves until the "good guy"—your client—says to his colleague: "Listen, why don't you get a cup of coffee and settle down." Once the raver is gone, the idea is that you'll let down your guard to the good guy, who actually turns out to be the much tougher negotiator. Be careful and watch your flank.

◆ **The knee-jerk.** Here, your client tends to overreact, automatically showing disdain or astonishment at your first offer, whatever it is. In this situation, it's important to know your bottom line and not be intimidated. You might be tempted to speed things up at this point. Don't—that's probably what he's counting on. The better strategy might be to slow things down.

Incidentally, if your knee-jerk client starts hitting you with intimidation tactics, such as "You don't understand. We're representing Multibillion Corp., Ltd.," don't cower. You can come right back with, "Yes, and we're representing Magazine Y, the largest-circulation monthly in the industry, and that's exactly why you belong with us."

✦ **The emotional outburst.** Often people use anger or disappointment to manipulate an outcome. You might have one client who's a continual naysayer, spouting, "You know, I've been very disappointed with the response rate lately" every time you bring up additional advertising. Of course, this could be a legitimate objection. But let your experience guide you. This "disappointment" might also be a ploy to throw you off—especially in a rate-cutting environment.

Most of us want people to be happy and we feel guilty or powerless if we disappoint them. If you recognize that an emotional outburst is simply a ploy, you will not be thrown off. You won't take it personally. You'll retain your personal power that, in turn, can make all the difference during negotiations.

✦ **The bully.** Beware of prospects who are overly emotional or negotiate unfairly. In my experience, bullies are the first to cause problems later on and the last to settle issues amicably. The best approach is not to react emotionally, but intellectually. You can quietly say, "Perhaps there are other ways we can help you reach your business goals." Or, "How else might we solve this problem?" To speak *softly* and *calmly* often stops bullies cold.

✦ **The nibbler.** My niece is a master at this. She knows Aunt Helen is always good for a trip to the frozen yogurt store. Once there, I'm immediately informed that she wants two scoops. Okay. She *must* have a topping. I agree. She believes life isn't worth living without a waffle cone. I give in. How can I resist such pressure?

With a nibbler, it's critical to know where you're negotiable

317

and where you're not. While my niece can waffle-cone me to bankruptcy, she is not permitted to choose where we sit in the movies. Since her infancy, sitting no closer than the first seven rows has been nonnegotiable. No argument here. She always picks row eight.

✦ **The ultimatum launcher.** Some clients won't negotiate at all, but simply hit you with an ultimatum: "If you don't give us the second cover, you're off our list." When this happens, you can choose one of several responses. You can back up and summarize, buying time in order to steer the client to Plan B or C. Or you can acknowledge what's happening: "It looks like we've reached a deadlock here. I don't believe either one of us wants that. Let's summarize what we've agreed on and see what else we can do."

Sometimes, though, you can even close on the ultimatum. Perhaps you can say, "If I get you the second cover, do we have a deal?" or, "If you give me three more pages and I get you the second cover, do we have a deal?"

✦ **The "guidelines" stickler.** Sometimes, clients stick to the rulebook in an attempt to make salespeople fold. The usual tactic goes like this: "Our guidelines say we don't pay rate increases," or "Our guidelines say we have to be in the first 10 percent of the magazine." Your response? Remember, your magazine has its own guidelines, too. "Our guidelines say all clients have to pay 10 percent increases this year on four-page schedules," or "Our guidelines say if you want to be in the first part of the magazine, you have to run at least six pages." Once you've established that both you and your client have rules, steer the negotiation back: "Now that we know what we have to work with, let's try again and see what we can do from here."

✦ **The silent treatment** Some prospects simply stop talking or stare in an attempt to unnerve salespeople in negotiations. Believe me, it works! Consider your options carefully, and decide what might release or break the tension. According to some negotiation experts, he who speaks first, loses. If you believe that

318

Try to truly understand where your client is coming from, and you'll always smooth the path toward a better deal—and a better relationship.

applies to your situation, keep quiet. Or, if you deem it helpful, work up your nerve and try to bring your client out of his shell. If you still encounter resistance, you might go on to explain that the more you all talk, the better the chances of everyone walking away with a solid agreement. After all, you can't read your client's mind, and your client can't read yours.

Silence is counterproductive. Help your client understand that it's in his interest to talk. If he walks out without a discussion, he may miss out on something that could help his business.

◆ *The client from hell.* Sometimes a client will dump everything on the negotiating table in an attempt to "win." You might hear self-pity about shrinking budgets and hard economic times. You might hear ultimatums and cursing. You might hear how every other magazine is giving a better deal than your own. What to do?

When in doubt, use empathy. "Look, Harry, I know you're under pressure to get the best price. I'll tell you what: If I can give you special position and you can give me an extra page, do we have a deal?" Or, "I know your budget's been cut, but we can't give you the rate you're talking about. So let's see what else we can do to help you to make this work."

Empathy defuses your client. It builds a bridge between his needs and your own. That's critical, since negotiations are rarely one-time transactions. Chances are, you'll have to deal with these clients again and again. Try to truly understand where your client is coming from, and you'll always smooth the path toward a better deal—and a better relationship.

THE BORN-AGAIN RATE CARD

Maybe you can't go home again or regain lost youth, but you *can* get back on your rate card—even if you've already slid down that slippery slope to rate-cutting. It's not easy, but it can be well worth the effort. Here are some tips to help you get there:

319

✦ *Hold the line.* Simply let your new clients know that your company's new policy is to stay on the rate card. Some publishers now even print this policy directly on the card itself. Once you make it clear that rates are not negotiable, steer your clients to other negotiating areas, like merchandising programs. You can also defuse your obstinance with humor. One sales rep I know tells clients, "You wouldn't respect me in the morning."

✦ *Present a united front.* It can be easy, of course, to tell the client that the rate-card policy is simply out of your hands. But if you do that, make sure you also stand behind company policy. Don't make an issue of disagreeing with management by saying, "If it were up to me, I'd cut the deal." If necessary, bring in your ad director or publisher to back you up.

✦ *Look for alternatives.* Let your clients know about your merchandising ideas; about value-added services, such as customized research, sweepstakes and special mailings to your advertiser's customers. Merchandising, as you know by now, is great to offer to advertisers who want *more.* And it's a lot easier to give away services than price—especially when you have to get clients back on the rate card later.

✦ *Analyze your rate-cutting position.* If you're currently rate-cutting, make a list of every client off the rate card and the amount of dollars you're giving away. Determine which accounts you'd jeopardize by enforcing your rates. Then determine which is greater: the amount of money you risk by taking a firm line, or the amount you're now giving away.

✦ *Create a rate card you can live with.* Some publishers pad their rates to make room for negotiating. I don't believe in that. Your rate card should *already* be the bottom line your publisher wants to take. Salespeople should not be asked to take the risks necessary to negotiate those rates. Asked to do so, they'll usually hit emotional overload and will concede much too quickly.

✦ *Develop your plan.* Commit yourself to bringing wayward clients back on the rate card. Then decide whether you'll take a cold-turkey approach or if you'll try gradually to nudge them back in place.

Of course, the best solution is to avoid the rate-card problem in the first place. When faced with the temptation to negotiate, do what's right. Sometimes, that may mean negotiating—*carefully*. Most times it means just saying "no."

SECTION V

SALES LETTERS THAT GET ACTION

18

The PEN CAN BE a MIGHTY TOOL

"Writing is no trouble: you just jot down ideas as they occur to you. The jotting is simplicity itself—it is the occurring which is difficult."
—Stephen Leacock (1869-1944)
Canadian humorist and economist

In times of fax machines, e-mail and cellular phones, written correspondence seems about as obsolete as carbon paper. But it' a smart sales rep who knows the selling power of a captivating letter.

I'm not talking about the usual boring and poorly written sales letter. I'm talking about a letter that grabs your client in the first sentence and pulls him through to a solid close. In fact, good sales letters can help you do the following:

✦ *Prospect effectively.* A sales letter can help you weed the *suspects* from the prospects. Moreover, a powerfully written sales communication improves your chances of getting that callback or sales appointment.

✦ *Reach that elusive client.* Mr. Stein may never answer his phone, but eventually he reads his mail. That gives you the opportunity to introduce yourself.

✦ *Differentiate yourself.* You can set yourself apart from competing salespeople by demonstrating professionalism, concern for your client's particular sales and marketing problems, and desire to help your client accomplish his goals.

✦ *Summarize and reinforce sales points.* If you've won over your prospect in a face-to-face or phone conversation, a letter can help you sustain the momentum.

✦ *Speak to several parties at once.* You can tell your client what happened at that meeting with his agency. You can inform several decision makers of new changes in circulation. Written sales communication can bring all the players up to speed and present the sales process as a smooth, straightforward operation that you control.

✦ *Increase the number and frequency of sales contacts.* After all, you tell your clients how crucial frequency is to their advertising success. Frequent contact by letter proves your point.

✦ *Advance the action of the sale.* Letters allow you to make new sales points or provide the data your clients need to move closer to a buying decision.

✦ *Recommend specific action.* If your client is at the "I'll think about it" stage, letters can stimulate action. You can suggest a next meeting, recommend your publication to other decision-makers, determine an ad schedule, or select ad copy.

✦ *Put agreements on the record.* If you've got an oral "okay" for a schedule, or simply need to clarify a point, letters can eliminate confusion and establish confirmation.

TYPES OF CORRESPONDENCE

Many salespeople, if they write letters at all, tend to restrict them to follow-ups or thank yous. Both are important, but don't limit yourself! Letters can assist you at just about any point in the sales process—when making introductions, during presentations, confirming orders, you name it. Think of letters as tangible reminders of you and your magazine. You want them out there often and working!

Letters can assist you at just about any point in the sales process...

People most often forget those great points you made on your last sales call. Studies show that only 50 percent of information is retained after 48 hours; only 10 percent after 30 days. So, if you're calling on each of your clients an average of four times a year, you can expect that they won't remember much about your magazine and market between visits.

Letters, notes, clippings and other correspondence fill the void left in your absence. They keep your magazine in the forefront of your prospect's mind until that next personal call.

Here's how letters work. Let's say you sell for a magazine called *Potato Farmer*. You're interested in pursuing a new client that sells fertilizer. In addition to your calls and requests for appointments, consider sending the following letters:

The "teaser." Assume Ms. Warren of Acme Fertilizer has a rock-solid secretarial screen. Not a single call has come back to you. Your weapon—the "teaser"—is a short introductory letter that grabs her attention, casts out your sales bait and closes with the next sales step: an appointment.

A good teaser letter is not about your magazine. It's about *your client's marketing needs*. In other words, you can use the teaser to say: "Your company is ranked 10th in buyer recognition among small-time farmers in the Midwest. Think what would happen to your sales if you were ranked 5th! Let's talk about getting that position. I'll call you for a convenient time."

Hint that much more information is available for the price of a conversation. But don't send the media kit. Not yet! Save it for when you know your prospect wants to hear more. Otherwise, she might get back to you with, "We've read your information and we're not interested."

The media kit. Good news! Ms. Warren's decided to speak with you by telephone. Now it's time to confirm your client's marketing needs. Following that initial conversation you can introduce the benefits of advertising in your magazine.

Your goal, of course, is to get that all-important appointment for a face-to-face presentation. But Ms. Warren wants more information about your publication first.

At this point, your media kit can support the next stage of the selling process. But don't just mail a standard folder and rate card. Customize it! Arrange your audit statements, rate cards, charts and graphics so the most important materials get the client's attention first. Attach Post-It notes that refer to Ms. Warren's market. Highlight circulation data to which you've alluded in your teaser.

Most important, reinforce your sales benefits with a strong cover letter:

> *You know that increased recognition is critical to capturing market share in the highly competitive fertilizer industry. You also know that small farmers, who buy more than 65 percent of fertilizer today, are your best prospects—and the hardest to reach.*
>
> *Here's how we can help. Meet your new customers! You'll reach more high-growth small farms through* Potato Farmer *than through any other magazine. Collectively, our readers own more acreage than the entire state of Massachusetts, and last year spent more than $1.5 million on fertilizer. Take a look at our circulation data. You'll discover exactly the customers that are looking for your product!*

You might think of your cover letter as an "executive summary" of the kit. Make it work hard! Don't wade through your entire selling story; instead, *highlight* the benefits that would most interest your prospect. Keep it short and punchy. It's this letter that makes Ms. Warren decide whether or not she wants to look at the rest of the kit.

The "leave-behind." When you finally meet Ms. Warren face-to-face, you'll have a lot of tools at hand during your presentation. You'll have intriguing visuals, charts, overheads, and a great market analysis.

Arrange your audit statements, rate cards, charts and graphics so the most important materials get the client's attention first.

328

But one tool will ensure that Ms. Warren remembers you after you've left. That's where the "leave-behind" comes in. It's a kind of mini-sales presentation: a summary of your major points coupled with the appropriate graphics. Although you don't want to distract your prospect with too many materials, the leave-behind is great to hand out as you make your closing remarks. You might even want to tell Ms. Warren during the presentation that you'll be leaving information for further review.

The sales follow-up. This letter, mailed after the presentation, incorporates what you've learned in the sales meeting about Acme with Ms. Warren. Here, you remind her of the points of your discussion and tie them into an additional sales push: "Your desire to increase distribution among Eastern farmers makes a lot of sense. An article in *Potato Farmer* reported that potato acreage and yield will double in this region during the next four years. Acme is in a prime position to capitalize on this expansion. Here's how we can help."

The sales proposal. More specific than the follow-up letter, the sales proposal actually outlines advertising programs. You might want to propose, for instance, that Ms. Warren run a special six-time full-page, four-color campaign to follow up on a direct-mail drop. You could even suggest special positions, discounts, and merchandising offers: "With a six-time schedule, you not only receive a 15 percent discount, but preferred use of our subscriber data and research."

Be careful about spelling out specific approaches if you haven't been in touch with your client's agency. After all, you'll lose if you suggest running full-page ads when the agency might actually be considering spreads!

If you're not clear about what to propose, talk about your client's need for a *dominant, consistent* communications effort. You might, for instance, show your client tear sheets of your competitor's campaigns. You could suggest how the competition has effectively used advertising to gain higher recognition in key markets: "Acme's need to move up will likely require a bigger communications effort. Clearly, your agency specializes in working out the details, but here are some general options for making your advertising big, bold and consistent." You can then list suggested approaches without irritating the agency.

IN ADDITION TO LETTERS...

Written correspondence doesn't stop at the word processor. Besides sales letters, you can send clients the following:

Notes and cards. These are great for shorter, faster and more personal communication: "Really enjoyed the lunch," "Congratulations on your promotion," "Great cocktail party," or "Thanks for your business." Some salespeople—like those at *Rock & Dirt* and *Trade A Plane*—even have customized note cards printed.

A customized card can help keep you in touch and out in front.

Personally, I also like to keep on hand both fun and serious greeting cards for such events as birthdays, anniversaries, career promotions, illnesses, or just general coping. Personal correspondence can strengthen your relationship with your client. If you are careful to be tactful, this can give you an advantage over your competitor.

A nice way to send congratulations.

News and industry tidbits. If *Industry Week* runs a small piece on trends in farming equipment, send it along to your client! Include a handwritten note, or news clippings that not only show that you're on top of the market, but that you're also keeping your client's interests in mind.

Marketing newsletters. Often, today's publishers produce newsletters, fax reports or online services for advertising clients. Most are designed to help clients sell product, keep them informed of the magazine's activities and demonstrate the magazine's industry expertise. In fact, some salespeople produce such reports on their own! That kind of initiative is bound to impress advertisers.

Direct-mail promotion. With an up-to-date promotion list, your magazine can regularly send advertisers timely, intriguing and useful information about the publication, including new research, special issues, or updates on industry events. One promotion, for example, could introduce a new industry-awards issue, outlining who'll be reading it and how your client could use it. Perhaps another mailing could summarize a highly technical article on, say, topsoil replenishment, indicating how Acme Fertilizer could benefit from the trend. To double the impact, just add a personal note when you mail it to your sales clients.

331

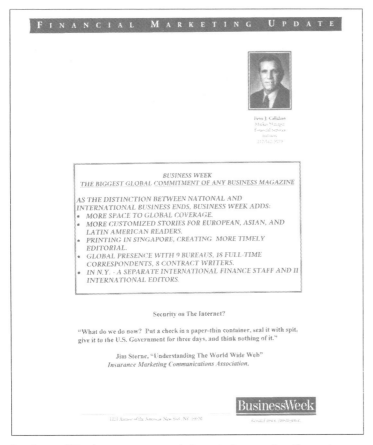

Business Week *creates newsletters to keep advertisers in touch with the magazine's features.*

And don't shy away from gimmicks. They can score you extra points, or at least get advertisers to open the envelope. *Pizza Today* once sent out a pizza-scented promotion that was perhaps the next best thing to the pizza itself.

Problem-solving letters. You can use these to untangle client/agency problems, billing snafus, and other details. If you've got significant news, such as "The printer lost your mechanicals," call first; then put it in writing.

Advertising contracts, letters of agreement, and insertion orders. You can't pass the finish line of the sale and forget a signed agreement. Use the fax machine to confirm verbal agreements immediately and speed along the orders.

332

WHEN TO CALL? WHEN TO WRITE?

For each prospect, you need to alternate calls and writing, but the order in which you do it is up to you. Your strategy will depend mostly your own comfort level and intuition. If you'd just met a friendly prospect at a show, you'd probably feel comfortable making a call for that first appointment, then sending a follow-up letter. But if you're pursuing a more formal, elusive client, you might want to drop a teaser or promotion piece to warm him up before you make that call.

It takes some skill to properly follow up a letter with a call. When you do call, first confirm that your prospect received the letter. If she tells you she didn't receive, read, or remember your mail, don't stop selling. Many prospects use "I didn't get it" as a brush-off.

The best way to handle it is to just keep moving through the sales conversation. You might say, "When you *do* have an opportunity to read my letter, you'll see that I've outlined how we can reach your target market." Then tell her what you said in the letter, but keep it in a conversational tone.

Don't let too much time go by before making your follow-up call. Assume a first-class letter arrived in two days, and was probably read within the week it arrived.

Moreover, keep following up your calls with more letters. A typical correspondence might go like this:

1. Teaser letter

2. Phone call to confirm receipt of letter and say, "Let's take a few minutes to review some other market data you'll be interested in looking over."

3. Media kit

4. Phone call or face-to-face

5. Written sales proposal

6. Follow-up call

Different sales reps may prefer different approaches. Your personal policy, for instance, might be to make that first contact by phone. Find whatever sequence works most effectively for you.

The point is that selling must be done *sequentially*. Every phone call, every letter, should confirm agreement at each stage in the process before moving on. In other words, you don't send a media kit to a client if she hasn't agreed with your assessment of her marketing needs, and you don't create a sales proposal if she hasn't confirmed that your publication's features match the benefits she's looking for.

Finally, don't get overly dependent on written communication, no matter how persuasive. These materials should support your personal sales efforts, *not substitute for them.*

Consider one salesperson I met who told me he had problems closing sales. When I asked him to describe his sales process, I realized the problem. He would go though the probing and discovery process with his prospect by phone and follow up with a media kit. His next call would begin by asking the prospect if he or she had received the information. When the prospect said yes, this salesperson would attempt to close the sale immediately.

Obviously, not only did this salesperson have a lot to learn about being a marketing consultant, he'd wrongly decided that written materials could sell the magazine better than a professional salesperson could!

19

"DOS" and "DON'TS" for EFFECTIVE SALES LETTERS

"The most valuable of all talents is that of never using two words when one will do."
—Thomas Jefferson (1743-1826)

❖ ❖ ❖

When it comes to the "dos" and "don'ts" of writing good letters, one finds no shortage of letter "don'ts." To demonstrate this point, allow me to reprint for you an all-too-typical sales letter, borrowed from the files of Greenwich, Conneticut-based advertising sales consultant Jack Sweger:

Dear Al:

Enclosed please find our media kit and a current copy of Trends Magazine.

Trends reaches 200,000 stockbrokers, security analysts and investment brokers in the U.S. It is published by Richardson & Smith Publishing Company, the second largest publisher of special interest consumer magazines and business publications.

As we discussed, our ten editors all have practical experience in the investment market. In fact, Art Jones, the senior editor, was a senior vice-president with Lynch & Fenner, the largest stockbroker in the country. He brings twenty years of experience to us.

A recent survey by Media Associates shows that Trends has outstanding readership. Three out of four readers surveyed said they read the magazine from cover to cover! Also, it has six readers per copy.

Trends has grown every year in advertising acceptance. Ten years ago we carried 305 ad pages. This year we'll run 2,800 pages. This is proof of how advertisers view the magazine.

If you have any further questions, please do not hesitate to call on me.

Cordially,

Bill Smith
Trends Magazine

Why does this letter make one's eyelids flutter? It embodies several classic letter-writing mistakes of which most salespeople are guilty. Consider the following:

It's about the magazine, not the client. This letter smacks of narcissism: it's about me, me, me, not you, you, you. Good salespeople don't sell the product; they sell the *customer*. They embrace the client's goals and they work for solutions to the client's needs. The magazine is merely the tool they use to help their customer meet their goals. In this letter, the magazine is the star, not the client.

It's generic. To which advertiser is the letter addressed? Who knows? Frankly, it wouldn't matter if it were mailed to a bank advertiser or a pizza advertiser. Beyond the salutation, this letter does not address the recipient as an individual. For that reason alone it could end up in the garbage heap.

It doesn't address the client's needs. Surely Bill Smith must have had a conversation or probing session with this client. Otherwise, why send a media kit? But there's no indication that the salesperson learned one thing about the client's marketing needs; never mind addressed them in this letter.

A good letter mentions features *only in the context of providing benefit to the advertiser.*

It's about features, not benefits. Who really cares that editor Art Jones has 20 years' investment experience? What does it mean that *Trends* has six readers per copy? This letter merely lists the features of the publication without any concern, or even understanding, of how they apply to advertiser needs. A good letter mentions features *only in the context of providing benefit to the advertiser.*

It's all over the place. What exactly is the point of this letter? Is it to brag about editorial expertise? Is it to show advertiser acceptance? This sales rep is throwing everthing at the client, hoping something will make an impression and stick.

It doesn't ask the client to "do" anything. Sales letters must move the sale along. They must take the client to the next action step in the sale, whether that's setting up a business lunch, confirming agreement on marketing needs, smoothing the way toward a presentation, or simply committing to a future conversation. This letter, closing with a feeble "do not hesitate to call," basically leaves the client shrugging. Since this sales rep clearly is kicking back and passively waiting for a call, why should the client bother?

STEPS TO GOOD LETTERS

It's easy enough to pick apart bad sales letters. Just about anyone can be a good critic! What's tougher, though, is knowing what goes into a good letter, and then developing good letter-writing habits.

Let's look at the four steps for writing good sales letters:

1. *Know your reason for writing*

2. *Know how to back it up*

3. *Know what the reader wants*

4. *Know how to organize it*

Let's look at how each of these works.

Know why you're writing. Figure out the purpose of writing your particular letter. Do you want to talk about the client's desire to increase sales in the Pacific Northwest? Do you want to clarify a discussion of rates? Do you want to introduce the new editor?

Whatever your theme, stick with it, and make sure it *addresses your client's needs.* If you want to make a point about circulation, tie that point directly to your client's need to boost sales among upscale homeowners. If you want to introduce a new editor, show how the direction of the magazine can help your client fulfill his marketing vision. Don't mention editorial awards, new columns or other features that have nothing to do with your point. Stay focused on the *specific benefit* for which your client is looking, or on the *specific action* you want the client to take.

Abraham Lincoln was once asked how long his legs were. His reply was, "Long enough to reach the ground." Your letter should be long enough to express your main purpose, whether that's upgrading the client's program or drawing attention to new research. Don't stretch it out with irrelevant details.

Back it up. If you're writing about targeted circulation, have the facts at hand. Do you have specific data about your readers or have any relevant anecdotes about their buying habits? Can you specify how this information will serve your client's sales needs? For instance: "We've got 75,000 pedigree dog owners that can boost your product's current recognition factor by 10 percent."

Be careful, however, with numbers. Use as few as possible but use them when necessary to clarify vague statements, such as "We have the cream of the crop" or "We look forward to being a part of the Acme marketing team."

Appeal to your reader. No matter what the topic of your letter, it's your job to make it exciting. By that I mean you have to grab the reader from the first sentence and hold him to the last.

Maybe your prospect needs to build enthusiasm around a new product he'll be introducing at the industry trade show. Trade show issues are commonplace, and so are letters that promote them. Most of them simply announce that clients can find their customers at the show, and therefore should advertise in the show issue. Since that's obviously not much of a grabber, it's your job to make your letter *sell* the trade show issue.

How? Play to your client's needs! Show how you can *presell* prospects on his new line. Here's how Sweger suggests you can grab a prospect's interest in the first paragraph:

> *$250,000! One quarter of a million dollars! That was what the average company paid to exhibit at last year's Chemical Expo Show. Money spent in hopes of getting prospects with current and/or future equipment needs to come to their booths, talk to their salespeople, and learn about their new planning systems—sometime during the fourteen hours of exhibit time. It's a real crapshoot!*
>
> *Here's how we can help you improve the odds. The fact is, 82 percent of show-goers pre-plan their show contacts before arriving at the show. Getting on their itinerary requires a pre-show contact...and our pre-show issue can do just that.*

Take care to use the language of the industry, incorporating buzz words and industry shorthand. And try to visualize your prospect, whether you've actually met him or not. Think about his personality; about the kind of relationship you have. Some prospects may require a more formal approach than others.

Organize your points. I'll address this more fully in the next chapter. But keep in mind that clear organization helps the reader focus on your message. You might want to outline your letter before you begin, or write it first and *then* outline it to check for gaps in logic. Many letter-writers also like to use bullets for clarity.

Even sentences can be organized for maximum impact. As an experiment, try underlining the key words in the letter. Do they hide behind long, empty phrases?

> *If you decide to take advantage of our advertising program, we <u>guarantee</u> you'll reach more <u>buyers</u> in our magazine than in any other.*

Move your most powerful words to the beginning of the letter, the beginning of paragraphs, and the beginning of sentences:

> *We guarantee you'll reach the buyers you need—more buyers than in any other magazine."*

Make it easy for your reader to find out what he needs to know.

POOR LETTER, REVISED

Now that we've gone over the steps for writing good letters, let's look at how one might revise that first brain-numbing missive. Here's how Sweger rewrote the *Trends* letter for maximum impact:

> *Dear Al:*
>
> *You must be doing a lot of things right! True Copy's sales are booming. Equally interesting was your comment that you were looking for new market opportunities for your latest Speedi-Print Model 200.*
>
> *A recent research report forecasts that the stockbroker-analyst*

---

market will double its buying of two-side copiers in the next 36 months. True Copy's Model 200 seems like an appropriate contender for a disproportionate share of that spending. Here's how we can help:

1) Your advertising in Trends *reaches some 200,000 broker-analysts actively using and influencing copier purchases.*

2) Your sales message will share pages with one of the most experienced, hands-on group of editors writing in this business. Art Jones, our new chief editor, was the former Senior VP Operations at Lynch and Fenner. He knows this market and its readers' needs.

3) Your advertising gets maximum exposure. Trends *has again proved itself the leader in readership. A new study shows three out of four readers go cover-to-cover with every issue.*

4) You'll be in good company. Other advertisers already know these values. They've made it possible for Trends *to hit another record year in advertising pages.*

You'll also be interested in some new market data on copier buying patterns. Let's review these reports together, Al. I'll call Monday to check your schedule.

Cordially,
Bill Smith

Take a look at what this letter does right:

It's specific. From the first sentence, the salesperson refers to the client's company by name, flatters the client on great sales, and even uses the client's very own words ("your comment that you were looking for new marketing opportunities") in the first paragraph. Does that get the client's attention? You bet.

It addresses needs. The client's own words state that he's looking for new marketing opportunities for the company's latest copier. Here, the salesperson homes in on those needs by discussing copier needs

341

among stockerbroker-analysts—who just happen to be the magazine's readers.

It's about the client, not the magazine. Notice how the writer has inserted "you" throughout the letter. That little pronoun not only engages the client, but subtly suggests that he may have something to gain from reading this letter. By speaking directly to the client and addressing his needs, this salesperson has guaranteed the client's attention.

It's about benefits, not features. Notice that every feature of the magazine—its veteran editors, its increased advertising—is presented *only in the context of giving benefit to the client.* Why is it important that Art Jones has stockbroker experience? "He knows this market and its readers' needs." Why does it matter that three of four readers read cover-to-cover? "Your advertising gets maximum exposure." This letter gives the client specific reasons to care about the magazine's features.

It's to the point. This sales rep is focusing on his target. He states right up front that his client needs to find new marketing opportunities for his latest copier model. He then responds to that need by showing exactly how each feature of the magazine—editorial expertise, reader loyalty—helps to accomplish the client's goal. Every point finds its target, cleanly penetrating the client's defenses.

It summons the client to take action. Look at the last paragraph. Here, the sales rep has dangled some tasty bait ("new market data on copier buying patterns") to lure the client's final attention. Even better, the sales rep offers an invitation ("Let's review these reports together") to move the client to take action. Instead of leaving the client on the hook with "Please call if you need more information," the salesperson has already swept in the next selling phase of committing to face-to-face contact. And, by specifically stating "I'll call Monday to check your schedule," the salesperson makes an assumptive close—a close that assumes that the client will want to get together to hear more.

Using the same information, this final version presents a much more compelling story to tell the client. Look how it follows the four steps to good letters:

1. The writer knows the reason for writing. The salesperson isn't mumbling, "Enclosed please find our media kit." Right from the start it's clear that his reason for writing is to increase his client's new copier sales.

2. The writer backs it up. Once the salesperson has established his client's need, he backs his solution (magazine advertising) with survey data, reader data, and critical editorial information. He uses only enough information to make his point, no more. Each feature forges a link in the chain of client benefits.

3. The letter appeals to the reader. "You must be doing a lot of things right!" the letter states up front. This letter pulls in the client from the first sentence, and the word "you" throughout makes the client the star.

4. The letter is organized. Each selling point in the letter logically follows the next. Just as in a presentation, the salesperson first establishes the client's needs, and then outlines the benefits and features that play into that need. The short paragraphs, bulleted points and concise length get the selling job done fast.

Most important, the letter sets the premise for the next call, and ultimately the final sale.

In the next chapter I'll show you the nuts and bolts of how to structure letters for maximum selling power.

20

STRUCTURING
YOUR LETTER

"Don't write merely to be understood.
Write so that you cannot possibly be misunderstood."
—Robert Louis Stevenson (1850-1894)
Scottish novelist, essayist and poet

❖ ❖ ❖

Like a good sales call, a well-structured letter commands your client's attention, holds his interest to the end, and then gets him to take action.

To write a letter that does all that, I've found it's best to follow the steps outlined by L. E. Frailey, author of *Handbook of Business Letters* (Prentice-Hall, 1989). Good letters, Frailey states, take readers through four steps: *attention, interest, desire,* and *action.* Moreover, letters need to take these steps in sequence. Obviously, there's no point trying to get someone to take action when you haven't given them any desire to do so.

In brief, as Frailey points out, you get a reader's *attention* with a strong beginning, one that flatters or teases the reader. You then establish *interest* and *desire* by describing benefits and appeals. And you conclude with *action* by closing with a compelling finish, one that acts on the desire you've created in the reader's mind.

It's no easy task. Your letters, after all, go to politely indifferent readers who are well-versed in objections and reasons not to buy. They're smart, defensive, and turned off by high pressure. Try to persuade your reader too soon—often the case with sales letters—and you've got a frightened or irritated reader. Approach too softly, and your reader won't catch on. Either way, your letter ends up in the trash.

The trick is to lead your prospect from point to point, paragraph by paragraph, subtly weaving a story that creates interest and overcomes objections. To do it well, Frailey also recommends what he calls the *Star-Chain-Hook* formula. It's the framework of good communication; a skeleton that can hold up any type of letter—teaser, follow-up or sales proposal.

The STAR, CHAIN and HOOK Method

Briefly, the *Star* is the opening that gets a reader's attention. The *Chain* outlines compelling sales appeals and benefits. And the *Hook*, as it implies, closes the letter and gets your reader ready for action.

The following chart outlines the process. Note how the Star-Chain-Hook formula moves a reader inevitably from "indifferent" and "cold" to "hot" and "needs only a push."

S T A R	Indifferent Cold Mildy attentive	**REASONS ARE** *RATIONAL*
C H A I N	Casual interest Lukewarm Deeper interest Visualization of benefit Begins to want Desire increases Objections pushed aside	
H O O K	Ready for action Hot Needs only a push	**REACTIONS ARE** *EMOTIONAL*

The Star, Chain and Hook push through a client's defenses and get him to take action.

Sound hard to believe? If you look at most sales letters, it is. Most are written in a hurry and end up being incomplete. They expect and ask for action while the reader is still cold or only luke-warm. They disregard the need for readers to change from *rational* to *emotional* reactions. They're the equivalent of the salesperson who starts his close as soon as he hears the prospect received the media kit!

Take some time and look over the following letters and examples. If you can use Star-Hook-Chain well in your initial letter, you can save yourself a lot of time, calls and letters that would otherwise make up for one that didn't do the job.

The Star

Right at the outset, your job is to make the reader the star. Let him know that he has won favor; entice him to read on.

In fact, why not quote his own words? As Sweger points out, most people think of their own words as priceless prose. Quoting them back, particularly in the opening, is the quickest route to their attention. Consider this example:

> *Dear Bob:*
>
> *You made an interesting statement during our get-together last week. You said that today's machinery market was the toughest, most competitive sell that you've experienced in your 25-year career. And that it takes smarter, more aggressive marketing to be successful. I agree!*

You can then move on to discuss the market trends, opportunities and the growing role of magazine advertising in marketing products—keeping your eye on how your own magazine can help.

What else works for an opening? You might refer to your client's new promotion, upcoming birthday, or other personal reference. You could note your client's current position in the marketplace, or his current sales. The point is, your reader won't be interested in your magazine unless he first knows you're interested in *him*.

347

It helps, of course, to start with the words "you" and "yours." That automatically personalizes whatever point you make: "You know the importance of good marketing: That's why you're operating one of the top 20 manufacturing plants in the bedspring industry."

You can add power to that appeal by mentioning names of people in the company or agency. You might also name the products or services the company provides. Even better, drop in a titillating industry tidbit to get attention. It's important to sound knowledgeable, like this marketing representative of *NOW* magazine:

> *You'll undoubtedly agree that having a dynamic music retailer like Tower Records in Toronto can only mean good news for music-hungry consumers.*

Other attention-getters might include industry quotes. Here's one from the advertising manager of *State Legislatures*:

"No man's life, liberty or property is safe while the legislature is in session." Gideon J. Tucker, 1866. The writer then acknowledges Tucker's extreme point of view and reminds the reader, *You know the power of reaching state and federal lawmakers.*

Industry knowledge is another "star-maker." This shows the reader that you share his concerns and know his market. A salesperson for *Pennsylvania Medicine* reminds the reader of changes in healthcare that may affect his marketing strategy:

> *As you know, the past few years have seen many changes in the structure of healthcare services and institutions. Everywhere, hospitals are reassessing their operations, reorganizing their services, and responding more aggressively to their community's changing needs.*
>
> - *Are physicians aware of your services?*
>
> - *Do they recommend your institution?*
>
> - *Do they view your hospital facility as a progressive institution?*

> Pennsylvania Medicine *wants to help you to let them know about you!"*

Finally, you can get a reader's attention by speaking in his voice; proving you can identify with his passion. Here's a strong start from a sports enthusiast-magazine, *Bowhunter*:

> *That moment's here! You've been waiting the entire year! The excitement grows, the huge buck is coming within range! Everything is perfect, he steps out at fifteen yards: broadside! You draw, anchor and . . . WAIT! Don't forget to AIM..."*

The letter then addresses the importance of "aiming" for the right advertising audience.

Any number of methods can make your own reader a star. Put yourself in his shoes. What marketing issues does he worry about? What excites him? What appeals to him? Use probing to get a sense of what you need to say from the start to get him to keep reading.

The Chain

The Chain is the body of your letter where you present the benefits of doing business with your publication. Here's where you arouse the reader's deeper interest and build desire to work with you.

Often, this part of the letter can look quite literally like a "chain." Take a look this letter from a title I'll call *Modern Footwear*. Each paragraph states a *benefit* to the reader ("Your ad reaches more buyers"), followed by a corresponding *feature* ("the highest circulation to retail jewelers").

> *Here are some strong reasons for making* Modern Footwear *your vehicle to reach retailers:*
> * *Your ad reaches more buyers.* Modern Footwear *has the highest circulation to shoe retailers—31,355. Higher than* JCK, *higher than* National Shoe Buyer.

349

- *Your ad is in a superior environment.* Modern Footwear *has won more awards for editorial excellence from the American Business Press in the last nine years than all our competitors combined.*

- *Your ad looks better.* Modern Footwear *leads the way in quality graphic design, photography and paper stock.*

- *You get more value for your ad dollar.* Modern Footwear *has the lowest rates and the lowest cost-per-thousand to reach the shoe retailer. Lower than* JCK, *lower than* National Shoe Buyer.

- *Your ad in* Modern Footwear *produces sales leads that build your business.*

At times, you might be tempted to create your Chain simply by presenting a laundry list of facts and statistics. Don't! By doing so, you risk a big "So what?" from your reader. Take this example from one sporting magazine:

- *Guaranteed circulation - 178,000*

- *The only audited archery publication*

- *Over 600,000 total readership*

- *#1 read archery magazine since 1971*

- *94% of readers look to ads for buying information!*

A better Chain would list what each of those statistics *mean to the reader.* If the letter writer knows, for instance, that the advertiser is looking for a quality publication, she might have emphasized the magazine's number-one status first, and described what makes the publication a leader.

A Chain, incidentally, doesn't have to touch on *every* benefit your magazine offers. If the purpose of your letter is simply to reinforce a particular sales benefit, like new research, you could create a Chain that specifically lists how that research would help your advertiser better reach his market. Look again at the revised *Trends* letter in the previous chapter to see how its chain of benefits played into the client's specific marketing needs.

The Hook

The Hook closes your letter persuasively. Its job is to get the reader to take a positive buying step. A letter with a weak Hook is like a sales call with an ineffective close.

Like a close, the Hook indicates what you want your reader to do. Your letter's goal may be to gain an ad schedule, or it may simply be to get your prospect to read your subscriber data, or return your phone call, or to recommend your magazine to an agency.

Also, like a good close, a good Hook is specific and positive, avoiding hedge words like "if" and "should." "Let's reserve space for you," for instance, is the kind of phrase that moves readers to act (provided, of course, you've already whet their appetite to buy).

What's important in the Hook is that *you*, the salesperson, continue the selling process. Don't leave it up to your client, waving him off with "call me for more information." Instead, keep the ball in your court. Say, "I'll call you next Wednesday to get your reaction to this idea. We can plan the next step from there."

Consider, for instance, this letter to the Toronto Argonauts Football club. Here, the marketing representative from *NOW* magazine concludes with a strong request to meet:

> The Hot Summer Guide *presents some unique opportunities for the ARGOs to score a touchdown in ticket sales. I will call you early next week to set an appointment.*

A letter from *Family Circle* to an ad agency closes with a request for a recommendation to a client:

351

> When these first ads run, your skeptical client will want to see action from the ad. Can you risk not using the leader in response?"
>
> Steve, good luck with your planning. I'll be in touch on Monday to discuss your decision.

Notice how the conclusion, in each case, makes a strong *assumption* that the reader will *want* to take action. That's the power of a good hook. It's not a plea; it's assurance that both the writer and reader are on the same wavelength. As with a good presentation, it takes confidence and sincerity to pull it off!

Here are some ways you can create your Hook:

✦ *Introduce an idea.* Balance the major idea of your letter with a new thought: "Let's talk about some ways our targeted circulation can work for you..."

✦ *Make a direct appeal.* Ask for the business. For example: "Let's reserve space for you in our January issue."

✦ *Make a prediction.* Here's one based on general economic trends: "According to the Index of Leading Indicators, the economy should be on a strong upswing next year. We're ready to help you make next year a winner!"

✦ *Use rhetorical questions:* "Can you really afford to ignore the buying power of architects?"

✦ *Refer back to opening comments.* Restate those all-important marketing needs and again note how your magazine can help.

✦ *End with a strong quotation.* Here's one that refers generally to the power of advertising: "Let us help you capture the market. In *The Art of War* Sun Tzu reminds us, 'When in difficult country, do not encamp. In country where high roads intersect, join hands with your allies.'"

✦ *Add a postscript.* We're all suckers for a good P.S. I like to use them to drop in another juicy point and create a sense of urgency.

352

◆ *Be brief!* As you conclude, ask yourself again what you want the reader to do or think about. Then state it concisely. Too many words distract from the main point and from your call for action.

It's hard to overestimate the power of a strong Hook—and a strong Star. Get both right and you can grab your reader, even if he skips the body of the letter. Remember, most readers fall under the doctrine of primacy and recency: People tend to remember beginnings and endings. Your Star and Hook may be the *only* part of your letter that the prospect reads.

PUTTING IT TOGETHER

Let's take a look at how all three elements—Star, Chain and Hook—can work together in a variety of letter styles.

The "Cold" Letter"

Granted, it's tough to write a cold letter to a prospect, particularly if you haven't even managed to get him on the phone for a little probing. What can you say to stimulate your prospect to answer your call? It's tempting, of course, to simply brag about your magazine and hope that your prospect will catch on. Take this example:

> *You'll find Convenience Store News to be the best medium for your sales message. Here's why:*
>
> • *We reach the largest available number of in-store retailers (114,000+)*
>
> • *We have the greatest circulation at the chain-headquarters level (27,000+)*
>
> • *We reach more independent operators than any other publication (33,000+)*
>
> *Please look over the enclosed materials. I'm sure you'll find that we will work hard on your behalf! I'm available to answer any of your questions. Please call me at...*

What's better in a cold letter—or in any sales letter, of course—is to *address marketing needs.* Even if you haven't yet spoken to your client, you can still touch on needs and benefits. And you can still use the Star-Chain-Hook formula to motivate your reader to act.

Here, for instance, is how the rewritten *Convenience Store News* letter might do it:

> *Like most marketers to convenience stores, you need to send your message to an enormous, fragmented—and very lucrative— retail segment with a tight budget. And you'll want creative, useful ideas for making your marketing dollars work harder for you.*

In this Star, the writer identifies with the reader's sales challenges. You can bet this salesperson knows that market fragmentation is a big issue in the convenience store industry, and one which *Convenience Store News* can help resolve.

The next two paragraphs comprise the *Chain*, detailing the publication's major benefits and features:

> Convenience Store News *delivers. For 23 years, we've been the #1 publication to this industry. And we want to be <u>your</u> marketing partner in successfully penetrating the c-store business with the most comprehensive circulation, plus readership and services no other magazine can reach.*
>
> *With* Convenience Store News, *you can:*
>
> - *Bring your message to the entire industry.* Convenience Store News *reaches the largest available number of c-store retailers (114,000+)*
>
> - *Reach decision-makers at the highest level in the business.* Convenience Store News *has the greatest circulation at the chain-headquarters level (27,000+)*
>
> - *Find retailers no other publication can bring you.* Convenience Store News *reaches more inde-*

> *pendent operators (single store owners) than any other publication (33,000+)*

The final paragraph—the *Hook*—asks the prospect to examine evidence of the magazine's strength. Here, the writer makes the assumption that the reader will want to go further, and will check out the sales materials and want to discuss them.

> *In short, your sales message deserves the most powerful, best-read medium in the convenience-store industry. But don't take our word for it—just refer to the enclosed Simmons Market Research study ("A Test of Strength") which shows precisely <u>why</u> readers prefer* Convenience Store News *and why advertisers prefer <u>our</u> readers.*
>
> *Thanks for reviewing the enclosed materials. I will call next week to answer any questions you may have.*

The Follow-up Letter

Let's face it. It's very tempting for most salespeople to get lazy on the follow-up letter, particularly if they're coming off a great face-to-face call. If they've already "bonded" with the client and sense that he's excited about advertising, they think, "Why not just keep that casual, friendly tone in the follow-up letter?" After all, the task of a follow-up letter is less to sell than to remind.

That's how most sales reps seem to think, anyway. And that's why we frequently see follow-up letters that look like this:

> *Thanks for meeting with me last week. I know you'll find that Bride's is exactly the publication to meet your marketing needs! Don't forget that we now offer wonderful marketing opportunities with "Bride's Choice," "New Essentials," and "Living Graciously at Home." I've enclosed materials for your perusal. Let us know which ones fit your needs!"*

Unfortunately, this letter does nothing to sustain the excitement of the sales call. Follow-up letters must *sell!* Don't forget that most people do not retain information. After one day your client will likely have forgotten half of what you discussed during your conversation. Worse, your client's enthusiasm will have faded as well. Rare is the client who becomes *more* enthused after the presentation than during.

So, follow-up letters must still follow the Star-Hook-Chain formula and they must reflect your conversation with the prospect. They must be customized for *that reader alone.* The letter must be clear about how your publication can solve your prospect's *specific* marketing problems.

Take a look at this effective follow-up letter from *Bride's* to a prospective advertiser, the maker of a line of high-quality cutlery. Notice how the writer compliments the company (Star), provides information specific to its product category (Chain), and concludes the letter with a warm and personal Christmas greeting—as well as (of course) the promise of a meeting (Hook).

It was a great pleasure to meet you last week. It's good news— and not all too common lately—that Henckels is doing so well.

As we discussed, your target consumers are used to acquiring <u>the best</u>, and that certainly doesn't stop when a young couple registers for housewares. Bridal couples are savvy consumers with a high recognition for quality, and Henckels Knives epitomize fine craftsmanship for real cooks.

Our Primary Reader Survey has shown that Bride's readers are <u>3 times more likely</u> to cook for pleasure than the average U.S. woman. Additionally, they spend $225 on cookware within a 12-month period. This is <u>beyond</u> what they may have already received from the $171 average of gift-givers.

As we both agree, the bridal market is important for Henckels as you are acquiring young couples who will build a collection of cooking knives. With this in mind, I was most pleased to

---

> *personally explain our new programs at* Bride's *for next year. "Bride's Choice," "New Essentials" and "Living Graciously at Home" have wonderful marketing programs for advertisers. We would be most pleased with the presence of Henckels in these high-profile programs. For your reference, I'm attaching the relevant details for each program.*
>
> *I hope that your budget for next year will include* Bride's, *and I will be happy to develop a strong bridal marketing program for Henckels through our Creative Services department. Within the bridal market, our in-store event list is unbeatable. Henckels will reach the bridal consumer first within our editorial environment, and second, through our store shows.*
>
> *I look forward to speaking to you next week. (In the meantime, I'm sure <u>all</u> your Henckels knives are ready to carve your Christmas feast!)*

LETTER KILLERS

Before you send out your next sales letter, check it against the following list. If you spot any of these "letter killers," take another shot at it. You only get one chance to make a good first impression!

"The usual" first graph. Try not to sound like every other salesperson. I've read hundreds of letters from advertising salespeople, and most of them begin with some version of the following:

> *Thank you for your interest in* National Business Magazine. *I have enclosed a media kit for your consideration and trust that once you have reviewed the material, you will see the many sales benefits our advertisers have realized.*

That's generic and boring. Be specific! Put your client first. What are his needs? What does he want to hear that will make him take three minutes from his packed schedule to pay attention to your magazine?

If you put some thought into that opening graph—the Star—you're halfway home to the close.

A laundry list. It seems most salespeople just can't wait for an excuse to get into their magazine data: "We have the biggest circulation among pet-store retailers," blah, blah, blah. Resist! Don't tell your reader everything that's in your media kit.

> *It was nice speaking with you today. Please find enclosed the current media kit of* XYZ *magazine that I promised to send to you today. Included is advertising information on current rates, publishing schedule and mechanical specifications, as well as circulation facts on newsstand distribution, subscriptions and demographics of our readers.*

Who cares? Your reader is perfectly capable of rummaging through a media kit. Stick to the highlights! Remember, you have to build the *client's* interest. That means talking about needs and benefits *first*, then features.

The unknown magazine. Consider the following:

> Wisconsin Technician *has the most targeted circulation in the industry.*

Excuse me—what industry? Don't forget to *position* your magazine right away. Your prospect may not read your magazine, know about it or have heard of it. You can't afford to let him guess.

The professional blunder. Remember that whatever you put in writing—especially in a fax—may be read by people other than the ones you addressed. Be discreet!

A client of mine once asked me for new agency suggestions. I happily obliged—in writing—since his current agency was blocking our business. Guess what? His current agent evidently read my letter while in the advertiser's office. He swore to me he'd never recommend our publication to his dying day. (And he didn't.)

The veiled insult. "You're shortchanging your sales team by not advertising in our publication." How would *you* like to be told how inept you are? Take a more positive approach: "Advertise with us and your sales team will make your investment grow."

Sometimes, however, a well-worded "caution" can carry a lot of weight with the right client. Consider, for instance: "Your salespeople are being blind-sided by the competition—and they don't even know it! Here's what's happening..." You can then go on to list how your client's competitor has taken more ad space than your client, or how it has invested more budget into marketing programs. Then, of course, you can recommend your client increase his own exposure to stay ahead.

Be careful, though. A strongly worded caution can sound a lot more like a veiled insult than you'd like. Advise your client—don't snipe.

Exaggerations. "Our publication gives you the only chance you'll ever have to triple your sales." Really? This kind of grandiose posturing invites skepticism. Don't weaken your argument by soapboxing.

Bullying. "Your right to first refusal on the inside front cover expires at midnight on Tuesday. If you do not respond by that time, we will be forced to release that position to your biggest competitor." Only weaklings succumb to threats. Don't underestimate your advertiser's intelligence.

Competitor abuse. "No doubt you've heard Magazine B's annual special issue was a big bust!" Guess what? Your client might have bought into that special issue, or seriously considered it. Even if he hadn't, such comments sound weak. Take the high road. Stick to your client's own needs and strengths.

Carnival barking. "Our publication will out-sell your salespeople and astonish you with more buyers than you ever thought you'd see in a lifetime." A first cousin to exaggeration. Don't make promises you can't keep.

Too many passive verbs. "The results will be seen in increased sales." That's a slow, boring way to make your point. Give your sentences actions verbs and subjects: "You'll see the results in increased sales."

Redundancies. "Your ad is in close proximity to the special section." You might be tempted to dress up your points with redundancies (like "close proximity") and unnecessary adjectives ("very" or "really"). Resist. Such padding weighs your letter down.

Too many words! "I would like to take this opportunity to congratulate you on the launching of your new line." Hone your sentences; keep the letter lean. In short, "Congratulations on your new launch."

Stilted language. "We regret to learn from your communication that you are unable to advertise in our publication, inasmuch as you found it to your advantage to accept our competitor's rate deal." You might feel that such stuffiness gives you an elitist bent, but it's pretentious and dull. Come across as a real person: "We're sorry to hear that you chose not to advertise with us."

If you're in doubt, read your letter aloud. If it doesn't *sound* natural, it isn't.

Poor sentence rhythm. Make your points concisely. Too many long sentences are confusing. Too many short ones are choppy. Vary your sentences to create a pleasing, natural rhythm. Again, judge your letter by reading it aloud.

Repetition. Try not to overuse "If . . ., then . . ." and other sentence crutches. Vary your structure.

Lack of transition. Don't jump from point to point as if randomly stacking groceries on a cabinet shelf. Make sure one idea leads smoothly to the next. Use transitions: "moreover," "clearly," "of course."

Poor spelling. With the array of excellent word-processing programs available, there's no reason for typos or grammatical errors in professional sales letters. Run each letter past spell-checkers and grammar-checkers. If your company has proofreaders, use them!

360

But don't rely on them entirely. The biggest spelling blunder: getting the client's name wrong. Double- and triple-check all names.

Too much emotion. *Never* send a letter you've written in anger or distress. At the very least, save it to reread when you've calmed down.

Lack of close. Don't forget to ask for action! And ask for it directly. Many sales letters hold forth on important benefits, only to back out the door with "if I can be of any assistance, please do not hesitate to call."

STILL DON'T LIKE TO WRITE?

Okay, I'm with you. You're a salesperson, not a writer. You probably take pride in your verbal skills, your ability to think fast, and your success in building personal and business relationships.

You may think that none of that has anything to do with writing. You're wrong. If you *write* as well as you *speak,* you're bound to be persuasive in your letters. Trust yourself! The more you worry over the gap between your verbal and writing skills, the less likely you'll come across strongly in your letter.

Besides, the real payoff in writing intelligent, persuasive letters is the *carry-over* effect. In other words, the better your sales letters, the more likely you'll give better presentations.

Think about it. Salespeople who write poor, disorganized, feature-ridden sales letters frequently give poor, disorganized, feature-ridden presentations. On the other hand, those who train themselves to write *benefits* into their letters find those benefits start showing up in their face-to-face sales practices.

Good letter-writing practice teaches a lot about what to do and expect in personal sales contacts. When you've got an intelligent, persuasive sales letter, you can always use it—again and again. Create form letters and letter modules. Many computer programs for account management let you customize letters, which means you can increase your number of written contacts and speed the sales process. (More about account management tools in the next chapter.)

Just remember to add your own specific, personal touch to *each* written contact. Don't let your letters become a litany of dull magazine facts. Keep selling as you write, and keep writing as you sell.

> Dear Mother and dad,
>
> I want on a camping trip. Whent you get back fome San Francisco put me up. I hat it hear.
>
> I Love
> Helen
>
> P. W.
>
> X X X X X X X X X X

Early example of effective letter writing. No Star, but the Chain and Hook ("I hate it here") certainly captured my parent's attention. My folks also believed that my "P. W." (for "please write") stood for "prisoner of war."

SECTION VI

TIME and TERRITORY MANAGEMENT

21

DON'T GET SWAMPED—GET ORGANIZED

"A definite goal and a specific deadline—
these are the keys to achieving one's destiny."
—Anonymous

❖ ❖ ❖

Let's face it: we've all had selling months when we had no idea where the time went. We didn't close enough sales and our ad pages were less than impressive. How did we manage to waste so much time with Client A, who only gave us three lousy pages? Why didn't we communicate more effectively with Client B, who dropped from a 12-time schedule to a 6-time schedule without warning? Why didn't we see that Client C was getting wooed by the competition?

Without some kind of sales management program, these months happen more often than we'd like. And if you're like most sales reps, you find getting organized about as much fun as getting your teeth drilled.

365

I can relate. I had always believed that a clean desk was the sign of a sick mind. So, once I started selling ad space, I let my work pile up and spill over my desk, then onto a chair, and then onto a second desk. With hundreds of clients to handle, I found that the price of my disorganized "sanity" was that I spent too much time looking for contacts and phone numbers and too little time doing my job: *selling*.

Eventually, I discovered six steps that solved my dilemma, making me a far more effective salesperson. They were the following:

1. *Situation analysis:* What's worth selling? Who's worth selling to?

2. *Identifying problems and opportunities:* What sales can I accomplish? What can get in my way?

3. *Ranking prospects and clients:* Who can best help me achieve my sales goals?

4. *Setting goals:* What are my specific sales goals?

5. *Implementing sales tools:* What can I use to help me achieve my sales goals?

6. *Sales control:* How well did I meet my sales goals?

It may take some time to adjust your schedule to the neater realities of sales management. Be patient! You didn't create that messy desk in one day, and you won't clean it up in one day, either. Think of it this way: every moment you spend prioritizing your time and energy is one less moment wasted on accounts that won't pay off for you.

For this chapter, let's assume you sell for a title called *Gems Today*, which covers the fine-jewelry marketplace. Here's how you might apply those six steps to your selling success.

STEP ONE:
SITUATION ANALYSIS

In magazine sales, I'd say selling is 65 percent preparation and 35 percent presentation. You can't present without prepping. So the first step in sales is to find out what's worth selling and to whom.

> In magazine sales, I'd say selling is 65 percent preparation and 35 percent presentation.

That's a *situation analysis*. You're assessing the opportunities in your territory and in your marketplace to establish where you are now and where you need to go.

To get there, you need to look at four areas:

- *Your marketplace*
- *Your readers*
- *Your competition*
- *Your prospects*

Let's look at each area in more detail.

1. *Your marketplace.* First, you need to find out the size and scope of the jewelry marketplace and how it may be changing. You should know not only how big the fine jewelry market is, but how many gem dealers are in the business, which are the largest, who their customers are and whether the market is shrinking or growing.

You also need information that can help you decide how to approach advertisers. For instance, is the industry dominated by two or three large wholesalers, or defined by a variety of smaller dealers with smaller ad budgets? Is it a mature or aging market, where your energy is best spent upgrading current accounts or going back to recalcitrant ones? Or, is a new consumer interest in unusual semi-precious stones creating opportunities to push for new accounts?

2. *Your readers.* After you've looked at your marketplace, take a look at your own audience—your client's customers. This step, after all, is the heart of the Advertising Syllogism: *Your prospects are our readers.* Who are these readers? How do they buy? What do they buy? Do they buy as individuals, or do they place orders by committee? Are they buying influencers rather than the buyers themselves? Do they buy mostly in certain seasons? Do you know size and sales volume of their companies?

3. *Your competition.* Now it's time to see how your competitors are doing in ad pages, revenues and circulation. This will give you some idea of whether the market is growing or declining. Don't forget to check editorial and graphics. A sudden improvement or redesign in this area might tell you whether your competition is gearing up for a strong advertising push.

4. *Your prospects.* Although you might have a general idea that the largest companies in your marketplace might be your best advertisers, you'll have to do some digging to pull together a full plate of potential clients—dealers, cutters, manufacturers, gold jewelry producers and wholesalers.

For that, you'll need sources. Listed below are places where you can find prospects, regardless of whether your magazine addresses textile mills, beauty parlors or car enthusiasts.

✦ *Ads in your competition.* Which advertisers do they have that you don't?

✦ *Promotion lists.* Are you familiar with everyone who receives information about your magazine?

✦ *Market advertising reports.* Have you listed all the advertisers in your market? Find out where they advertise, ad size, use of color, frequency, seasonality and products they display.

✦ *Exhibitor lists* at industry trade shows.

✦ *The Yellow Pages.*

✦ *The Standard Directory of Advertisers and the Standard Directory of Advertising Agencies.* These directories list advertisers, agencies and clients nationwide by product category, name and geographic area.

✦ *Editorial.* Maybe your magazine or a competitor's has a section on new product releases or industry news. Look for details that could turn up potential prospects.

✦ *Industry contacts.* Those you know in the industry can introduce or lead you to their peers and competitors.

Now, the results

Once completed, your situation analysis should list the critical information you need to weigh your selling opportunities. Let's assume your *Gems Today* analysis reveals the following:

◆ 75 percent of fine jewelry sales come from the top 17 percent of dealers and manufacturers.

◆ The top 17 percent of dealers deal only with precious gems and popular semi-precious stones.

◆ The precious gems market is large, but seems to have plateaued due to recession.

◆ Gold is still the leading consumer choice as a precious metal jewelry setting.

◆ Consumer interest in unusual semi-precious stones, like moonstone, has pushed that market from 10 percent to 22 percent of the fine-jewelry business, and continues to grow.

◆ Consumer interest is also rising in fine costume jewelry.

◆ The competitor, *Fine Jewelry Illustrated*, runs with 15 unusual-stone accounts and 12 costume-jewelry accounts that *Gems Today* doesn't have.

◆ A study of industry sources turned up another 22 small accounts in the unusual-stone dealer market

Now that you have a clear picture of your marketplace and sales opportunities, its time to move to the next phase of planning.

STEP TWO:
IDENTIFYING PROBLEMS AND OPPORTUNITIES

Clearly, you've spotted many changes in demand among *Gems Today* readers. How do you translate those changes into selling opportunities?

Once you've sifted through your findings, you might decide the following:

1. Top prospects for advertising might be larger gem dealers and larger gold dealers.

2. Diamond merchants, a mainstay of the publication, might fall off unless you can plan some kind of value-added advertising opportunity for them.

3. Given consumer trends, costume jewelry presents a selling opportunity as well. Though costume jewelry isn't a natural fit with your publication, a talk with your magazine's editor reveals that *Gems Today* intends to run a costume jewelry column or special issue.

Now you can try "plotting" these prospects by drawing a simple chart of concentric circles. Put your top-drawer prospects, the ones most worth your time and effort, in the center. Surround them with your strong potential prospects, and then with your less valuable ones.

Drawing a chart like this helps you determine how much time you should spend on each client.

In this case, you decide that even though diamond jewelry has plateaued in demand, the market is still big enough and stable enough to remain your primary target. Meanwhile, small gem dealers are still a relatively small market, but the growth in unusual

370

stones makes them worth pursuing as a secondary target. Finally, you decide costume jewelry manufacturers are a tertiary target. These accounts are primed for growth, but will never be a mainstay in a fine-jewelry publication.

Notice that you can target a prospect with any measurement tool you like—type of business, product category, sales potential or geographical region. If you work for a city lifestyle magazine, for instance, it could be that your strong, city retail accounts would fit in the center circle, regional accounts might occupy the second circle, and national advertisers—which are hardest to sell—might take third place. Though it sounds simplistic, this "bullseye" evaluation can help you size up your prospects quickly and organize your selling time.

Now, Try It Backwards

You might also try the "bottom-up" approach when putting together this end of the sales plan. That means *first* deciding which prospects are worth pursuing, based on the sources we've listed above. From there you can define your magazine's marketplace and universe.

Let's say that you decide to pursue costume jewelry advertisers primarily because you've spotted them in your competition. You can go back and perform your situation analysis to find out the strength of demand for costume jewelry among your readers and in your marketplace. Then, you are able to present your findings on the costume-jewelry market to prospects.

Once you've established your sales opportunities, you're now free to decide which prospects to pursue first. That's Step Three.

STEP THREE:
RANKING PROSPECTS AND CLIENTS

In planning your territory, your biggest concern is *account analysis*. Basically, this means identifying and ranking your accounts, identifying their needs, and figuring out how much value they'll bring to your magazine.

You'll need to ask yourself some questions about each account. Does the client run a quarter page every once in a while, or can she be counted on to run a full schedule of inserts? Is the client accessible or tough to contact? Does she have a product that fits well with your magazine, or is it a stretch? The right answer will let you know how much of your time can be spent profitably with each client.

The easiest way to measure value is to decide whether a client is an "A," "B," "C," or "D" account. The following chart can help you decide how each category measures up. Notice how your sales strategy will reflect the "attractiveness" of each prospect.

STRENGTH OF POSITION

Strong	**Weak**
A **Attractiveness:** Very attractive. High growth opportunity; sales department has strong position. **Sales call strategy:** High level of calls.	**C** **Attractiveness:** Somewhat attractive. Limited growth opportunity, but sales department has strong position. **Sales call strategy:** Moderate level of sales calls to maintain the current strength of the sales organization's position.
B **Attractiveness:** Potentially attractive. High growth opportunity, but sales department has weak position. **Sales call strategy:** High level of sales calls to strengthen the sales organization's position.	**D** **Attractiveness:** Very unattractive. Low growth opportunity; sales department has weak position. **Sales call strategy:** Minimal level of sales calls. Replace personal sales calls with telephone sales calls, direct mail, etc.

Source: Increasing Sales Productivity Through Improved Sales Call Allocation Strategies, *by Raymond W. LaForge, Clifford E. Young and B. Curtis Hamm; appearing in* Journal of Personal Selling and Sales Management.

Although this evaluation seems fairly cut and dried, keep in mind that a prospect's value can change at any time. At *Gems Today,* for instance, a diamond merchant may eventually drop from an "A" prospect to a "C," while several small gem dealers might rise from "B" to an "A." You need to continually monitor your position with each prospect to best focus your sales energy.

The Lure of the "C" Client

Incidentally, it always surprises me how so many salespeople actually end up spending the *most* time with "C" accounts. Why? These reps may feel there's less risk with these clients. They may know they probably won't get those accounts anyway, but they still enjoy dealing with them. Or it may be that the companies are smaller and more receptive to a sales call.

Whatever the reason, it's clear that the energy spent on "C" accounts is better spent with prospects likely to bring the greatest returns. You want to pursue clients that you know have the potential for 12-time schedules, for color ads, for full- or half-page ad buys, and for participation in your value-added programs.

At times you may be tempted to cover everyone and everything. But experience will show you that blanket coverage of too-small accounts is often at the expense of the time more profitably spent by making an extra effort against key prospects. Even if your sales territory is only small accounts, you can still find ways to rank your prospects, and to use your time and energy accordingly.

Now, "Grade" Your Time as Well

Once you've established which of your accounts are "A," "B," "C" or "D" status, the next organizational step is easy. All you have to do is allocate your time according to the "grade" you've given each account. The following chart makes it simple. On top, you list your current accounts by grade. Below, estimate how many accounts are in each category, how many calls you'll likely need to close each account, and how much estimated time you'll need per call. You can then calculate the percentage of your sales time each account will consume.

Naturally, the higher priority the account, the more of your time it's worth. A chart like this helps you organize your accounts and evaluate how much coverage you can or should devote to each. You can clarify not only which accounts are worth your time, but how much of your time they're worth.

Grade Definitions

Current Accounts   **Prospects**

"A" _____   _____
_____   _____
"B" _____   _____
_____   _____
"C" _____   _____
_____   _____
"D" _____   _____
_____   _____

ALLOCATION OF MY SALES TIME BY ACCOUNT GRADE:

	Current Accounts	Total # Accounts	# Calls to make in period	Estimated time per call	Total percent of sales time
"A"					
"B"					
"C"					
"D"					
Prospects					
"A"					
"B"					
"C"					
"D"					
Grand Totals:					

Grade your accounts to better allocate your time.

STEP FOUR:
SETTING GOALS AND OBJECTIVES

Once you've determined the value of your accounts, it's time to set some realistic goals for your territory.

Essentially, a goal is a non-budgeted forecast—something that a salesperson could realistically achieve if the right effort were behind the account. Think for a moment about your top clients. You might ask yourself what percentage share of their advertising market your magazine can claim. What was the past performance of your territory? What new business could you gain from it?

To establish your goals properly, you need to project future ad sales. In fact, most sales reps are required by the publisher to make a formal sales projection at least once a year. This not only helps sales reps establish targets, it helps the company know exactly where the magazine is going. Based on the amount of business you project, your publisher can determine how much editorial the magazine will need, how much ad revenue it can count on (and from where), and how much revenue it may need to get from other sources, like subscription sales. Sales forecasts like these help publishers make financial decisions about the magazine.

Let's walk through a sample forecast report, column by column. You'll find it on page 376.

1. *Account name.* Each account and prospect is listed on the far left.

2. *Target accounts.* A "Y" (for "yes") under this category flags that account for special sales attention. (We'll discuss target accounts in detail in an upcoming chapter.)

3. *Client/Agency.* The "C" code tells you that you're dealing directly with the client, while the "A" code says this account is being handled by an agency.

4. *Sales split.* If the account is marked "sales split," that mean you're splitting the commission with someone else. Perhaps another sales rep for instance, handles the New York corporate office while you work with the Chicago-based line manager.

5. *Prior year pages.* Listed here are the number of pages that ran the previous year with each account. Diamond Mine, for instance, ran 24 pages last year; Smith's Semi-Precious ran three; Dillard Gold ran 12 and Providence Costume ran none. From this background, and using information from your situation analysis, you can start to gauge how much business you'll pick up with each of these accounts in the future.

6. *Forecasting.* The next columns indicate how much confidence you have that you'll pick up pages from these accounts. Obviously, you base your confidence level on what you know about the company and the marketplace.

ANNUAL FORECAST REPORT

Account	Target	C/A	Sales Split	Pages Prior Year	75% Pages	20% Pages	5% Pages	Potential Pages
Diamond Mine	Y	A	Y	24	16	24	30	18
Smith's Semi-Precious	N	C	Y	3	3	10	12	7
Dillard Gold	Y	C	N	12	12	14	16	12
Providence Costume	N	A	N	0	3	6	8	4

Projecting future ad sales helps you establish targets and helps the company know exactly where the magazine is going.

Perhaps you've discovered Providence Costume ran three pages in competing magazines last year and has shown signs of growth and willingness to try new markets. So you might feel it has a 75 percent chance of giving your magazine three pages, a 20 percent chance of generating six pages, and a 5 percent chance of an eight-time schedule. When you multiply 75 percent times three (2.25), 20 percent times six (1.2), and 5 percent times eight (0.4), you find that you can list the potential pages as 3.85. We'll round that off to four.

Likewise, Diamond Mine, a large but less stable advertiser, ran 24 pages last year. Business for the company is down, so you're 75 percent confident they'll drop to 16 pages. You're also 20 percent confident, however, that they'll stay at 24 pages, and you're 5 percent sure that with an extra sales boost, they might bump up to 30 pages. Add that up, and you can list your page goal as 18.3 pages. We'll round that down to 18.

You can then follow the logic to determine your page goals for your other clients. Your optimism about Smith's Semi-Precious, for instance, gives you a page goal of seven, compared to last year's three pages. And your confidence about the stability of Dillard Gold, another target account, lets you peg your page goal at three pages above last year's 12-time schedule.

Incidentally, you can forecast your pages with any percentage numbers you like (provided they add up to 100 percent). Let's say that you're 100 percent confident that you can keep Diamond Mine at 24 pages, no more, no less. Fine: your sales projection would be 100 percent times 24, or 24 pages. But if you're only 50 percent confident Diamond Mine will stay at 24 pages, and 50 percent confident it will drop to 16 pages, then your page goal would be 50 percent times 24 (12 pages) plus 50 percent times 16 (eight pages), which would bring your sales projection to 20 pages.

Once you've nailed down your projections for each client, it's time to prepare for the sale itself. This means putting into practice a few more sales tools, which we'll talk about in Step Five.

STEP FIVE:
IMPLEMENTATION OF SALES TOOLS

Okay, you've defined your market and prospects, you've ranked your accounts and you've put together a sales forecast. It's time to organize the sales calls themselves. You can now decide which of your clients deserves your time and energy. Listed below are the tools you'll need:

1. *An individual account strategy.* At this point, spend a little time checking off key points about your clients. A short customer profile, like the one on the next page, will prove very handy in guiding you in how to approach each prospect and in determining the probable success of each sales call.

Customer Profile Checklist

☐ **Client's primary decision maker** _____

☐ **Agency's primary decision maker** _____

☐ **Fiscal year** _____   ☐ **Product's competition** _____

☐ **Planning month** _____   ☐ **Product's market share** _____

☐ **Budget** _____   ☐ **Why do consumers buy this product?**

☐ **Media used** _____   _____

☐ **Product** _____   ☐ **Where can this product be purchased?**

☐ **Product's price** _____   _____

☐ **When is this product purchased?**

_____

☐ **Who is the client's primary target?** _____

☐ **Who is the client 's secondary target?** _____

☐ **What are the client's objectives?** _____

☐ **What are the client's strategies?** _____

☐ **What does your magazine have to offer?** _____

☐ **Who needs to know about this?** _____

☐ **What is my strategy with this client?** _____

_____

☐ **How will my competition try to sell this client?** _____

_____

With a client profile, you can decide specifically what kind of a marketing program you might need to put together.

With this information, you can decide specifically what kind of marketing program you might need to put together. What information do you need to sell this client? How can you get it? Is your research up to date? How organized is your data? Do you know what your sales story will be?

2. *A call schedule.* This schedule allots the amount of time appropriate to each client. If you sell in the field, you ideally want to reach the point where you make two effective calls in the morning and two in the afternoon, along with a productive business lunch. And by business lunch, I don't mean chit-chatting with your favorite client at the diner. I mean an 11:30 presentation with a client, then lunch.

How do you decide whom to call, and when? Take a look at your account rankings and your sales projection. If Diamond Mine, for instance, is an "A" account and in danger of dropping precious pages, you would need to arrange your call schedule to get a maximum amount of time selling this client. If Providence Costume is a "C" account, capable of giving you a small number of pages with little effort on your part, arrange to have just enough face-to-face exposure to make the sale. (Just keep in mind that some smaller clients may need more marketing education than your larger, more sophisticated clients.)

In other words, don't arrange your call schedule on gut instinct, calling the clients you like and avoiding those you don't, regardless of the sales potential for each. Use the guidelines you've established to determine how and when to contact your clients.

3. *A travel schedule.* Like a call schedule, a travel schedule also helps you allot time appropriately to each client. Here, you need both short-range and long-range planning. Long-range, you must make sure you get the most exposure with the clients and agencies who'll represent the bulk of your business. And short-range, you should arrange your travel plans so that you see clients in a time-efficient manner.

Here's a general sense of how to plan effective sales travel. Assume you're a salesperson in Chicago covering several key states and cities in the Midwest. Your plan requires that you spend 50 percent of your travel time in the Midwest territory and 50 percent at your home base and its environs.

If you intend to make six trips to Indiana, for example, you should create a long-term schedule first in a yearly planner. Then, as the dates draw near, you can route your individual appointments so that you can give your best Indiana clients your most productive time while ensuring that other accounts also have a place on your schedule. It may be that by your second trip to Indiana, your "A" Indiana account may have slipped to "C," and several of your "B" accounts may have moved up to "A." Obviously, you would arrange your travel time for your second trip to give more face-to-face to your newly elevated clients.

Don't neglect your home base. Treat it like a territory in itself, dividing Chicago, say, by its three distinct sections: Chicago A, the North Side; Chicago B, the South Side, and Chicago C, the Loop. Don't make the mistake of spending more time than necessary in the office when you could be in the field, following up on your own home territory.

4. *A sales tracking report.* For each call you make, you can fill out a simple form (like the one on the following page) that details whom you've contacted, their titles and functions, the purpose of your call and the results. Even better, you can write down the objections you might need to overcome with each account. You can also make notes on future selling strategies and write out the next action you might take, as well as the target date for taking action.

Sales tracking reports help you analyze your time and effort as you go. (For the easiest sales-tracking reports, use account-management software.) By looking at these reports, you might find that Providence Costume is proving to be a tougher sell than you thought, requiring a lot of face-to-face time while showing little commitment to a schedule. With that information, you might drop this prospect from a "C" to "D" ranking, or perhaps drop it altogether in order to focus on clients with more potential.

380

SALES TRACKING REPORT

Company	Salesperson
Date	Grade Account
1. Person(s) Contacted	**Title Function**

2. Purpose of Call:

3. Result of Call:

4. Objections to be Overcome:

5. Strategy to Make the Sale:

6. Next Action and Target Date:

Comments:

Tracking reports help you analyze the effectiveness of your work.

STEP SIX:
CONTROL

Sales, of course, is a never-ending process. Just as you've closed one account, you're researching another, scheduling presentations with a third and monitoring the progress of a fourth and fifth.

381

But, at certain points, you must step back and realistically monitor and evaluate your progress. By collecting data on your time spent versus your goals accomplished, you can identify areas that need more of your attention, as well as those that may deserve less.

So after closing each issue, take a look at your standards of performance. Did you set your goals too high or too low? Did you feel rushed and/or lack confidence with your clients? Were you able to counter objections? Did you overprepare for your presentations? Underprepare?

You can self-evaluate by going back to your sales projections and results. Did you reach certain sales goals in less time than you thought? Did other sales goals prove impossible to meet? By looking at your results, you can clearly evaluate your progress towards meeting your sales projections and moving forward with your career. Each month, instead of becoming more and more overwhelmed with your sales tasks, you should be seeing greater efficiency, more confidence, and a greater understanding of your market and client needs.

After this self-analysis, you may feel the need to take *corrective action*. Perhaps that means resetting your time priorities. Maybe it means downscaling your goals, or shifting account priorities. You may find that you're spending too much time on the phone and not enough in the field (or vice-versa), or that much of your time is unproductive when you're on the road. You may find you habitually overestimated or underestimated expected sales.

To prepare for your next issue or sales period, summarize your findings into an *estimated revenue projection form*. You might want to create this report during your down time after each issue, once you've made your follow-up phone calls to close sales.

This form differs from the long-term forecasts we discussed earlier. This method helps determine what kind of short-term business you can expect for the next issue. At the end of the sales cycle, you can refer back to these estimates to review how well your projections matched up to reality.

Estimated Revenue Projections

Salesperson		
Date	Sale period	
Territory		

Contracted Business
Estimated New Business
Total Estimated Business

Account	Size/# Pages	Color	Contracted 100%	Confidence Level 90%	50%	25%	Next Action	Date for action

Estimating revenues prepares you to sell the next issue.

This form is a good way to review each issue and to evaluate how your sales are going. Maybe you've got a gut feeling that several hot accounts are ready to close, or you fear some of your better accounts are losing interest. Preparing an estimated revenue projection form will give you solid information either to back up your confidence or refute your fears. Here's how to do it:

1. *Note the account.* Write down the names of the clients already scheduled for your next issue.

383

2. *Note the details of the contracted ads.* Are they full pages? Color? Insertions? Be sure to compare those notes with your production department and ad-trafficking staff to make sure the records agree. It's easy to overlook an ad change. Perhaps a client called to replace a full-page ad with a half-page island, or to upgrade from black-and-white to color. Naturally, it's important to make sure you've got the details straight so your own records are accurate.

3. *Consider your prospects.* Which ones are "maybes" for this upcoming issue? How many pages are under consideration?

4. *Project your confidence level.* As with the earlier sales projection form, make a note of how confident you are that your accounts can be upsold, or will at least stay on into the next issue.

5. *Project your sales action.* Based on your confidence level and your experience with each account, note the kind of action you need to take next. Should you have more face-to-face time with Diamond Mine? Do you need to create a mini-presentation for Smith's Semi-Precious?

6. *Estimate your new business.* When you've finished combing through accounts, calculate the number of pages and amount of revenues you can expect from your accounts for the next issue. Once you add this number to your *contracted business*, you can arrive at your *total estimated business projection* for the next issue.

You can now compare this figure with your annual projection. How are you doing? If you're close on comparison, congratulations! You have an entire issue to enjoy or build on your success. Are you way off? If so, go back, and with great care look to see if you've missed anyone.

IT'S CIRCULAR LOGIC

Notice that these six steps take the guesswork out of sales. Instead of using your gut to decide who gets your time and attention (as in, "I think I can close Client X with three more calls," even though Client Y may be far more lucrative), you can turn to these steps to organize your sales process and prioritize your accounts.

Notice, too, that the six steps actually follow a circular logic. Consider the diagram below:

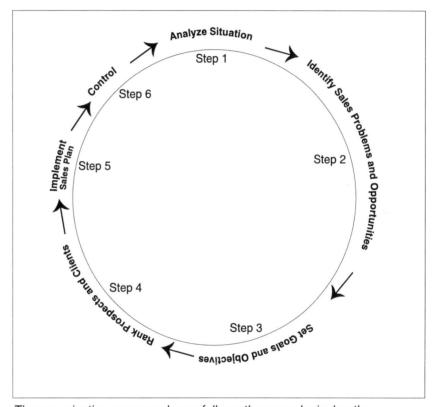

The organization process always follows the same logical path.

So, for instance, say you've closed out your issue. During your "control" phase (Step Six), you discover that, despite the information you found during your "analysis" stage (Step One), your costume jewelry dealers were actually your strongest accounts. They exceeded your sales projections, they were easiest to close, and the payoff was the greatest in sales versus effort. What do you do now?

You return to Step One. Now you can use your new information from your sales control to *re-analyze the situation*. Your new analysis might help you *identify new opportunities* (Step Two). From there, you can *re-rank your prospects* (Step Three), *set new sales goals* (Step Four), and *reconfigure your call and travel schedules* (Step Five).

Once you've put the whole process in motion again and closed more new business, you can proceed to your *sales controls* (Step Six) to find out how well this new information paid off.

This circular logic means you can work your account management from bottom to top, using your sales results to determine which accounts need priority attention. Or you can work top to bottom, investigating information about the market in order to set your sales goals. You can work from the middle, basing your time and territory management on, for example, new sales goals determined by your sales manager. You can even work simultaneously on the steps, to see if the results are a close match to the goals you set out to achieve. However you choose to work the steps, you'll find that they'll stay in the same logical order. Moreover, they allow you to have greater confidence in your projections and sales plans.

Keep in mind that lots of events can trigger a change in your account management process. A new competitor in the marketplace might trigger a return to Step One, forcing you to reassess your situation. Or, if the costume jewelry trend proves short-lived, you might need to go to Step Two and identify new opportunities. Or, if your "A" and "B" clients have less time for you than you'd like, a Step Four analysis can help you reconfigure your call and travel schedules. Either way, every time you return to a step, you just continue around the circle again, following up on your new opportunities and new information and organizing your sales calls for maximum efficiency.

IT ALL ADDS UP

On first reading, it may seem that getting organized is a pretty laborious process. Between sales tracking reports, revenue projection forms, call schedules and client profiles, it's a wonder there's any time left for actually selling.

Notice, though, that each of these steps is designed to keep you moving forward. Each time you apply an organizational technique, you're helping yourself find out:

◆ *Where you are*

◆ *Where you're going*

◆ *What you need to do to get there*

◆ *How much progress you've made*

That, remember, is what efficiency is all about.

My father once told me, "Whatever happens, good or bad, don't let it be a surprise." Surprises come from broken expectations and lack of planning. You don't want to be surprised by clients who suddenly disappear into the competition's magazine, and you don't want to be ambushed by a backlog of paperwork. Most certainly, you don't want to disappoint your company executives with a lack of ad pages. And you won't—not if you've planned your time and territory well.

22

GETTING the MOST from YOUR TIME

"O, call back yesterday, bid time return."
—William Shakespeare (1564-1616)
English poet and dramatist

Time is money, and in your job, money equals sales. Some sales gurus say the average close takes five calls. That means the more time you can spend talking to clients, visiting prospects and making presentations—in short, the more time you can spend *selling*—the more money you can bring in.

The problem is, however, that many other demands are made on your time. There's travel time. There's calling time, waiting time, creative time, preparation time. There's follow-up time and administrative time. None of these directly net sales, but they're all critical for ensuring that your sales time is profitably spent.

Obviously, you can't control how long an hour lasts, or how

389

many days are in a week. But you *can* manage yourself, and your job, with respect to time. Do you know how much of your time is productive? Who wastes your time? How much time do you spend even finding contacts who deserve your time?

In this chapter, I'll show you how to get more value from your time. At first glance, you might think a lot of the following methods are, yes, time-consuming. Don't be daunted. Once you start practicing how to measure and allocate time, you'll find yourself freer than ever to spend it making sales.

MEASURE YOUR SALES BY TIME

In sales, we value our accounts by the amount of revenue they produce, both for our publication and for our personal commission. But have you ever tried to measure each account's value by *time?* Each sale you bring in should be roughly equivalent to the time you spend selling it. In short, your 12-time clients deserve more of your time than your occasional half-page buyer.

This may sound obvious, and you might think you're already allocating time efficiently. But try putting real numbers on it. Try this three-step process.

1. Starting with your "A" accounts, calculate the time required to sell ad space to each one, along with the dollar value of each.

2. Divide your earnings on each account by the number of hours you worked to close it.

3. Calculate the difference between the "ad cost" and the "time cost." That's the return on your (time) investment.

Let's look at an example:. You have spent roughly 35 hours to close a sale with Client A, bringing your magazine 10 pages at $10,000 per page. This includes time spent preparing for the sale, traveling, meeting with the vice president of sales, meeting with three regional managers and making phone calls. With Client B, you've spent 10 hours closing a two-page sale. And Client C got 15 hours of your time, but in the end didn't buy any pages.

Your return on investment—if you just measure it by a 10 percent commission—was $286 per hour for Client A; $200 per hour for Client B; and of course, a net loss for Client C because that was time you probably could have spent profitably elsewhere.

What's that tell you? To maximize your selling, you should spend *only as much time on each to give you a return.* And you should avoid overinvesting time on less promising accounts that usually give a negative return.

Naturally, you'll always have some sales that come easily, and some efforts that will never pay off. Nobody bats a hit each time. But if you evaluate your "return on investment" in this way, you can determine how to better spend your time on your next client. Perhaps Client B could have been upsold if you'd prepared better research. Perhaps you'd overestimated the potential of Client C based on faulty projections. Now's the time to reset priorities for your calls and decide how much time to devote to each.

Don't think in terms of calls. Think in terms of sales. Before you pick up the phone, ask yourself if this call will lead to closing a sale. If you're not sure, you need to focus on the value of that client.

THE TOOLS OF TIME ANALYSIS

Now that you've actually measured some of your sales by time, chances are your eyebrows are lodged permanently at your hairline. How did you manage to waste so much time with your "favorite" clients? Why didn't you spend more time closing business with the clients who made you real money?

Well, relax. Now that you know a little bit more about how you've spent your time, you can start to manage it. Here are a few tools you might find handy to keep track of time and use it better. Although this logging process may not be critical to your job, it's a potent way to evaluate your time when you feel out of control.

The time log

Did you ever reach the end of the day and wonder where all the time went? If you knew exactly how you spent your time, you could probably find ways to use it much more effectively.

HOUR	TIME FRAME	ACTUAL TIME	DESCRIPTION OF ACTIVITIES	COMMENTS FOR BETTER TIME USE
11	0-30			
	30-60			
12	0-30			
	30-60			
1	0-30			
	30-60			
2	0-30			
	30-60			

Time log for_____ Date_____ Day_____ Analysis

Use a time log to analyze how you spend time during the day.

In the beginning, the only way to know how you spend your time is to write it down. For 10 days, try this: Log how you've spent your time every 15 minutes. It may sound impossible at first, but remember lawyers must log their time all day, every day. Try not to let an hour go by without recording what you've done. It will be a habit in no time.

Now at the end of 10 days, analyze the time logs. Look for the *six most important* activities you engaged in over that time. Then write down the *six least important* things you did. Find out how much time you spent on each.

Then, look for patterns in your time logs. What went right? What went wrong? At what time did you start working on priority tasks? What were your three biggest time wasters? Which activities needed less time? Which need more?

TIME LOG ANALYSIS

MY SIX MOST PRODUCTIVE ACTIVITIES   Between (Dates) _____

1.   Total Time: _____

2.   Total Time: _____

3.   Total Time: _____

4.   Total Time: _____

5.   Total Time: _____

6.   Total Time: _____

MY SIX LEAST PRODUCTIVE ACTIVITIES   Between (Dates) _____

1.   Total Time: _____

2.   Total Time: _____

3.   Total Time: _____

4.   Total Time: _____

5.   Total Time: _____

6.   Total Time: _____

Look for patterns in your time log.

You can relate all this information to your goal setting. Let's say your time log revealed that you spent an hour preparing a teaser letter about some editorial features, or trying to get past a secretarial screen to get your client's attention. Perhaps you might delegate these tasks in the future to gain more valuable time for yourself and your client. Or say your time log showed that you chit-chatted with a friendly but unproductive contact for half an hour. You might make a note to use your time better on the next call.

Remember, the goal of your job is *sales*. If you know what you want to achieve, a time log will show you if you're using your time effectively to get there.

393

The annual plan

An old friend and mentor of mine, the late David Hagenbuch, used to plan his sales time backwards. He'd start with the 240 working days in the year and plan an itinerary. That is, he wrote on a yearly calendar the goals he wanted to achieve for the year, whether that meant increasing his magazine's market share by two points, or selling 20 percent more pages than the year before, or landing an account that had eluded him in the past. He'd note every goal, and then work back to monthly, weekly and daily planning.

In this way, he could see the overall challenge he had ahead of him. By focusing on long-range goals ("How do I close 12 more accounts by June?") not short-range issues ("Should I have lunch with Miller Petroleum?"), he could avoid getting hung up on nonproductive activity.

How does an annual plan enable productivity? Think of it this way: Sales are a result of exposure. Research shows that most sales close after five calls—but only a small fraction of salespeople actually make those five calls. Hagenbuch believed that 35 percent of salespeople sell 65 percent of the business. If he wanted to be in that 35 percent, he needed to know where he was going and plan how to get there. He needed to spread out his goals over time so he could allot the proper amount of time to each account. If he didn't plan long-range, he knew he'd be caught up in the panic of trying to jam his selling messages into two or three calls before each issue closed.

His advice to me was this: don't plan week-to-week and have only a hazy idea of what the year will bring. If you set your goal ahead of time, and keep it in front of you, chances are better that you'll achieve it.

394

PLANNING CALENDAR

	JAN	FEB	MAR	APR	MAY	JUNE	JULY	AUG	SEPT	OCT	NOV	DEC
1	WED NEW YEAR	SAT	SAT	TUES INDIANA	THUR	SUN	TUES CHICAGO B	FRI	MON LABODAY	WED	SAT	MON OFFICE
2	THUR OFFICE	SUN	SUN	WED	FRI	MON CHICAGO A	WED	SAT	TUES ST. LOUIS	THUR	SUN	TUES
3	FRI CHICAGO A	MON CHICAGO A	MON CHICAGO A	THUR	SAT	TUES	THUR	SUN	WED	FRI	MON ST. LOUIS	WED THUR
4	SAT	TUES Association MEETING	TUES	FRI	SUN	WED	FRI JULY 4TH	MON ARC	THUR	SAT	TUES	THUR
5	SUN	WED	WED	SAT	MON CHICAGO C	THUR	SAT	TUES CONVENTION	FRI	SUN	WED	FRI CHICAGO A
6	MON VACATION	THUR CHICAGO C	THUR	SUN	TUES	FRI OFFICE	SUN	WED	SAT	MON CHICAGO C	THUR	SAT
7	TUES	FRI CHICAGO A	FRI	MON CHICAGO A	WED	SAT	MON VACATION	THUR	SUN	TUES	FRI	SUN
8	WED	SAT	SAT	TUES	THUR	SUN	TUES	FRI OFFICE	MON CHICAGO	WED	SAT	MON OFFICE
9	THUR	SUN	SUN	WED	FRI	MON SALES	WED	SAT	TUES	THUR	SUN	TUES
10	FRI OFFICE	MON OFFICE	MON OFFICE	THUR	SAT	TUES MEETING	THUR	SUN	WED	FRI OFFICE	MON	WED
11	SAT	TUES INDIANA	TUES CHICAGO B	FRI	SUN	WED	FRI	MON MINNEAPOLIS	THUR	SAT	SAT N. ILLINOIS	THUR
12	SUN	WED	WED	SAT	MON INDIANA	THUR	SAT	TUES	FRI OFFICE	SUN	WED	FRI CHICAGO B
13	MON KANSAS CITY	THUR	THUR	SUN	TUES	FRI OFFICE	SUN	WED	MON KANSAS CITY	THUR	SAT	
14	TUES ST. LOUIS	FRI	FRI	MON ST. LOUIS	WED	SAT	MON N ILLINOIS	THUR	SUN MEMPHIS	FRI	SUN	
15	WED	SAT	SAT	TUES	THUR	SUN	TUES	FRI INDIANA	MON LOUISVILLE	WED	SAT	MON VACATION
16	THUR	SUN	SUN	WED OFFICE	FRI CHICAGO C	MON	WED	SAT	TUES ST. LOUIS	THUR	SUN	TUES
17	FRI	MON MINNEAPOLIS	MON N ILLINOIS	THUR KANSAS CITY	SAT	TUES	THUR WISCONSIN	SUN	WED	FRI OFFICE	MON CHICAGO A	WED
18	SAT	TUES	TUES WISCONSIN	FRI	SUN	WED	FRI	MON CHICAGO C	THUR	SAT	TUES	THUR
19	SUN	WED	WED	SAT CHICAGO B	THUR	FRI	SAT	TUES	FRI	SUN	WED	FRI
20	MON OFFICE	THUR CHICAGO B	THUR	SUN	TUES GOLF	FRI	SUN	WED	SAT OPEN	MON	THUR	SAT
21	TUES CHICAGO B	FRI	FRI	MON OFFICE	WED OUTING	SAT	MON OFFICE	THUR LOUISVILLE	SUN	TUES OFFICE	FRI	SUN
22	WED	SAT	SAT	TUES CHICAGO B	THUR OFFICE	SUN	TUES	FRI MEMPHIS	MON OFFICE	WED	SAT	MON OFFICE
23	THUR	SUN	SUN	WED	FRI	MON ST. LOUIS	WED INDIANA	SAT	TUES	THUR	SUN	TUE
24	FRI	MON OFFICE	MON CHICAGO C	THUR	SAT	TUES	THUR	SUN	WED N ILLINOIS	FRI INDIANA	MON	WED KMAS PARTY
25	SAT	TUES ST. LOUIS	TUES	FRI	SUN	WED	FRI	MON OFFICE	THUR WISCONSIN	SAT	TUES	THURS XMAS
26	SUN	WED	WED	SAT	MON MEMORIAL DAY	THUR	SAT	TUES	FRI	SUN	WED	FRI OFF
27	MON N ILLINOIS WISCONSIN	THUR	THUR	SUN	TUES MEMPHIS	FRI KANSAS CITY	SUN	WED CHICAGO B	SAT	MON OFFICE	THUR	SAT
28	TUES	FRI	FRI	MON MINNEAPOLIS	WED	SAT	MON CHICAGO A	THUR	SUN	TUES MINNEAPOLIS	FRI	SUN
29	WED		SAT	TUES	THUR LOUISVILLE	SUN	TUES	FRI	MON CHICAGO B	WED	SAT	MON OFFICE
30	THUR		SUN	WED	FRI	MON OFFICE	WED	SAT	THUR	THUR	SUN	TUES
31	FRI		MON OFFICE		SAT		THUR	SUN		FRI		WED

DAVE HAGENBUCH & ASSOCIATES, INC.,

An annual plan can produce more sales by enabling you to better focus on long-range goals.

The itinerary

Just as the annual plan helps you figure your long-term goals, so does a weekly itinerary keep you focused on what to do each day of the week. First, you break down your annual goals into monthly goals. Then you break your monthly goals into daily and weekly goals.

WEEKLY CALL SCHEDULE

Salesperson:				Calls Planned -- Week of:		
CALLS TO BE MADE				**CALLS MADE**		
Date	Company	Contact(s)	Objective	Results	Action To Be Taken	Date of Next call

Weekly call schedules help prioritize your time.

So, for instance, if your monthly goal is to "Close Golden Hotels account by July 30," you can plot your weekly goals like this:

Week 1: Phone contact with ad manager and agency. Schedule appointment.

Week 2: Send media kits, letters in preparation for presentation.

Week 3: Presentation.

Week 4: Follow-up with letters, calls. Finalize sale.

You can then use *a weekly/daily planner* to fill in all the details. You can schedule the calls you'll need to make to Golden, as well as to your other target accounts and prospects. You can note what you need to do to prepare for your presentation. You can track your sales progress each day, figure your lunch dates, and write down the phone numbers of those you're scheduled to call during and after hours. That way, when you're on the phone preparing appointments, you can see how your week is unfolding. (Most account-management software programs allow you to fill out this "to-do" calendar automatically.)

Particularly when you're traveling, you might find it useful to supply a copy to of your itinerary to your support people. That way they'll know what you're doing when they need to contact you.

The sales call or sales tracking report

Memory is perishable. Do you recall the last discussion you had with a "C" client? Do you remember how the call ended? Do you know whether you'd promised anything unusual, or when you were due to call him again?

A sales call report (or sales tracking report, as shown in the previous chapter, page 381) isn't strictly for recording how many pages your client wants to schedule. You use it simply to record what your clients tell you. For every client, you should be able to call up from your computer a history of all your calls and discussions. Without this record, you might find yourself wasting time going over old ground or trying to remember long-ago conversations. With a sales call report, you can stay on top of your clients effortlessly.

The weekly call-schedule summary

Each Monday, try to write down your expected call schedule for the week. Then, at the end of each week, use your sales call reports to fill out a quick call summary. You might not think it necessary, but a weekly summary is a great way to find out whether you're making productive calls. Are you in touch with too many agencies? Too few? Is your volume of calls up or down? You might not be able to tell your progress on a day-to-day basis, but a weekly report can keep you abreast of your movement.

The call summary is also a good reference point for past sales contacts. At a glance, for instance, you can see how often you'd contacted Client B in the last three weeks, or whether Client A has been neglected of late.

ITINERARY

SALESPERSON_____ WEEK BEGINNING_____

	DATE	CITY & STATE	HOTEL	KEY ACCOUNTS
MONDAY				

SALES CALLS - WEEK BEGINNING

SCHEDULE

TIME	SUNDAY	MONDAY	TUESDAY	WEDNESDAY	THURSDAY	FRIDAY	SATURDAY
8 AM							
9							
10							
11							
NOON							
1 PM							
2							
3							
4							
5							
EVE.							

NOTES

An itinerary and a call summary help you keep up with your clients efficiently.

TOO MUCH PAPERWORK?

All this probably sounds like a lot of paperwork, and like most salespeople, you probably hate paper and reports. You want to sell.

I'm with you. Paperwork that doesn't make you more efficient is a waste of time. But you'll find, at most, you'll only spend about half an hour a day using forms to keep track of your business—and if you're like most sales reps today, you'll have the advantage of good computer software to do it for you. (Take a look at Chapter 24 to find out what you need in account-management software.)

That's a half-hour very well spent. If you doubt it, consider how many hours you'd otherwise waste trying to play continual catch-up with your accounts. Don't diffuse your energy. Organize completely the first time, and you'll free yourself of the paperwork anxiety that would otherwise overwhelm you later.

WORKLOAD ANALYSIS: ARE YOU DOING TOO MUCH?

Once you've put your paperwork in order, this part should be easy. Here's where you take an honest look at your workload and decide if the amount is working against you. You'll find that you're either overloaded or that you're spending too much time on too few accounts and could effectively take on more.

Time and Duty Analysis   Day_____   Date_____

| | SALES CALLS | | TRAVEL | WAITING | ENTER-TAINMENT & LUNCH | ORDER EXPEDITING | REPORT WRITING | TELEP-PHONE CONTACTS | MISCEL-LANEOUS |
| | Customers | Prospects | | | | | | | |
	A	B	C	D	E	A	B	C	D	E							
8:00 - 8:30																	
8:30 - 9:00																	
9:00 - 9:30																	
9:30 - 10:00																	
10:00 - 10:30																	
10:30 - 11:00																	
11:00 - 11:30																	
11:30 - 12:00																	
12:00 - 12:30																	
12:30 - 1:00																	
1:00 - 1:30																	
1:30 - 2:00																	
2:00 - 2:30																	
2:30 - 3:00																	
3:00 - 3:30																	
3:30 - 4:00																	
4:00 - 4:30																	
4:30 - 5:00																	
5:00 - 5:30																	
5:30 - 6:00																	
Total Time																	
Percent of Day																	

This time log helps to analyze your workload by breaking down duties performed with each client.

399

To come up with an honest estimate, just take a look at how many accounts you have. Now try and estimate the number of calls you need to make for each account. Are certain kinds of accounts taking up more of your time then others? Estimate the travel time spent on accounts you see face-to-face. And don't forget nonselling time, when you may be writing letters, going to meetings, working with production and so on.

If you do feel overloaded, this kind of analysis would prove far more helpful than a mere complaint to your boss. You need to *justify* that you use your time effectively but have too much to do. That way, your superiors would be in a position to help you, not to square off against you.

23

The CARE and FEEDING of TARGET ACCOUNTS

"It was a friendship founded on business, which is a good deal better than a business founded on friendship."
—John D. Rockefeller (1884-1960)
oil magnate and philanthropist

In Chapter 22 I touched briefly on target accounts as I discussed sales projections. Remember, these are accounts you and your sales manager have set aside as priorities. Perhaps they're accounts that run exclusively with your competition. Perhaps they're growth accounts ripe for an upgrade, or account categories that you're trying to crack.

In this section, I'll talk about how to fit target accounts into your time and territory management. Because these are priority accounts, they'll need priority attention. Here's how to make sure they stay at the forefront of your schedule.

TYPES OF TARGET ACCOUNTS

Generally, you'll deal with two types of target accounts: *indigenous* and *non-indigenous*. The first are accounts that have a generic, direct relationship with your magazine. The second are not directly related to your title, but can benefit from its audience and market.

Say you sell for a fine-jewelry magazine. Here, you might consider small gem dealers indigenous target accounts. That's because the magazine covers fine jewelry, and you know that unusual gems have recently become a consumer trend.

But costume jewelry, meanwhile, could become a non-indigenous target account for the title—something the magazine doesn't currently include, but could prove worthy of special consideration. Now that the title is adding costume-jewelry articles to its editorial mix, the time could be right to break into an account area currently dominated by the competition.

Target accounts also break into one of two *placement* categories: *full schedule* and *specific*.

The first are those that can be developed into your full schedule of issues. These accounts are a logical fit with your magazine on a month-to-month basis, and generally fall into one of four types:

- ✦ New business
- ✦ Significant increases in existing business
- ✦ Business exclusive to your magazine
- ✦ Vulnerable current accounts (accounts you might lose and want to keep)

Other accounts make sense for specific issues during the course of a year. They would either fit with a certain editorial focus, a special event, or a particular time of year in which to introduce a new product.

If your magazine decides to include costume-jewelry editorial just once every quarter, for instance, you would pursue those target accounts only on that basis. Or, if costume jewelry sells best only around Christmas, Mother's Day and Valentine's Day, you might find that pursuing a full schedule of ads would be a wasted effort, even if you do carry costume editorial year round.

Should you go the extra mile? How do you determine whether an account is worth priority status? Ask the following questions:

◆ Does the account have sufficient immediate *and* long-term **potential**? If the jewelry magazine decides to carry costume-jewelry editorial only as a special issue, it wouldn't make sense to put long-term energy into building costume accounts.

◆ Is the client a **leader** in the field and able to influence competitors?

◆ Does the client have a **favorable attitude** toward your magazine? Perhaps costume-jewelry clients would feel uncomfortable among fine-jewelry advertising and editorial.

◆ Is there a **weak spot** in the client's media plan? If you know that your costume-jewelry prospects aren't happy with the circulation of your competitor (their current buy), you might be able to use that disappointment to your advantage.

◆ Can you apply any **special promotions** for this account to other accounts? If you set up a value-added plan for your costume-jewelry prospects, for instance, could you use the same plan to upgrade your fine-jewelry clients?

◆ Do the client's advertising and media **objectives** logically fit into your story?

◆ Is the **timing** right in the next few months for the extra effort?

◆ Will the effort result in a particularly high **return** for your company?

Let's say after all your consideration, you feel costume jewelry deserves target account status. Now that you've decided that, be sure to keep this in mind: The process of managing a target account program is something that must be done *every day*.

TARGET-ACCOUNT ANALYSIS

Company Name: _____

1. What type of product do you sell?

_____

2. Who are your best prospects?

   A. By industry:

   _____   _____

   _____   _____

   B: By title:

   _____ General Management   _____ Sales/Marketing Management

   _____ Technical Management _____ Advertising/PR Management

   _____ Other: _____

3. Why do customers buy from you? (price, quality, service, selection, location, etc.)

_____

4. Who are your competitors?

_____

5. What is your competitive standing? What's the main difference between you and your competitor?

_____

6. Is your business growing? Stable? Declining?

_____

7. What are you doing to attract new customers?

_____

8. How is your budget allocated among the following ($/%):

   Magazines _____   **Direct Mail** _____

   Trade Shows _____   **TV**   _____

   Catalogs _____   **Radio**   _____

This chart helps you keep on top of the needs for your priority clients.

TARGET-ACCOUNT ANALYSIS (cont'd)

9. Which magazines do you use? What are the ad schedules?

_____

10. How do these magazines fit your criteria and marketing needs?

      a. Circulation _____

      b. Editorial _____

      c. Readership_____

      d. CPM Efficiency _____

11. What would you like to accomplish with your advertising? What are your objectives?

_____

_____

12. Who is involved in making the advertising decisions?

_____

13. How do you sell this market?

    _____Direct-Sales Force

    _____Reps

    _____Brokers

    _____Telephone

    _____Direct Mail

Say you spend two intensive weeks closing costume-jewelry clients. You've showered them with special offers and value-added programs. If, after the issue closes, you return to them with a plain old media kit and rate card, you'll probably find a rather dismayed client. No one likes to be courted and then taken for granted.

We'll now talk about how you can give target accounts priority in your time and territory management.

PICKING THE ACCOUNT

Once you've decided that costume jewelry is a target category, now comes the tricky part. How do you choose, among 145 potential advertisers, which ones deserve priority attention? This is no simple matter of gut instinct or picking the biggest players. Instead, it's a process in which sales reps and managers sit down and prioritize prospects based on a long menu of solid criteria.

Here's how you start: first, categorize your present accounts and prospects under the following categories: Top 15 Running Business Accounts, New Business Accounts, and Split Accounts. (At least once a year, you and your manager should go over these top accounts and prospects in detail.)

Starting with your *top 15 running business accounts*, list the names of current advertisers in descending order by size of schedule (see illustration on next page). Next to them, list the number of pages each account currently runs in your title, as well their page counts in your competitors' titles.

Alongside each account, be sure to list your personal sales goals over the next two years. Let's say Client A now runs 15 pages a year. If you feel this client is ripe for growth, you might indicate that 20 pages are possible for next year.

This goal would not be the sales projection you give each year to your company's publisher and financial managers. Instead, this number would be a *personal* goal—something you feel is realistic and possible. In some cases, as with troubled clients, a realistic goal might simply be to maintain the current page count. In other cases, the goal might be to upgrade the client from six pages to nine, or to take 20 points in market share from your competitor.

Move on to your *top five new business accounts*. These are *not* new accounts who've recently started running in your magazine. Instead, these are top accounts that *do not yet* run in your magazine, but which you feel have the best advertising potential over the next few months or years. Make sure you list your personal sales goals next to each of these five accounts.

Finally, list the *top five split (or non-exclusive) accounts* from the past year. These are clients who may advertise with you, but give the lion's share of their business to your competitors.

(Salesperson)			(Date)	

PRIORITY & TARGET ACCOUNT LIST

Territory Total	ACTUAL PAGES		GOAL	
Top 15 Running Business Accounts (Division or Brands)	Competitor	Our Publication	Competitor	Our Publication
	Last Year	Last Year	This year	This year
1.				
2.				
3.				
4.				
5.				
6.				
7.				
8.				
9.				
10.				
11.				
12.				
13.				
14.				
15.				
Subtotal				
New Business (Divisions or brands)				
1.				
2.				
3.				
4.				
5.				
Splits or Exclusives To Be Resolved (Divisions or brands)				
1.				
2.				
3.				
4.				
5.				
Subtotal				
Total				

Prioritize your accounts to see who deserves the most attention.

Here, make sure you list personal goals for resolving the split on each account. If, for instance, Client B gives 8 percent of her advertising to your competitor and is pleased with the results, you might realistically feel you can take only one point in market share from the competitor. But if the competitor has 8 percent of Client B, and you sense Client B is restless, you might feel you could bring 15 percent of her business your way.

407

Now that you've listed your accounts, look them over and make one adjustment. Go back to your top 15 running accounts and put an asterisk next to those *five* that should get top billing for the next year's sales effort. These may be accounts with the strongest growth prospects, or perhaps they're clients with whom you feel a particularly good rapport. They may also include accounts that pose a problem for your magazine, such as those clients who lately have cozied up with a competitor.

After you've completed your list, meet with your manager for a planning session. Make sure you agree on priorities and goals. Are you leaving out any important accounts? Are the goals realistic? Should certain clients receive more of your attention than others? Which ones?

Finally, you and your manager should periodically (perhaps monthly) review these target accounts in strategy sessions. Where do you stand on your goals? What's the next step? What do you need to prepare for the next step? Who can help with the account? Make sure you follow up your discussions with a target-account commitment memo that sums up what steps you'll be taking next with your priority clients.

THE STATUS REPORT

Now that you've set your goals for target accounts, it's important to take two steps to keep on top of them. The first step ensures that your account records are complete and accurate. The second step assesses where you stand with each client.

For both those steps, you need a *status report*. A status report lists each account with the following information:

✦ Name, address and telephone number of the company

✦ Names of contacts and their titles

✦ An asterisk next to the names of prime decision makers

✦ A "status" symbol, which indicates how the decision makers feel about your magazine. (You could rate their feelings from 1 to

10, with 10 being "extremely positive." Or you could use plus and minus signs to indicate how open they are to advertising in your magazine.)

Here, the goal is to manage the relationship between your magazine and the client. The more complete the form, the better you can service your target accounts.

Date: _____

TARGET ACCOUNT STATUS REPORT

+ + = very positive
+ = supportive
- = negative
/ = indifferent
0 = not called on

ACCOUNT	STATUS	AGENCY	STATUS
Company:	☐	Name:	☐
Address:		Address:	
City, State:		City, State:	
Phone:		Phone:	

☐ President:

☐ V. P. Sales:

☐ V. P. Mktg:

☐ Ad Director

☐ Ad Manager:

☐ Other (please state):

☐ President:

☐ Mgmt. Supervisor:

☐ Account Super:

☐ Account Executive:

☐ Other:

☐ Media Dir.:

☐ Asst. Media Dir.:

☐ Media Supervisor:

☐ Media Planner:

☐ Other Potential Accounts at Agency:

1.

2.

3.

4.

*NOTE: Prime Mover/Decision Maker

You can service your target accounts more efficiently by keeping up on your Target Account Status Report.

THE PLANNING CALENDAR

By now, you've put together a weekly, monthly and yearly calendar scheduled with your sales goals and activities. Your goal now is to make sure you highlight target-account activity. This will help you plan for sales thrusts throughout the year.

A good itinerary for a target account covers about three or four months. That's because many of your clients' decision makers plan their strategies about two to three months in advance. If you're going to meet with target accounts on a regular basis, you must have a plan that takes that time frame into account.

Say you're working on costume-jewelry accounts for the next fiscal year. If you want to wrap up sales by September, you might need to start developing a sales plan for this account in June. That means in June you'll prioritize to research the costume-jewelry marketplace, review your client's needs and put together your own magazine's research to prove your reader value to the client.

In July you should start preparing particular selling strategies. Perhaps you might construct a value-added package, offering the client access to readership surveys and special positioning in exchange for a six-time schedule. As a backup plan, you might offer exclusive placement, or access to the magazine's mailing list, or perhaps a special presentation at an industry trade show. In addition, you might organize your readership and market data to show how advertising would help the client reach a top marketing goal, such as increasing business 20 percent among fine-jewelry counters in major department stores.

By August, you should be discussing advertising options with your target account. Here's where you make your final presentations and close your schedule for the next fiscal year.

Also review your target accounts for seasonality. Perhaps some clients only advertise during holidays or trade shows, while others introduce new products during the fall or spring. Your sales plan, then, should fall comfortably within their planning schedule.

THE MASTER FILES

Once you've started working on your target accounts, keep a set of master files organized alphabetically by client. These should include:

◆ Insertion orders, contracts and other miscellaneous paperwork

◆ Sales letters, call reports, proposals

◆ Articles on your client, annual reports, executive profiles

◆ Your client's company profile, complete with a "needs analysis" (see on following pages)

You'll find this file will come in handy as you service your accounts. The more information you keep on your target clients, the better off you'll be constructing ongoing sales strategies.

Organizing your target accounts will take you a long way toward organizing your entire sales schedule. This way, you'll have managed your time and territory to give priority to clients who can give you the greatest return.

Consider these questions to address with your client:

TARGET ACCOUNT NEEDS ANALYSIS

Account_____   Contact_____

What are the company's expectations for growth this year?

_____

_____

Who is responsible for sales?_____

Marketing? _____

Advertising? _____

What products does the company make? _____

_____

Which of these products is the priority product line for advertising? _____

Who buys these products? _____

What are the buying considerations? _____

What is the job title or responsibility of the person who specifies this product?_____

How is the product positioned compared to competition? _____

What makes the company's product better than the competition?_____

_____

_____

Who are the company's biggest customers?_____

Who are the company's biggest prospects? _____

Who is the company's primary competitor?_____

What is the company's market share? _____

Is there any seasonality to the company's sales? _____

What role does advertising play in the company's marketing mix?_____

What other types of marketing does it do?_____

_____

What are the key trends in the market that affect business?_____

What was the objective of the company's last advertising campaign?_____

How did this particular ad do? _____

When does the company do marketing planning? _____

How does the company set the budget for advertising? _____

What publications does it use? _____

What about Bingo Cards? _____

What is the single largest objection or myth the company's salespeople need to deal with in the field? _____

_____

What is the company's pricing strategy? _____

What is the company's opinion about my publication? _____

If I come back to the company with an idea, would it be willing to listen? _____

What promotions has the company used in the past that have been successful? _____

Does the company plan to make changes in allocation of marketing funds this year? _____

24

CLICK! USING COMPUTERS to ORGANIZE

"When it comes to computer technology, what is top-of-the-line today is passé as soon as you buy it."

— Anonymous computer user

I've been in the magazine advertising business since 1977, and I still can't believe how much paper we used to consume. In ad sales B.C. (Before Computers), logging notes, schedules, phone lists, contact sheets and the like took up much of my day—and most of my available desk space.

Of course, we all still need paper. Personally, I'm lost without my schedule book. That being said, however, I'd feel more lost without a good contact-management computer program. Just about anything I used to do by hand, or in my head, I now do on my laptop. It's simpler, and I have to admit that a computer program has a much better organizing capacity than I do.

415

It's not just that computers can shuffle information around with such efficiency, or that they're great for sending e-mail and faxes on the road. Computers increase *productivity*. A good program reduces your busy work, giving you more time to sell. In an informal survey of sales reps at my seminars, I found that those who used computers completed an average of 23 to 32 sales phone conversations a day. That's compared to the 13 to 22 daily calls made by the average sales rep operating without a computer.

Without a doubt, that kind of efficiency is a sizable payback for the relatively small investment in a good laptop and a top contact-management program. Here's what a good system will do:

+ Help you to organize and target prospects according to sales potential

+ Allow you to react faster to client needs

+ Help you to communicate faster and more effectively by fax and e-mail

+ Enable faster sales follow-up

+ Reduce nonselling and administrative time

+ Increase your confidence in your ability to meet client needs

+ Allow you to sell anyplace, anytime

THE ELECTRONIC DAY

Of course, when you're new to ad sales, it's hard enough to figure out your job, much less how to manage a computer system. Eventually, given the right program and experience, any sales rep can use the computer as an untiring assistant with a boundless capacity to track, monitor, and keep things organized—a faithful "Cyber-Secretary."

The right system should help your day look something like this:

1. *Review and Organize.* You arrive at the office and ask your computer to list everyone you are scheduled to call today, or have

416

not yet reached from the prior day. Yesterday you called up your list by top show exhibitors. Today you'll call up everyone in your costume jewelry category. Press "enter," and the computer looks for your target accounts, organizing them by "A," "B," "C," and "D" priority.

2. *The Call List.* When you return from pouring a cup of coffee, the monitor displays the day's call list. You press "print" and direct the computer to dial the first client, Providential Fakes. The computer also automatically dials each progressive client after you hang up. Later, you might decide to disconnect the automatic dial and instead "point and shoot" your calls, skipping over a few "C" prospects to go back to some "A" accounts you called yesterday.

3. *Account Review.* In between calls you record your notes under each contact's file. You access your Providential Fakes file. Presto! On the screen you see the company's list of product categories, target customers, advertising history and sales priority.

Here you can look at the notes you made of your previous conversations. When you called on 6/16, Mr. Important said he'd know more about his budget figures by today. On 5/29, he'd indicated he'd take six pages if he could get prime positioning. You'd written, "PFakes runs 9X with competitor; need to assure him we deliver better value. Also, he may do full schedule in next budget cycle." (I even write down phrases or expressions my clients use so I can repeat them in my conversations and letters!)

Mr. Important is a steady client. You have his birthday noted, and a reminder to send a congratulatory card on his latest promotion. You've also noted that you sent him a sales letter on 5/14 and a personal note on 5/19. Both letters are in your word-processing program—only a keystroke away.

As you speak to Mr. Important, it's a good idea to wear a headset so you can type notes into the file as you talk. Later, you'll go back to your word processing program to enter another sales letter or customize a previous proposal.

417

4. *Reminders.* After speaking to Mr. Important's secretary, you post an electronic memo in a tickler file to send him a media kit.

5. *Calculations.* In a call to Pseudo Sapphires, you discuss changing an ad schedule from 4-time half-page to 3-time full-page ads. Within a few minutes, you calculate the new charges, discounts and commission for the change, and send an electronic message to production inquiring about late schedule changes. Then you call up Pseudo Sapphire's account, noting changes to previous contracts over the past year. You make a note to discuss the account with your ad manager.

6. *Research.* After lunch, your sales manager hands you a contact and phone number for Diamond Dupes, a new account. You do a quick electronic search of the name, looking for editorial mentions in the magazine and for your title's share of the prospect's ad market. You then calculate page potential for Diamond Dupes based on company size, share of market, media buying habits and other information you access electronically.

7. *Letters.* You've just had a promising initial phone contact with Diamond Dupes. So you head to your word-processing program and call up your letters file, retrieving the standard form letter you use for media kits. Alongside it, you pull up your notes from your conversation with Ms. Dupes and prepare a customized version of your form letter. You note how Diamond Dupes has great word-of-mouth (based on that recent article in *Fakes Today*), but lacks awareness among small costume retailers. Press "print," and your letter shoots out on company letterhead, ready to send. Or, fax the letter directly from your account-management program via modem.

8. *Management Review.* You and other sales reps gather to review business for an upcoming issue. Back to the computer. You print out your sales projections, goals, target account progress and comparisons to the previous issue. You also print out your projections and goals for the year, and quickly calculate the progress you've made in reaching them.

418

9. *Day's Review.* You call up the list of accounts you've contacted today and list action you want to take tomorrow. The tickler file indicates that you have three media kits to send out, six names to add to the magazine's comp list, and two letters to fax. You compare this week's closing ratio with last week's, and look at last week's call schedule to see how you're measuring up. Finally, you access your calendar to see which clients you'll be meeting with next week—where and when.

WHAT YOU'LL NEED

You might think you need a computer programming certificate to get all this done. All you really need is a computer, a comfortable chair, a high quality headset and letter-quality printer. Add a scanner, and you can attach your clients' ads to their file.

Confer with your magazine's MIS manager. He or she will advise you as to which easy-to-use account-management and word-processing software programs will help you put all your information in order and at your command.

As of this writing, you can choose from about 400 different generic account-management programs and several magazine-specific systems now available. Rather than recommend specific programs (which change too quickly), I'll discuss some features you'll probably want your program to have. Consider the following:

✦ **Sufficient file capacity** for recording thousands of names, addresses, phone and fax numbers.

✦ **User-defined sorting** for recording and reviewing client data. This feature allows you to retrieve files by last name, zip code, company, hair color or whatever other criteria you choose.

✦ **Ability to record** advertiser history by issue date, description, size, color, position and frequency.

✦ **A notepad** to keep track of conversations. It should be unstructured and vast, enabling you to write freely and as much as you want.

419

- ✦ **Automatic dialing** to save time and prevent misdialing.

- ✦ **Automatic time and date stamp** to record the last time you contacted the client and duration of the call. You should be able to access your contact records by date and time, as well as by name.

- ✦ **Calendar** to schedule events, travel plans and calls.

- ✦ **Ability to "mark"** so you can "cache" your file and immediately return to it after handling another client or task.

- ✦ **Ability to code** in order to designate results and reports of action, such as "sent media kit" or "called agency."

- ✦ **Word processing** for creating form and customized letters. Be sure it includes a spell checker and grammar checker! Look for an account-management program that allows you to import your favorite word-processing program.

- ✦ **Contract acknowledgment,** which tracks contract terms and contract expiration dates.

- ✦ **Standard forms** for insertion orders and advertising confirmations.

- ✦ **Database management** to keep and update your comp list file.

- ✦ **Pop-up menus** that contain selections for quick data entry. In other words, it should take you no more than a few keystrokes to get to "Letters" or "Callbacks."

- ✦ **An onscreen coach** or a "HELP" menu to guide you when you get stuck.

As mentioned above, you'll also need a modem for sending e-mail and faxes, and for gaining access to the Internet. Don't forget that access to the 'Net can be a huge asset in your quest for information, statistics, company histories and related materials. (My bet is that probably most of your advertisers have a Web page!)

WHO'S GOT WHAT

True, I said I wouldn't recommend specific programs to you. Still, you should be aware that (as of this writing), SpaceMaster (Seacau-

420

cus, NJ) is one of the few sales-management programs specifically designed for magazine ad sales. The list of its features includes the following:

✦ Contact directories

✦ Comp/promo lists

✦ Call reporting abilities

✦ Ad placement reporting, including ability to calculate charges, account splits, premiums, etc.

✦ Contract management

✦ Sales forecasting

✦ Invoicing/accounts receivable

✦ Financial reporting

✦ Production reporting

Moreover, one of the most popular sales-management programs is ACT (Activities, Contacts and Time), manufactured by Symantec (San Jose, CA). ACT allows sales reps to track contacts, make notes, sort by user-defined fields, and schedule callbacks. Although it's not specifically designed for ad sales, it's easily adapted to most sales needs.

Before you settle on a program, make sure you talk with your ad manager and MIS manager. At the very least, you need to know that your software interfaces with your magazine's computer hardware, and that your program meets all your publication's specific needs.

Whatever program you choose, using contact-management software is like keeping a running journal of your work—a journal you can review anywhere or anytime you need to. It's the fastest and easiest way tie up the loose strings of your business, and it frees you from having to memorize all the discussions, letters and information that pass between you and your client.

If you're serious about managing your time and territory, you'll find that the right computer program—and your practiced, consistent use of it—will help make it happen.

SECTION VII

ON THE ROAD AGAIN: SHOWS AND TRAVEL

25

WALKING the HALLS to SALES SUCCESS at SHOWS

"The world is before you, and you need not take it or leave it as it was when you came in."
—James Baldwin (1924-1987)
American writer

Want to know how to compress weeks of selling into a couple days? Get thee to an exposition. One walk through an industry show on printing processes, for instance, can put you in touch with more printing shops and manufacturers than a dozen flights around the country.

But you have to *know* just how to take that walk. A great trade show to a unprepared sales rep is like a Porsche turbo to a 14-year-old. It may look like a dream, but it's useless (even dangerous) if

425

you don't know how to handle it. So in this chapter, I'll show you how to make the most of your show time to prospect, sell to current advertisers and make important contacts. I'll also show you how to survive a show, physically and emotionally. It's more of a challenge than you might think!

ON WITH THE SHOW

Picture all your prospects and clients captive under one roof. It's an ad salesperson's dream! One East Coast ad director I know even called selling at shows "shooting ducks in a barrel."

Shows can give ad salespeople more face-to-face contacts per hour than any other selling opportunity. Moreover, these are *motivated* contacts. Successful shows run on a kind of adrenaline rush. People want to buy, sell and make deals. They'll talk day and night about ceramic tiles, framing materials, industrial screws—the kind of thing they would normally stop thinking about as soon as they leave the office. It's the perfect atmosphere for selling.

Shows also give you other opportunities. You can make "reader calls" and see firsthand what and how your readers like to buy. You can view products up close, and get a quick but thorough mini-education about your industry. Best of all, you can watch advertisers sell to their customers. You get a free course in marketing consulting by tuning in to what your advertisers emphasize about their products and services.

At shows, your market comes alive. Instead of merely *talking* about your clients' business, you're seeing it firsthand. Industry suppliers are meeting customers, distributors and wholesalers. And you're in the mix.

Get To The Hotshots

One of the best things about a show is that your clients and prospects can't hide. There's no secretary to screen your call; no voice mail to be returned. If you've been having trouble getting to a VP of marketing, or if the marketing director never returns your calls, you might find your golden opportunity within the show walls.

426

Just pick a way to move up the decision-making ladder. Your client contacts may be happy to introduce you to their associates and superiors. Or, if your contact is a recalcitrant prospect, you might find a way to "accidentally" meet her superior without the usual risk of offending her. You might also ferret out hidden decision-makers with some quick detective work.

Network! If one of your clients is pals with a marketing head at that manufacturing prospect that keeps dodging your calls, ask for an introduction. To some people, merely seeing you in friendly conversation with an exhibitor who is an advertiser can act as a third party testimonial. Once you're accepted as one of the gang, you'll find it easier to land and keep your prospects.

You might also find that many executives who wouldn't take your calls will be pleased to speak with you once they see your smiling face. If you sell primarily by phone, you know that it's tough to develop rapport without face-to-face contact. Prospects find it easier to say "no," or even to act rudely, when speaking with an anonymous "someone" on the phone. Shows are critical for establishing those personal relationships that often lead to sales.

LAYING THE GROUNDWORK

How well you do at a show depends a great deal on your pre-show planning. You need to outline and discuss your expectations, objectives and strategies long before you get on the plane. Do you know which clients will be there? Do you have time to meet them all? Do you know if anyone you need to see is free to meet with you? If you're not careful, you can let those crucial prospects slip by without even a "Hello."

So here's how to get started:

✦ *Review the exhibitor list.* Decide, prospect by prospect, what you want to achieve. Maybe Smith Tool & Die is ready to close a specific ad sales contract, while Jones Industries, which never returns your calls, rates an in-person introduction. You can circle a few unfamiliar companies for a fact-finding mission, and drop in on other friendly clients for a public-relations call.

◆ *Organize your floor plan.* First, make sure you've got an accurate floor plan from the show producers. Then figure out how you'll walk the aisles, organizing yourself by exhibitor booth numbers. Consider color-coding the floor plan or exhibitor list to indicate your "A," "B," and "C" prospects. You might make additional notes on index cards to cue you when you start walking.

Especially at large shows, you may want to visit with "A" prospects on the first round, circle a second time for "B" prospects, and so forth. That way, you'll ensure that you meet with the most important advertisers before the close of the show. Bear in mind that the higher up the executive, the less time she'll spend at the show. Many leave after the first day, so be sure to visit them first.

◆ *Make appointments.* As you talk to clients in the weeks before the show, make specific plans to meet with your most important contacts. Send confirmation notes or faxes. Set up a breakfast (or two) plus some lunch, coffee, cocktail hour and dinner appointments. If a client simply invites you to "come by the booth," though, prepare yourself for a cool reception. That might be less of an invitation than a brush-off.

◆ *Fill up your time.* At a good show, just about every moment creates an opportunity. Use it! One West Coast sales manager requires his ad salespeople to schedule 8 to 10 appointments a day at the show. In order to spend time with his most important clients, he also gets a dozen tickets to a major evening sporting event.

Your own publisher may decide to sponsor an advertiser/ exhibitor breakfast or party. Schedule time for special events, such as opening-night receptions and exhibitor cocktail parties.

Remember, though, even at a party you're still working. These aren't times to let off steam or hang out with your buddies. Develop your networking skills, learn to work a room. You'll find yourself making contacts with top executives and industry leaders you might not otherwise meet.

Shows are a perfect time to break a salesperson into a new territory or to "pass the baton" from one salesperson to another.

✦ *Walk with your associates.* Schedule time to cover the hall with the publisher, editor, or even the circulation director. They may have relationships with important prospects, or could introduce you to key decision makers. They can also bring a different perspective to advertisers, such as emphasizing the value of your magazine circulation or editorial.

Shows are also a perfect time to break a salesperson into a new territory or to "pass the baton" from one salesperson to another.

SELLING "SOFTLY" AT SHOWS

Once you know whom you'll be meeting, it's crucial to know *how* to meet with prospects at a show. A trade show is *not* your client's office; it's not where you bring out the dog-and-pony and the three-ring presentation. (On the other hand, if you've got a set appointment with a client, he might find it the ideal time to hear your presentation. See if he invites you to speak.)

Remember, your prospects—the exhibitors—are there to sell, not to buy. True, you've got most of your customers under one roof, but not all of them want to be sold there. In fact, when I first started selling, I was kicked out of a booth by a grumpy exhibitor who thought that all ad salespeople were piranhas. To sell at a trade show, you must be sensitive and sell *softly*. It's crucial that you create the right impression.

Consider the following suggestions as you make your contacts:

✦ *Courtesy counts.* Be sensitive to your client's schedules, moods and needs. If your client is alone at a booth, he may not be inclined to chat with you if it means ignoring buyers. Exhibitors need to feel that you're there to *support* their success, not to impede or distract them. Use good judgment.

✦ *Approach with care.* You know the feeling. You're at a cocktail party and that attractive person you've had your eye on is maddeningly engrossed in talk with someone else. How to cut in? Discreetly.

Same thing with that attractive prospect. Don't give him

429

the chance to see you as the stereotypical space hustler. Be careful with your approach. Watch for body language that indicates whether he's in deep conversation or just shooting the breeze. Check the badge color to see if he's speaking with another exhibitor or an attendee. Stay back if it looks like your prospect is in selling mode, but if he's is speaking with another exhibitor, move closer and wait. You may get a signal to wait a moment, or to come on over as the means to ending a boring conversation. If he ignores you, take the hint and move on.

BOOTH COURTESY

For many sales reps, the real test of trade-show skills is in crossing that invisible line to an exhibitor's booth. That's where you can find out who a company's real decision makers are, what they sell and how they like to sell it.

Entering a booth offers a great opportunity to get acquainted with your prospect. You want to make sure that every moment in that booth is productive, both for you and the prospect. Here's how to do it:

◆ *Get some knowledge.* Take a moment to look at what the company exhibits, particularly if it's a new prospect. Quickly review the sales literature before you ask to be introduced to the decision maker. Your first booth contact will probably be a salesperson, and she'll usually know what's going on in the company. She'll also be a good person to help you to find the real decision makers.

◆ *Be careful of the dreaded question.* If a show seems so-so, avoid asking, "How's the show going?" Trust me, you'll get an earful of all that's wrong at the show, the hotel, the world, and maybe your jacket. You don't want to begin your conversation on a negative note (particularly if it's *your* company putting on the show!).

◆ *Bring goodies.* Just as a good guest brings a bottle of wine to dinner, a good sales rep tends to prepare special material when visiting a prospect's booth. Great "gifts" might be, for instance, advertising lead-evaluation reports from reader response cards.

430

Exhibitors and advertisers are obsessed with leads, so you'd hit their hot buttons immediately.

Other "goodies" might be market tidbits you've scavenged at the show. Exhibitors know that ad salespeople meet with lots of other exhibitors—which means they're inevitably asked to play reporter. Pass along information about how certain customers are looking for pre-press materials, or how Marvel Enterprises is thinking of changing distributors. (Just don't give away secrets!) One salesperson I know scores lots of points by bringing potential buyers to exhibitor booths. There's no better booth-warming gift!

✦ *Sit in on a sale.* If you can, use this opportunity to learn about the sales challenges your advertisers face. Just ask an exhibitor if you can watch him in action for a while! Even a few moments of eavesdropping on a sales conversation can yield precious information about which benefits the company emphasizes, or how it handles a prospect's objections.

✦ *Let the prospect guide the sale.* In a normal sales presentation, you're the one in charge of the turf. But an exhibitor's booth is your prospect's turf. Let him make the rules. Act as a marketing consultant, and let him tell you how far into the selling process he's willing to go.

Many ad salespeople believe it's better to concentrate on prospecting, fact-finding and relationship-building at shows, rather than on presentations and closing. I take each situation case-by-case. Especially when dealing with new prospects, you can simply ask if they'd like to continue the sales discussion. You can then ask if they'd like to talk now or later. Some clients consider shows the perfect time to analyze advertising options; others consider you an intrusion.

Just be careful once you find yourself closing a sale with a new and excited customer. Many clients get caught up in the adrenaline rush of a show, then forget all about (or cancel) that insertion order once they get back to the real world. When this happens, don't pressure your advertiser. You'll only create ill-will. Instead, re-sell your advertiser. He had good reasons for buying the first time!

◆ *Leave notes.* If you can't catch an exhibitor's attention after several passes by the booth, write a note on your business card and leave it with one of the booth staff. A simple "Came by to say 'hi'—glad to see you so busy with prospects" can put you in good stead.

A note is also a record of your interest in your client. I remember the frustration of going by an exhibitor's booth a dozen times, unable to make contact. Later, on the phone, the client complained I never came to see him!

◆ *Take notes.* You might *think* you'll remember that Jargen Industries has a six-time schedule in your competition, or that Rothco Imports is introducing a new product line. But once you walk out of that exhibit booth, memory fades quickly. Take notes as you go along, or talk into a microcassette recorder. One organized sales rep I know even carries a stapler to staple a prospect's business card right into her notebook. You'll be glad you can save yourself a lot of time and hassle.

◆ *Collect your notes.* Once you've finished your rounds, you'll likely find yourself with a briefcase full of paper scraps, flyers, scrawled phone numbers, business cards and other unholy detritus. Don't despair.

First, cut and paste your handwritten notes into alphabetical order and read your report into a tape recorder. Send the tape overnight to the office, or take it with you for immediate transcription.

Set aside the exhibitor brochures and fact sheets. You can later use these as fact-finding tools when you talk with the client again. Perhaps that brochure of new mold-making services can help you recommend ad copy for a potential ad.

Add the business card information and phone numbers to

your client and prospect file. Again, write any odd notes or observations you recall. Do this while you're still fresh from the show. With your show report and sales literature in hand, you're ready to follow up on the show immediately.

IT'S ABOUT ATTITUDE

Working an exhibitor floor takes guts, energy, charm, flexibility. But mostly, it takes attitude. If you're exhilarated working the show floor, your clients will react more positively toward you and your sales message. If not, you'll drain your clients' energy as you shuffle in to see them. It's tough enough for most exhibitors to maintain their spunk. Don't make it harder. A positive attitude will help them recharge *their* batteries, and they'll love you for it.

Besides, you need humor to survive the chaos and overwhelming aspects of a show. It's the perfect place to witness Murphy's Law ("If anything can go wrong, it will") in full operation. Every show veteran can regale you with horror stories of lost luggage, botched appointments, disappearing clients, missing business cards. I once got the flu during setup, missed the entire show, and spent several miserable days by myself in a Mexico City hotel room. Be prepared to earn your show trooper badge!

Working the show floor demands both physical and emotional stamina. You'll be on your feet longer than a coffee-shop waitress, and talk more than a game-show host. You'll need to pace yourself, respect your nutritional needs, and stay off the high-fat junk foods and liquor that may slow you down.

So make sure you're comfortable. Wear appropriate business dress for your market or industry. In most cases that will mean a business suit (with pockets for business cards), although I've seen salespeople in the sports market wear sweats with their publication's logo. Keep to the comfortable shoes—even tennis shoes if you must. Those heels may look great, but you'll be lucky if your feet make it to a coffee break.

Carry as little as possible. Keep it to a clipboard, floor plan, note paper, and media material or research. If possible, arrange to have someone stop by certain booths and pick up sales literature for you. This material will prove invaluable after the show! If your publication has its own booth, use it as a storage and message center. Don't rest idly in the booth and pretend that you're working the show.

TURN IT ON AND KEEP IT ON

When does the show start? As soon as you register at the hotel, if not in the cab ride down from the airport. And from the moment it starts, remember that you're "on" and highly visible the entire time.

Being "on" is hard work, but important. Being "on" means keeping your badge on at all times, worn on your right side so your prospect can see it as he shakes your hand. It means smiling, even though your face may crack. It even means being careful what you say in places where you may be overheard. You may not know who's standing next to you in the elevator, or sitting at the next table in the hotel restaurant.

When I first started selling at shows, I attended a cocktail party with my editor. We left for the bathroom and continued our conversation from inside the stalls. As I exited my stall, I was horrified to find the person I had been talking about washing her hands.

Don't forget that you'll meet contacts everywhere—aisles, escalators, coat checks, even the hot-dog line. I find the best day to find prospects is the last day of setup: Top managers are often around, and there are no attendees to distract them. The only problem may be identifying who's important due to the lack of badges. I confess to having walked right past a bluejean-clad worker who turned out to be a long-term client!

But for all the hard work and chaos, a show is perhaps the most rewarding experience in selling. You'll get more of an education than you ever expected, and meet more potential clients than you could ever hope. Make the most of it. Make your plans, but be ready to switch gears and be spontaneous. Keep your antennae up and follow your instincts. Walk the halls to sales success.

26

TRAVEL TIPS for ROAD WARRIORS

"Its a funny thing about life; if you refuse to accept anything but the best, you very often get it."
— Somerset Maugham (1874-1965)
English novelist, dramatist and short-story writer

When someone asks where I live, I'm tempted to say, "at 35,000 feet on an airplane." When you're in sales, travel is a given. It's also a physical and emotional drain. I love to travel, but without careful planning, physical stamina and emotional fortitude, traveling can make me a selling wreck.

So when you travel as long as I have, you learn a lot about how to do it right, based on everything that's gone wrong. If you haven't traveled much, take these travel tips from me. They'll make your miles more enjoyable and less frenzied. More importantly, they'll help keep you in top form for successfully meeting with clients.

FIND A GOOD AGENT!
The best advice I can give is to find a professional and caring travel agent. He or she can understand your travel and personal needs, look out for the best fares, give you good advice on anything from

foreign currency to hotels, and prevent you from making travel mistakes.

At some point soon, I expect we may do most of our ticket buying directly from the airlines online. Technology would allow us to select all our fare information, enter our travel profile data and even select hotels and restaurants at our destination. Such a service would save time and money for everyone. But until that day comes, a good agent is invaluable.

Here's just a short list of what good agents can do for you:

◆ *Play the airline fare games.* Airline fares are designed to penalize the business traveler, and the rules change constantly. Let your agent be your guide. Make sure he takes advantage of lower advance fares, but leaves you the flexibility you need.

◆ *Provide tickets and itineraries.* You can get your boarding pass from your agent and save yourself an airport line. Just check the accuracy of your tickets as soon as you get them; even the best agents make errors. Cross-check your itinerary as well. Once, I almost left on a business trip a week early.

◆ *Set up a file of preferences.* You can, for instance, have a permanent file of seat preferences (I request aisle seats, far forward). You can also pick special meals (coach meals not only taste terrible, they're very high in fat and sodium).

◆ *Select the right airlines.* With experience and your agent's help, you can find which airlines have the best routes, times or most flights to your frequent destinations. I once found one airline that had great fares, but on my *first flight* I was delayed four times and missed appointments! It pays to fly a good airline, even if it's a bit more expensive.

AIRPORT SURVIVAL

◆ *Be a frequent flyer.* Pick one or two airlines that you will use most frequently and accumulate frequent flyer points. Many major credit cards also give you points for each dollar you spend. Use your points to upgrade to business or first class, or,

436

like me, buy frequent flyer "sticker books" that charge a set dollar amount per 1,000-mile upgrade.

Frequent flyers also get early boarding privileges on most major airlines. That can also protect you on an overbooked flight. After all, possession, as they say, is nine-tenths of the law.

✦ *Join airline clubs* of the airlines you use most. You need only one stranded evening in a storm for the club to pay for itself. Airline clubs provide welcome respite from airport hassle. The agents handle any of your problems, and the people are friendly. You can relax, watch the news or conduct business. The clubs are set up with plenty of phones, faxes, modems and other necessary services. If you have your notebook computer, an airline club is like an office wherever you go.

GETTING THERE

✦ *Don't take the last flight out.* If you miss the last flight of the day, or if it's delayed, you'll miss your appointments the next day. Let the problems happen on the way home, when you have less to lose.

✦ *Fly nonstop, if possible.* That's especially important during winter, when there's a greater risk of long delays and cancellations.

✦ *Choose reliable ground transportation.* Balance convenience, reliability and finances. Maybe a car service is more expensive than a bus, but it will at least get you to the airport on time.

✦ *Allow time for errors.* I always tell the pickup service to come early so that I can jump in my car in case it doesn't show. (Recently, I was thankful I left early for one training session because I discovered my car wouldn't start. I called a taxi from my cellular phone and got to the training site with time to spare.)

✦ *Arrive early at the airport.* This will help lower your stress level and take care of any last-minute boarding snags.

✦ *Avoid lines.* You should already have your boarding pass from your agent. Check your luggage at curbside, but make sure the porters put correct flight and destination tags on your luggage.

437

PACKING REMINDERS

◆ *Take what you can carry on board.* It's always a good plan, but personally I can't pull that off unless I'm going away only for a day or two. I bring along one piece of luggage to check and fill it to capacity with all my personal items. A luggage cart holds my luggage and work materials, and my carry-on can roll through the aisles.

◆ *Don't forget medications.* I try to bring essential medications on board, and keep a list of medications to which I'm allergic. From now on, I'll also carry a thermometer. I learned my lesson on a trip to Spain where I became ill. I had someone locate a thermometer for me—only to find I has a 102° fever and I hadn't even packed an aspirin!

◆ *Don't check the sales materials.* NEVER place the next day's sales materials into checked luggage. If you're taking a lot of handout materials, consider shipping them in advance. If you must check materials, keep an original with you for emergency copying.

◆ *Write it down.* Always put your business card and hotel destination address and phone number on the inside as well as outside of your luggage. For safety, use your business address rather than your home address.

◆ *Keep the itinerary with you.* Include the hotel confirmation number. I once inadvertently left this information in my checked luggage. Guess what? The scheduled car service never arrived; the airline lost my luggage; it was Sunday so I couldn't call my client—and I was lost. Luckily, I remembered that I was going to a hunting lodge, and after playing "name that place" with the driver, I finally recognized the name.

◆ *Protect yourself.* Never pack anything you can't afford to lose, such as jewelry, money or medicine. And make sure your homeowner's policy covers loss and replacement value of your clothes, since the airlines are liable for only a minimal amount. Two major airlines in the same year sent most of my spring and winter business wardrobes to luggage heaven. So now I keep a list as I'm packing to make sure (a) I'm packing all that I need (plus a little more) and (b) I've got a record for insurance purposes. I even keep all clothes receipts in a file in case the airlines lose my luggage again.

WHILE ON THE PLANE

✦ *Eat healthy.* Consider packing a picnic lunch or at least some of your favorite healthy snacks. Be careful not to add an extra meal to the day if you're crossing time zones.

✦ *Stay hydrated.* Air inside the plane is oxygen-poor and can result in dehydration. Avoid alcohol, drink lots of bottled water and use moisture lotion often. Some people even bring a mini-spray bottle of water. Every hour or so, take a walk around the plane.

✦ *Dress comfortably.* Obviously, you should dress appropriately if you're going directly to see a client. Even if you're not, most experts suggest you dress for business anyway. If the airline loses your luggage, you can have the hotel press what you're wearing and still be presentable for your meeting. (Personally, though, I prefer to dress for comfort on long trips and take my chances. True, I once had to sell at a two-day trade show in my sweats—but at least I had a wonderful ice breaker at the show.)

JET LAG

Jet lag is a killer, particularly traveling west to east. Westerners like me have to get up at about 4 a.m. California time to get to an 8:30 New York City appointment. I'm the first in line the day they develop an effective and safe jet lag pill. Until then, I'll share these tips.

✦ *Set your body clock.* Start going to bed earlier and getting up earlier a few days before your west-to-east trip.

✦ *Adjust early.* Soon after you board the plane, set your watch to the time zone of your destination. Now try to eat and sleep on that clock.

◆ *Stay in the light.* Experts say that natural light tells our body what time it is. If possible, take a walk when you land, especially if it's still light.

WHEN YOU ARRIVE...

◆ *Choose your transportation carefully.* Picture me, a native Southern Californian, trying to drive through a snow storm in a rental car in Montreal. I swerved to a stop, my hubcap fell off, and I ran after it, slipping and sliding, tears in my eyes, screaming I would never drive in the snow again.

What's easy for a native may be very difficult for you. You may not know the streets, weather or driving habits of your destination city. When in doubt, take a cab.

◆ *Know where you're going.* Too obvious? Once, in Ohio, I rented a car from an agency that didn't have a map. Instead, they gave me verbal directions for my two-hour drive. Two hours later I arrived at a major city—the wrong one and in the opposite direction I needed to go! My two-hour trip became a four-and-a-half-hour disaster.

◆ *Get a cellular phone.* It's great for safety as well as convenience. You can call 911 from anywhere in the country. You can also call for traffic reports and directions, not to mention emergency road services like AAA. And if you're hitting heavy traffic or running late for a sales appointment (a major sin in selling) at least you can call your client's office from the road.

YOUR HOME AWAY FROM HOME

Pick your hotel carefully, and make sure it meets your location, financial and personal needs. You might prefer small, quaint European-type hotels. I like those with all the services, such as 24-hour room service, exercise rooms, massage and stores. Whatever hotel you choose, be comfortable. Keep these tips in mind:

◆ *Make it familiar.* If you travel to the same city frequently, pick a hotel you like and stick with it. The staff will probably give you a corporate rate, and you'll have the comfort of a familiar place.

440

That takes the edge off feeling like a stranger.

✦ *Let the hotel take care of you.* I love room service, especially in the morning. Most hotels will honor your special dietary requests. Get a wake-up call and set an alarm for back-up. And if you're overly tempted by the mini-bar (those frozen Snickers bars always give me pause), refuse the mini-bar key.

✦ *Put safety first.* Take control of your environment so that you feel secure and comfortable. Personally, I stay away from rooms where the front door opens to the street, especially on the first floor. I also use the room safe, if available, to secure valuables.

Before you leave home, make a copy of all your credit cards and leave the information with a family member or trusted friend. If your wallet gets stolen, you can make the necessary calls to protect your credit.

Never let anyone in your room, even the hotel staff, unless you've requested service or can double-check by phone first with the front desk. Remember, a "please clean" sign on the door also alerts thieves.

Be aware of your surroundings. Notice who follows as you walk down the hall or into the elevator. Avoid being alone anyplace with a stranger who makes you feel uncomfortable. Use common sense and trust your instincts.

If you take a cab out, be sure you can get one to take you back to the hotel. If necessary, make arrangements to be picked up by the cab driving you, or at least bring along the cab company's number. Always take along the hotel's phone number and address. I once found myself stranded late at night at a mall in Puerto Rico. My Spanish is poor, and after several failed attempts to get a cab, I had to stand there, feeling like a four-year old, as the police called a cab for me and stood guard until it arrived.

✦ *Have fun!* Business trips can leave you with nights off and energy to spare. I might go to a gym, or ask my hotel concierge to direct me to a safe mall that has a movie theater and a food

441

court. Even on winter nights I can walk around and relax by watching a movie.

I've had many wonderful experiences while traveling and met people I would never have met at home. Take special care to ensure that your travels add to your life experience while you conduct business successfully. Come home safe and sound.

SECTION VIII

SECRET SKILLS
OF THE
TOP SALES PROS

27

USING YOUR INTUITION to BECOME a SALES VIRTUOSO

"...in much of life, imagination is more important than knowledge."
—Albert Einstein (1879-1955)

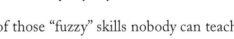

Intuition is one of those "fuzzy" skills nobody can teach you. All the intuition you will ever have is already inside you, and it's enough to make you the best salesperson you can be. All you have to do is learn to access it.

What can intuition do that an office full of subscriber research and audit reports can't?

✦ It signals when you're wasting energy with a client who's just not interested.

◆ It helps you "know" when it's okay to close, even if you haven't finished your presentation.

◆ It is that gut feeling that the person you're talking to isn't the real decision maker.

◆ It can jump to the rescue with ideas when your client is stuck in a marketing rut.

In other words, using your intuition can get you into the game of selling, which is a fluid, creative activity between people. Sure, you can read this book again and again, and you'll know something about selling. In fact, you'll know quite a lot. But you'll never really *know* how to sell until you're out there taking risks and interacting with people.

Years ago, I took a college course in music appreciation. The professor, a world-class pianist, told us right away that all our exams would be based on the book. That meant that we didn't even have to attend the lectures or listen to concerts! But he also said that if we *didn't* actually listen to music, we would never get a thing out of the course.

At the time, I only wanted a good grade. I read the book and got an A. I didn't go to concerts; I never "felt" the music as he so clearly did, bobbing and gesturing as he carefully listened to recorded music he shared with us.

To this day I don't know much about music. I wasted my time, and I regret it because I didn't understand what it was to really learn.

Take the time to listen and tap into your intuition, your creativity, and develop a style. If you sell strictly "by the book," you'll end up with cliche techniques that your prospects will see through like a wet T-shirt. Present your magazine in a way that's as unique as you are. Use your intuition to guide you through the morass of CPMs, demographics, audits and rates. Then use the information to spark your creativity, rather than kill it.

With imagination, you can make your magazine come alive.

446

You can develop winning solutions for your client's marketing problems. You can find ways to make your job interesting, exciting and profitable.

TAPPING THE RIGHT SIDE OF THE BRAIN

Like many activities, selling is a combination of linear logic *and* creativity. For instance, if you're about to cook dinner, you take out the six ingredients the recipe calls for and mix them in a bowl. But then as you taste the mix, as all the ingredients start to blend, you might get an idea to add some in cumin or ginger. Now you might want a few raisins in it as well, or maybe some currants. That's the process at work—the linear logic, like a long fuse, erupted by a creative spark. Often, our analytical minds lead us only partway down the path to a fruitful decision. Our intuition guides us the rest of the way when we listen to it.

Imagine that your client tells you his restaurant equipment sales have declined in the South. Without thinking, you reach for your publisher's statement showing the geographic strength of your readership. You begin to give the usual presentation about making a demographic buy. But then, in the back of your mind, you start to get a flash about southern restaurants, southern food—and you get a sudden crazy notion about sponsoring a Pierre Prudhomme Cook-Alike and Look-Alike Contest. Wacky idea? Sure! But it gets you and your client talking about marketing plans and exciting ways to promote his product.

Don't be afraid of this wacky side of yourself. We all have one. I learned a lot about creative thinking from a book by Roger van Oech called *A Whack on the Side of the Head*. In it, he talks about how to break out of "mental locks" and not let routines imprison our thinking.

I gave myself a whack once by taking a drawing class. It was great because my teacher released us from preconceived notions of *seeing*. She asked me, for instance, to copy a picture of a dog scratching its tail—but I had to copy it upside-down. That way, I couldn't be influenced by my idea of what a scratching dog looked like. My attention was on the lines and forms in the picture. Interestingly, by drawing it this way, I created a picture that looked very much like the original!

The point, I learned, was to confuse the left side the brain, the part that controls our logical and rational thinking. With the left brain shut down, the right brain, in charge of creative thinking, has a chance to take over.

I quickly saw how this applied to sales. Good sales is "looking at the same thing as everyone else, but thinking something different," to paraphrase Nobel Prize winner Albert Szent-Gyorgyi. In other words, you don't just peddle space for the sake of giving advertisers a place to sell. You don't give a presentation that's nothing but ready-made answers. You act as a sales and marketing consultant, solving problems and planning strategies with your clients.

As a further right-brain exercise, our drawing teacher had us perform "gesture drawing," which involved drawing a live model who switched poses every 60 seconds. We learned how to perceive the whole being quickly, without getting stuck in details. How many times do we find ourselves groping for answers in a selling situation because we're stuck in details?

I've also tried communication exercises. In one, I went on a 24-hour silence marathon—quite a challenge for my expressive personality! At first, I panicked. For a while, I wrote notes to communicate, but somehow that seemed to defeat the purpose.

Finally, I gave in—and discovered that I didn't need to talk to get the attention and support I wanted. In fact, I was getting even more support by quietly watching what was going on around me and feeling that I was not alone. I was able to observe and understand on a deeper level.

Don't get me wrong. I'm not suggesting you hand-draw your next presentation chart, or perform your next sales call in mime. But if you've got the guts to take an occasional excursion into your intuitive powers—and yes, it takes guts—you'll find yourself a better salesperson for it.

448

28

The SALES CHAMELEON

"Within the self, there is a central force that unifies thoughts and actions. When you are not in accord with your goals, you may feel indecision, conflict and malaise; when you are, a sense of self-confidence and well-being will surround you."
—I Ching No. 45

Remember Zelig? In the old Woody Allen film, he was the lead character who took on the personality of everyone he met—acting, shouting, nodding or waving his arms around in a mirror image of the people around him.

He wanted to fit in and make people like him. He was a chameleon. Which brings up this point: If you're going to be in this people business—if you're going to sell—you've must make people feel comfortable with you. And the best way to do this is to be a sales chameleon.

Don't get me wrong. I'm not advocating that you suddenly change personalities in order to make a sale. After all, your clients need to see you as you are, a genuine, real and trustworthy person.

But what I *am* advocating is that you spend a little time observing your client's personality and adjusting your own to his or her comfort level. For instance, if you're meeting with a passive, low-key prospect, you don't want to wring his hand like a dishrag. Nor do you want to avoid eye contact with someone who's clearly used to being in charge. You don't want to fast-talk anyone who's reluctant to move to business matters, and you don't want to waste time with another who's giving you those "get on with it" cues.

Adapting a chameleon skin helps your prospect relax and listen. Just observe what happens if you don't pay attention to your client's cues. Start spouting like an auctioneer around a slow-paced talker, and he'll think you are untrustworthy, suspicious, a con artist. Start foot-dragging around a fast talker, and she'll think you're slow or dimwitted.

LEARN TO DANCE WITH YOUR PROSPECT

It takes two to tango in dancing and sells. If you're out of sync with your partner/prospect, you'll step on his toes, and you may not get asked for another round. But if you're on to his rhythm, you'll make the dance look easy, graceful and natural.

Like bad dancers, many salespeople stick to one basic selling style. They don't use their observation skills, experience, intuition and creativity to think fast on their feet and tailor their strategies.

To learn the dance of sales, pay attention to your prospect. You may not always know what he's thinking, but he'll certainly put out behavior signals. One prospect, for instance, may physically pull away or look stone-faced at your attempts to be friendly. Another may start talking about the Knicks game as you're pulling out your latest audit figures. They're both giving signals that they're uncomfortable with your style. Take the hint. These clients are coaching you on how to sell them.

Resistance is the killer, whether you're selling or dancing. Good communication puts your partner in a positive mood. When you recognize your partner's style, you begin to treat him as he wants to be treated.

450

Keep in mind that your prospect wants to know how much you *care* about his problems and business before he wants to know how much you *know*. You may have the greatest presentation in the history of the world, but he won't listen to it if he doesn't like who's delivering it.

EVERYBODY'S DIFFERENT

If you're in sales, chances are pretty good you're persuasive, a big thinker, an idea person, spontaneous and fun. You are, in other words, an *expressive* personality, and you're probably comfortable around others who are expressive, too.

But not everyone is expressive, persuasive or spontaneous, and your client may fit into another personality category. In fact, there are four basic personalities, and it helps to be familiar with each so you'll know how best to communicate with any type you'll meet.

One behavior model divides personality types between *assertiveness* and *responsiveness*. Assertiveness is the amount of control people try to exert over themselves, others and their environment. Responsiveness refers to the person's ability to show emotion.

Very low-assertive people may appear submissive, introverted, and indecisive. They may have a soft handshake, intermittent eye contact, a quiet voice and protective body movements. Very high-assertive people appear aggressive, decisive, energetic, ego-driven or manipulative. They have a firm grip, steady eye contact and dramatic speech and gestures.

Very low-responsive people come across as cold fish, poker faced, secretive, cautious and difficult to read. They may be less expressive, less likely to share feelings, more interested in learning facts and details than in talking about personal issues.

A high-responsive person, by contrast, may be dramatic, talkative, outgoing—someone you can read like a book. These people tend to tell stories and anecdotes with plenty of body movement, and provide immediate nonverbal feedback.

Observable Responsive Behaviors

High Responsiveness	Low Responsiveness
Animated facial expressions	Somewhat expressionless
Much hand and body movement	Controlled and limited hand and body movement
Flexible time perspective	Conversation focuses on issues and tasks at hand
Tells stories and anecdotes	Pushes for facts and details
Little emphasis on facts and details	Little sharing of personal feelings
Shares personal feelings	Noncontact-oriented
Contact-oriented	Slow at giving nonverbal feedback
Immediate non-verbal feedback	

Observable Assertive Behaviors

Low Assertive	High Assertive
Soft handshake	Firm handshake
Intermittent eye contact	Steady eye contact
Low quality of verbal communication	High quality of verbal communication
Questions tend to be for clarification, support information	Questions tend to be rhetorical, to emphasize points, challenge information
Makes tentative statements	Makes emphatic statements
Limits gestures to support conversation	Gestures to emphasize points
Low voice volume	High voice speed
Slow voice speed	Emphasizes points through challenging voice intonation
Little variation in vocal intonation	Communicates readily
Communicates hesitantly	Fast moving
Slow moving	

Look for behavior traits to determine personality types.

ADAPTING YOUR SALES STYLE

Naturally, most people fall somewhere between the extremes. But the combination of assertiveness and responsiveness form four distinct personal styles. **Expressive, Driver, Analytical** and **Amiable.** Your job is to determine which of the four styles you're working with, and to learn how to adjust your sales technique appropriately.

High Responsive

1. Amiable

Makes decisions carefully
Likes close personal relationships
Dislikes interpersonal conflict
Supports and actively listens to others
Doesn't pay attention to goal setting
Has ability to gain support from others
Works slowly and cohesively with others
Seeks security and belonging
Good counseling skills

2. Expressive

Spontaneous actions and decisions
Likes involvement
Dislikes being alone
Exaggerates and generalizes
Tends to dream
Gets others caught up in acitivity
Jumps from one activity to another
Works quickly and enthusiastically
  with others
Seeks esteem and belonging
Good persuasive skills

3. Analytical

Cautious actions and decisions
Likes organization, structure
Dislikes involvement
Asks questions with specific detail
Prefers objective, task-oriented work
Wants to be right
Relies on data collection
Seeks security, self-actualization
Good problem-solving skills

4. Driver

Decisive actions and decisions
Likes control
Dislikes inaction
Prefers maximum freedom to manage
Cool, independent, competitive
Works quickly and impressively alone
Seeks esteem, self-actualization
Good administrative skills

Low Assertive (left side) — **High Assertive** (right side)

Low Responsive

Once you recognize your clients' behavioral styles, you can better put them at ease.

1. The *Amiable* Prospect. With these low-assertive, high-responsive prospects, you show an interest in their personal goals and feelings. Amiables need to move slowly from casual personal conversation to business discussion. Don't try to push the rate card and media kit. Let them get to know you first; acquaint them with your magazine and readership through case studies and testimonials. Amiables are less impressed with data than with trustworthiness and service.

2. The *Expressive* Prospect. Expressive people—high-assertive, high-responsive—like to act on opinion. They like variety; they tend to overgeneralize and create drama. They want full and per-

453

sonal service, and they want it now. (Sound familiar? Most sales-people are expressives who find it easy to sell to other expressives. For them, the big problem is selling to other personality types, especially analytics.)

When selling to an expressive prospect, get him talking about his ideas, dreams and goals. The expressive personality is interested in hearing about possibilities—about how that marketing event you've talked about will bring customers to the company's trade show booth. These prospects welcome your enthusiasm and excitement for the magazine. Don't give them a pile of statistics. They want to hear all about case histories, stories and testimonials.

3. The *Analytical* **Prospect.** Low-assertive, low-responsive analytical prospects will want to explore your presentation in detail. They'll be concerned with efficiency, cost, stability and proof. Make sure you present this prospect with a sales story that is organized and structured; don't try to "wing it" with lots of color and drama. Include hard data, price comparisons and audit figures. And be sure to follow up in writing, providing additional facts or evidence he might find useful. Most salespeople report that media buyers tend to be analytical, making for frustration, indeed!

4. The *Driver* **Prospect.** Drivers are high assertive, low-responsive. They're goal-oriented, impatient, efficient, blunt and direct. Drivers want results. They want evidence of your competence, capability and effectiveness.

Want to impress a drive? Let him be in charge. Give him all the research that shows exactly how your title fits his marketing goals. Then ask him questions such as, "Are you satisfied with your current coverage in the Midwest?" That allows him to discover possibilities and draw conclusions.

In the end, of course, you're going to find that you're more comfortable with some prospects than others. Love to tell stories? You'll get a stony look from your analytical client. Are you detail oriented? You can just picture the yawns from the expressive prospect.

So make sure you adjust yourself to your client's level. Try not to let your sales relationship with your client get too much out of sync. If you do, tension may destroy the sale. It's your responsibility as the salesperson and communication leader to adopt the appropriate chameleon sales style.

Take the time to identify your own style. Then check out your prospect's style. Make sure you sell in a way that makes it easy for your prospect to buy, not merely easy for you to sell. If you make clients comfortable, you'll assist them toward a positive buying decision.

29

TAKING YOUR CUES FROM COMEDY

"Whether you think you can or think you can't, you're right."
—Henry Ford (1863-1947)
U.S. automotive manufacturer

In Volume I, I talked about fear. Now I'd like to follow up with "funny." It turns out the two have a lot in common, as I found out explicitly in front of hundreds of people at the National Speakers Association.

I'd attended an NSA workshop on the topic of using humor in public speaking. During a breakout session of smaller groups, each of us told a funny story that we traditionally present in our own seminars. Before I stood up to tell mine, I wrapped up the gum I was chewing in a piece of paper and set it aside.

Later, each group voted to pick one member to tell his or her story to the whole audience, which included several hundred members and several professional comedians. I was among the lucky eight chosen.

It's an honor and a terror to be called before the NSA. Even the most experienced of us are afraid to be judged by our public-speaking peers. I'd always pictured my first time as something I'd carefully planned and rehearsed. Now that it was happening, all I could do was fantasize about speaking last so that time might run out before my turn.

Once I concluded that probably wouldn't happen, I decided to go first instead. I jumped up and headed to the podium, all poise and dignity. The audience roared. I reddened, becoming confused. "Am I not supposed to come up here yet?" I asked. Hysteria. I suddenly noticed people were pointing toward my rear end. I looked around, and there was my chewing gum, stuck smack in the middle of my derriere in full view of the National Speakers Association.

Fortunately or not, the audience assumed the gum was part of my act. I went along. I simply removed the gum, stuck it on top of the podium and told my story. After I finished, I took the gum off the podium, stuck it back on my behind and walked back to my seat as my peers rolled in laughter.

HUMOR TO THE RESCUE

That's humor. That's improvisation. That's the kind of thing that can turn a wrong remark, a foot-in-mouth catastrophe, into a triumph.

Don't get me wrong. Salespeople shouldn't be stand-up acts. But neither should they be too serious. If you can't lighten up, you can't expect your prospect to do so either. To reach your full potential in this career, you need to enjoy the game of selling, to break out of your old routines, release your creativity and intuition.

Psychologists have already measured the benefits of a good belly laugh. According to *Psychology Today*, laughter causes your blood pressure and heart rate to drop, inducing profound relaxation. Laughter also breaks up rigid thinking, a killer in the fast and flexible sales world. John Morreall, Ph.D., president of HUMOR-

WORKS, says in *PT,* "Humor loosens up the mental gears. It encourages out-of-the-ordinary ways of looking at things."

It seems some salespeople are naturals at this, born spontaneous, free-thinking, hail-fellow-well-met types. But even they could get a lot out of *consciously* putting humor into practice. For my part, I decided to try a workshop on comedy improv at the University of California, Los Angeles. What I learned there has helped me enormously in selling situations.

Broadly speaking, comedy improvisation is a great place to learn about creativity and spontaneity. As salespeople, we're continually challenged to think on our feet. Despite our best plans, our clients have their own reactions, opinions and agendas. They might want to ignore 98 percent of our presentation and stick like a crab to the fact that we missed rate base 12 issues ago. They might want to gossip about who'll be the new editor at our competitor's title. Whatever they throw out there, improv helps us go with *their* flow and thereby keep them interested in what we have to say.

HOW "IMPROV" LEADS TO "IMPROVE"

In comedy improv, I've done everything from pretending to prepare a meal 300 years ago to reviving a wilted colleague in a stuck elevator by preparing fruit cocktail from a portable blender. While none of this had anything strictly to do with selling, I've found that every one of my sales situations has been, more or less, an improv routine. Here's what I've learned to apply from my comedy practice:

You must risk looking foolish. In fact, in sales you must be absolutely ready to look foolish and fall on your face. You must take creative risks, fail miserably and persevere despite the setbacks.

An ad manager I know for a regional magazine spent many years in theater and improvisation. As she puts it, both improv and selling share the same traits: You face a conflict, apply available information to it, and then communicate a solution.

Once, for instance, she was selling to a retail store owner in a Chicago suburb. He wondered why he should bother to advertise,

459

since it seemed unlikely city people would travel to his little suburban shop.

She asked what he had to offer customers. He mentioned service: personal gift wrapping, custom tailoring, free UPS shipping and free parking. Given her improv background, this ad manager immediately clicked into a creative mode, and on the spot designed an ad headlined, "Tired of No-Service Mall Stores?" The owner bought a schedule, and became a satisfied repeat customer.

Clearly, this ad manager was comfortable taking risks and thinking on her feet. She could have gone for the usual route, which might have involved showing her magazine's suburban penetration. Instead, she let the store owner become her improv "partner," allowing him to suggest information that led to a solution.

You must work in ensemble. Comedy improv, like good selling, only works if the team works together. In an exercise called "Who Knows?", for instance, I was isolated while my colleagues told a secret about me (I was a notorious bicycle thief). When I rejoined the group, I had to guess my secret by the way others behaved *silently* toward me.

Think that's tough? It is. But each actor contributed a different hint or expanded on hints given others. The solutions were an *ensemble* performance.

That's the way it is with you and your prospects. Your prospect may start off as your audience, watching you "perform" your presentation. But your goal is to bring her into the skit as quickly as possible. She needs to brainstorm with you, become an active member of the selling process. That way, you're not "selling" her; you're coming up with solutions that involve both of you.

How can you do this? I recommend open-ended questions that encourage her to talk about problems, opportunities and strategies. Say your client produces heavy-duty automotive-braking equipment, and you're trying to sell her into a special issue on trucking safety. You might say: "Tell me about your trucking equipment. What does it offer to customers? What do truckers say about it?"

Good probing techniques will encourage her to jump into a conversation with you about truck brakes. This helps you build trust with her. You can demonstrate your ability to hear her problems and assist in coming up with solutions. Once she's confident enough to lay her sales problem on the table, you can build on each other's ideas through brainstorming.

Brainstorming is a great way to build sales. Because it's informal, interactive and nonjudgmental, it allows for a lot of great ideas to pop out. Best of all, your client is fully participating. The ideas are hers as much as yours, so she'll be much more inclined to take action!

You must get excited. In comedy improv, you never know what you have to say or do, but you have to say and do it with 100 percent commitment. If you're asked to talk about wet socks, you have to act as if wet socks were more important and twice as interesting as Mom, the president and apple pie. That's because if *you* can't get interested, neither can your audience.

That's something every sales rep needs to know. I've seen many salespeople drone on about their publication, betraying with every shrug and monotone how they've dragged out this audit statement hundreds times. Too bad. Why should prospects get excited about a magazine if the sales reps aren't?

You must listen. In one improv workshop, we were asked to pretend we were first listening to a bird chirping, then to a bulldozer moving concrete, and finally to African drums. In each exercise, I noticed that my body language changed. As I listened for the bird, my head tilted upward. As I "heard" the drums, I felt my shoulders move to the beat.

In selling, you must not only listen to your clients, but *clearly demonstrate* that you're listening. Imagine, for instance, that you're listening to a child tell you about her scraped knee. You listen in a way that communicates your caring. And you also listen between the lines to interpret how serious her injury is. Why shouldn't you listen to your clients the same way?

461

FOLLOW YOUR PROSPECT'S LEAD

In comedy improv, listening breaks down three ways:

+ *Paying careful attention*

+ *Demonstrating that you're listening*

+ *Letting the information guide your next move*

The important concept behind all this is what my teacher called "giving up your good idea." For instance, say two people are told to act out a scene in which they're watching a parade. Person A starts to think about the things that remind him of parades, so he says, "I love pink elephants." Person B might respond by saying, "I love elephants, too."

Or the remark may lead her to someplace totally different. She might say, "When I was a child, I remember having a hard time seeing those elephants because of the crowd." At this point, Person A has to "give up his good idea" and pick up the story line set out by Person B. Otherwise, he'd be denying his fellow actor.

It's the same way in selling. Let's say you start out talking with your client how effective your magazine will be in spreading the word about his soap products. Instead of agreeing, your client starts reminiscing about inventing soap powder in his basement 35 years ago. At this point, you need to give up your good idea and pick up your client's cues. Perhaps you can encourage him to talk about how he'd built sales over the past 35 years. He might then explain how tough it was to promote his soap powder in an immature market. You can point out how much easier it is to do now—especially to the audience of your magazine.

THE *SUD* FACTOR

Finally, comedy improv taught me something about positioning.

Ever notice in a circus that no two clowns are the same? Clowns actually learn—yes, in clown school—that they must develop a unique clown personality, one that no one has seen before or since. That's what my teacher called *SUD—special, unique, differ-*

ent. In comedy, you need to give the audience information about what makes you special, unique and different from the thousands of performers they'd otherwise see.

Likewise, everything you communicate about your magazine should reflect this *SUD* factor, moving your publication away from the pack and positioning it as the best and most appropriate media buy. You can use the same *SUD* concept to help your client position his product as a breakout from the same old stuff in the marketplace.

It might take some effort to find your *SUD* factors where you need them. But that's why subscriber research, audit statements, positioning research and many other selling tools are at your disposal. Use these tools with insight and intuition. Use the loosening power of humor to connect your client's needs with the benefits and features of your own magazine. You'll find your "improv" selling will soon improve your sales.

Glossary

A

A counties See *Counties*

AAAA See *American Association of Advertising Agencies*

ABC See *Audit Bureau of Circulations*

ABP See *American Business Press*

ARF See *Advertising Research Foundation*

A.C. Nielsen Company A firm that offers research and marketing information, particularly for television media. Nielsen's Television Index and Station Index measures and reports on audience size and demographics for national and local television programs.

Account A client of an advertising agency.

Account executive The advertising agency executive who maintains client relationships and helps develop advertising plans for clients.

Account supervisor The advertising agency executive who supervises the account executives and who may interact with the clients.

Added value In advertising sales, services or opportunities offered by a publisher to give extra marketing power to an advertising page buy. Added value can include directory listings, inclusion in postcard decks, classified advertising and other marketing tools. Added value can also be offered as an incentive to close a sale. See also *Merchandising*.

Additions and removals Changes to a magazine's circulation file that are counted in an audit report.

Advance renewals A subscription renewal order received before the end of the current subscription term.

Advertised price The advertised subscription price for a publication.

Advertiser copies Current copies of a publication provided to advertisers who are running ads in it. Also *checking copies*.

Advertising agency A firm that contracts with advertisers to develop and manage their advertising. The agency works for a fee or commission derived from a standard media discount on the advertiser's spending. Also *agency*.

Advertising allowance Payment made by the manufacturer of a product, or that manufacturer's representative, to a wholesaler or retailer who advertises the manufacturer's product or brand.

Advertising budget The detailed breakdown of costs involved in advertising a product, including agency expenses and time charges as well as cost of advertising media, such as magazine pages or broadcast time.

Advertising contract A detailed agreement between an advertiser and a publisher (or other media company) regarding advertising in that publication or media. The details of the contract, including schedules, frequency, costs and other considerations, are usually negotiated by an advertising agency.

Advertising director The executive at a magazine who directs and coordinates all advertising sales.

Advertising/editorial ratio In a publication, the percentage of advertising space to editorial pages. An ad/edit ratio of 60/40 would mean that 60% of a publication's pages are adver- tising; 40% are editorial material.

Advertising impression One person exposed to a single advertisement. On a gross basis, the sum of all impressions to the ads in a schedule, including duplication. A billboard, for example, may register 100,000 impressions a week, though most would be duplicate impressions by people seeing the billboard more than once.

In some instances, advertising impression refers to those persons or homes exposed to a media vehicle, such as a magazine or TV show. Impressions are calculated by multiplying the audience of each vehicle (on a household or person basis) by the number of advertisements or commercials. A magazine reaching 500,000 readers and carrying 100 ads would register 50 million advertising impressions, for example.

Advertising linage The amount of advertising carried by a magazine or newspaper during a given period. Usually expressed in page totals.

Advertising manager The company executive who reviews and approves advertising plans. The ad manager usually oversees advertising execution and sometimes sales promotion plans as well. Typically reports to a marketing director.

On a magazine staff, the advertising manager manages the ad sales effort and reports to the advertising director.

Advertising Research Foundation (ARF) A foundation whose purpose is to advance advertising research methodology and maintain research standards. ARF also audits and endorses research projects that meet its standards. The foundation is sponsored by advertisers, advertising agencies, advertising media, and researcher associations; ARF publishes the *Journal of Advertising Research*.

Advertorial A special advertising section of a magazine that includes informative editorial-style copy and display ads relating to a particular subject.

Affinity studies In advertising research, studies that reveal how readers see themselves and their relationship to the magazine. The higher readers score in affinity to a magazine, the more likely their interest in that magazine's advertising.

Agency See *Advertising agency*.

Agency commission A commission paid by a publication, TV or radio station to an advertising agency, usually in the form of a 15% discount on the total advertising rate billed to a client by the agency.

Agency of record The advertising agency that purchases media time or ad pages for another agency or a group of agencies that serve the same client.

Agency sold In subscription sales, refers to subscriptions sold by independent agents, primarily large "stampsheet" direct mass mailers such as American Family Publishers and Publishers Clearing House.

Aided recall In advertising research, a method of testing a respondent's recall of an ad or series of ads by having a researcher provide clues.

American Association of Advertising Agencies (AAAA, or the Four As) A national association of advertising agencies whose purpose is the promotion of advertising, the improvement of the advertising business, and service to member agencies and their employees.

American Business Press, Inc. (ABP) An association of business publishers that promotes, conducts research for and serves business-to-business magazine publishers.

Ancillary products In advertising sales, products, other than magazine pages, that a publisher provides to enable advertisers greater

466

marketing reach. Ancillary products can include postcard decks, directories, marketplace sections and other advertising opportunities. Publishers sometimes also sell ancillary products to readers as a way of extending their affinity with the magazine. Such products can include books, videos or T-shirts with a magazine logo.

Annual discount A discount given to an advertiser based on the number of advertising insertions or units purchased during a contract year. See also *frequency* or *volume discount.*

Arbitrary In advertising sales, refers to a budget-setting process in which advertising expenditures are decided on arbitrary benchmarks. Example: A company's sales increased 3%, so it will spend 3% more on advertising.

Arrears Unpaid subscription orders that continue to be fulfilled after a paid subscription has run out. It is standard practice for publishers to drop arrears from circulation files after three months. Also known as *grace copies.*

Association subscription A subscription sale of a publication to members of an association in which the membership fee includes the cost of a subscription.

Audience The number of people or households exposed to a publication or another medium.

Audience composition A classification of individuals or households by various demographic factors, such as age, education, sex or income.

Audience, pass-along Individuals other than newsstand buyers or subscribers who are exposed to a publication.

Audience, potential The total potential audience for an issue of a publication, including pass-along.

Audience, primary All readers who live in households where someone purchases a magazine. Also *primary readership.*

Audience profile The characteristics of the people who make up a magazine audience, in terms of age, family size, location, education, profession, income, and other factors.

Audience, secondary Pass-along readers who read a publication they did not purchase.

Audit Bureau of Circulations (ABC) An independent organization of publishers, advertising agencies and advertisers whose purpose is to verify circulation figures. ABC is mostly known for auditing consumer magazines and newspapers. ABC distributes audits by request to any member. All ABC member publishers issue a publisher's statement of circulation every six months, which is verified by an audit report.

Audit, circulation An audit bureau's review of a publication's circulation file. Primarily ensures that a magazine actually reaches the number of newsstand buyers and subscribers it claims to reach, and (in a business publication circulation audit) that the magazine reaches the audience described in its publisher's statement. Most circulation audits are performed by recognized circulation audit bureaus, such as the Audit Bureau of Circulations (ABC) or BPA International (formerly Business Publications Audit of Circulation).

Performed yearly, a circulation audit typically includes the original source documents that support the names currently on the mailing list. Other supporting documents, such as printers' invoices and postal statements, are used to confirm mailing dates and the number of subscribers.

Audit report The statement usually provided annually by auditors as the result of reviewing a publication's circulation files.

Average Frequency The number of times the average home (or person) is exposed to ads

467

that are part of a media schedule. This is measured over a specific period, such as six issues.

Average paid circulation The average paid circulation of a publication per issue. The average is established by dividing the total number of copies sold for the period by the number sold per issue. So, if in three months a magazine sells 115,000 copies, 165,000 copies and 127,000 copies, the average paid circ for the period is 135,666.

B

B counties See *Counties.*

BPA International An independent organization that audits the circulations of paid and controlled/nonpaid, publications. The primary audit bureau used by business/trade magazines.

Back start A new subscription order that begins with an issue, or issues, prior to the current issue. Back starting, while not looked on favorably by advertisers, is sometimes used to pump circulation figures if a publication has been having trouble meeting its rate base.

Base rate See *Open rate.*

Basic price (or rate) The cost of a subscription as stated by the publisher in the magazine's masthead. Subscriptions sold above basic price are *premium priced.* Those sold below are *discount priced.*

Benefit/feature In sales presentations, the correspondence of a prospect's needs and goals to the magazine's specific features. Example: For a beef distributor, *Magazine A*'s strong circulation among metropolitan restaurants (feature) would give the distributor access to the top New York steak houses (benefit).

Billboard An upright structure to display outdoor advertising; usually a panel of 24 or 30 poster-size sheets. Billboard can also refer to a brief television or radio announcement that

identifies the sponsor of a program.

Bind-in card An insert card in a magazine that is bound in with the printed pages and is often used to sell subscriptions. Bind-ins can also be used by advertisers as coupons. A bind-in card is called a *bingo card* or *reader service card* when used as a request form for information on products and services advertised in the publication.

Binding The finishing process in printing a magazine, involving folding, collating, stitching, gluing or stapling and trimming printed pages.

Bingo card A card printed or bound into a magazine that a reader can mark up, tear out and mail back to the publisher for advertiser information. Also *reader service card.*

Black and white (B&W, B/W) Refers to the printing process that includes only black ink on white paper. Sometimes called *monotone.*

Bleed To print an illustration or photograph to the very edge of a page on one or more sides, running beyond the typical border or margin. Bleed ad pages are usually sold to advertisers for a 5-15% premium.

Blueline A proof of offset printing work, made on photosensitive paper, that is typically printed with blue ink. Also called *blue* or *blues.*

Bonus circulation Circulation delivered above and beyond the circulation on which an advertiser's rate is based.

Bottom line Net profits or losses, usually before taxes.

Brand differentiation The degree to which a brand has succeeded in establishing an image as unique, especially when its unique attributes are perceived as beneficial.

Brand extension A line extension or item

marketed under a single brand name.

Brand image The feelings, associations, and ideas held by the general public in regard to a specific brand. Also *brand personality.*

Brand loyalty The loyalty of a customer to a particular brand of goods.

Broadcast media Radio and television.

Budget In advertising sales, money earmarked for planned spending on marketing activity, such as advertising, during a certain time period.

Bulk discount The discount offered by a media company to advertisers who place large orders. It is measured by the number of pages or total linage placed by one advertiser in a given magazine. See also *frequency* or *volume discount.*

Bulk distribution Distribution of a publication via bundles placed in high-traffic locations (such as campus student centers) for the public to pick up free of charge. For business publications, also refers to distribution of more than one free copy to the same individual (also known as *duplication*). In an ABC audit report, bulk circulation is reported separately from subscriptions or single-copy sales. Also *bulk sales.*

Bulk mailing A mailing of third-class matter (also called *direct mail*), usually in quantities of thousands of pieces or more.

Business classification A code to describe the primary business activity that takes place at a magazine reader's place of business. This is a necessary classification for business/trade magazines, normally referred to in ABC and BPA audit statements. See *Standard Industrial Classification.*

Business magazine A non-consumer publication that serves the interest of a particular industry or profession. Also *trade magazine.*

See also *horizontal* and *vertical* publications.

Business plan An outline prepared by the publisher of a new magazine describing its editorial content, staff, market and financial projections.

Business Publications Audit of Circulations (BPA) See *BPA International.*

Business reply card (BRC) Generally, a card addressed to the sender and sent with a third-class solicitation (such as a subscription solicitation) to be used as a response device. Business reply cards are generally postpaid by the sender.

C

C counties See *Counties*

CPM See *Cost per thousand*

Cable television Television paid for by subscription and transmitted by cable to a subscriber's home.

Call report The daily or weekly reports submitted by sales representatives that convey the results of a particular sales call with an advertiser or prospect.

Camera-ready In production, material suitable for photographic reproduction on film or printing plate.

Campaign A program of coordinated advertisements and promotional materials designed to achieve a specific sales objective.

Campaign tracking In advertising research, a study that determines whether a particular campaign boosted reader awareness of a product and service.

Cancellation date The final date for canceling a planned advertisement. This can also be the final date for supplying printing material for advertisements. Also called *closing date.*

Card deck See *Postcard deck.*

Card rate The advertising rates printed on a rate card. These are the official charges for purchasing ad pages and do not take into consideration special agreements or discounts.

Cash discount A deduction allowed by a publisher to an advertiser (usually 2% of the net) for prompt payment (within 15 to 30 days). Generally passed along by the agency to the advertiser to encourage collections.

Category In advertising sales, refers to any general grouping of types of advertisers. Typical categories are beauty, health, fashion, direct response, food, high tech and so on.

Category discount In advertising sales, a discount granted to certain advertising categories, such as real estate, retail or direct response.

Center spread The two facing pages at the center of a publication. Desired by advertisers who want a continuous image with little or no visual interruption at the gutter.

Charter rate The reduced rates offered by a new magazine to potential subscribers and advertisers.

Checkerboard The placement of portions of an ad in a checkerboard arrangement, alternating with the editorial content of a page.

Checking copies See *Advertiser copies.*

Circulation The total number of distributed copies of a publication, including subscriptions and newsstand sales. Also *Distribution.*

Circulation director Publishing executive responsible for maintaining and increasing the level of subscriptions and newsstand sales.

Circulation, effective The part of a publication's circulation that is received by individuals or companies that an advertiser desires to reach.

Circulation grantee The minimum total circu-lation of a magazine offered to its advertisers.

Circulation, nonpaid The circulation of a publication that is sent free to qualified recipients. Also *controlled circulation.*

Circulation, paid The circulation of a publication that is paid for via subscription or newsstand sales.

Circulation, qualified That circulation, either paid or nonpaid, for which the mailing address, conformance to the field served, recipient qualification, and the correct business and/or occupational classifications are able to be audited and verified. Example: If a publication claims to reach 43,000 muffler shops, and an audit shows 2,000 recipients have either bad addresses or are in different businesses, the qualified circulation would be 41,000.

Qualified recipients must also receive every issue of the publication, subject to normal removals and additions.

Circulation, request Recipients on a publication's circulation list who have completed a questionnaire in order to receive the publication.

Circulation statement The publisher's report of circulation data for a six-month period. Although the statement may be unaudited when it is issued, the information contained is verified during an annual audit. For consumer publications, this statement is called a *pink sheet;* for business publications, it's known as a *BPA* (after the auditing agency). Also *publisher's statement.*

City magazines Sometimes referred to as *metropolitan* or *regional* magazines, these publications cover the special interests of readers in a particular city or area.

Classified advertising A type of small-space

advertising subdivided according to products or services offered to or sought by readers, such as real estate, employment opportunities, special health products, and so on.

Client An account or advertiser.

Close-ended question A question to which the answer is generally yes or no. Often used in surveys, or in closing a sales presentation. Example: "Would you be interested in reaching this market?"

Closing date See *Cancellation date.*

Clutter Excessive amounts of advertising in print and broadcast media.

Collapsing In magazine research, combining totals from several study responses to create a single response. Example: In a survey, 70% of respondents rate a service as "good"; 5% as "excellent." By collapsing the data, the following statement results: "75% of respondents rate the service from good to excellent."

Collateral Advertising material other than that presented through communications media. Examples are brochures, wall posters and so forth.

Collection stimulant An action that urges subscribers to pay for their orders.

Color print In production, a positive full-color reproduction, on photographic paper or in printed form.

Color proof In production, a proof made from color plates, printed separately or in combination.

Color separations In production, a set of photographic color negatives made with color filters for the creation of color printing plates. In four-color printing, three different color separations—yellow, magenta, cyan—are combined with a black plate to create full-color images.

Column in production, an area of print composed of lines of equal width that runs down the page of a publication. Column also refers to the typical or standard width of such an area of print, used as a measure of size.

Column inch The unit of space one standard column wide and one inch deep in a publication.

Combination rate A rate, often discounted, for purchasing advertising space in two or more magazines that are usually owned by the same company.

Commission The compensation to a sales representative or agent, as a percent of sales.

Commodity In advertising, refers to a product category in which it is difficult to distinguish a particular brand from its competition.

Comp A complimentary subscription to a publication.

Comp letter A sales letter bound into a magazine that is sent to its complimentary subscribers, most of whom are advertising prospects.

Comp list The list of a publication's complimentary subscribers.

Company size For circulation auditing purposes, company size codes are usually based on different measurements (annual sales volume, square footage or office space, number of employees and so on) for each publication.

Competitor In advertising sales, a rival in business and advertising.

Composition The percentage of a medium's total audience that is part of a specific demographic group. Example: If 3 million women read *Woman Today*, and 1.5 million are 18-34, then 50% of the total audience is composed of women 18-34.

471

Consumer An end user of a product or service; a person who purchases goods.

Consumer advertising Advertising directed at end users rather than at the members of a particular profession or industry.

Consumer magazine A magazine for the general public rather than for a trade or profession.

Consumer profile The demographic, geographic, and psychographic characteristics of the users of a product, especially as they differ from the total population.

Continuity A method of scheduling advertising so that its messages appear at regular intervals. Continuity patterns can range from daily advertising to monthly to quarterly.

Continuous circulation The number of qualified readers who continuously receive a publication for a minimum of six consecutive months. All audited circulation is continuous.

Contract In advertising sales, an agreement as to terms of purchase between an advertiser or agency and an advertising medium, such as a publication. A contract can also be an agreement between an advertiser and an advertising agency or other advertising supplier with specific terms of service and compensation.

Contract year A contractual relationship of one year between a publication and advertiser. The contract year begins when the first ad is placed.

Controlled circulation Refers to business publications distributed free of charge to a select, targeted audience. Also *nonpaid circulation*.

Controlled Circulation Audit (CCA) An audit service bureau for controlled circulation publications.

Conversion The first renewal on a paid subscription order. The subscriber converts from new subscriber to renewing subscriber.

Conversion factor Refers to the number of subscription leads that are converted to actual or renewing subscribers.

Cooperative advertising Advertising run by a local advertiser in cooperation with a national advertiser. A typical coop ad may feature a local department store—say, Saks Fifth Avenue—and mention of a national brand product sold there, such as Gucci watches. The national advertiser usually supplies the copy, plates, or reproduction materials; the two share the cost of the advertising.

Copy The written portion of an advertisement. Copy can also refer to the text and graphic material for reproduction on a printing plate.

Cost efficiency The effectiveness of an advertising medium calculated by the cost of reaching an actual or potential audience. Example: If one publication offers a rate of $8.50 to reach 1,000 marketing professions, and another offers a rate of $10.50 to reach 1,000 of the same audience, the first publication is more cost-efficient in reaching marketing professionals than the other—even if the second publication has a lower overall card rate.

Cost per inquiry The cost of obtaining an inquiry from prospects through the use of ad media, computed by dividing the media cost by the number of inquiries received. Example: If a $10,000 ad receives 150 inquiries, the cost per inquiry would be $67.

Cost per order A measure of the effectiveness of mail-order advertising in terms of the sales received divided by the cost of the advertising.

Cost per thousand (CPM) The advertising cost required to reach 1,000 persons, homes or other audience units. In publishing, the adver- tising page rate is divided by the circulation to reach a CPM. Example: A publication with a $6,000 page rate and 24,000 circulation would have a CPM of $4. With television and radio, CPM refers to the rate charged for commer- cial placement divided by the average number of persons or homes tuned in.

Counties, A-B-C-D Demographically and geographically defined areas for target marketing purposes. Defined by A.C. Nielsen Company, **A** counties belong to the 25 largest metropolitan areas, including the largest cities and consolidated areas in the United States. **B** counties are those smaller than A counties but are in metropolitan areas with over 150,000 population. **C** counties have populations that fall between 40,000 and 150,000. **D** counties are classified as rural.

Coupon A certificate issued by an advertiser that offers a discount on the purchase price of an item.

Cover The outer pages of a magazine. *First* cover refers to outside front cover; *second* cover is inside front cover; *third* cover is inside back cover; and *fourth* cover is outside back cover. Advertising is often sold on the second, third and fourth covers, seldom on the first cover.

Cover position Refers to the four various cover options. See *Cover.*

Coverage The geographical area reached by a publication or other communications medium.

Creative Refers to the process of conceiving, developing and executing advertising ideas.

Creative director The advertising agency executive responsible for managing the operations and personnel of a creative group or department.

Cumulative audience The net audience of a campaign, either in one medium or a combination of media. Also *cume.*

Current subscription order The subscription order with a start and end that includes the current issue. A reader may have a current subscription order and one or more previous and future orders—each with start and end dates that do not usually overlap.

D

D counties See *Counties.*

Database Electronically stored information that can include lists of individuals or companies. Each record (or group of linked records) contains all relevant information pertaining to a specific person or company or subscription order. Example: A typical database subscriber record may contain name, address, subscription duration, payment record, company name and size, and so forth.

Dealer listing A listing of local dealers who carry an advertiser's product. Dealer lists are added to advertisements that cover geographical areas. For national ads, dealer listings can be altered by city, state or region.

Decision maker In advertising sales, that person or group of people on the client side who ultimately makes the decision about whether to buy advertising.

Demographic edition An edition of a publication intended for a specific demographic group. Advertisers generally pay premium rates to run in demographic editions.

Demographics Identifying data gleaned from studying a group. Demographic details might include job title, family size, age, income and sex.

Derived demand In marketing, demand for a product that depends on demand for related products. Example: Demand for cellular phone cases is derived primarily by demand for cellular phones.

Direct mail Advertising that is sent through

the mail (usually third-class mail) to prospective buyers of a product. Direct mail can include catalogs, credit card offers, financial advertisements and other materials sent to either a wide or targeted audience. Direct mail is also used by a magazine's circulation department to recruit potential magazine subscribers.

Direct request For business publications, refers to a request made by a recipient to receive a controlled-circulation publication. To qualify, the recipient must meet the magazine's "field served" requirements and adhere to audit rules about how the request should be made. Most direct requests are submitted in writing.

Direct-response advertising Advertising that allows prospects to respond directly to the advertiser rather than going through a retailer or other middleman. Direct-response ads can take many forms: third-class distributed mail, such as catalogs; magazine print ads with a coupon or toll-free order number; or television commericals with an advertised address or toll-free line. In magazines, direct-response advertisers often receive a discount off the standard page rate.

Directory advertising Space advertising that appears in a directory of products or services regularly consulted by consumers or businesses.

Discount Any reduction from a stated price or rate of payment. Magazine publishers almost always grant discounts for frequent or volume advertisers.

Display advertising Print advertising that often uses illustrations as well as type. Display ads also appear in standardized formats on a page, such as a quarter-page, half-page, junior page and so on.

Distribution Used in some instances as another word for circulation.

Distributors In newsstand circulation, the national organizations that distribute magazines to local wholesalers.

Dollar-volume discount A discount to an advertiser (or other purchaser) who buys above a certain dollar volume. Example: Advertisers who spend more than $100,000 on advertising space might receive a 10% discount from the publisher. Generally, the greater the amount purchased, the greater the dollar-volume discount.

Double postcard A postcard in the form of a folded and perforated double-sized sheet. Often used for subscription solicitations, the double postcard features one leaf addressed to the recipient, the other addressed to the sender as a business reply card. Double postcards are often mailed bulk rate.

Double spread Two facing pages in a periodical. Also *double page spread, double truck* or simply *spread.*

Duplication The amount of exposure of a known magazine audience to another magazine carrying the same advertising. Example: Duplication happens when an advertiser runs the same ad in the same issue of two competing magazines with similar audiences, or in successive issues of the same magazines. See also *Readership duplication.*

Duplication audit An audited report of the extent of duplication between the circulation of two or more publications.

E

Earned rate The actual rate for advertising space charged to an advertiser, taking into account all discounts for volume and frequency.

Editorial environment The standard content and tone of a publication.

Efficiency The effectiveness of an advertising buy, expressed by comparing audience size with the cost of placing advertising. See *Cost efficiency.*

Estimated revenue projection form In ad sales management, this form, used for managing time and territory, enables sales reps to analyze the value and estimated future value of each account.

Exclusivity In advertising sales, an agreement by a publisher to run an advertiser's message without competing advertising messages in the same issue. Example: Pepsi may negotiate for soft-drink exclusivity in an issue, precluding other soft-drink advertisers from buying space. For the privilege, such advertisers usually pay a major premium.

Expire date or expiration date The date of the last issue a subscriber will receive as part of a paid subscription. Copies sent after this date are *grace copies or arrears.*

Expire inventory See *Renewal inventory.*

Exposure In print media, the presentation of a magazine ad to an audience, expressed in terms of the total number of people who may see it. Exposure can also refer simply to opening a magazine page to an advertisement.

Extrapolate In magazine research, to estimate unknown data from projections of known data. Example: Six hundred of 1,000 subscriber respondents say they are pet owners. A researcher may extrapolate that 60% of the magazine's 600,000 subscribers are pet owners.

F

Field served A clear statement from an audited, controlled-circulation publisher that precisely defines the recipients of a publication. This defines the limits of who may and may not receive the publication. Example: The field served for a BPA-audited publication may be "Licensed mechanics in the car, motorcycle and small truck repair business." This statement, and any changes to it, must be registered with the audit bureau.

Fifth color In production, refers to an ink color used in addition to the standard four color process. Fifth colors generally command a premium.

Film In production, the transparencies used to transfer graphic information to a printing press. In *filmless production,* digital information is used instead.

First cover See *Cover.*

Focus group interview A research technique that employs small consumer group discussions led by trained moderators to obtain insight into consumer behavior and perceptions. Publications use focus groups when considering editorial changes; advertisers use them to gain marketing insight.

Format In production, the trim size of a book or publication, or the number of pages in a signature. Format can also refer to the general design of a book or magazine page, or piece of graphic art. (In radio, format refers to the type of programming.)

Four As See *American Association of Advertising Agencies*

Four color (4/C) The combination of yellow, magenta (red), cyan (blue), and black, mixed in varying percentages, to give a complete range of hues and tonal values in a piece of magazine art. These standard four colors are used for virtually all magazine reproduction.

Four-color process The process of color printing using four-color separations to reproduce color artwork. To begin, full-color artwork is reduced to its basic four colors by a filtration and separation process, which produces four pieces of film. The film is used to engrave the printing plates and determine where the ink should be placed on the page.

475

Fourth cover See *Cover*.

Fractional page space Advertising display space that consumes a percent of the page, such as 1/3 or 1/6. Also *fractional*.

Franchise position A specified position in a publication, such as back cover or inside front cover, for which a advertiser is granted a permanent right to use (or franchise). Some franchises are negotiated for specific issues, while others may be granted by frequency of use, such as six of 12 issues.

Free copies Copies of a publication mailed free of charge to a reader. Most free circulation is sent to qualified/controlled readers, but free copies can also include those sent to adver- tisers, potential advertisers, and business associates (also called *comp copies*). Some bulk-distributed copies are also free to readers, as on college campuses.

Frequency In advertising sales, the number of exposures of an advertisement to its readers over a given period of time. In magazine publishing, frequency refers to the number of times in one year a magazine is published. Example: A magazine publish with monthly frequency. In that magazine, an advertiser may appear with quarterly frequency.

Frequency discount A discount offered to advertisers who agree to run a certain number of ads within a specified period. See also *Quantity discount*.

Front of book The section of a magazine preceding the main editorial section.

Fulfillment The process of maintaining a subscriber database and sending magazines to subscribers.

Full-service agency An advertising agency offering clients a full menu of services, including marketing, planning and management, creative, media, research, accounting and often merchandising and advertising-related legal counsel as well.

G

Galley proof The proof of a page or of the type that will make up a page. Galley proofs are sent to a magazine's proofreading staff for checking and correction before shipping to the printer.

Gatefold A special two-part page in a magazine, with an outer part that folds over an inner part that is slightly narrower than the trim size of the magazine. Often appearing on inside front covers, gatefolds usually are used to expand a double spread into a three-page spread.

Geographic split run A print run that is split so that different ads appear in different regional editions of a publication. Example: An advertiser could run one type of ad for Northeast editions, another for Southwest, and a third for the Midwest. See also *Split run*.

Grace copies Issues mailed to a "bill me" subscriber during the invoice process to encourage payment for the subscription.

Grace copies-renewal Issues mailed to a paid subscriber after the expire date to encourage a subscription renewal order.

Graphic A visual device of an informative, symbolic, or decorative nature used to illustrate or enhance information presented in the text.

Gross audience The combined audience of a combination of media or of a campaign in a single medium. If an advertiser buys a page in one magazine with an audience of 200,000 and a second page in a magazine with 400,000, it will reach a gross audience of 600,000. Gross audience, however, does not take duplication into account.

Gross billing An advertising cost billed to an advertiser, including charges for agency commission. Gross billing can also refer to the charge for a one-time rate; or the total amount of advertisers' funds handled annually by an advertising agency.

Gross impressions The total audiences of all media used in a media plan. Example: If an advertiser in one week buys a page in a magazine with a total audience of 500,000 adds a TV spot with a total audience of 2.5 million, and places a billboard that receives 500,000 impressions per week, the ad will that week register 3.5 million gross impressions. This number represents the *message weight* of a media plan, or *tonnage*, given that the number can be so large.

Gross rate The published rate for space quoted by a publisher (or other advertising media), without regard to agency commissions or discounts. See *Card rate.*

Gross rating point (GRP) A unit of measurement of audience size for television, radio, or outdoor advertising audience, equal to 1% of the total potential audience universe. Example: If a program scores 10.2 GRPs, the advertising on the program reaches 10.2% of the total potential audience. GRPs do not take into account multiple exposure of the same advertising to individuals.

Group subscriptions Subscriptions purchased in lots of five or more. Companies often purchase group subscriptions for employees. These may be mailed either to one address or to individual addressees furnished by the employer.

Guarantee A commitment from a publication (or other medium) assuring an advertiser of an agreed-upon rate, audience or circulation level.

Guaranteed circulation The circulation level of a publication on which the advertising space rate is based. Although similar to *rate base*, in guaranteed circulation no advertiser is assured of a rate reduction if the circulation level is not achieved.

Gutter In a publication, the margins at the crease formed by a pair of facing pages at the place where they are bound or folded.

Gutter bleed An ad that runs beyond the gutter of a magazine to the binding edge of the page. Gutter bleeds are typical for spreads.

Gutter position An advertising position beside the gutter on a magazine page.

H

Half-page spread A spread of advertising material that consists of the upper or lower halves of two facing pages.

Halftone The tonal variation used for the reproduction of black-and-white photographs. The original graphics are photographed through a halftone screen, which breaks down the image into a small, varied dot pattern that can be duplicated on press.

Hook Any device in a advertisement intended to stimulate an immediate response or inquiry. Example: The words "free," "this week only," "never offered before," or similar inducement are all advertising hooks. A hook may also be a premium, such as a clock radio offered with a new subscription.

Horizontal business publication A magazine for persons holding similar positions in different types of industries. A magazine for MIS engineers, for instance, would go to any business that employs managers of information systems, from publishing to warehousing. See also *Vertical business publications.*

Horizontal half-page The upper or lower half of a publication page.

Horizontal selling Selling to all legitimate buyers regardless of their area of industry. Ex-

477

ample: Tile manufacturers would sell to all users of tile, whether grocery stores, factories or convents.

House agency An advertising agency owned or controlled by an advertiser.

House organ A periodical published by a company with editorial content devoted to company activities. An internal house organ is edited for company personnel; an external house organ is for customers and readers outside the company.

I

Image In graphics, the visual composition of a photograph or illustration. Or, the impressions and opinions the public holds of a company or product.

Image advertising Advertising designed less to sell a specific product than to improve or upgrade opinions held by the public about the advertiser.

Impression A person's or household's exposure to an advertisement.

Impression studies Conducted primarily by Daniel Starch and Associates, these are studies of print ads that evaluate what kind of an impression the ad made on readers.

Impulse buy A consumer purchase motivated more by chance than plan.

Incremental spending Increased advertising or promotional expenditures for a product or service.

Index In publishing, a directory of contents in a publication. In magazine research, the comparison between two quantities by using one quantity as the norm. Ratios with a 1:1 relationship are usually expressed as an index of 100. Example: Say the average height of an American male is 5'9". Males who are 5'9" would be indexed at 100. A man who is 6'4"

would then index at 108.5, while a man of 5'6" would index at 94.9.

Indigenous/non-indigenous accounts In advertising sales, indiginous accounts are those clients and prospects that have a direct, generic relationship with the magazine. Non-indigenous accounts have no obvious connection to the magazine, but can still reach a target audience. Example: For a medical news publication, pharmaceuticals would be indigenous accounts. For the same publications, airlines and travel agencies wishing to reach doctors would be non-indigenous. Such accounts may advertise only in, say, the magazine's annual travel issue.

Industrial advertising Advertising of capital goods, supplies, and services directed mainly to industrial or professional firms that require them in the course of manufacturing.

Industry classification See *business classification* or *Standard Industrial Classification*.

Inquiry A request, usually for information on goods and services, from a potential consumer made in response to an advertisement. For publishers and advertisers, inquiries—which are generally noted on inquiry cards or "bingo" cards—are primarily useful in determining advertising effectiveness.

Inquiry card In publishing, a reader service card or "bingo" card returned to the publisher for processing. Inquiries are then passed onto respective advertisers for fulfillment.

Insert A separately printed section of a publication bound with or tucked into its regular pages. Printed either by the publisher or by an advertiser, an insert is usually printed on special stock so that it stands out from the rest of the magazine.

Insertion order The order an advertising agency sends a publication that contains infor- mation regarding advertising placement, including its size, rate, frequency, date and any other relevant information.

Installment billing In subscription sales, installment billing allows subscribers to pay for a subscription over a series of months.

Integrated marketing communications A co-ordination of an advertiser's total marketing efforts into a single, unified plan with one cohesive message. Integrated marketing may also involve reaching customers and prospects via a targeted message strategically placed in a mix of advertising, direct marketing, telemarketing, sales promotion, public relations, and/or retail marketing.

Interim statement A publisher's sworn circulation statement that is made quarterly to the Audit Bureau of Circulations. The interim circulation statement is issued unaudited, but is subject to a later audit. Interim statements are not the normal course of business; publishers make them in cases of dramatic circulation growth or if one magazine purchases and consolidates a competitor's circulation file into its own.

Invoice In publishing, a bill for advertising or for an ordered subscription. Invoices generally itemize goods purchased, along with quantity, price and size.

Issue All copies of a magazine published on a given date; hence carrying uniform editorial and advertising content within its various editions.

Issue life The period during which a given magazine issue is assumed to be read by the average reader. Weeklies typically have an issue life of three weeks; monthlies, three months.

J

Joint demand In marketing, demand for a product that depends equally on demand for related products. Example: Screws and nuts, guitar pegs and strings, or interlocking engine parts would all be products jointly demanded by manufacturers.

Joint venture A cooperative business enterprise involving two independently owned business firms, established on the basis of licensing, joint ownership, or contract. Many consumer magazines are launched as joint ventures between an entrepreneur and a well-heeled publishing company.

Junior page In advertising sales, typically refers to a standard-size ad that appears in a tabloid-size publication. This allows advertisers to run advertising in larger-format magazines without going to the expense of creating larger-format ads. In a tabloid publication, a junior ad is wrapped with editorial. Also *junior unit.*

Junior spread An advertising layout in which two junior ads occupy portions of a page spread.

K

Keycode In direct response promotions, a code printed on a mailing label or order form that identifies the list and type of package mailed. Analyzing orders by key code makes it possible for advertisers to discover which lists and packages received the best response.

L

Layout In production, any drawing intended to show the planned contents and visual appearance of printed page or advertisement.

Leading question An interview question worded to influence the answer. Leading questions, such as "You'd prefer a higher-quality product, wouldn't you?" are generally considered unsound in conducting research, but may be used effectively in closing a sales presentation. Also called *bias questions.*

Leave-behind In sales presentations, sales material left behind to summarize major sales points.

Letterhead Stationery, usually used in formal correspondence, with the name of a business firm printed or engraved. Other information, such as the address, telephone number, and principal executives, may also appear.

Libel A legal term in publishing relating to a written statement that is either: 1) defamatory, 2) conveys an unjustly unfavorable impression or 3) tends to expose an individual or group to public contempt. Libel is a criminal offense usually punished by fine.

Life cycle See *Product life cycle.*

Light-bulb research Research conducted by binding a reader-survey card into the magazine itself. Results are not statistically valid, but the methodology is considered a good way to get "bright" ideas.

Limited distribution Distribution of a product or magazine to one or more specific geographical areas rather than nationwide. May also refer to less-than-complete distribution within an area. A magazine mailed only to Upper East Siders, for instance, would be considered limited distribution within Manhattan.

Line copy Artwork suitable for reproduction as a line illustration, as opposed to a halftone.

Line extension A new product or magazine marketed under an existing brand name, intended for use in the same category as the parent product line. Example: *Sports Illustrated for Kids* may be considered a line extension of *SI.* Also *brand extension.*

List broker A firm that helps market a publication's circulation list, or that helps rent other companies' lists for promotion. The list broker is paid a commission by the list owner.

List seeding Inserting phony names with valid addresses into a mailing list in order to track unauthorized use of a mailing list.

Literature/product showcase The section of a magazine in which different advertisers can display products and services in the same category. These small display ads are usually grouped together, catalog style, with a response device for information requests.

Live matter That part of a magazine ad page where copy and illustrations are placed in a fixed field in order to avoid being trimmed off in the publication's binding process.

Local media Media whose coverage and circulations are confined to or concentrated in their market of origin.

Loss leader A retail item advertised at an unusually low price in order to attract customers into a store. Loss leaders are generally unprofitable or only marginally profitable for the retailer.

M

MPA See *Magazine Publishers of America*

Magazine A periodical, often published on glossy paper stock, that offers comprehensive coverage of a subject area and is published with regular frequency.

Magazine Publishers of America (MPA) An organization of consumer magazine publishers dedicated to promoting magazines to both advertisers and readers. MPA also supplies member publishing companies with information and services. The Magazine Advertisers Bureau is its sales arm.

Magazine supplement A preprinted tabloid or standard-size consumer publication usually distributed in a newspaper's Sunday edition.

Mailing list A list of prospective buyers prepared for direct mail solicitation.

Mail-order advertising Advertising sent as third-class mail that solicits direct orders for a product or service. See also *Direct mail*.

Makegood In publishing, a rerun of an advertisement or other compensation for an advertisement incorrectly inserted or published in the magazine.

Make-ready The process of preparing a press for printing, particularly four-color printing.

Makeup The arrangement of type, illustrations and photographs of a printed advertisement or editorial page.

Market penetration The degree to which a service or product is used by the audience for which it is designed. Example: If a bicycle manufacturer has sold 10,000 mountain bikes among a measured group of 100,000 mountain-biking enthusiasts, it has penetrated 10% of the the market.

Market potential The potential sales volume for a product or service. Example: The market potential for selling to all 100,000 mountain-biking enthusiasts, with an average product price of $600, Would be $60 million. Market potential is also influenced by category development: as mountain biking grows, so does its market potential.

Market profile A summary of the characteristics of a market, including information on typical purchasers, competitors, economic factors, distribution patterns, suppliers, and so on.

Market share The percentage of a category's sales, in terms of dollars or units, attributed to a specific brand. Example: If the total mountain-biking universe is measured at $6 million, and Best Bikes has $600,000 sales in that category, Best Bikes has a 1% market share.

Marketing director The company executive responsible for reviewing and approving marketing plans. In some companies, a marketing director may be responsible for sales management.

Marketing mix The levels and interplay of marketing efforts for a product or service. The marketing mix can including product features, pricing, advertising (whether print, broadcast or direct mail), merchandising, distribution, and spending.

Marketing plan A strategy for marketing a product or service; or a comprehensive document that details a marketer's goals, objectives and strategies.

Marketing research Research designed to supply information relevant for effective marketing of goods and services. Such market research might include demographic studies, focus groups, surveys and other forms of gathering information.

Marketplace section The section of a magazine that lists advertisers' products and services as a reader resource.

Mass circulation Refers to consumer magazines with large circulation distribution—at least 1 million or more—to a widespread audience. The newsweeklies, for instance, are mass circulation, as are most women's magazines.

Mass magazine A magazine edited for the general public.

Mass medium A communications medium, like broadcast TV sitcoms or mass circulation magazines, that reaches the general public as opposed to special-interest consumers.

Mass merchandiser A retail outlet or chain handling general merchandise lines.

Master files In sales account management, an all-inclusive list of a publication's accounts, including such relevant information as annual reports, insertion orders, proposals, sales letters and so on.

Masthead In publishing, the page or section

in a magazine set aside to list the publication's title, personnel, and publishing policies. It often appears near or alongside the table of contents.

Mean and median In statistics, within a set of numbers, the *mean* is the average; the *median* is the middle. Example: if a magazine has nine readers aged 12, 22, 34, 46, 52, 67, 72, 75, and 89, both mean and median age is 52. But if readers are aged 12, 22, 34, 35, 40, 67, 72, 75 and 89, the mean age is 49 (all numbers added together, then divided by the number of individuals), while the median is 40 (the midpoint number). Median is generally considered the more accurate representation.

Mechanical In production, the composite of the physical elements of an ad or editorial page, also known as a *pasteup*. Mechanicals are no longer created by publications that compose their pages directly on computer.

Mechanical requirements In production, the layout and makeup specifications of a publication. These specifications, or specs, indicate to advertisers the size requirements, special handling and other requirements that their advertising material must meet in order to run in the magazine.

Media Plural of the word medium. Refers to the general mix of communications vehicles available to advertisers and to the public: magazines, newspapers, TV, radio, outdoor advertising, the Internet, and so on.

Media buyer Advertising agency executive responsible for the purchase of advertising space or time in communications media. Reports to media supervisors and media director.

Media director Advertising agency executive responsible for supervising the selection and purchase of space or time in communications media for a client's advertising.

Media kit A package used by magazines to promote advertising sales. It contains a rate card, research survey results, reader demographics, a magazine issue, trade advertising, publisher's letter and often, publicity or testimonials about the magazine.

Media survey A survey of the extent to which specific communications media reach specific markets and audiences.

Medium Any communications vehicle used to convey an advertising message to the public. See *Media*.

Merchandising In advertising sales, offering an advertiser additional services in exchange for advertising placement. Merchandising can include use of a magazine's subscriber file, assistance in designing direct marketing materials, inclusion in directory listings and so on.

Metropolitan Statistical Area (MSA) An urban area that meets certain standards pertaining to population, metropolitan character, and economic and social integration within its county and outlying counties. In essence, an MSA is the urban center of a region. MSAs are determined by the Bureau of the Budget with the advice of the Federal Committee on Standard Metropolitan Areas. Also known as *metro areas* or *standard metropolitan statistical areas (SMSAs)*.

Minimum frequency The lowest level of advertising exposure or advertisement sched- uling that will produce effective results with the advertiser's audience.

N

National advertising Advertising delivered to a nationwide market that serves a common marketing objective.

National advertising rate The rate charged by a publication for exposure to a national audience. This rate is usually higher than the rate charged for local or regional advertising.

Net audience The number of individuals or households reached by a communications medium over a specified period. Unlike gross audience numbers, net numbers count each individual once, regardless of the number of exposures.

Net number In advertising research, refers to a conclusive number. Example: In research, a magazine finds 67% of readers bought a garden hose, 17% a rake and 23% a shovel. In totalling responses, however, the magazine finds 94% of readers purchased some form of garden tool. That 94% is the net number of garden-tool buyers.

Net paid circulation Circulation consisting of the average number of mail subscriptions plus the net single copy sales. Publishers may or may not include arrears in this figure.

Net unduplicated audience. The actual number of persons who may be exposed to advertising, regardless of how many exposures each person may have.

Newsletter A publication of a limited number of pages, not usually sold on newsstands, that addresses itself to the special interests of a particular group. Newsletters may or may not run advertising.

Newsstand circulation Retail magazine sales, as opposed to subscription sales. Also *single-copy sales.*

Nielsen Clearing House (NCH) A company that handles the administrative work associated with processing coupons.

Non-qualified A reader who is not qualified to receive a controlled-circulation magazine, usually because the reader does not fall under the publisher's statement of field served.

Non-qualified distribution For a controlled-circulation magazine, that portion of circulation that does not conform to the field served and definition of recipient qualification.

O

Objection In advertising sales, a challenge or point raised by the client or prospect as an obstacle to placing an ad schedule.

Occupational classification Grouping recipients by business or industry, or by the position they occupy in a business organization.

Off card In advertising sales, sales achieved at a price not printed on the rate card.

One-time rate See *Open rate.*

Open-end questions Interview questions to which respondents may answer in any way they please, without being confined to a predetermined choice. Example: "How do you plan to market your new product?"

Open rate The rate for a single, unrepeated ad page. Also called *base rate* or *one-time rate.*

Outsert An advertising supplement polybagged with a magazine.

Overrun Additional copies of a magazine, or any printed material, printed in excess of that required for general circulation.

P

P4C Abbreviation for page/four color. *P2C* stands for page/two color; *PB&W*, page/black and white.

PMS See *Pantone Matching System.*

Packaged goods Broadly used consumer products wrapped or packaged by the manufacturer, typically sold through food, drug and mass merchandiser retail stores.

Page In advertising, the basic unit—one magazine page—used in calculating advertising rates. All display ads are an expression of a

483

page: half-page, quarter-page, double-page spread and so on.

Paid distribution The number of copies of a publication distributed to individuals who have either purchased a single copy or have an active paid subscription order. A subscription must sell for at least 50% of the basic price to be considered "paid."

Paid subscriber A reader of a publication who has paid, or plans to pay, for the issues delivered. A subscriber cannot be considered "paid" unless he or she has paid in the past and/or is currently in the renewal or invoice cycle. In other words, a reader receiving a trial magazine copy (or copies) is not considered paid until he or she agrees to pay for a complete subscription.

Pantone Matching System (PMS) In production, a palette of standardized ink colors that advertisers or publishers can use to enhance four-color or other graphic work. Also known as *match colors*.

Pass-along readership The number of persons who receive a publication from the original subscriber or purchaser. This does not include others who live in the same household as the purchaser, but it does include readers in doctor's offices, airplanes, and so on. Also known as *pass-along readers, secondary readership*.

Penetration The effectiveness of advertising in reaching and persuading the public, principally measured by sales volume. Also, the percentage of homes or consumers in a geographical area that own a given product. See *Market penetration*.

Penetration study The study of the effectiveness of advertising on consumers.

Per-inquiry (PI) advertising An agreement between a publisher and a direct-response advertiser in which the publisher agrees to accept payment of advertising based on the number of inquiries or sales generated from the ad.

Percent coverage In print media, the audience of a publication as a percent of the total population of a given category or area. Or, the circulation of a publication as a percent of total homes. Example: a magazine that reaches 200,000 nurse-practioners in a total population of 350,000 nurse-practitioners would have a 57% coverage of that group.

Perfect binding In magazine printing, the process of binding a publication with glue rather than staples or stitching. This results in a square spine. Frequently used with upscale magazines or those that carry many pages. Also *adhesive binding*.

Pickup advertising Advertising material repeated, or "pickedup" from a previous ad.

Pickup material Advertising material created for one advertisement and used in some form in a different or later ad. Also *pickup*.

Planning calendar In sales account management, a calendar that enables scheduling for all sales activity.

Plant A production facility or factory, such as a printing plant.

Point of purchase Refers to advertising displays mounted at retail stores to encourage the purchase of a product.

Polybag A clear plastic bag used to enclose and protect a magazine and its outserts, if any.

Pop-up In publishing, a special die-cut folder that rises from a center fold when the publication is opened.

Position The place in a publication where an advertisement will appear. A *preferred position* would be any area in which advertisers believe they will have maximal exposure. Such positions are often near the table of contents, front of book, facing popular editorial, and so

484

on. Preferred positions are generally granted to heavy advertisers, or sold at a premium.

Position request A request by an advertiser for a certain location in publication.

Postcard deck In advertising sales, a group of different postcard-sized advertising messages mailed together to subscribers or to other mailing lists. Often offered by publishers to advertisers as an ancillary product. Also *card deck.*

Premium rate In advertising sales, an extra rate charged for a preferred position, or for special color, bleeds, covers or other extras that go beyond the standard page rate.

Premium sold In subscription sales, subscriptions sold through an offer that includes a free product or service as an inducement. Common premiums include editorial, such as special editions of the magazine, a directory or calendar; or products, such as a coffee mug with a magazine logo. All premium-sold subscriptions must be reported on a publisher's statement.

Pre-press In production, the preparatory process, such as typesetting and camera work, accomplished before a magazine goes to press.

Presentation A formal face-to-face exposition before prospects and advertisers of factual information about a publication, along with plans, visuals and other material, designed to support a proposed course of action.

Press run The actual number of copies produced by the printer. This number is used to determine if the publisher has met the 51% direct-request rule to meet the U.S. Postal Service's second class mail requirements. In other words, a magazine cannot mail second class unless 51% of its total press run is direct-requested by subscribers.

Primary audience The audience a publisher or advertiser wants most to reach with a specific message.

Primary households Households that contain the primary subscriber or newsstand buyer of a publication.

Primary readers The readers of a publication who reside in primary households.

Primary readership The total number of primary readers of a periodical.

Print run The circulation manager's count of the number of copies that are to be printed of a specific issue. This includes copies that go to paid and controlled subscribers, bulk copies, comp copies and newsstand copies. Also included are copies needed for distribution at trade shows, for customer service, or for back-issue requests or any other purpose.

Probability In statistics, the percentage of times, in a given number of occurrences, that certain results should appear if the sample chosen is truly random and if the occurrences under study are subject to chance alone.

Probing In advertising sales, asking strategic questions to gauge a prospect's marketing needs, goals and readiness to buy.

Product life cycle In marketing, the arc of a product's existence. Initially, sales are derived primarily from trial purchases. In the growth stage, sales increase from new trials while repeat purchases form a base. In the mature stage, sales level out and repeat purchases fluctuate. In the declining stage, sales diminish as fewer consumers purchase the product.

Product research and development (R&D) The process in a corporation of researching and furthering product and corporate marketing objectives.

Product usage information In advertising research, information regarding consumer use of product types and brands. Such information is usually categorized demographically or psychographically.

485

Production The process of converting editorial material, illustrations, images, general design and layout into a printed magazine or advertisement.

Production manager At an advertising agency, the person responsible for the development of advertising materials. At a publication, the person who oversees the production of the advertising and editorial pages.

Projection In statistics, the process of estimating unknown figures on the basis of existing ones, usually with known probability for error. Example: If a magazine finds 245 gardeners in a random sample of 1,000 readers, those results can be projected onto the readership as a whole. Thus, among 100,000 readers, the magazine projects that 24,500 are gardeners.

Promotion director The magazine executive charged with promoting subscriptions, newsstand sales, and advertising sales efforts.

Promotions A broad base of marketing activities geared towards obtaining more primary readers and/or advertisers. Promotions can include posters, brochures, events, contests, direct mail, publicity and so on.

Proof In production, an impression on paper of type and graphics for the purpose of checking correctness and quality before final printing.

Prospect A person or company considered eligible for purchasing a product or service, such as advertising.

Psychographic In research, descriptive characteristics of personalities, attitudes, and lifestyles of individuals and groups. Like demographics, psychographics can be used to classify readers: 43% of readers are Democrats; 13% are highly religious, 8% are gay and so on. Psychographics are sometimes seen as better predictors of behavior than demographic characteristics.

Public relations (PR) Activity intended to promote understanding of, and/or good will toward, a company and its products and services. PR often seeks to assess and favorably influence public opinion without incurring direct media costs, usually by seeking positive press coverage.

Publisher's statement A notarized statement of a magazine's total circulation, including amount of circulation, how readers were acquired or qualified, geographic distribution, and so on. Publisher's statements are issued every six months and are subject to audit by the Audit Bureau of Circulations or BPA International.

Pulling power The effectiveness of an advertisement in persuading the public to buy a product, make inquiries, send in coupons, or take some action. Also *pull*.

Pulsing In advertising sales, a media scheduling technique that alternates periods of heavy activity with periods of less activity.

Q

Qualification date The date a reader issued a request to receive a publication. This date is used to determine the age of the qualification information. Qualification information more than three years old is no longer considered valid in auditing reports.

Qualified circulation That portion of subscribers that has met the specifications for receiving a controlled-circulation magazine.

Qualified recipients Recipients who receive every issue of a publication and who meet the publisher's definition for recipient qualification within a field served.

Qualitative research Research conducted to broaden insight and understand opinions and impressions. Such research is less numbers-oriented; more interpretative. Example: A subscriber survey that seeks opinions about a new graphic design. Also *subjective research*.

Quantitative research Statistical research that analyses specific degrees of differences in responses, usually conducted to reach conclusions. Example: A subscriber survey that asks whether respondents are homeowners or apartment dwellers. Also *objective research*.

Quantity discount A graduated discount on quantity purchases, or periodic refund based upon the value of purchases over a period of time. In advertising sales, see *frequency* or *volume* discount.

R

ROI See *Return on investment*

Random sample In statistics, a sample of potential research respondents, each of which has had an equal chance of being selected to be part of the research. Example: Selecting every 10th subscriber in a database. Also *unrestricted sample*.

Rate The amount that a publisher charges an advertiser per unit of advertising space.

Rate base The minimum number of copies of a publication that a publisher guarantees advertisers are purchased by or mailed to qualified readers.

Rate card A list of a publication's advertising rates. Rate card information also includes mechanical requirements, issue dates, closing dates, cancellation dates, and circulation data.

Rate holder An advertisement placed primarily in order to qualify an advertising schedule for quantity or frequency discounts.

Rate protection A publisher's promise to an advertiser to honor previously agreed-upon advertising rates or unexpired ad-rate contracts, despite current or expected ad-rate increases.

Reach and frequency The criteria for evaluating the level of an audience's exposure to an ad over a given period of time. *Reach* is the percentage of all people, companies or households exposed to the advertising. *Frequency* is the average number of exposures for each member of the audience.

Reach, cumulative The total number of homes reached by a publication (or other medium) during a specific time period.

Reach/frequency, effective. The extent to which a media or media schedule reaches into an advertiser's targeted audience. Example: A magazine has 100,000 subscribers, but 20,000 are in Italy. For an advertiser with no market in Italy, those 20,000 subscribers are deducted from the title's effective reach.

Reader A person who regularly reads a copy of a publication. Publisher's statements are forbidden from using the term when describing circulation since it cannot be demonstrated that all magazines received or purchased by an individual are actually read.

Reader response Actions on the part of readers, either by mail or telephone, to respond to print advertisements.

Reader service card See *Bingo card*.

Readers per copy The average number of readers of a magazine per copy derived through totalling circulation and pass-along numbers. When multiplied by a magazine's circulation, the result equals its audience, or total readership.

Readership The total number of people exposed to a publication as measured by syndicated research services, such as Simmons Market Research Bureau.

Readership duplication In print media, the overlap of readership or circulation exposure between different issues of the same magazine or among issues of different magazines. Example: Two competing nursing magazines may have a readership duplication of 45%, meaning 45% of one title's audience is also exposed to the competition.

Readership study A survey of the characteristics or interests of the readership of a publication; or a survey of the attention given to a publication by any part, or all of its readership.

Reading time The average amount of time a reader spends with a copy of a publication.

Rebate In advertising sales, a discount or deal offered to advertisers who have exceeded spending the contract minimum. In retail marketing, a rebate is a consumer refund offered off the listed price for merchandise.

Recall In readership studies, the measured ability to remember the content of a publication or advertisement.

Recent reading In readership or magazine studies, a measurement technique in which respondents check a list of publications they have read recently.

Recognition In media research, the recall of prior exposure to an advertisement provoked by a repeated exposure. In advertising sales, a publisher's agreement to regard an advertising agency as competent, ethical, and entitled to discounts.

Red Book See *Standard Directory of Advertising Agencies; Standard Directory of Advertisers.*

Regional edition An edition of a national publication distributed in a certain geographical area. In most cases, advertising space in regional editions can be purchased separately from the national edition.

Remnant space "Leftover" magazine advertising space sold at a discount to ensure that it will be occupied.

Removals Names of individuals or companies removed from a publication's mailing list during periods of reader re-qualification. Names are generally removed because they have failed to respond to re-qualification solicitations or because they no longer fit the definition of "field served."

Renewal A subscriber's order to continue receiving a publication. Money may or may not be included with the renewal order. This renewal order must be received within six months of the previous order's expiration date and paid for within six months following receipt of the renewal order. Orders received later qualify as new subscriptions.

Renewal at birth An extension of a subscription order received within a very short time (usually less than 60 days) after the original subscription order is received.

Renewal inventory The number of records with a specific expire date that could potentially renew. Though original order dates may vary, a two-year subscription, a one-year subscription and a six-month subscription may all be available for renewal (expire) on the same date.

Renewal rate The rate at which subscribers renew their subscriptions for another term. It is described as a percentage of all subscribers expiring in the period covered by the magazine's audit report. Example: *Magazine X* has 200,000 subscriptions expiring during its audit period. A total of 115,000 renew, giving the title a renewal rate of 57%.

Repetition In advertising, reiteration of an advertisement, slogan, or theme to strengthen its impression and awareness.

Representatives A general term used to describe salespeople who work for media companies. Also called *reps.*

Reprint A re-issue of an advertisement or editorial content, usually done only with permission from the publisher or advertiser.

Research director In publishing companies, the executive who supervises market and surveys, and who develops research into usable information for assisting advertising sales and circulation efforts.

Response rate In advertising sales, the percentage of persons, out of the audience reached, who respond to an advertisement. In surveys, the percentage of people within a sample population who provide useful information.

Return card A self-addressed postcard sent with advertising to encourage customer inquiries and orders. See also *Business reply card.*

Return on investment (ROI) The amount of profit gained from an investment.

Returns Unsold Newsstand copies returned by a distributor or retailer for credit from the publisher. To save shipping charges, only covers are generally returned, or a signed affidavit representing the unsold or destroyed copies.

Role-playing technique In sales training, a technique in which participants are encouraged to act out imaginary sales presentations or resolve hypothetical sales problems.

Run See *Press run.*

Run-of-book In advertising sales, refers to ads positioned in a magazine at the publisher's discretion. Some publishers honor advertisers' demands for preferred positions while others treat all advertising orders as run-of-book. Also *run-of-press.*

Running business accounts In advertising sales, those clients currently doing business with the magazine.

S

SIC code See *Standard Industrial Classification.*

SRDS See *Standard Rate and Data Service.*

Saddle stitching In magazine printing, the process of binding a publication with staples at the folded edge.

Sales incentive In advertising sales, a reward, beyond salary or commission, offered to sales reps in return for achieving stated sales goals.

Sales tracking report In ad sales management, a record of all sales contacts, purposes of calls, results and expected actions.

Sampling error In statistics, the deviation between the characteristics of a sample and that of the population from which it is drawn. Also called *sample variation.*

Saturation Blanketing an advertising message across an audience. Saturation implies wide coverage and high frequency designed to achieve maximum advertising impact or coverage. In broadcast, *roadblocking* is a form of saturation in which the same advertisement appears in the same time slot on all networks.

Schedule In media planning, a list of media to be used during an advertising campaign. In magazine advertising, a list of issues in which a campaign will run.

Screen In printing, the number of rows of dots per linear inch in a halftone. Screens indicate the level of graphic detail that can be achieved during a print run. Screens range from 55 dots per inch for ordinary newspaper work to 300 dots per inch for finer magazine printing.

Seasonal Used to describe a product, service, or category normally purchased only at a certain times of year.

Secondary audience The readers of a publication beyond those for whom its editorial content is intended. Also *secondary readership* or *pass-along readership*.

Secondary research Research information attained indirectly from a published study or from another person or group.

Segment An subgroup of buyers within a market who share a common trait or need. Also *market segment*.

Segmentation A marketing strategy that subdivides a market into different groups to be targeted by specific advertising. Also *market segmentation*.

Separation negative In production, any of the negatives produced in making a color separation.

Share of mind Among all brands for any given category, share of mind is the percentage of brand awareness enjoyed by any one brand.

Short rate In advertising sales, the additional charge incurred when an advertiser fails to use enough advertising page space to earn the contract discount agreed upon during the original order.

Show See *Trade show*.

Show issue See *Trade show issue*.

Signature A portion of a publication created through printing, folding, trimming, and binding a sheet so as to form a number of pages. Signatures generally run in groups of 8, 16 or 32 pages.

Simmons Market Research Bureau (SMRB) A media and marketing firm that provides syndicated data on magazine audience size, composition, turnover, and duplication. Simmons also provides measures on broadcast exposure and data on ownership and usage of consumer products.

Single-copy sales See *Newsstand circulation*.

Single-rate card A magazine rate card that has no separate rates for special considerations, such as local and national editions.

Size See *Company size*.

Source code A code on a promotion effort that identifies the source of the name—whether from a list, directory, request card or invoice. Likewise, *effort codes* are also used on promotion pieces to find which promotion effort the customer responded to.

Space In advertising sales, term used to denote advertising linage.

Space discount A discount given to advertisers for buying a certain amount of ad pages. See also *frequency discount* and *volume discount*.

Space schedule A schedule submitted by an advertising agency to a client that lists the amount and frequency of advertising space to be bought in various media.

Split accounts In advertising sales, those clients who do business with one magazine, but give the lion's share of business to the magazine's competitor. Also refers to accounts running with one magazine but managed by two or more sales reps.

Split run In magazine printing, a press run that carries two or more different forms of an advertiser's message in different copies or issues. Split runs are used to test the effectiveness of one ad message against the other, or to appeal to regional or other specific markets.

Split series In magazine circulation, a renewal promotion or invoice series that is split among the same group of subscribers. Normally, subscribers up for renewal would all receive identical promotions. With a split series, the subscriber list is divided into two or more groupings, each of which receives a different series in order to test the effectiveness of one series against another.

Spread See *Double-page spread.*

Staggered schedule Advertisement schedules in two or more publications, arranged so that the dates of insertion are alternated or rotated. This ensures the ad won't appear simultaneously in the same issues of two different magazines.

Standard Directory of Advertising Agencies; Standard Directory of Advertisers. Directories that list advertising agencies and their accounts, as well as advertisers in large metropolitan areas. Also known as the *Red Book*, These directories also run classified advertising.

Standard Industrial Classification (SIC) A standardized business classification, published by the U.S. Department of Commerce, that assigns a numerical code to a type of industry. SIC codes are particularly valuable for business magazines in describing "field served."

Standard metropolitan statistical area See *Metropolitan statistical area.*

Standard Rate and Data Service, Inc. (SRDS) A Chicago-based firm that issues monthly directories of circulation and advertising rate information for magazines, TV, radio and other media.

Star, Chain and Hook In advertising sales letters, a method for structuring a sales message. The "star" is a pointed and personal observation to encourage reading; the "chain" explains benefits and features of the magazine; the "hook" offers a sales inducement.

Starch Daniel Starch and Associates, a company that conducts advertising and mediarelated research studies.

Starch rating Magazine and newspaper advertisement readership ratings gathered by Daniel Starch and Associates. Ratings include "noted" (readers recall seeing the ad) and "most read" (readers read more than 50% of ad's copy).

Status report In ad sales management, a list of a magazine's accounts, with name, address, contacts, decision makers, and a "status" symbol that represents that account's friendliness or unfriendliness toward the magazine.

Stratified sampling In magazine research, taking samples from various groups to draw comparisons and conclusions. Example: In marketing, also used to describe companies that supply goods or services to an advertiser. Example: Sewing machine manufacturers are suppliers to the apparel industry. *Dog Owner* magazine surveys samples of its readers and of heavy pet-store shoppers to draw psychographic conclusions about shopping habits of its readers.

Subscriber Usually refers to readers who pay to receive a magazine subscription. Can also refer to those who qualify to receive free, or controlled, subscriptions of business magazines.

Subscriber source On a publisher's statement, description of how a recipient placed his or her order. For consumer publications, common sources are direct-mail sold and agency sold.

Subscriber study A demographic or psychographic study of a publication's subscribers, usually commissioned by the publisher.

Subscription A publisher's contract with a subscriber to send every copy of the publication for a determined period of time. A subscription term is usually expressed in months or weeks.

Subscription director The magazine circulation executive whose duties include generating and maintaining subscription sales.

Supplement Any of various separate publica-

491

tions added to the main editorial section of a magazine or newspaper.

Supplementary audit For business publications, an audited report attesting to the number of secondary or multiple products, functions, or buying influence of the qualified recipients of a publication.

Supplier Any firm, such as a printer, graphic arts, film or art studio, that prepares material for a publisher, advertising agency or advertiser.

Suspend To temporarily stop service to a reader. This process is normally used when a copy is returned by the post office as undeliverable due to wrong address.

Sweepstakes A promotion that involves rewarding prizes to a randomly selected group of respondents who have submitted qualified entries. Such promotions, often used as part of new subscriber solicitations, do not require entrants to make a purchase.

Syndicated research Research conducted by an independent firm that measures the same reader characteristics for different magazines. This enables one magazine to accurately compare the psychographics and demographics of its readers to another's.

Synergy The mutual strengthening of and by various media used in an marketing effort. When used effectively in a coordinated campaign, such media as TV, radio, newspapers and magazines can combine synergistically to create marketing power greater than the sum of the parts.

T

Tabloid A magazine larger than the standard size (8 1/2" X 11") trim; usually 11" X 14 1/2".

Tag line In magazine publishing, the line or phrase that appears under the magazine's logo. Example: The tag line for *Folio:* is "The magazine for magazine managment."

Target accounts In advertising sales, those accounts deemed most valuable to a magazine's busienss.

Target audience The audience an advertiser intends to reach in a media effort.

Target market An occupational, demographic, or psychographic group of consumers that a marketer designates as his best sales prospects. Also *target, target group, target consumers.*

Tearsheet An unbound, printed page from a magazine; often sent to advertisers to show the position and appearance of an ad in a particular issue.

Teaser In advertising sales letters, a short, introductory letter that grabs a prospect's attention and is designed to encourage a face-to-face appointment.

Telemarketing The sale of goods and services via telephone. *Inbound* telemarketing, often used for customer service, relies on consumers to call with questions or product orders. *Outbound* telemarketing calls are placed by a telemarketing firm to potential customers.

Term The length of a paid subscription order, usually expressed as the number of issues—12, 24, 36—or as the number of years.

Territory In advertising sales, a geographical area or product category assigned exclusively to a salesperson.

Test market A geographical area in which a test of an alternate, or new marketing plan or product is conducted.

Testimonial Recommendation of a product by a user for promotion or advertising purposes.

Three color Refers to color printing that uses yellow, red (magenta), and blue (cyan), but not black. Also *3C.*

Through-the-book In magazine research, one technique for determining audience size. Readers are asked whether they recall reading certain magazine, and then they are given stripped-down issues to review and discuss which articles interest them. Those who accurately recall reading a particular magazine are counted as readers.

Tie-down In sales presentations, the act of confirming a prospect's willingness to advertise by asking close-ended questions.

Tie-in The effort to develop a cooperative marketing effort between products, brands or marketers. Example: An ad effort that gives away Spiderman cups at McDonald's would constitute a tie-in for Marvel Comics.

Tie-in advertisement A print ad that refers to another advertisement in the same issue. Or, a single advertisement that pitches more than one product or service, often involving more than one advertiser.

Tip-in A distinct insert glued or stitched into a publication.

Tombstone An all-print advertisement, small or large, with no graphics.

Top of mind In awareness research, the first brand or advertising campaign that comes to a respondent's mind.

Total audience Combined total of a magazine's paid circulation and pass-along readership.

Total distribution In marketing, a situation in which an item or brand has maxed out all opportunities for enhancing distribution in retail stores.

Total paid Total of all classes of a publication's distribution (bulk, subscription and newsstand sales) for which the purchasers have paid in accordance with the standards set by the auditing bureaus.

Trade advertising Business-product advertising. Also *business-to-business advertising*.

Trade association Any organization established to promote the interest of a trade or industry, to establish and enforce standards of quality and practice, or to offer information to members.

Trade magazine See *Business magazine*.

Trade show A sales exposition in which buyers and sellers in a particular industry meet and display products and services. Also *show, exposition, expo*.

Trade show copies Copies of a magazine distri-buted free at trade shows. Also *show copies*.

Trade show issue Special issue of a business magazine designed to reach the audience of a conference or trade show. Also *show issue*.

Trading out The practice by which a magazine exchanges space with another magazine, or with a supplier of goods or services, with no cash involved.

Travel and entertainment (T&E) Expenditure for travel, meals, lodging and client entertainment for business purposes. T&E can also refer to a company's travel and entertainment budget.

Two-color Noting or pertaining to printing in black and a single color, or in two colors other than black. Also *2C*.

Two pages facing Two advertising pages opposite one another without a gutter.

U

Unique selling position (USP) The unique benefit claimed for an advertised product or service.

Unit Refers to a single copy of a magazine or a single ad run in a specific medium.

493

Unit audit For business publications, an audited report of the number of companies, plants or other establishments reached by the publication.

Universe The total number of potentially qualified readers or buyers that exist within an industry.

V

VAC See *Verified Audit Circulation Corporation.*

Value Refers to the usefulness of a product or service to a user or prospect as measured by the rate of sales or interest. Value can also refer to the usual retail sales price of a product or service.

Vehicle An individual advertising medium, such as a magazine or a TV station.

Vendor Any person who, company or organization that sells products or services.

Verified Audit Circulation Corporation (VAC) A magazine audit bureau that particularly specializes in auditing bulk circulation.

Vertical half page A half-page ad that consumes vertical space rather than horizontal.

Vertical publication A publication intended for persons in specific trade, profession, interest group or lifestyle. While a horizontal magazine is intended for people who work the same occupation in various industries—such as financial officers—a vertical publication is edited for a specific group, such as glassmakers.

Vertical selling Selling to buyers in a specific limited range of industries.

Visual A rough sketch depicting an advertising layout or illustration. A visual can also refer to any aid, particularly in presentations, that helps an audience grasp an idea visually. Charts and graphs are common sales presentation visuals.

Volume discount A discount offered an adver- tiser for the purchase of a certain specified amount of advertising, either in pages or price. See also *Frequency discount.*

W

Waste circulation Magazine audience members who are not prospects for a particular advertised product. This could include circulation in a geographic area where an advertiser does not distribute, or it could include circulation among readers who are not typical consumers of the product. Example: For a golf-equipment advertiser, all non-golfing readers of a sports publication would constitute waste circulation.

Weight In advertising sales, the amount of advertising in support of a marketing effort, expressed in terms of gross-rating points (TV), reach and frequency, impressions or spending levels.

White space A blank area on a printed magazine page.

Women's service magazine A magazine that largely provides information to women, many of whom are homemakers. The Seven Sisters—*Woman's Day, Good Housekeeping, McCall's, Better Homes & Gardens, Ladies' Home Journal, Redbook* and *Family Circle*—are all women's service magazines.

Z

Zapping Using a remote control to change television stations during commercials.

Zero-based In advertising sales, a budget-setting method of allocating advertising expenditures based on a prioritized "wish" list of marketing methods. Example: A company has a $40,000 budget for marketing a new product. After prioritizing a "wish" list of promotion methods and costs ($23,000 for business magazine advertising, $15,000 for trade shows, $7,000 for sales reps, $5,000 for signage, $10,000 for public relations and so on), it simply decides to commit to those methods at the top of the list, dropping off any methods at the bottom of the list that would exceed the budgeted amount.

Zipping Using a remote control device to fast forward through commercials during a playback of a recorded TV show.

Index

HELEN BERMAN'S
ADVERTISING SALES SEMINARS

HELEN BERMAN'S INTENSIVE 2-DAY SEMINARS

GREAT SALESPEOPLE AREN'T BORN—THEY'RE TRAINED! In her 2-day intensive seminar, nationally recognized advertising sales trainer, Helen Berman, changes run-of-the-mill "space peddlers" into highly successful ad marketers. She shows how to win new prospects, increase market share, increase ad frequency, sell bigger space units, win back lost business, minimize sales costs, maximize productivity, and increase motivation to gain the competitive edge.

CUSTOMIZED IN-HOUSE TRAINING

Helen Berman can tailor seminars to meet the unique needs of your publication and sales team through analysis of your market position, readership, media kit and promotion—along with mind-expanding exercises, motivational discussions, in-depth coaching, case studies and more.

"Helen gave us a road map, her strategies resulted in immediate sales. The light went on for our salespeople."

—Jim Johnson
Group Publisher, McGraw-Hill, Inc.

"When Helen's seminar is finished—you've learned! One of the few seminars I've attended where I thought my time and money were well spent."

—Charley Tomlinson
Director of Marketing, *Delaware Today Magazine*

"Helen's own motivation and enthusiasm create the kind of 'fire in the belly' you want to have in your sales force."

—Robert Krakoff
Chairman and CEO, Advanstar Communications, Inc.

"Helen's workshop is a powerful sales tool! As a manager, the workshop gave me great insight and direction."

—Deborah Holtschlag
Associate Publisher, *D Magazine*

FOR MORE INFORMATION:

BERMAN PUBLISHING COMPANY
12021 Wilshire Blvd., Suite 177
Los Angeles, CA 90025-1200
Phone: (310) 820-7312
Fax in U.S.: (800) 538-3083, International Fax: (310) 312-9757
E-Mail: Bermancorp@AOL.com

HELEN BERMAN'S
BOOKS and TAPES

THE ADVERTISING SALES SOLUTION:
Audio Learning Cassette Program
Recorded at Helen Berman's Seminars (8 Cassettes/8 Hours)
$195.00 per set (plus $4.50 shipping and handling)
ISBN: 0-9649716-3-1

"The first step we take with new salespeople is to have them 'Bermanized.' With Helen's training audio tapes, our senior salespeople demonstrate marked improvement in their performance!"

—Carolyn Flick
Associate Publisher, TAP Publishing

AD SALES: Winning Secrets of the Magazine Pros
VOLUME 1—ISBN: 0-9649716-1-5—$69.95 Hardbound (plus $6.00 shipping & handling) 448 pages, 8.5x11 inches, Illustrations, Index, Glossary

VOLUME 2—ISBN: 0-9649716-2-3—$69.95 Hardbound (plus $6.00 shipping & handling) 512 pages, 8.5x11 inches, Illustrations, Index, Glossary

**SET (Volumes 1 & 2) ISBN: 0-9649716-0-7— $119.95
(plus $8.00 shipping and handling)**

"Every ad salesperson should read this book! It's full of great selling tips...a reference source that should be kept handy and referred to constantly."

— William R. Facinelli
President, Facinelli Media Sales

"...an ideal training tool for the novice, a stimulating refresher for the veteran...covers every skill the ad-sales professional needs to succeed. A must read!"

— Richard Hathaway
Group Publisher, Intertec Publishing

"A comprehensive look at the advertising sales process for the magazine industry."

— Mitchell Marchesano
President and Chief Executive Officer, BPA

ORDER FROM:

BERMAN PUBLISHING COMPANY
12021 Wilshire Blvd., Suite 177
Los Angeles, CA 90025-1200
Phone: (310) 820-7312
Fax in U.S.: (800) 538-3083, International Fax: (310) 312-9757
E-Mail: Bermancorp@AOL.com